M000223288

Crystals are Mother Earth's gift to mankind. We must not forget that crystals are not only beautiful as jewelry and decoration, but they also have energetic properties that play a part in different fields, such as healing, channeling, and other realms of awareness and enlightenment. Moreover, they are used in various areas of mysticism such as color therapy, pendulums and so on.

Since ancient times, mystical and healing properties have been attributed to crystals. However, only in the last few years, prior to the Millennium and the New Age, has mankind acknowledged the important function and great power of crystals.This book teaches you everything you need to know about crystals and stones: their properties, the energies they contain, and the correct and most effective use that you can make of them in fields such as pendulums, jewelry, healing, and so on.

USA-born Connie Islin divides her time between Israel and the USA. A consultant and lecturer on mystical subjects and alternative medicine, she has written on the subjects of healing, crystals, parapsychology, and mysticism. Her books on numerology and dream interpretation have become bestsellers, and have been translated into several languages. Connie Islin purchases crystals and jewelry for a major chain of New Age stores in Israel.

Connie Islin

ALL ABOUT
CRYSTALS

Astrolog Publishing House

Series editor: Sara Bleich

Editor: Marion Duman

Cover design: Na'ama Yaffe

Layout and Graphics: Ruth Erez

Production Manager: Dan Gold

© Connie Islin 2001

ISBN 965-494-111-2

All rights reserved. No part of this publication may be reproduced, stored in a retrieval system, or transmitted, in any form or by any means, electronic, mechanical, photocopying, recording or otherwise, without the prior permission of the publisher.

Published by Astrolog Publishing House 2001

Astrolog Publishing House

P. O. Box 1123, Hod Hasharon 45111, Israel

Tel: 972-9-7412044

Fax: 972-9-7442714

E-Mail: info@astrolog.co.il

Printed in Israel

10 9 8 7 6 5 4 3 2 1

Contents

The qualities and properties of the various metals:

The contents of this book are based on the experience and the knowledge of the author. Neither the author nor the publisher claims that the book is a medical or therapeutic prescription. In the case of any disorder or disease, a qualified physician must be consulted.

Crystals and minerals

The various crystals and minerals - the children of Mother Earth - have fascinated and impressed human beings since ancient times. Their incredible beauty, the special sensations that they inspire, and frequently their rarity, have always inspired people's affection and admiration for these unique objects.

In ancient times and, in fact, up until recently, the rarity and costliness of the special crystals meant that they were unavailable to many people. They belonged to kings, nobles, and the wealthy, who used them to flaunt their riches and glorify themselves in people's eyes. Various religious leaders, healers, and alchemists also used crystals.

The sages and philosophers of all eras know how to identify the special properties of the crystals. They examined their properties in depth, healed with them, and used them to develop their wisdom and their minds. They used crystals for treating physical and mental problems, for protection, for making magic, for reinforcing amulets, and for incantations. Moreover, they used certain minerals and crystals for linking up to exalted spiritual planes, and for receiving divine knowledge. The protective properties of minerals were effective for all those who possessed them. Those qualities were the source of the stories of wonders and miracles that were attributed to crystals. Some of them are actually true.

Today, the various crystals and minerals are spread out before us in all their glory, and are available to one and all. However, certain extremely rare minerals such as moldavite, diamonds, sapphires and so on are very expensive, and not everyone can afford to purchase them. Various minerals that have been polished to the point of becoming precious stones are not cheap, either. In contrast, the range of minerals that can be purchased inexpensively is enormous.

Nowadays, everyone can enjoy the marvelous properties of crystals. We can use these beautiful objects to balance body and soul, to learn from them, to be cured by them, to develop our awareness, and to gaze into infinity.

In this book, we will embark on a journey to discover the wondrous properties of crystals. We will learn about the qualities of each of the most commonly used minerals, how to take care of them, and how to use them for healing and for balancing body, mind, and spirit. A vast amount of information will be revealed to the reader, but it is your own crystal that will provide you with the most profound information about itself. Listen to it, and let it guide you into the wonderful world of crystals, and into your own world.

The formation of crystals and their path from the earth to man

The gorgeous minerals that we use for such a variety of purposes are all products of the earth (except for meteorites, which come to us from other worlds). They were formed and crystallized in different conditions and ways. The range of conditions for their formation is one of the parameters that create the huge variety of minerals that are found on the face of the earth. It can even be said that the crystal "remembers" the conditions of its formation - ultimately, those conditions made it into what it is. The conditions of the crystal's formation frequently teach us about its unique properties and qualities. Basalt, for instance, which originates from a volcanic eruption that cooled down and solidified, helps people cope with their rage. The diamond, too, is formed in conditions of tremendous heat and pressure, and crystallized into a stunningly beautiful precious stone. In its hardness (it is the hardest mineral) and beauty, it symbolizes the agonies that cleanse the soul, and bring it to full perfection and strength.

Some of the crystals originate from burning gases or molten magma that erupted from the flaming bowels of the earth onto its surface. Some of them originate from volcanic eruptions. After cooling down and solidifying, they began to form crystals, and the form of the particular crystal began to take shape. These crystals are called "magmatic crystals." Quartz, for example, is created in these conditions, and is thus considered a magmatic mineral.

The volcanic eruption, which is the source of some of the magmatic crystals, emits steam containing various mineral compounds. This steam may create the crystallization of various minerals. The steam thickens, becomes denser and more solid, and creates the mineral. Copper, for instance, originates from the steam that is released during volcanic eruptions.

Residual minerals are minerals that are formed from various hydrous solutions, and develop as a result of the natural activities of various organisms, or as a result of the actions of the forces of nature - ice, air, water, and wind.

Existing minerals may sometimes undergo "another crystallization." Out of the same minerals, this additional crystallization creates new crystals that are different than the minerals from which they were formed in their texture and shape, and even in their properties.

The minerals are mined from various strata. Some of them are found in mineral-rich veins of the earth and in rocks of a different type that contain veins of the mineral. In contrast, there are minerals that are found in high concentrations in riverbeds, or on the shores of rivers and oceans.

After the mineral has been located, it undergoes polishing in accordance with its type and quality. Some minerals, such as emeralds and rubies, are polished and made into exquisite gemstones. Polishing emphasizes the beauty of the stone, causes it to reflect light and sparkle impressively, and renders it more prestigious and suitable for being set in jewelry.

In addition, there are organic products that went through a process of transformation and crystallization, such as fossilized wood, pearl, amber, and so on, which are considered to be "stones."

The structure of crystals

The difference between an ordinary mineral and a mineral that is defined as a crystal lies in the structure of the mineral's crystallization. Crystals have a unique atomic structure that creates the crystalline structure. There are seven basic crystalline shapes, and each one has a unique geometric and molecular structure. Despite the "long" names for the crystalline shapes, it is ultimately possible to recognize them by sight according to the examples that follow, since the crystalline shape is what gives the crystal its unique shape.

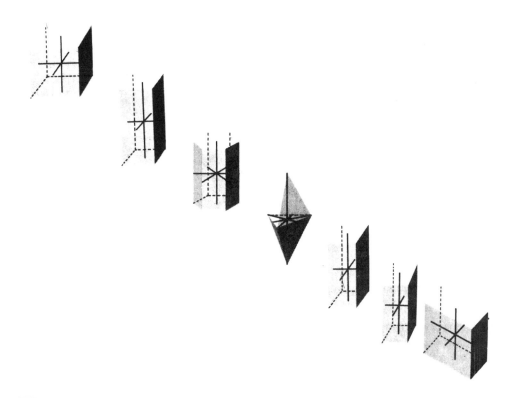

The isometric shape: This shape is that of a cube with angles that are not necessarily perfect. For example - fluorite.

The tetragonal shape: This shape has four corners. For example - **wulfenite**.

The hexagonal shape: This shape has six corners. For example - emerald.

The trigonal shape: This shape has three corners. For example - tourmaline.

The orthorhombic shape: This shape is reminiscent of a diamond shape. For example, acanthite, celestite.

The monoclinic shape: This shape has a single slope. For example, azurite.

The triclinic shape: This shape has three slopes. For instance, turquoise.

The shapes of crystals

The shape of a crystal may exert a significant influence on its mode of action. Some of the shapes of crystals are natural, and some are man-made. In each one of its configurations, the basic natural energy of the particular crystals is preserved. The uniqueness of the shape lies in the fact that by means of the particular shape, it is possible to program the crystal to receive or transmit energy in various ways, and to dedicate it to various roles. When you wish to use a particular crystal for a specific purpose - one of those that will be discussed later - you can choose the configuration or the structure that suits the crystal. Quartz crystals have their own unique configurations that will be described separately when we discuss the properties of quartz crystal.

The cluster

A cluster of crystals is a natural configuration that consists of a group of crystals. The formation of the cluster reinforces the power of the crystal, and helps it spread its energies in a stronger and more diverse way. The crystals in the cluster reinforce, charge, and purify one another.

The cluster is used for purifying other crystals. For this reason, the quartz cluster is used, in the main. The citrine cluster is considered to attract abundance and prosperity. The amethyst cluster is very soothing, and purifies the atmosphere and the air in a room.

Because they are groups of crystals that co-exist and cooperate in perfect harmony, clusters are superb for placing in rooms in which group activity takes place. The energy of cooperation and unity that they transmit exerts a beneficial influence on groups that work together, on workplaces, on classrooms, and on groups that meet for meditation and spiritual development. Because of the multiple crystals they contain, the clusters transmit powerful energy and spread harmony wherever they are placed.

The egg shape

Many crystals are industrially fashioned into an egg shape. Using an egg-shaped crystal, it is possible to cleanse the aura (by holding the crystal between the thumb and the fingers), locating holes in it and filling them. Some people use egg-shaped crystals as an aid in Shiatsu, reflexology, and acupressure treatments, because it is easy to hold (its shape fits the palm exactly), and it can reinforce the therapeutic energies. The pointed end of the egg can be pressed into the area being treated, or onto an acupressure or reflex spot.

The spherical shape

Many legends have been linked to the spherical crystalline configuration during the course of history - some of them true. The famous crystal ball, which is used for predicting the future, is actually a sphere of quartz crystal, but other minerals also serve that purpose.

Spherical crystals can occur naturally, or can be shaped artificially. They are suitable for use during group activities, in order to create better communication between the members of the group. Moreover, they are used for linking up to events or people who are not present, or are not in the same time-frame that we are at the moment. It is possible to use these crystals to issue especially strong energetic orders, as we will see in the chapter on the crystal ball. By means of gazing profoundly, it is possible to "read" past and future events in them. This gazing requires depth, constant practice, and development. In the same way, the spherical crystal also serves to fortify introspection, and is very instrumental in the development of intuition and extrasensory perception. Small spherical crystals can be used as amulets and for the prevention and alleviation of degenerative diseases.

The star shape

Some crystals form naturally into a four- or six-pointed star configuration. In addition, there are industrially fashioned star shapes, but they do not contain the properties that are unique to the natural star shape. A star-shaped crystal is suitable for use during meditations for linking up to the universal light and to superior forces. This shape stimulates the person's superego while helping him to operate according to divine will.

The pyramid shape

There are industrially fashioned pyramid-shaped crystals, and natural ones as well, but they are rare. A pyramid-shaped crystal gets the crystal's energy "into focus" and hones it. It is widely used in meditations for stimulating and enhancing spiritual development, and in third eye meditations.

The ankh shape

The ankh is a famous shape, known principally from ancient Egypt, although there is evidence that it was used in other ancient civilizations. The shape of the ankh comprises a cross whose upper arm is replaced by a circle. It is considered the symbol and amulet of longevity. Crystals that have been fashioned into the shape of an ankh (this shape does not occur naturally) can be used for increasing fertility - not just physical fertility, but mental and creative fertility.

Crystal bowls

Natural crystal bowls are extremely rare. In general, they can only be found as industrial products. Crystal bowls are used for recharging energy, and for reinforcing and stimulating other crystals that are placed in them. Moreover, they are used in meditations (held in both hands), mainly to receive divine abundance of any kind.

Polished crystal

The polished crystal is a crystal whose apex has been polished in order for it to be smoother. This crystal can be used for promoting creativity. The polished crystal is used in massages, and it is also possible to use it for stimulating the meridians in the body.

Crystals and energy fields

Crystals are extremely powerful tools for raising consciousness. They can fit into many meditations, and are among the best and simplest tools that exist for balancing the chakras, the energetic bodies, and the various layers of the universe. In this book, we will deal extensively with the link between crystals and the various energetic bodies, and the influence of certain crystals on the different chakras. In order to facilitate the reading and use of this book, we will clarify the various terms that are connected with the energetic bodies and the chakras, and the way in which the energies of the crystals influence them.

Everything that exists on earth vibrates at different frequencies, and these frequencies surround and affect matter. Colors have their own unique frequencies, as do sounds, light, the human body, minerals, and the plant and animal kingdoms. Although the various frequencies have different qualities, they have an interreactive ability. The frequencies of light, color, and sounds, as well as the special frequencies of minerals, have a strong and significant influence on the frequencies that envelop and activate the human body. It will be easier for us to understand this concept if we compare it to the movement of atoms. The atoms that constitute the apparently material, solid, and stable world are in a state of constant vibration and resonance. Although the naked eye cannot perceive these vibrations, they exist regularly and unceasingly.

When the energies of crystals are added to human energies, a new blend of vibrational power is created. This can be compared to two stones that are thrown into a pool of water. Each of them creates a circle in the water, but ultimately, the two circles blend into the movement of the pool. The combination of human and mineral energies causes man to rise to a higher and more open state of awareness (while the mineral carries out its function and its vocation). When we link our energies to mineral energies, we gain additional knowledge and understand of our physical, emotional, and spiritual state. The frequencies of the various crystals operate in a balancing and cleansing way on the frequencies of our physical body, as well as on the frequencies of the energetic bodies - the etheric body, the emotional body, the mental body, the intuitive body, and the karmic body.

The bodies

Besides the physical body, human beings have several energetic bodies. They can also be called auras, and there are people who can see some of them. Many people can see the aura of the physical body easily, when the person stands next to a white wall. By the same method, and after a bit of practice, it is possible to discern the etheric body.

Some people count five bodies - the physical body, and four energetic bodies. Some people count five or six energetic bodies in addition to the physical body. This increase stems from the ability of various people to look in depth into the finer strata of the comprehensive energetic being - the person. In the book, we will focus on the five best-known bodies, which we will treat by means of crystals and healing. The sixth energetic body, which is also profoundly influenced by crystals, will also be mentioned in this introduction.

The human aura - the person's electromagnetic field - is the result of the magnetic and electrical current of the conscious bodies. For this reason, any imbalance in one of the bodies, including, of course, the physical body, is manifested in the state of the whole aura, and influences it.

The energetic bodies are perpetually affected by the person's spiritual, mental, and physical state, and they influence these states. These interactions cannot be separated. Everything that influences the energetic bodies influences the person. Everything that influences the person physically, mentally, or spiritually, is manifested in the energetic bodies and in the aura.

The first body is the **physical body**. The physical body operates on the existing physical planes and is composed of substances that can be sensed physically, and examined and discerned by means of the instruments that we have at our disposal today. It is affected and activated by various biochemical processes, and subject to the laws of the physical world. It obeys the laws of time, space, and gravity, and is not infinite, but subject to the constant processes of degeneration and regeneration. Having said that, it must be remembered that our physical body is made up of atoms. Atoms are in constant motion, and in fact, their perpetual movement is what creates matter, as the eye sees it.

We will treat the physical body with many crystals that balance its actions, improve its functions, and accelerate its regeneration.

The second body is the **etheric body**. The meridian channels, which convey life energy (chi), and are connected to the body's nervous system, are located in the etheric body. The meridians of the etheric body convey energies and recharge energies in the body. The reaction of this body to the crystals' energy is especially strong. A large part of the treatment of problems and diseases by means of crystals is performed on this layer. It is in the etheric body that diseases actually start - the diseases that are later manifested in the physical body. This body is responsible for the general health and varied activities of the human body, and nourishes the physical body energetically via the meridian system in it.

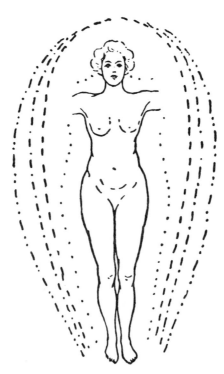

The third body is the **emotional body**, which is also called the **astral body**. All of our emotions are expressed in the emotional body. It is influenced by its feelings, and influences them. Every state of emotional imbalance is manifested in this body.

The fourth body is the **mental body**. The mental body contains our thought patterns. Via this layer, we attract the situations in which we believe to our lives. The thought patterns in which we choose to believe are embodied in this body, and affect the energies and the situations that we attract to our lives. With the help of meditations with crystals to which we add mantras of positive thinking, we work very powerfully on this body.

The fifth body is the **intuitive body**. This body contains the sum total of the higher knowledge that we are able to contain and understand, even if we have not grasped them with the full power of our intellect and logic. Via the intuitive body, we sense the large range of gut feelings, unexplained knowledge, message-bearing dreams, and so on. Work with crystals causes us to be more connected to this layer, and to develop the link between the more conscious layers and the intuitive layers.

The sixth body is the **karmic body**. The karmic body contains our inherent knowledge about our soul's previous incarnations, the reasons for our being in our particular physical body, our vocation, and the repairs we have to perform in this world. Many of the channeling stones and crystals that help us recall previous incarnations operate via our link to this high layer.

The problems, or imbalances, are liable to begin, ostensibly, in any one of the bodies, but it is not easy to diagnose which came first, "the chicken or the egg," if there is any "precedence" like this at all, because, as we said before, the interaction is extremely close. For this reason, when there is a blockage or problem in one of them, it will affect all the others. By means of the use of crystals, the blockages in the various bodies are released, and our conscious connection to the different layers of our existence becomes stronger, clearer, and better understood.

The chakras

Since the containing and flow of energy is not identical among all the bodies, owing to the fact that some of them are finer and more delicate, and others are thicker, there are centers in the human body for the conversion of energy when it passes between the various bodies. The meaning of the word "chakra" is "wheel." The higher energies, cosmic energies, are channeled through the chakras. This energy, which is also called life energy that flows through the chakras, is of cardinal importance to our lives and physical, mental, and spiritual health. When a situation arises in which the energy does not flow through the chakra in a harmonious way, or when one of the chakras is blocked, or open too wide, an imbalance is created that is manifested in all areas of life. All the conscious bodies, as well as the material body, have their own vibrational frequency that responds to the frequencies transmitted by the crystals. For this reason, the chakras respond marvelously to the energy of the crystals. Certain crystals may help open certain chakras. Others will stimulate and balance them. The state of the chakras reflects the state of the link between the various conscious bodies, and our ability to receive energies and abundance from the infinite source of energy of the cosmos. When one of the chakras is unbalanced, it affects all the chakras. Moreover, an imbalance in a particular chakra leads to a disruption in the functions for which that chakra is responsible. This imbalance is manifested in the physical, mental, and spiritual planes together.

Each chakra is stimulated and activated by a particular color that is unique to it. It reacts to certain sounds, and to the energetic frequencies of various crystals. In this book, we will relate extensively to the influence of the various crystals on the chakras, and we will present a broad range of techniques for balancing, stimulating, and opening the chakras. However, we will start off by giving an overview of the actions and functions of each of the chakras.

The first chakra - the base chakra (Muladhara)

The base chakra symbolizes man's most basic needs - those of survival. It is located between the anus and the genitals.

The base chakra stimulates our innate, basic survival instinct. It links spiritual, intellectual, and emotional abilities with their physical manifestation. When the chakra is balanced and in a state of harmony, the person is strong, stable, and full of life. He functions well sexually, and feels active, energetic, vital, and stable. He expresses himself assertively, makes decisions easily, and copes well on the material level. When the chakra is in a state of imbalance, suffering either from lack or excess, or is blocked, the person can experience existential fears, or may suffer from sexual imbalance that is liable to manifest itself in sexual urges that are either too strong or too weak. The person may suffer from anxiety, from an aggressive attitude, from a tendency toward unnecessary risk-taking, or from spinelessness.

An imbalance of the chakra is liable to lead to an exaggerated focus on the world of money and material things, and a lust for sex and mammon. On the other hand, it is liable to lead to a feeling of "detachment," a lack of interest in sex or physical functions, and an inability to cope on the material level. States of disharmony in the action of the chakra are liable to lead to a lack of confidence and stability, to living in a world of illusions, or to seeing only the physical layers of the universe, and to extreme egocentricity. From the physical point of view, the imbalance in the base chakra is manifested in various spinal, skeletal, and joint problems, in constipation, hemorrhoids, venereal diseases, and problems connected to sex and infertility.

The colors of the base chakra are black and red. For this reason, most of the crystals used for balancing it are in these colors.

The second chakra - the sex chakra (Swadhisthana)

The sex chakra symbolizes sexuality and sensuality, emotions and creativity. It is located on the pelvis, between the pubic bones.

The sex chakra represents the change and individuality that comes from the understanding of the uniqueness of the self and that of the other. When the chakra is balanced, the person knows how to enjoy life. He expresses his creativity, experiences a feeling of self-satisfaction, and realizes himself in his own way. States of imbalance of the chakra are liable to be expressed in sexual problems that stem mainly from an emotional source. The person is liable to feel that he is full of passion that is not expressed. He is unable to satisfy himself and realize his abilities. Sometimes, this situation causes various addictions. When the chakra is blocked and in a state of imbalance, the person may feel that he does not enjoy life, and that his creative ability, on whichever level it may be, is blocked. There could be a decrease in libido, or alternatively, unbridled sexual passion. The social aspects and his ability to establish both conjugal and social relationships are influenced by the functioning of this chakra. The person is liable to feel a lack of motivation and direction, and that he is unable to fulfill his wishes on the practical levels. He may experience loneliness or an unbalanced relationship that is disrupted by emotions such as jealousy and dependence.

The sex chakra is responsible for the organs of the circulatory and lymph systems, the adrenal glands, digestive juices, the kidneys, the bladder, the muscles, and the sexual organs. A blockage or imbalance in the chakra is liable to be expressed on the physical layer in the form of kidney and gallbladder problems, in frigidity and impotence, in muscular problems, in problems in the sexual system and urinary tract, and also in certain problems in the digestive system.

The color of the sex chakra is orange, and yellow that tends to orange. Crystals in these shades, such as carnelian and fire agate, are used to balance and open the chakra.

The third chakra - the solar plexus chakra (Manipura)

The solar plexus chakra symbolizes the "I," the ego, personal power, the development of the personality, our ability to influence others, our range of emotions, and the practical expression of the intellect. It is located beneath the diaphragm.

The solar plexus chakra is the seat and source of sensations and emotions. The way we fulfill our desires, our will power, and our personal power derives from the state of this chakra. We interpret the world and relate to it via the solar plexus chakra. When the chakra is balanced, this state is manifested in creativity, courage, ego, good emotional control, respectful behavior toward others, great personal strength, and a tolerant and caring attitude toward other people. When the chakra is not balanced, the ego will also not be balanced. This is liable to be expressed in manipulative, domineering behavior, in the person's desire to impose his will on other people, in dependence, in a lack of motivation and action, in feelings of fear and anxiety, in conceit or feelings of inferiority.

The solar plexus chakra is responsible for the functioning of the diaphragm and the respiratory system, the digestive system, the stomach, the pancreas, the liver, the spleen, the gallbladder, the small intestine, the adrenal glands, and the sympathetic nervous system. A state of imbalance in the chakra is liable to be expressed physically in liver, gallbladder, digestive system, and eye problems.

The color of the solar plexus chakra is yellow. For this reason, most of the crystals used for opening, stimulating, and balancing it are yellow, such as amber, citrine, and yellow topaz.

The fourth chakra - the heart chakra (Anahata)

The heart chakra symbolizes love, balance, giving, devotion, and healing. It links the three lower chakras to the three upper ones, which means that a state of imbalance in this chakra is manifested immediately in the other chakras. The heart chakra is located in the center of the chest, parallel to the heart.

Our abilities to love, give, surrender ourselves, worry about others, receive love, and forgive, depend on the chakra being in a balanced state. When the chakra is balanced, the person is generous, caring, unselfish, full of compassion, and eager to help. When the chakra is not balanced, there could be difficulties in his ability to give and receive love, as well as various forms of selfishness and stinginess - both emotional and financial. A state of imbalance in the chakra is liable to make the person hesitant, indecisive, avaricious, uncaring, frightened, anxious, and hard-hearted. An extreme state of an unbalanced heart chakra - almost blocked - is liable to be expressed in a state in which the person sees no one but himself, and even in cruelty.

The heart chakra is responsible for the condition and functioning of the heart, the circulatory system, the lungs, the immune system, the thymus gland, the skin, and the hands. An imbalance in the chakra is liable to be manifested physically in circulatory, cardiac, and respiratory problems, including asthma.

The colors of the heart chakra are pink and green. Thus, mainly pink and green crystals such as rose quartz, rhodochrosite, and green tourmaline are used to balance the chakra.

The fifth chakra - the throat chakra (Visuddha)

The throat chakra symbolizes our ability to express ourselves. Since it links the heart chakra to the third eye chakra, it represents the ability to express verbally what we think and feel. It is the source of communication, creativity, and belief.

The throat chakra is responsible for all the communicative and expressive abilities - the ability to understand our inner desires and express them inwardly and outwardly, the ability to communicate effectively with our surroundings, our self-image in our own eyes, and the way in which we express our opinions, beliefs, and thoughts. When the chakra is in a state of balance, the person experiences good communication with himself and with his surroundings. He expresses himself and his emotions easily, expresses his creativity, knows how to translate his thoughts into words in a satisfactory fashion, and knows how to give a verbal and cerebral form to his intuitive layers. When the chakra is in a state of imbalance, or is blocked, this is liable to be manifested in a broad range of communication problems, from angry communication, unwillingness to listen, and inability to express thoughts and feelings, to stuttering. A state of imbalance in the chakra is liable to cause a lack of creativity and inspiration, a low self-image, apathy and indifference, conflicts between emotion and reason, and a lack of faith.

The throat chakra is responsible for the neck, the vocal cords and organs, the thyroid gland, the nerves, the ears, and the muscles. A state of imbalance in the chakra is liable to be manifested physically in recurring ear-nose-throat infections, in throat inflammations, and in vocal problems.

The colors of the throat chakra are blue, light blue, and turquoise. Most of the crystals used to balance and stimulate the chakras, including blue lace agate, blue topaz, and blue sapphire, are in these colors.

The sixth chakra - the third eye chakra (Ajna)

The sixth chakra symbolizes intuition, intellectual power, will power, and knowledge. It is responsible for the balance between the two cerebral hemispheres - the right and the left - and between intuition, emotion, and mysticism on the one hand, and logic and reason on the other. When the third eye chakra is open and balanced, the person is properly linked to his subconscious and intuition. If the third eye chakra is open, the person is fortunate enough to have the ability to understand cosmic insights and pick up non-verbal messages. When we go back and open our third eye chakra, and listen to its intuitive message, our intuitive ability increases amazingly, and the sixth sense becomes more developed and accessible. The state of the third eye chakra affects the person's physical balance, his ability to concentrate, his wisdom, and his peace of mind. When the chakra is balanced and open, the person is popular, wise, clear-thinking, intuitive, and highly moral. A state of a lack of balance in the chakra is expressed in states such as depression, dependence, unrequited passions, indecisiveness, imbalance, mental exhaustion, hearing and sight problems, and learning and comprehension problems. An imbalance in the chakra is liable to be expressed physically in headaches, nightmares, a lack of equilibrium, vertigo, nervous problems, and problems in the ears and eyes.

The colors of the third eye chakra are indigo and purple. For this reason, most of the crystals that are used to stimulate and balance the chakra, such as sodalite, azurite, and sugilite, are in these shades.

The seventh chakra - the crown chakra (Sasharata)

The crown chakra symbolizes enlightenment and cosmic knowledge, linking up to the highest levels of awareness, and spiritual openness. It is located in the middle of the head, on the crown.

The crown chakra is the chakra that links human beings to infinity. It is the source of cosmic knowledge, and it is the link to divine wisdom and to cosmic awareness. When the crown chakra is open, the person has the ability to receive divine and cosmic insights, and to link up to divine knowledge and to universal light and love. A state of openness and optimal balance of the chakra means enlightenment and harmony. When the crown chakra is not balanced, the person is liable to feel boredom and a lack of purpose in his life. A state of disharmony in the chakra is liable to lead to an inability to open up to spiritual dimensions, and a lack of awareness. Extreme states of blockage of the crown chakra can lead to coma and even death.

The crown chakra is responsible for the functioning of the brain and the pineal gland.

The colors of the seventh chakra are purple and white. For stimulating and opening the chakra, we use crystals in these colors, as well as channeling stones, stones that develop our ability to open up to the highest spiritual levels, such as selenite and apophyllite.

When we set about treating the chakras with crystals - cleansing, stimulating, balancing, and opening them - we can simply look at the color of the crystal in order to know the chakra for which it is appropriate. Of course, it is possible to use the list of crystals that appears at the end of the description of the actions of each chakra in order to choose a suitable stone for our needs and purposes. However, if you feel that you are drawn intuitively to placing a particular stone (purified and cleansed, of course!) on a particular chakra, try it. The possibilities for combinations and matches are endless. If by chance you need a particular stone for treating one of the chakras, and you do not have it, you can use clear quartz crystal. You will have to program it with the same properties that you wanted in the crystal that you do not have.

The colors

As we have already mentioned, colors also have frequencies that exert a significant influence on human beings. In order to understand this statement in a concrete manner, we need only describe the feeling of being in a room that is painted entirely red, as opposed to being in a room that is painted blue. We react constantly to the colors around us, and they have a healing and balancing effect on our electro-magnetic field. Our aura contains all the colors. That is the optimal condition. When there is a lack of a particular color, this will be felt both emotionally and physically.

When we know the significance of colors, we can very easily use crystals. Even if we do not know the name of the crystal, and its properties, its color will give us an initial indication regarding the qualities of its basic action, and regarding the chakra it is supposed to balance.

First of all, when we approach any crystal, we must distinguish between the warm colors and the cool colors. This distinction will give us an initial indication concerning the crystal's action. If the color belongs to the group of warm colors - red, orange, and yellow - it almost certainly has a stimulating and energizing quality, and is likely to have masculine energy - yang. This is not an axiom, but it works for most of the crystals. When the color of the crystal belongs to the group of cool colors - blue, purple, and indigo - it is likely to have soothing and cooling energy. Many of the crystals in these shades are considered to be crystals with feminine energy - yin. The color green, which is found between the two groups of colors, and is composed of a mixture of a warm color (yellow) and a cool color (blue), is therefore considered a balancing color, as are most of the green crystals.

It is a good idea to learn the basic aspects of each color. They will be useful for us in better understanding the nature of the crystal, both in matching it to the chakras, and for various higher activities that take place with the help of crystals, such as reading crystal balls.

In the chapter dealing with projecting color, we will discuss the significance of the different colors in depth, and their various healing powers. It is imperative to learn and understand the significance of the colors well before using them in sets of stones (laying on of stones) and in meditations with stones.

The qualities and properties of the various minerals

Acanthite

Acanthite is iron-black in color, and it crystallizes in orthorhombic shapes. It is a relatively soft stone, and for that reason cannot be used for preparing an elixir in the regular ways.

Physical healing properties: Acanthite helps preserve the health of the body, mainly by inspiring the person to look after his body and take care of his health. Moreover, it helps find the correct ways to solve health problems and to improve general health. It is used for treating flu, colds, viral and bacterial infections, and for more effective expulsion of toxins from the cells. Some people use it to improve the action of the immune system when its functioning is impaired, and to help absorb vitamins.

The mineral's effect on the mental and emotional layers: Acanthite helps balance the emotions and the intuitions by operating on the energetic plane for the regulation of emotional and intuitive energies. It fortifies during difficult times and periods of hardship, helps remove obstacles from the person's path, and engenders a sensation of general well-being.

Spiritual influence: Acanthite helps the person see the reason for and manner of the onset of diseases, especially in the case of internal or chronic diseases. In the past, acanthite was used as a stone that strengthened the predictive abilities and stimulated wisdom and inner knowledge. In former times, warriors would wear it in a bag or container for protection, and for eliminating evil and maleficent forces.

Agate

Agate comes in many different forms, and in a wide range of colors. Some of the forms are adorned with patterns, stripes, elliptical and circular shapes, and so on. The stones belong to the chalcedonic family, and are used in the treatment of many layers of existence in unbalanced emotional and physical states. Since there are so many types of agate, there are various kinds that are named after the place where they were discovered. Carnelian, rhodochrosite, and many other well-known stones belong to this extensive family.

As early as Babylonian times, widespread use was made of the various agates, both for decoration and for healing. The ancient Egyptians and Greeks used them, and they were also common in central and east Africa. Agate was one of the stones in the High Priest's breastplate, representing the tribe of Naphtali.

All types of agate are considered to reinforce the connection to the earth and to the plant kingdom. In ancient Rome, it was customary to wear agate in order to bring about abundance, as well as to increase agricultural prosperity. Agates were used in various rituals for increasing the harvest, as well as in fertility rites. They were frequently added to and combined with other stones for treatment, in order to ensure the maximum efficacy of the stones. In general, in order to increase the action of the other stones, an agate of a similar color was added to them (pink, orange, and so on). The combination caused an increase in the vibration of the color of the stone. In ancient times, agates were used in order to guard the water reservoirs against harm, poisoning, or drying up, and for protecting young children. It is said that the person who wore or carried agate gained strength, courage, and confidence, and was cured of his fears.

Physical healing properties: The agate is used for treating problems of sight, especially for strengthening weak sight.

The mineral's effect on the mental and emotional layers: Agate increases the analytical ability and accuracy, and stimulates hidden or overt abilities and talents, as well as inspiration. By means of agate, the person can assess his current situation correctly and accurately, and act judiciously. Agate reinforces the qualities of fidelity in the person's character. It gives confidence, courage, and support. Moreover, it strengthens our link to nature, helping us feel part of it. All the types of agate are emotionally soothing, and diminish tension and stress.

The mineral's effect on the chakras: This depends on the color of the stone. Most of the types of agate stimulate the third eye chakra. They can be used in linking-up rituals to the spirits of nature.

Spiritual effect: Agate balances the yin and yang energies. It balances the physical, mental, and emotional bodies with its etheric energy. It cleanses and dispels negative or inhibiting energies, removes them, and sometimes transforms them into positive frequencies. It stabilizes the aura and helps the person introspect.

Money, profession, occupation: Agates are suitable for artists. They stabilize the imagination, inspiration, and creative forces. They have varied protective abilities, and are considered to be beneficial for bakers and chefs, because they protect them against burns. Since they strengthen the physical body, they are useful for dancers and athletes. In addition, they are recommended for people in professions that require very steady hands, such as surgery, dentistry, and so on. Since they help emotional balance, and preserve it, they are recommended for social workers, teachers, and people who are liable to suffer from emotional burnout in their professions. Together with petrified wood, agates are recommended for people who work in agriculture and with the soil, especially exhausting physical labor.

Banded Agate

Banded agate is agate that contains layers of quartz that look like stripes or bands.

Physical healing properties: Banded agate helps improve the absorption and assimilation of vitamin B complex. It fortifies the body generally, and helps relieve spasms and external and internal spastic conditions.

The mineral's effect on the emotional and mental layers: This is a wonderful stone for people who are particularly sensitive. It bolsters their personal strength and provides them with a feeling of protection. It helps the person face others courageously, especially people who have difficulty doing so. It helps people who are inclined to have their energy "sucked" out of them easily, as well as people who are easily influenced by the negative energies in their surroundings. It is very soothing, and helps people release feelings of stress and tension.

Spiritual effect: Banded agate is an extremely powerful protective stone. It helps keep negative energies at bay, and does not allow them to penetrate the energy field of its holder.

Money, profession, occupation: Banded agate is thought to provide protection against falling objects, and is very suitable for people in the building or haulage business. Moreover, it is useful for people who are exposed to violent attacks in the course of their work, such as police officers and wardens.

Blue lace agate

Blue lace agate crystallize in masses, and it has a delicate light-bluish hue. Sometimes it contains white stripes that are reminiscent of lace.

Physical healing properties: Blue lace agate helps preserve general physical health. Moreover, it serves as a treatment for various blockages in the nervous system, in the glands that are connected to the digestive system, and the pancreas. It helps release blockages in the circulatory system and in the eye capillaries (in the form of an elixir); it is good for irritations in the eye, and it helps treat skeletal problems and rheumatism. It safeguards and cares for the "hard" parts of the body - the skeleton, the bones (after fractures and sprains, too), and the nails.

The mineral's effect on the emotional and mental layers: Blue lace agate is a stone of love, peace, and joy. It creates a feeling of tranquillity and serenity in its holder, and is very helpful in stressful and tiresome situations. It is very good for people who are shy or find it difficult to speak out and express themselves. It helps people express themselves more easily, even on levels where they had difficulty doing so. It is recommended to place blue lace agate in the house, at work, or in any other place, so as to cleanse non-positive vibrations and to make the atmosphere cleaner and more pleasant. It removes and releases blockages from the nervous system, and helps dispel feelings of depression and despair.

The mineral's effect on the chakras: Blue lace agate is, of course, suitable for treating the throat chakra. It is one of the most popular stones for doing so. Moreover, it also does good work with the heart chakra, the third eye chakra, and the crown chakra.

Spiritual effect: Holding blue lace agate during meditation, or placing it on the region of the third eye or crown chakra, is likely to give the person a pleasant feeling of floating and lightness, while transporting him to new and lofty places. By placing the stone on these chakras, it is possible to get into new and high states of awareness. It is very delicate and pleasant.

Money, profession, occupation: Blue lace agate is very appropriate for people who hold management positions. They will most likely find it very useful for calming and soothing the brain after great mental exertion. Moreover, it is recommended for homemakers, or for people who feel that their work is unfulfilling. It stimulates work satisfaction. It is considered to be very suitable for postal workers, especially for those who have a huge workload.

Botryoidal black agate

Botryoidal black agate is the stone of courage and peace, a protective stone that removes obstacles and affords the accomplishment of objectives. It is black in color.

Physical healing properties: Botryoidal black agate is used for alleviating pains of varying intensity. It is effective for the treatment of a variety of digestive problems, for irregular intestinal action, and problems in the digestive tract. It has a beneficial effect on the veins, and is useful for treating ear, nose, and throat problems.

The mineral's effect on the emotional and mental layers: Botryoidal black agate gives its user courage, but courage that stems from peace. It teaches how the these two properties blend together in order to help the person accomplish his objectives with determination but gentleness. It reinforces communicative abilities and enhances the powers of concentration and the ability to focus. By means of botryoidal black agate, the person can get to the root of things, situations, and problems, and find ways to solve them.

The mineral's effect on the chakras: Botryoidal black agate can be placed on the base chakra, but it is not the most widely accepted stone for placing on the chakras. If you have a botryoidal black agate, and you want to place it on the base chakra while balancing or opening the chakras, go according to your intuition, and see whether this specific stone is suitable.

Spiritual effect: Botryoidal black agate can be used in order to strengthen the link with other worlds, and with creatures and beings from other worlds. Some people use it to increase the power of divining rods (rods that are used for discovering water, quarries, lost objects, and so on), and some use it for enhancing their predictive abilities. By meditating with the stone, it is possible to try and hear with the spiritual, extrasensory sense of hearing.

Money, profession, occupation: Botryoidal black agate was once carried by people in the military and military commanders, whose aim was victory by peaceful means. It is suitable for soldiers, people in the permanent forces, and people who deal with various aspects of warfare and security (politicians, too), for reinforcing determination, courage, and even the ability to compromise from a standpoint of courage and wisdom.

Botswana agate

Botswana agate is widespread in Africa, hence its name. In ancient times, it was used by African tribal healers in fertility rites for reinforcing physical and sexual energy. It is easy to identify this stone. It is "painted" purple-gray, and contains oval and circular white spots.

Physical healing properties: The stone is used for detoxifying procedures, helps people who suffer from depression, and regulates nerve action.

The mineral's effect on the emotional and mental layers: The stone helps people express repressed emotions, stimulates creativity, and is very helpful in solving problems - it guides the person to the depths in order to find the solution to the problem rather than getting embroiled in the problem itself. Moreover, it helps us see the whole picture in all its details. It stimulates the conscience, alertness, and honesty. It is good for very sensitive people, especially when they are compelled to cope with or be near large crowds, in which they do not feel comfortable. It cheers people up immeasurably when they feel lonely or bereaved, and helps people who are not sure what their personal vocation is.

The mineral's effect on the chakras: The stone stimulates the crown chakra, and helps us link up to its lofty properties.

Physical effect: Botswana agate is used by people seeking enlightenment and the unknown, and gives them strength and encouragement on their path. It recharges the aural body, and stimulates divine love.

Money, profession, occupation: It is a very good stone for people whose jobs require supreme alertness and great caution. It ensures alertness and wakefulness while doing their jobs, as well as deliberation and attention to details.

Dendritic agate

Dendritic agate can appear in an opaque or transparent form. Its color is milky white, with kind of stars in blue or brown. Sometimes it contains branch-like intersections, whose source is manganese. Because of its brown or blue "stars," it symbolizes the starry night skies under which the vagabond roams. It is considered to be one of the strongest protective stones for wanderers and hikers. According to many legends, dendritic agate has the ability to prevent the traveler from becoming fatigued, and to protect him from accidents along his way.

Physical healing properties: Dendritic agate helps alleviate pain. In accordance with the shape of the branches that appear in the stone, it helps treat the person's skeleton, and repair defects in the skeleton and in the bones that support the body. Moreover, it helps treat irregularities in the nervous system and in the blood capillaries (especially stones with axon- or capillary-like branching).

The mineral's effect on the emotional and mental layers: Dendritic agate helps the person move easily and safely along life's paths - physically, emotionally, and energetically. It enables the person to be more amiable toward others, especially to people who want to "get closer," but are prevented by shame or embarrassment. It helps the person be connected with himself, even in times of crises and in difficult situations, and helps him understand and know his personal vocation.

The mineral's effect on the chakras: Dendritic agate opens and activates all the chakras.

Spiritual effect: Dendritic agate helps the person feel closer to nature, and link up to and communicate with the plant kingdom. It is suitable for earth- and nature-healing rituals, and for linking up to the natural consciousness of the universe. It allows the spiritual receptive vessels to grow in order to receive an abundance of insights from the universe.

Money, profession, occupation: This is an excellent stone for travelers, airline stewards, pilots, drivers, and truck-drivers. It safeguards against traffic accidents (although it is not a substitute for alertness and caution, of course!), and against fatigue and exhaustion while driving. In addition, it is recommended for traveling salespeople and for those who fly frequently. It is a superb stone for keeping in one's suitcase, backpack, and car. Farmers use it to increase the yield of their crops, and business people use it to increase their turnover. It is considered to be a stone that increases abundance and prosperity on every plane of life. Moreover, it is thought to be a very effective stone for secretaries, as it helps stabilize the energy levels and the work distribution when it is necessary to work on many different levels under pressure.

Fire agate

Fire agate ignites the inspiration that is within us, and enables us to realize our vocation. Its appearance is special because of the presence of thin strata of the mineral limonite. It occurs in a variety of colors - brown, bronze, orange, light green, and blue.

Physical healing properties: Fire agate is used to treat eye problems and for improving night vision. In acupressure and acupuncture, the stone is used for removing blockages in the circulatory system and the central nervous system by means of work on the meridians. It also helps treat hormonal problems.

The mineral's effect on the emotional and mental layers: Fire agate has a powerful action in calming deep, real fears, and, as a result, it is excellent for those who are afraid without knowing why, or find it difficult to liberate themselves from incessant fears. It helps weaken inhibiting and disruptive lusts, and, by so doing, cause the person to experience a sensation of extra energy, which was previously used time and time again to satisfy those lusts. It reinforces the memory, stimulates inspiration, and helps the person advance along his unique path.

The mineral's effect on the chakras: In accordance with its colors, the stone is suitable for the various chakras. If it is orange in color, it can be placed on the sex chakra.

Spiritual effect: Fire agate is said to be able to "send back" threats and harmful wishes to the people who want to hurt the user, so that they will understand the consequences of their thoughts and actions (from the point of view of "everything comes back to you"). It is a good stone for profound introspection. In addition, the stone grounds the person, and is good for people who feel detached or spaced out.

Money, profession, occupation: Fire agate is suitable for people who work in the air or at sea, airline stewards, pilots, and sailors, because of its protective powers, especially when passing over seas and oceans. Moreover, it helps provide safety and protection to people who work in the vicinity of high voltage, so it is recommended for electricians and technicians (but is not a substitute for caution and alertness, of course!)

Flame agate

When flame agate is split in two, it looks like red or white flames are erupting from its base. It sparks a holy fire in the person, and pushes and encourages him to seek the light. Because it also contains red jasper (which is what generally creates the "flame" appearance of the stone), it also has that stone's properties.

Physical healing properties: Flame agate stimulates and promotes energy and physical vitality. It is good for treating burns, infections, and eye problems, alleviates pain, and increases the body's regenerative properties.

The mineral's effect on the emotional and mental layers: Flame agate stimulates enthusiasm and energy, helps the person pay attention to the little details, and helps develop industriousness. In addition, it is said to be able to rekindle the love between lovers.

Spiritual effect: Flame agate spurs the person on and stimulates him clearly to persist in his quest for hope and light.

Indian agate

Indian agate is linked to many folklore legends, especially with stones in which a kind of eye shape is imprinted. They were used as a protection against evil and negative influences. In the Middle East and Africa, the stone was and still is used as a prophylactic against bodily harm and accidents. In ancient cultures, Indian agate was used to protect the locals against floods and natural disasters, and to protect the crops against pests.

The mineral's effect on the emotional and mental layers: Indian agate is suitable for people who experience difficulty or hardship in survival, or whose existential needs are not met, for whatever reason. It is suitable for reinforcing survival abilities under rough and difficult conditions. Some people give it to soldiers who are about to embark on campaigns or actions that may be perilous. Moreover, it is useful for people who suffer from a lack of emotional confidence, and for people who feel that they are physically or emotionally weak.

Spiritual effect: Indian agate helps the person feel protected, and keeps negative energies at bay. It is good for people who are afraid that they have the evil eye, or that someone is envious of them, bears a grudge against them, or thinks negative thoughts about them.

Moss agate

Moss agate is considered by the Indians to be a powerful stone. It strengthens, and replenishes power and energy. It was considered to be the tribe's healing stone, and properties of strengthening the warrior and safeguarding him against enemies and wild animals were attributed to it. In former times, it was used for extracting poisons and healing war wounds. Moss agate appears in many different varieties and in many shades - red, light green, dark green, yellow, brown, and brown-black. Moss agate is transparent, sometimes opaque, and contains various minerals that form plant- or moss-like shapes - hence its name.

Physical healing properties: Moss agate is used for treating dehydration, chills, colds, flu, fungal infections, and eye problems, and helps expel toxins from the body. Moreover, it improves the digestion and speeds it up. An elixir prepared from the stone can be spread on skin inflammations and diseases.

The mineral's effect on the emotional and mental layers: Moss agate endows its user with good persuasive abilities, strengthens his power to do things in every field, and refines behavior and appearance. It encourages efficiency, reinforces the person's positive properties, and is very good for people with a fragile or vulnerable ego and low self-esteem. The stone helps the person attain emotional balance, and gives joy and tranquillity by means of its quality of emphasizing the beauty and pleasantness of every existing thing. In addition, it helps the person feel that he is part of nature.

Spiritual effect: People who have intuitive knowledge, or knowledge that is linked to the ways of the Indians and their rituals, can use moss agate as a stone of power, in accordance with the intuitive knowledge that reaches them.

Money, profession, occupation: Moss agate is considered to promote greater sensitivity to food and food products, and for that reason it is recommended for chefs, bakers, and people who work in professions of food preparation and marketing (including homemakers). Moss agate, whose internal part is reminiscent of a kind of plant growing inside it, is used to fortify crops and encourage growth. It is a wonderful stone for farmers and field workers, and is also suitable for vets and farm animals in general. Moreover, it may help people who experience anxiety when they go for job interviews or are in the process of looking for work. It is said that moss agate is a stone that brings wealth and economic prosperity.

Plume agate

Plume agate is a form of moss agate with a warm, burning red color.

Physical healing properties: Plume agate is good for treating all aspects of flow in the body - blood, energy, neurotransmitters, and so on. It is able to balance the white blood cells in relation to the red blood cells, thus helping to improve and strengthen the immune system.

The mineral's effect on the emotional and mental layers: Plume agate stimulates creativity and imagination, and helps the person center and focus. To a great extent, it develops the person's visual powers. In addition, it is very helpful for people who fear the unknown.

Spiritual effect: Plume agate stimulates visualization and powers of the imagination, by means of which we can see in our mind's eye what we are longing for. Through this powerful work, plume agate helps us realize the dreams that have a physical form in the real world. It is used in rebirthing and in meditations that evoke events and experiences from the past, so that they can be seen in a different light, and fixed. Plume agate helps liberate us from these memories and experiences when they are no longer necessary to us, and its action is plainly felt on the energetic level. Moreover, by means of plume agate, it is possible to enter deep meditative states, receive answers to questions during meditation (the question must be defined beforehand and programmed into the stone), and feel meditative emptiness.

Money, profession, occupation: Plume agate, like moss agate, develops and encourages greater sensitivity to food and food products, and is recommended for chefs, cooks, bakers, and people who work in food preparation or marketing professions. Since it strengthens focus, as well as the fulfillment of wishes (mainly when we hold it and see what we desire in our mind's eye), it should be carried in our pocket when we go out to seek employment or have a job interview.

Alabaster

Alabaster is a kind of gypsum that crystallizes in white granules, or white with thin stripes.

Physical healing properties: Alabaster is used mainly for treating heart problems.

The mineral's effect on the emotional and mental layers: Alabaster dispels the anger and irritation that cause diseases, and in this way helps the feeling of emotional cleanliness and promotes a more profound treatment of physical illnesses. It helps people forgive, and makes these actions easier by clearing away grudges. Alabaster is a good stone to use during periods of stress and hardship, because it promotes maturity and the ability to cope, and encourages self-control, so that the person will not fall apart as a result of the load he is carrying.

Spiritual effect: Alabaster can be used to charge other treatment stones and augment their power. The stones are placed on the alabaster, and it recharges them energetically. It is used in guided meditations for linking up to the pharaonic period, and helps decipher the secrets of the pyramids. Moreover, it facilitates the moments of sinking into meditation by helping to concentrate in the correct way, and augments the perceptive ability during meditation.

Money, profession, occupation: This stone is very good for people who engage in volunteer activities and in service professions - it hones and reinforces the ability to give and the talents necessary for giving to others.

Alexandrite

Alexandrite is an exquisite stone, characterized by its tendency to change color in accordance with the light projected on it. It can be blue, green, orange-red, purple, and red, according to the light reflected in it and the direction from which it is observed. In addition to the properties that appear here, you should also read about the properties attributed to beryl, since alexandrite is a type of beryl. From the historical point of view, its name is linked with Russia, since it is named after the Czar Alexander. It is a very rare and expensive stone. Synthetic alexandrites have been manufactured successfully, too, and they are among the rare synthetic stones whose properties are almost the same as those of the original stone.

Physical healing properties: Alexandrite can be used for treating problems of the nervous system, for various anemic disorders, and for increased protein absorption in the body. In addition, it is used for treating intestinal, spleen, and pancreatic problems, and for regeneration of the cells of the nervous tissue.

The mineral's effect on the spiritual and mental layers: Alexandrite sparks creativity, and is very helpful to people who are involved with theatrical arts, painting, and writing, as well as in every art form in which it is necessary to keep on expressing the abstract and making it concrete. It helps the person's inner concentration, so as to evoke understanding and inner learning. It contributes to the increase of self-esteem, optimism, and emotional balance. It is an important stone for people whose love of life has been extinguished. In addition, it is thought to be a stone that brings good luck to its owner. During the day, when the alexandrite's color is blue-green, it can be used for inspiring a good mood, success, and good luck. At night, when its color becomes red, it can be used to make a person feel more sensual, warm, and loving.

The mineral's effect on the chakras: Alexandrite links the third eye chakra, the heart chakra, and the base chakra.

Spiritual effect: Alexandrite can be used during astral journeys. When it is used during meditation, it helps the person understand what his path up to this point has been, and what the path that stretches out in front of him is. Alexandrite helps tune and link the mental, emotional, and etheric bodies.

Money, profession, occupation: This is a marvelous stone for artists of all kinds.

Amber

Amber is not a stone, but rather fossilized resin. Its shades range between golden yellow and brown. Sometimes, the stone can occur in shades of red, blue, and green. The most famous amber "stones" are the ones in which an ancient insect has been trapped and perfectly preserved, with the resin solidifying around it and turning into clear amber. Because of its beauty, and the fact that it is rather prestigious, amber is widely used in various items of jewelry, and is thought to be one of the oldest stones to be worn - amber jewelry has been found in graves in northern Europe from 8,000 years ago. It was considered to be a favorite stone in ancient Egypt, and it is mentioned several times in the Bible. Some people claim that amber is appropriate for menopausal and postmenopausal women, since it enhances their power, prestige, and majesty. As opposed to "natural" crystals, which feel cold, amber feels warm to the touch (since it is not a "real" crystal). It has been said about it that it stores the sun's power inside it, and the ancients would use it in their primeval fire rituals.

Physical healing properties: Amber is used for treating goiter, which is a disease of the thyroid gland, and for various throat ailments, for clearing phlegm, and for coughs and colds. Moreover, it is used for treating kidney and urinary tract problems, especially the bladder. Its main action is helping the body heal itself by converting the non-positive energies into positive energies. In addition, it helps to calm and stimulate the nerves simultaneously. It has antiseptic and anti-infection properties. In ancient times, amber was finely ground, and its powder used for treating bacterial and infectious diseases.

The mineral's effect on the emotional and mental layers: Amber is very effective for stimulating the person's mental layers, and for linking the aware self to the universe, of which every individual forms a part. Moreover, it helps achieve various objectives during mental efforts, such as in cases of visualization, in a physical and tangible manner. It draws the person's attention to the free choice available to him, and helps him be aware of this ability and use it wisely. Amber helps the person feel unconditional love, and in bygone days symbolized the wedding vows and the binding of the couple. It is an excellent stone for people who are suffering from tremendous stress, and for people who need encouragement and morale-boosting. It is very helpful for people who are severely depressed - to the point that they do not want to go on living - as well as for sufferers from anorexia or other diseases rooted in a lack of will to live.

The mineral's effect on the chakras: A yellow piece of amber is suitable for balancing, opening, and cleansing the solar plexus chakra. It can be used for opening and cleaning the other chakras - the sex and base chakras, according to the color of the amber, which can also tend to be spotted or brown.

Spiritual healing properties: Amber contains unique purifying properties, and it can be used to purify rooms, as well as the body, mind, and spirit, of negative energies. It has the ability to draw diseases out of the body, and it must be purified after being used in this way.

Amethyst

Amethyst, which is very well known, is one of the twelve stones of the High Priest's breastplate, and is identified with the tribe of Gad. Amethyst is a kind of quartz, and is formed in masses and crystals. Different-sized clusters of amethyst are easily obtainable. The colors of the stone range from purple and pale lavender, sometimes with white speckles, to very deep purple. It occurs both in opaque and transparent forms.

This marvelous stone exerts a significant action on the third eye chakra, and is widely used in meditation, where it is placed on the third eye. It enables the person to enter a meditative state easily, and to remain there without being disturbed. Some people use or wear amethyst in order to bring an abundance of prosperity into their lives.

Physical healing properties: Because it is linked to the third eye and the crown chakras, amethyst is used for treating problems of the sympathetic nervous system and the endocrine system. It helps restore balance to those systems, and treat general problems of the nervous system. It is an excellent stone for repairing the damage caused by stress, tension, and pressure, and for treating headaches, vertigo, and insomnia. Overall, this stone is very good for treating various mental disorders. It is helpful in the treatment of auditory, digestive, stomach, skin, teeth, and heart problems. Moreover, it can be used for treating problems of a weak skeleton, and for improving defective posture. Some people use it for treating alcoholism and other addictions. If it is worn around the neck, the stone protects against radiation, such as the radiation that emanates from cell-phones, TV, microwave ovens, and so on. Alternatively, the stone can be placed on the appliance so that it absorbs the radiation and prevents its dissemination throughout the room. After being used in this manner, it must be cleansed and purified immediately (it should not even be held in one's hand, but rolled with a pencil or some such object straight into a glass of water).

The mineral's effect on the emotional and mental layers: Amethyst helps in the attainment of tranquillity, power, stability, and energy. It clears up mental and emotional confusion, encourages a feeling of caring toward others by making us understand that those are the demands of the universe, and inspires humility. It helps us make wise, responsible, and flexible decisions; it soothes, and helps us do things for our peace of mind. It is very good in calming down vibrations of nervouness and anger, and for releasing the person from various emotional patterns by helping him see the range of possible paths for coping with emotional situations. Amethyst is very effective for people who have difficulty falling asleep and for people who suffer from nightmares. It helps people who are in mourning, or who have suffered a loss, to link up to faith and the understanding of the essence of death, which is in fact a change of form. It is effective for calming tensions, and for treating fatigue and over-excitement. It is helpful for people who are agitated and excitable, as well as for people who suffer from anxiety. Moreover, it can be used for liberating a person of his dependence on others, or of others on him. It combines mental logic with intuition and the receiving of spiritual knowledge, and in this way greatly strengthens the person's abilities.

The mineral's effect on the chakras: This is one of the best stones for placing on the third eye. Its color falls into the highest vibrations of the third eye, and it helps induce a meditative state very easily. Moreover, it is also suitable for stimulating and opening the crown chakra.

Spiritual effect: Amethyst is an extremely powerful spiritual healing stone. It helps convert low energies into high energies, and balances the energies of the bodies by linking the mental body to the emotional and the physical bodies. In this manner, it helps the connection between the upper and the lower. It can be used for cleansing and purifying the aura, and for getting rid of non-positive energies, especially those that originate in the mental layer. It reinforces telepathic powers, and, as mentioned before, stimulates and opens the third eye. It lovingly and gently teaches the person the humility that is required for contact with high spiritual insights, from faith and a desire for truth. This stone is a "must" for anyone who engages in spiritual activity, and for anyone who is interested in developing his spiritual awareness. Since its frequencies are very delicate, and despite its high spiritual activity, it can be worn, carried on the body, or placed anywhere in the home or office, without any fear that it will cause the person to "levitate" at an inappropriate time. It is one of the most popular stones for placing on the third eye in laying on of stones and in healing treatments. Because of its many energies and great strength, albeit delicate and soft, it is wonderful for beginning meditation with stones. It is recommended that people who are inexperienced at meditation with stones begin their session with the help of an amethyst.

Money, profession, occupation: Amethyst is very suitable for people who engage in the different fields of art, because of its ability to stimulate intuitive powers and inspiration. It is considered to be a very effective stone for ministers and people in high positions that are fraught with responsibility toward the community. It encourages humility, and develops the spiritual layer. Moreover, it may help them cope with the numerous pressures to which they are subjected.

Amazonite

Amazonite is actually a kind of feldspar that attains a form of masses or prisms. It is mainly turquoise in color, but sometimes yellow, whitish, or gray areas can be seen in it. It is also possible to find amazonite in shades of pearl, blue, or pink. Some people maintain that this was one of the stones that was set in the High Priest's breastplate.

Physical healing properties: Amazonite can be used to treat problems of the nervous system by opening blockages that cause defective nerve impulse transmission to be even worse. It helps balance and improve the metabolic processes, and is helpful in problems of a lack of calcium, such as teeth problems, osteoporosis, and so on. Drinking an elixir of the stone may be very helpful in improving calcium absorption. It is used in treating scoliosis and muscle spasms, and helps treat headaches. Because of its spiritual properties, it is a stone that helps maintain general good health when it is worn or carried.

The mineral's effect on the emotional and mental layers: Amazonite is an excellent stone for treating worries and fears, because it relates to the process itself and permits these emotions to be experienced. It helps the person attain a feeling of calmness in times of hardship, it has a soothing action on the nervous system, and helps dispel nervousness and non-positive energies. It encourages hope and faith, and alleviates situations of loneliness. Amazonite is helpful in communication, in understanding the other person, and in conveying our thoughts to him correctly and understandably. Moreover, it strengthens the person's link to nature. Some people link amazonite to the Amazons, the female warriors, and consider it to be suitable for feminists and women who fight for female equality. On the other hand, it helps women who feel that they are weak and helpless in the "man's world," as they see it.

The mineral's effect on the chakras: Because of its color, amazonite, especially in its turquoise shade, links up with the throat and heart chakras. Since it consists of a mixture of two of the chakra colors, to make up the color turquoise, it is possible to consider it a stone that promotes more loving communication, and better communication between people who love each other.

Spiritual effect: One of this stone's special properties is its ability to link and blend apparently different things: between the astral and etheric bodies and the physical body, between masculine and feminine energies, and between the ostensibly clashing foundations of the human personality. Moreover, it is used in ceremonies to make contact with the spirits of nature.

Apache tear

The Apache tear stone is actually a type of obsidian. It originates in volcanic fire, and it is a kind of volcanic glass that occurs in opaque black, transparent black, smoky black, mahogany black, purple black and greenish black. It is rounded in shape, and on it there are shell- or spiral-like features. It is a stone with amazing consoling abilities. According to legend, it got its name because of the tears of the Apache women who lost their warrior husbands in battle.

Physical healing properties: Apache tear is used for increasing the absorption of vitamins, and helps combat poisons and toxins. In ancient times, it was used in different parts of the world to extract snake venom after a snake-bite. (I do not recommend, however, that the action of the stone be tested out at such a critical moment. It can be placed on the bite while the person is being taken for medical treatment *without delay*, but under no circumstances must it be a substitute for prompt medical treatment.)

The mineral's effect on the emotional and mental layers: As we mentioned before, this is an excellent stone for comforting mourners. When a person is in a time of crisis because of the loss of a dear one, especially in tragic circumstances, it is a good idea to give him an Apache tear as a gift. The stone should be programmed to dispel sadness, fortify the person, and protect him from plunging into prolonged grief. The stone helps the mourner understand the situation in a more profound manner, to accept it, and to go on living despite the fact that a near and dear one was taken from him. In addition to this powerful property, Apache tear helps a person adopt a more forgiving attitude toward other people and the universe. It helps free a person from emotional inhibitions, improves spontaneity, and promotes a better analytical ability. In general, it is not used for treating, opening, cleansing, or balancing the chakras, but more for general work on certain situations such as heavy mourning and a need for consolation. In these cases, it should be worn on the body or carried in a pocket.

Apatite

Apatite is a stone that is widely used in healing and channeling. It crystallizes in the form of a prism, and comes in a variety of colors: white, yellow, green, olive, blue, brown, reddish brown, purple, and so on. It is very common in the form of crystals that are yellow or greenish yellow in color.

Physical healing properties: Apatite is used as an appetite suppressant by carrying, wearing, or drinking as an elixir. Since it is a stone with abilities that focus mainly on the spiritual layer, it is possible to use it for physical healing by focusing the healing energies on the meridians, the endocrine glands, and on the various organs in the body, generally through healing work. Some people call it "the nutrition stone," because it teaches us how to nourish our body, mind, and spirit in a wise and loving manner.

The mineral's effect on the emotional and mental layers: Apatite is excellent for improving and stimulating the intellect, at the same time ensuring that the person stays away from condescension and from a negative use of the acquired knowledge. It is helpful in acquiring coordination and cooperation between the physical, the emotional, the mental and the etheric bodies, and balances situations of hyperactivity or sluggishness. In addition, it helps increase creativity, and in the attainment of a feeling of tranquillity and equilibrium between the yin and yang energies. It encourages self-confidence and greatly assists people with a low self-image. Since it teaches us using love and compassion, it helps people who help others keep up with their wonderful work.

Spiritual effect: As we said above, apatite is widely used for channeling and healing. It helps people learn and receive information via channeling, both personally and in a group. It not only helps people receive the information, but also apply it on the physical plane and correctly understand the insights that are received through meditation with it. Because of its far-reaching abilities in the field of channeling, it can be used for channeling with beings from other planets and galaxies, for understanding information from previous lives, and for developing telepathic abilities. This stone can be used for opening blockages in every one of the chakras, for balancing situations of overload or congestion in the chakras, and for developing senses of sight, hearing, and extrasensory perception (that are parallel to the physical senses). It helps the person achieve higher levels of awareness when it is combined with clean and correct spiritual work, and assists him in his spiritual work, by helping him overcome various mental embarrassments that are liable to appear during the work and the spiritual development.

Profession, occupation: This stone is highly recommended for people who engage in healing, channeling, therapy, and teaching spiritual professions, as well as for those who are involved on a volunteer or paid basis in care-giving professions, assistance, and social counseling.

Apophyllite

Apophyllite occurs in green, white, gray-white, and transparent. It crystallizes in grains or clusters, mainly on the surface of other minerals.

Physical healing properties: Apophyllite is good for the health of the body by encouraging us to pay heed and attention to our physical condition and needs. Moreover, it serves to rejuvenate.

The mineral's effect on the emotional and mental layers: Apophyllite helps the person go deeply into his personality and see into it. It presents to him whatever needs fixing in his character, his behavior, and his attitudes. It helps him discern what is in need of repair and change, and it also stimulates the power to repair and change. It helps him see the truth that is contained in various situations, and in physical existence, and to follow it. It arouses the aspiration to perfection on all levels, as well as to universal love. It inspires intuition and extrasensory perception, optimism, and joy.

The mineral's effect on the chakras: When it is placed on the third eye, apophyllite stimulates intuitive vision. Green apophyllite can be used for activating the heart chakra and for joining it to spiritual and enlightened levels.

Spiritual effect: Some people use apophyllite for predicting the future. Apophyllite provides a link to the higher dimensions. It is a famous channeling stone, and it can be used on all the different levels of channeling. By means of apophyllite, a link between our physical existence and our spiritual reality can be created. It is possible to use it during astral journeys, in order to safeguard the link with the physical body during the journey, and in order to preserve in the consciousness the impressions and insights of the journey. It can be used to channel with spiritual beings, to reconstruct incarnations, and to raise up insights that are linked to previous lives. It is a wonderful stone for channeling when the person wants to request help, receive guidance, or know how and in what way a friend or relative can be helped, and get a solution to the problems. Green apophyllite can be used to avoid the penetration of unwanted powers and eliminate them, both in the past and the present.

Profession, occupation: Apophyllite is very suitable for those who engage in healing and spiritual development for the purpose of therapy and learning. It helps them look inside themselves and listen to the components of their personality, so that they will function better on the therapeutic and instructional levels of the spiritual professions. In addition, it is a stone that helps channelers and people who engage in predicting the future, or people who are learning those topics.

Aquamarine

Aquamarine is the most famous of the beryl stones, and in addition to the properties that appear here, it shares many properties with stones in the beryl family. It crystallizes in the shape of a prism. The color of aquamarine is light, transparent greenish-blue, sometimes almost colorless. It was one of the stones in the High Priest's breastplate, and it might be the stone that is identified with the tribe of Asher.

Aquamarine is also called "blue emerald." It is linked to the power of the moon and water, as its name, "sea water," indicates. Its blue-green color symbolizes the rays of the sun reflected in the waves of the cosmic sea. The Romans were the first to give it this name, since the fishermen used it to protect them against storms at sea, and to promote good catches.

Physical healing properties: Aquamarine purifies the throat, the kidneys, the liver, and the spleen. It helps treat neurological pains, glandular problems, throat and jaw problems, and toothache. Moreover, it is also good for maintaining the teeth and bone structure. In cases of environmental pollution, it should be worn around the neck as a protection. In these situations, it is possible to imagine it enveloping us and moving around in the air surrounding us, so as to protect ourselves from air pollution. It is used for eye treatments, for making eyes healthy, for improving vision, and for balancing and reinforcing glandular action.

The mineral's effect on the emotional and mental layers: Aquamarine has far-reaching balancing properties in all the layers. It balances the mental, emotional, and physical layers, and soothes and assuages emotions. It is very good for people who suffer from nervousness and find it hard to calm down. It is helpful in times of change by helping us learn life's lessons. It is very effective for pupils and students because it stimulates mental activity and thought processes, and helps them learn not only about the things around them, but also about themselves. Aquamarine is called "the stone of heroism." It reduces worries and fears, and helps people refrain from judging and criticizing others by stimulating the energy of humility, gentleness, and moderation. Aquamarine is extremely powerful in the field of the person's communication with himself as well as with his surroundings, and helps the person take conscious responsibility for his words, conduct, and deeds.

The mineral's effect on the chakras: Aquamarine stimulates, activates and cleanses the throat chakra by helping people to "find their voice," be it from the point of view of speech or song. It purifies the chakra, and cleanses it of impure patterns and thoughts. It has a balancing and tuning action on all the chakras, and it directs the energetic equilibrium that links the various bodies.

Spiritual effect: Aquamarine stimulates the purity, the immaculateness, and the innocence that is within us, and helps us achieve clear visions. It performs a protective action on the aura and on the delicate bodies. It stimulates the superego, and helps the person tune into the frequencies of the spiritual planes. When using the stone during meditation, it is possible to reach the level of "diving" inward to the self, in order to understand the processes and the complexity that occur within the soul, and work on them with awareness. Aquamarine is especially suitable for people whose sign of the Zodiac is Aries, Gemini, or Pisces.

Money, profession, occupation: Aquamarine is considered to be a stone that protects seafarers, fishermen, sailors, divers, and people who go sailing. Some people claim that it prevents or alleviates seasickness. Moreover, it is wonderful for people who work on voice production, or who want to sing. It augments the ability to feel and react, and inspires ideas and the aspiration to perfection and truth. It is recommended for students and people whose profession requires that they frequently cope with new knowledge (researchers, computer people, and so on). It is considered to be one of the most excellent stones that can be given to researchers, zoologists, and marine archaeologists, especially when their work entails diving.

Aventurine

Aventurine is the name given to a crystal that is spotted with other minerals. Aventurine stones whose basis is quartz spotted with hematite are extremely common. Sometimes the basis is feldspar. Generally speaking, the color of aventurine is green, occasionally with gold sparkles.

Physical healing properties: Aventurine soothes the nervous system, and helps treat heart ailments and problems in the lungs, genitals, and muscles.

The mineral's effect on the emotional and mental layers: Aventurine is an excellent stone for working on the emotional layer. It is an exceptionally soothing stone, and induces well-being and calmness. It stimulates motivation and adventurousness, while linking us to creation and dispelling fears and anxieties. It stimulates and increases creativity, reinforces leadership ability and decisiveness, and arouses pleasant optimism.

It helps the person release himself from negative thoughts, encourages a positive attitude toward life, and raises self-esteem. It helps the person find a direction in life, and frees him of possessiveness and inhibiting thoughts. It balances emotions, and it is wonderful to hold an aventurine stone in each hand when one is feeling bad emotionally, or to stick it with a plaster to the heart region (or put it inside the bra). Using aventurine, it is possible to release oneself easily and pleasantly, gently and softly, from the traumatic experiences of early childhood. It is a very soothing stone that promotes tranquillity and quiet, and it should always be kept in the vicinity. This stone has a unique and exceptional action in men who find it difficult to express their feelings or are emotionally "closed" - men who love, but are unable to express themselves and say "I love you." Aventurine should be placed under their pillow for several weeks.

The mineral's effect on the chakras: This is a wonderful stone for treating the heart chakra. It cleanses the chakra, activates it, opens it to love, and even protects it against the "sucking" of energy.

Spiritual effect: Aventurine balances yin and yang, and helps create equilibrium between the physical, emotional, and mental layers in the whole aura. During meditation, when it is held in the person's hand or placed on his heart, he can feel a pleasant feeling of love flowing through his body and mind. Many therapists place it in the patient's hand, left or right, and place rose quartz in the other hand, especially when the purpose of the treatment is releasing traumas and emotional pains.

Money, profession, occupation: Aventurine is considered to be a stone that increases the "seizing" of financial opportunities. For this reason, it is recommended for bankers, business people, and stockbrokers. In addition, it is recommended for all those whose occupation entails a great deal of tension and mental pressure.

Azurite

Azurite is a dark blue stone with a touch of purple, and may also occur in a variety of shades of blue, starting with light blue. It crystallizes in masses or prisms. Azurite is the symbol of inner knowledge and wisdom, and some people call it "the stone of heaven." It is considered holy to the Native Americans and the Mayan culture, and writings about its uses can be found in various ancient cultures. It is considered to be one of the stones that is most linked to the third eye. Azurite *is not particularly recommended* for wearing as an item of jewelry.

Physical healing properties: Azurite improves the body's absorption of the minerals magnesium, copper, zinc, and calcium. In addition, it helps treat various problems with the spinal column, the vertebrae, the ribs, and the bones. Some people use it to treat circulatory problems, tics and convulsions, and situations of imbalance of the neurotransmitters. It is used in detoxification processes for eliminating toxins from the body. It helps reduce and disperse tumors *(only when an expert healer administers the treatment!)*. Drinking an elixir produced from the stone helps treat and cure rheumatism and skin inflammations.

The mineral's effect on the emotional and mental layers: Azurite is highly recommended for pupils and students who are studying for exams (it should be placed on the desk). It helps develop and deepen thought, and aids the comprehension and absorption of the information. It can be used in order to increase and even identify the abilities and talents that are hidden in the person. Moreover, it reinforces creativity and stimulates it. It is a good stone for freeing the person of worries, troublesome thoughts, decision-making problems, and feelings of uncertainty. It increases the ability to make decisions as well as self-confidence.

The mineral's effect on the chakras: Azurite is, of course, suitable for the third eye chakra. It opens, balances, and stimulates it. Moreover, it is possible to place it on the heart chakra as well, in order to open it, and for experiencing the feelings of humility and empathy. The stone is also effective when placed on the sex chakra, since it helps increase the creativity that emanates from this chakra.

Spiritual effect: Azurite develops sensitivity, spiritual comprehension, and intuition. It stimulates the ability to see lofty sights and visions. It takes us away from emotion and thought into a situation of an experience of simply "being." It is a wonderful stone for placing on the third eye during meditation, since it projects visions of cosmic truths and opens up the inner vision. In addition, it helps the person enter a meditative state that is free of any thought or feeling. It performs marvelous healing work for developing the person's spiritual layers. It can be used in order to identify the energetic channels necessary for solving a problem. By conscious focusing with azurite, and concentration of thoughts on dispelling obstacles and disturbances, it is possible to use it to remove every obstacle and disturbance from the person's path. Moreover, it should be placed on the body wherever there is an organic blockage.

Profession, occupation: The stone is highly recommended for students and pupils who are studying for exams. It is an excellent stone for beginner healers, and also for therapists who heal with energies.

Basalt

Basalt is a gray-black volcanic stone that is found in regions where volcanic eruptions occurred. It comprises hardened molten lava. It is considered to be a lunar-influenced stone in which all the moon's power comes to the fore at new moon or full moon.

Physical healing powers: Basalt is used for developing and strengthening muscles. Moreover, some people use it for fertility treatments, and for treating problems of the genitals.

The mineral's effect on the emotional and mental layers: Since it is lava that burst forth from the bowels of the earth during a volcanic eruption, cooled down, and solidified, basalt represent the ability to "cool off" when a person is enraged and angry. It helps assuage anger, and brings the person to understand and accept the situations that oblige him to retreat from his opinions and intentions. It strengthens the person in difficult situations and times, and helps him cope with changes that are not easy.

Spiritual effect: Basalt helps people who are working on assuaging their anger, and on their lack of moderation or tolerance, as a condition for and an important part of spiritual growth and development.

Beryl

The beryl family comprises several types of stones. Among them is aquamarine (blue emerald), emerald, golden beryl, and so on. You can read about aquamarine and emerald under separate headings in this book. For this reason, we will now relate to golden beryl.

Physical healing properties: Golden beryl can be used for treating problems of the spinal column, for cardiac disturbances, and some therapists use it to treat people who suffered concussion or skull injuries.

The mineral's effect on the emotional and mental layers: Golden beryl inspires self-confidence and the desire to succeed and achieve. It encourages the person's inherent initiative and helps him operate and think independently. It helps the person adapt to different situations in the best possible way, safeguarding his self, and enables him to overcome the obstacles that stand in the way of realizing his aspirations courageously and with inner strength.

The mineral's effect on the chakras: According to the color of golden beryl, we can understand that it exerts a significant influence on the solar plexus chakra. It opens and activates it, but, in addition, also opens and activates the crown chakra. In that way, it helps the person follow his path with a feeling of independence of thought and deed by linking him to the need to realize the gifts of the universe that are contained inside of him. It links intellect to spirit, thus creating a wise and relevant way of operating.

Spiritual effect: Golden beryl arouses the purity that is within us, on all the layers. It stimulates the potential in each person and supports it by creating a feeling of support and guidance from the Creator. Apparently, beryl was one of the stones in the High Priest's breastplate.

Money, profession, occupation: Golden beryl is considered to be particularly suitable for politicians. It arouses in them the abilities to overcome the many obstacles that stand in their path, and protects them from the manipulative influence of others and of their own ego. Moreover, it helps them adhere to an aspiration to purity in their ways and in their conduct, both personal and political. It helps them refrain from abusing their power.

Bloodstone

This stone is also known as "heliotrope." The stone was given its name because of its appearance - it is a green stone with red spots that are reminiscent of blood. Bloodstone is a type of quartz, which is formed in masses, and its green color is mainly opaque.

Physical healing properties: According to its name, one can understand the treatments administered by the ancients, as well as by healers today - this stone is used for treating and purifying the circulatory system. It is good for treating the spleen, cancer of the blood, and for increasing, decreasing, or stabilizing the blood flow, according to the patient's needs. Moreover, it has cleansing and detoxifying properties, and as a result is used for treating the kidneys, bladder, intestines, and liver - that is, the organs that excrete and expel the toxins from the body. Bloodstone is used for treating hemorrhoids and varicose veins, and can be used for the relief of congestion in the lungs, soothing rashes, and strengthening vision. Some people say that the stone can stop nosebleeds.

In general, it helps the person achieve physical equilibrium, mainly in states of pressure, tension, and anxiety.

The mineral's effect on the emotional and mental layers: Bloodstone helps concentration and facilitates the decision-making process. It is good for invigorating relationships and renewing them. It helps the person make practical applications moderately and logically, and stimulates wisdom and sensitivity so that things can be done in the right way. It increases creativity and hones various talents, while it directs the person to use his talents for the greater good. Of course, it safeguards the person against selfishness and a lack of ideals. It is a good stone for calming down, for treating negative or unclean thoughts, and for cleansing the aura.

The mineral's effect on the chakras: Bloodstone is suitable for treating several chakras together. Because of its green color, it is very appropriate for the heart chakra and the energy of the heart. It helps stimulate and balance the base chakra, and treat problems connected with the sex chakra. When we hold a bloodstone, we notice the color of the spots on it. They are likely to be in a strong red-maroon color, which renders the stone very suitable for the base chakra, or in shades of dark orange, which render it very suitable for the sex chakra. In any event, by means of the correct tuning, we can use the stone for treating any one of those chakras.

Spiritual effect: Bloodstone has a beneficial effect on the energetic bodies, and regulates the flow of energy. It helps the bodies achieve a higher level of coordination among themselves. It strengthens them and enables them to cope in a better way with changes, and with changes in the energy field.

Money, profession, occupation: Bloodstone is suitable for people who practice healing, because of its ability to regulate the energy flow and allocation correctly. For the same reason, it is considered to be suitable for nurses and veterinary surgeons. Because of its close connection to the circulatory system, it was used by the practitioners of these and similar professions in the ancient world.

Calcite

Calcite, which crystallizes in a variety of forms including grains, masses, dodecahedrons, and diamonds, is in fact a transparent, colorless stone. The mingling of different elements in the process of its creation is what give it a broad spectrum of beautiful shdes. Calcite in many different transparent shades of color can be found: light transparent green, orange, peach, pink, gray, black, yellow, red, and even blue. Calcite in the different colors have many common properties, and, having said that, each differently colored stone has its own uniqueness that derives from its color.

Physical healing properties: In general, calcite in the different colors is used for treating various kidney ailments, for problems with pancreatic and spleen function, for calcium outcrops in the body, and for the balance of calcium absorption in the body. **Orange calcite** helps get rid of waste products and toxins, and strengthens the bones. **Green calcite** is good for treating arthritis, tight, contracted muscles, and joints that are hard to move, as well as for infectious or bacterial diseases (it should be carried or held when someone in the vicinity has come down with an infectious or bacterial disease, in order to stop the disease and prevent it from spreading). **Pink calcite** helps treat headaches.

The mineral's effect on the emotional and mental layers: Calcite of all colors is good for people who are studying science or art, because it enables them, even unconsciously, to gain broader knowledge and understanding.

Orange calcite helps the person achieve clear and lucid thought. It is used as a great aid to people who are engrossed in learning - students and pupils.

Green calcite does wonderful work in helping understand negative and inhibiting patterns of thought, behavior, and emotion. It helps us cleanse the unconscious layers of these patterns. In order to bring about this action, it is mainly advisable to place the stone on the throat chakra. Its action in this area is really very powerful, and it has proved itself in its efficacy in an experiment that was performed in the encounter between a cat and a dog, when each one had a green calcite stone next to its neck. Within several hours, they had succeeded in overcoming their natural mutual hostility. It is considered a stone that helps people, or animals, free themselves of a genetic code. It helps people liberate themselves of painful childhood experiences, mainly when it is placed on the heart. It is recommended for people who do mental work for distancing and liberating themselves from unwanted lusts and ego problems. Moreover, green calcite helps in achieving mental balance. It should be carried or worn when a person is starting a new job, task, studies, or relationship - it helps the new beginning occur more easily, better, and more harmoniously.

Blue calcite stimulates communicative and expressive abilities. It helps the person express the material he has learned verbally, so it is recommended for students who have to lecture or present projects to their class and lecturers.

Pink calcite helps dispel old patterns of fear or sadness.

The mineral's effect on the chakras: The different types of calcite are good for purifying and activating all the chakras. Calcite in an appropriate color is placed on the relevant chakra. **Pink calcite** causes love to flow to the heart chakra very strongly. In addition, **green calcite** can be placed on the throat chakra in order to eliminate negative patterns of thought and emotion. **Yellow** or **transparent calcite** can be placed on the crown chakra in order to fill it with energy. **Transparent calcite** placed on each of the chakras increases the chakra's energy. **Diamond-shaped transparent calcite** has a unique effect on the third eye chakra.

Spiritual effect: The various calcite stones have a unique ability to increase the energy that is tuned inside them. For instance, if the energy of love is tuned into calcite, it will come back to us doubled and tripled. They expand the awareness and awaken in us respect and esteem toward Nature's creative powers. Moreover, they also stimulate creativity. Placing suitably colored calcite on the chakras activates the chakras and cleanses them, while influencing all the other chakras. Meditation by means of placing diamond-shaped transparent calcite on the third eye chakra, and asking any kind of question, is likely to bring us the answer to the question. As a rule, meditation by means of placing a diamond-shaped calcite on the third eye chakra is likely to stimulate wonderful visions while creating a clear link to the superego. It throws light on the reason for the occurrence of various situations and events in our lives, and their meanings. In addition, it provides an explanation for our dreams and flashes of inspiration.

Calcite liberates cellular and spiritual memories. This liberation is likely to induce a sensation of relief and comfort, sudden understanding of things, and even enlightenment. It helps reconstruct memories from previous incarnations, and understand the connection between them and our present lives.

Work, occupation: The various calcite stones in their different colors are especially suitable for holistic healers, students, scholars, and artists.

Carnelian

Carnelian, which is also known as sard, is a type of agate. The source of its name lies in the Latin word for "meat." It is mainly orange in color, but it can also be found in red, red brown, and shades of salmon and sienna. It generally crystallizes in masses. It is an amazingly lovely stone, and is widely used because of the warmth and cheerfulness it radiates.

In the days of ancient Egypt, the stone was used to assuage and soothe feelings of rage, fear, and hatred. In this ancient civilization, the stone was considered the "builders' stone," and was worn by the "master builders" and designers. Warriors from other ancient civilizations would wear it around their necks in order to increase their physical strength and the courage needed in battle.

Physical healing properties: This is an excellent stone to add to a combined treatment for sexual problems. As a general rule, it increases physical energy and fortifies the body. It is good for treating various nervous problems, as well as stones in the kidneys, gallbladder, spleen, and pancreas. By drinking an elixir prepared from the stone, problems of the blood vessels, colds, allergies to pollen and blossoms, problems in the spinal column, and radiation injuries and radiation from the sun can be treated. By spreading the elixir prepared from the stone, it is possible to achieve better and faster healing of cuts and wounds.

The mineral's effect on the emotional and mental layers: Carnelian is a wonderful stone for use in states of depression and a lack of *joie de vivre*. It reminds us of the *joie de vivre* that is always in us, even at the most difficult moments, and does so immediately. It stimulates self-confidence, inner courage, and the ability to accomplish objectives. When a person is in a serious state, or is depressed, he should suck a small, round piece of carnelian and keep it in his mouth. It has a beneficial action in the intellectual and mental sphere. It hones the intellectual abilities, the ability to make clear and correct decisions, precision, initiative, curiosity, and diligence. It helps overcome emotions of sadness and sorrow, anger, nervousness and fear. It safeguards the person against jealousy, whether his own, or of others. Carnelian is an excellent stone for treating conditions of apathy, inertia, passiveness, and inactivity. It arouses inner curiosity and helps the person advance and feel motivation. It augments creativity, arouses emotions of caring about others, and feelings of humility, and helps strengthen charisma and inner strength. It supplies the person with energy to make his ideas into a reality. This is a stone that stimulates the feeling of self-satisfaction, and balances the emotions in an effective manner. It is one of the strongest stones for arousing ambitiousness, motivation and independence.

Carnelian in a shade of pink inspires love and reinforces the connection between parents and children.

The mineral's effect on the chakras: This is one of the most excellent stones for working on the sex chakra. When we want to increase sexual energy, the stone should be kept in our pocket for about 12 hours before making love. Moreover, it is suitable for treating the base chakra, the solar plexus chakra, and the heart chakra.

Spiritual effect: Carnelian increases self-awareness and helps us understand, from an emotional point of view, why we have gotten into, or why we are in, a particular situation. It gives inspiration and stimulates the link with the upper and spiritual worlds.

Money, profession, occupation: Carnelian has the reputation of a stone that brings good luck in business. It is wonderful for people who engage in the arts of the theater. In general, it stimulates motivation and the appetite for business in every field. It is a wonderful stone to keep in one's pocket when looking for employment. It is considered to be a stone that is suitable for people in law enforcement and the military, for soldiers and cadets, for strengthening courage and physical endurance. It is suitable for people engaged in various selling professions and for salespeople, because it stimulates self-confidence and the motivation to succeed. The combination of carnelian and citrine is thought to increase productivity at work, especially for clerks and government employees. Since it helps shape and organize information, some people recommend it for journalists, and for those who are engaged in work that combines the need to collect information and organize it together with motivation and courage. Since it strengthens endurance and physical endurance, it is very suitable for athletes and sports people, mainly in combination with ivory. In addition, architects and people who are involved with design and building are likely to find it very useful. It is said that carnelian can turn an architect into a master-architect.

Cat's eye

Cat's eye is actually a phenomenon that is reminiscent of the character of a cat's pupils, which change in accordance with the amount of light. It appears mainly in quartz or beryl, which have a fluctuating sheen and an illusion of changing colors, which resemble cat's eyes. Since it is likely to appear in different minerals and in different combinations of minerals (generally, asbestos fibers are what give the mineral this property), its range of colors is tremendous.

Cat's eye that exists in star chrysoberyl is thought to be particularly superior. Its color is honey brown, and when light strikes it, shadows in a different color can be seen. The non-illuminated side looks like rich brown, while the illuminated side takes on a white-yellowish shade. This effect is called "milk and honey" and it represents the perfect cat's eye. This property is likely to occur in other minerals as well, and there is a great deal of importance to a mineral in which the phenomenon is present. It influences all of the stone's properties in addition to the ones listed here.

Many legends have been spun around this stone. In ancient times, there was a tendency to think that a person who carried or wore this stone could see everything, even through closed doors and through walls. It was widely used as an amulet, and for attracting luck.

Physical healing properties: Cat's eye reinforces night vision, and is used for various eye treatments. It helps treat the facial nerves, neuralgia, and nervous problems, and is used for alleviating headaches.

The mineral's effect on the emotional and mental layers: Cat's eye promotes balance, tranquillity, joy, and inner strength. It bolsters the person's confidence in his ability to accomplish his objectives and to acknowledge his inner wealth. It helps strengthen mental focus, alertness, and the ability to concentrate. It has the ability to direct the person toward the correct decision, mainly in cases of fear of taking the wrong steps. It helps the person think clearly before taking action, and helps him understand what the action will lead to, before it is applied. Impulsive people are recommended to wear it on one of their fingers. It promotes clear thinking, the ability to judge precisely, protection, and luck.

Spiritual effect: Cat's eye promotes spiritual development. It stimulates inner knowledge and lofty insight. It is used as a protective stone, and eliminates energetic disturbances in the aura.

Money, profession, occupation: Cat's eye is considered to be a stone that brings luck not only in business, but in other fields as well.

Celestite

Celestite occurs in masses, groups, and tablets. It is also known by the name "celestine." Its range of colors includes blue, light blue, white, orange, yellow, red, and red brown. Some people call it "the angels' stone."

Physical healing properties: Celestite is used mainly in treating problems of the upper chakras, of mental functions, of hearing and sight. Moreover, it is possible to use it to treat intestinal and digestive problems.

The mineral's effect on the emotional and mental layers: Celestite is a wonderful stone for alleviating states of despair and depression. It dispels troublesome worries, soothes, and helps the person find time for the things that he enjoys and for the occupations that he likes. It is good for mental activity, especially via meditation that combines awareness with the crystalline structure of the stone. It helps the person see the problem or the idea from all angles, stimulates higher logic, and helps the person find original and wise ways of action for solving the problem. It is a good stone for placing in the person's environment when he feels that external influences are undermining his equilibrium or affecting him. It promotes good and light communication, and refines the character. In that way, it helps the person be more pleasant toward those around him, and more likable.

The mineral's effect on the chakras: It is possible to cleanse and purify all the chakras with celestite. It improves the flow of energy in them, and makes their action more effective.

Spiritual effect: Celestite balances the yin and yang powers. It is used widely in meditation for channeling, because it provides legendary information and higher messages. In addition, it helps relay the messages that are received in a clear and precise verbal manner. It is a good stone to hold during astral travel, especially when the person knows where he would like to go - it helps him get to those places in a calm way. It helps the person remember dreams, so it is worthwhile placing it under the pillow or on the bed when "ordering a dream" (requesting a dream that will explain a problem or situation, or that will provide a solution or information). It helps the person remember the dream he was sent. In healing, it serves as a general cure, especially blue and light blue celestite by transforming the energies of the pain and the injury into the energies of light and love. It is used for deep cleansing in healing, and for cleansing childhood traumas that are connected to thoughts that affected the emotions.

Profession, occupation: Celestite, with its impressive beauty and delicate energy, is a wonderful stone for those engaged in art, especially the "delicate" arts: water colors, jewelry design, music, design, and the rest of the professions that are concerned with art and esthetics, and even the intangible fields. It helps the person link up to the delicate energy frequencies, the ones that are required for opening and cleansing in order to perform this delicate and greatly inspired work, and encourages him to link up to an enjoyable and soothing occupation in art.

Chalcopyrite

Chalcopyrite occurs in masses and grains, in a range of colors centering on copper yellow, which sometimes tends toward green, off-white, or pearl.

Physical healing properties: Chalcopyrite is used in treatments involving the brain and problems concerning the crown chakra. It helps treat tumors, especially in the glands. It is an extremely powerful stone for treating various inflammations, inflammatory diseases, and also serious infections, and it can protect those who work with people suffering from these diseases. Moreover, it can be used to lower fever, and it can be included in the treatment of pulmonary problems.

The mineral's effect on the emotional and mental layers: Chalcopyrite is important in raising the person to the level of understanding the perfection of the universe by understanding that every part of the universe contains perfection that constitutes a total unity. It helps him feel and understand this universal property. It is an important stone for evoking happiness in people who tend to sink into sadness and melancholy. It is good for depressive people who find it difficult to liberate themselves from their depression.

The mineral's effect on the chakras: Chalcopyrite can be used while working on the crown chakra. The stone cleanses, opens, and activates the chakra.

Spiritual effect: Chalcopyrite is a wonderful stone for facilitating entry into a meditative state and for maintaining the state of meditative awareness. There are people who use it for finding mislaid items, by holding it and paying heed to the sensation or the information that it creates and transmits to the user. By means of meditation with the stone, it is possible to link up to ancient civilizations. It helps the user receive clear and simple information and understanding about those civilizations, which may be significant for the person himself. In addition, it helps the person receive the information that is important to him for his spiritual development.

Money, profession, occupation: Chalcopyrite is considered to be the suitable stone for people who are engaged in the care-giving professions, in which they come into contact with people suffering from various inflammatory diseases. It protects them, and helps safeguard them against infection. However, it is not a substitute for essential precautionary measures.

Charoite

Charoite occurs mainly in the form of masses, and occasionally it can be found as a tiny clump on the surface of another type of crystal. Charoite's range of colors includes different shades of purple, purple-pinkish, and pink.

Physical healing properties: Charoite cleanses the body in a superb manner (when an elixir prepared from the stone is drunk). It is used for treating eye problems and heart disorders, heart rate and pulse, because it stimulates blood pressure and regulates it. It can be used to treat liver and pancreatic problems, mainly problems that were caused by the person himself as a result of eating bad food and drinking alcohol. The stone is very effective in alleviating headaches, pains in general, and also psychosomatic pains.

The mineral's effect on the emotional and mental layers: This stone can be of great help to people who tend to drift into daydreams and hallucinations. It can help them separate imagination from reality. It hones the analytical ability and promotes prolonged concentration. Charoite helps us accept others as they are, without going into their bad points, or the non-positive energies that flow out of them. Having said that, it helps us identify and understand those energies without being harmed by them. It helps us understand the essence of the lessons we go through by directing us to a state of pure giving and love, which exist in every one of us. Since it links the heart and the crown chakras, it creates a welcome link between love and spirit by helping us to accept ourselves as we are with love, and, as a natural extension of this situation, to feel much greater love and acceptance toward the people around us. Charoite is a welcome and wonderful stone for people who suffer from many diseases. It helps them understand the lessons and the repairs that they go through, be it consciously or through a feeling of conciliation, and helps alleviate the mental suffering of the patient.

The mineral's effect on the chakras: Charoite is used to treat both the heart chakra and the crown chakra. It links the two by letting love flow into us, and links us to the highest love in such a way that it can be realized and felt on the physical level. It has a purifying effect on all the chakras, and fills them with love.

Spiritual effect: By means of meditation with charoite, the intuition can be developed to a great extent, to the point of seeing scenes and visions. It has an important and exceptional action on the spiritual plane - it dispels the fears that hinder the person on his way to reaching heights while meditating and channeling. Moreover, it chases away unwanted entities.

Profession, occupation: Charoite is a very important stone for people who channel and engage in healing, because of its unique ability to dispel fears and entities. People who channel extensively and feel that there are disturbing entities in their vicinity that prevent them from sleeping, are advised to place charoite under their pillows.

Chrysocolla

Chrysocolla crystallizes in strata, masses, and clusters. As a gemstone, it is known by the name "silica." Its colors range between light green and deep blue, green-blue, sometimes turquoise. Occasionally veins of various shapes appear in it, in shades of brown. It crystallizes in a manner similar to that of turquoise, and has a high copper content. It is considered to be the stone of Venus, and symbolizes beauty, love, and harmony. Its action is gentle, but very powerful.

Physical healing properties: Chrysocolla helps alleviate various types of pains, as well as raise the body's level of general vitality. It helps treat pancreatic problems, balance the sugar level in the blood, and regulate the insulin level. It is used for treating various blood problems - cancer of the blood, and so on, for a variety of pulmonary problems, such as emphysema, tuberculosis, and asthma, and facilitates breathing and the actions of breathing. It is good for treating a range of muscular problems, especially in the feet, back, abdomen, and arms, and alleviates cramps and spasms in the muscles. It helps the digestion and absorption of food, detoxification processes, and the healing of wounds. It balances the hormones, and is helpful in regulating irregular periods.

The mineral's effect on the emotional and mental layers: Chrysocolla exerts a balancing effect on the emotional layer. It is very powerful for creating emotional balance and for soothing feelings and thought. It helps assuage anger, fears, and guilt feelings that prevent the person from calming down. It helps him express feelings of love, and helps withdrawn people to open up and communicate much more easily with their surroundings. It induces a feeling of harmony with the universe, and arouses the ability to understand and accept other people. It strengthens the person during crises and difficult situations, while granting him the mental powers to cope. It encourages initiative and action. Chrysocolla creates a harmonious sensation and helps release the person from non-positive feelings and tensions. It can stimulate the brain and the mental layer, and soothe the emotions at one and the same time. It helps develop both analytical and intuitive powers. In addition, it helps open up emotional blockages that are liable to disrupt thought processes.

The mineral's effect on the chakras: Chrysocolla is an excellent stone for treating the heart chakra. It helps relieve emotional heartaches and open up the heart to new feelings of love. It balances the chakra and strengthens it. Moreover, it can be placed on the solar plexus chakra, the sex chakra, and the root chakra, when they need soothing and a flow of vitality. When it is placed on the third eye chakra, it stimulates the ability to see visions and scenes.

Spiritual effect: Chrysocolla is suitable for use during meditations that link the person to the earth. It purifies the home and the surroundings, and disseminates a sensation of unity with the universe.

Money, profession, occupation: Chrysocolla is suitable for people who engage in the various arts, because it stimulates creativity to a great extent. Moreover, it is suitable for accountants, mainly in a stressful work environment, and a tight, pressured schedule, because it is very effective for soothing emotional pressures, and helps the person do his work more easily and with less pressure. It is also suitable for computer people, people who deal with systems analysis or data analysis, because of its beneficial effect on the analytical abilities. It is good for inventors and designers, because it encourages practicality, together with the inventive and innovative ability. In general, it is a stone that should be placed on the desk in order to improve results.

It is considered to be a stone that brings luck, success in business, and prosperity.

Chrysoprase

Chrysoprase occurs as stalactites, clusters, and sometimes as masses. In fact, it is a type of chalcedony. Its color is light green or apple green, and sometimes there are black sediments or particles.

Physical healing properties: Because it is a very suitable stone for the heart chakra, chrysoprase is used for treating heart problems and ailments. Some people use it to increase the absorption of "sunlight" in the body. Chrysoprase is widely used for treating problems concerning the sex chakra - prostate, testicle and ovary problems, fertility problems - in two principal ways: by drinking an elixir prepared from the stone, or by conscious tuning of the stone to treat these problems.

The mineral's effect on the emotional and mental layers: Chrysoprase is an excellent stone for improving self-expression. It helps people who have a hard time expressing themselves, and stimulates eloquence and thought. Using or holding chrysoprase develops the feeling of mercy and compassion that is within us, and promotes an uncritical and non-judgmental attitude toward people. It helps people adapt to new situations quickly, and make the most of them. It is useful for clarifying problems by raising solutions to problems from the subconscious to the conscious layers. Chrysoprase has the ability to help people extricate themselves from feelings of inferiority, or from superiority complexes and megalomania. It promotes a feeling of loyalty and forgiveness toward others, and it is advisable to hold it after crises that leave the person heartbroken.

The mineral's effect on the chakras: Chrysoprase is suitable for treating the heart chakra, for opening and balancing it. It stimulates the chakra and opens it up to love. When it is held, especially after conscious tuning, it is likely to help solve problems that originate in the imbalance of the sex chakra.

Spiritual influence: Chrysoprase inspires compassion, forgiveness, and love. It helps balance the feminine and masculine energies, the yin and the yang, and links the chakras to the etheric layer in a harmonious manner. It stimulates the creation of a balance between the physical body and the mental body. It is very helpful in developing higher awareness on the emotional and spiritual levels, and stimulates the person's inner vision.

Money, profession, occupation: Chrysoprase is considered to be a stone that promotes business loyalty very strongly. It is recommended for anyone who works with partners or a team.

Citrine

Citrine is a proud member of the quartz family. Many of the citrine stones originate from amethyst that lay under strata of blazing earth for a long time, thereby getting its golden color. This could be one of the stones in the High Priest's breastplate, but conversely, the stone in the breastplate might be opal. Citrine occurs in different shades of yellow, yellowish-brown, yellow-orange, and even amber-color. It crystallizes mainly in masses and clusters. It is considered to be the stone of peace and wisdom.

Physical healing properties: Citrine is very good for treating various problems of the digestive system, and aids the absorption of vitamins and minerals. It strengthens the circulatory system, blood flow, the production of red and white blood corpuscles, and is effective in stimulating the flow and reinforcing the blood vessels. It helps the body's detoxification process and cleansing the body of poisons, and constitutes an additional means for treating problems of vision and for strengthening the vision. Moreover, it can be used for curing inflammations in general, and can be included in treatments for balancing the thyroid gland and for stimulating the thymus gland.

The mineral's effect on the emotional and mental layers: Citrine hones thinking, stimulates the brain and the intellect, and simultaneously helps us link up to our intuition. It is a marvelous stone for pupils and students, and for people whose work demands clear, sharp thinking in order to solve problems. It stimulates the mental layer by helping the person reach optimal decisions and solutions as a result of a combination of intelligent thought and inner intuition. It is good to give the stone to people who experience difficulty in making contact with others, or people whose profession requires excellent communication channels. It is advisable to place a cluster of citrine in a place where several people work in order to make their communicative ability clearer and better. Citrine helps encourage good communication both at work and in people's personal lives, and by using it, the friction among team members and among family members can be reduced. It helps us understand more correctly the survival instinct that is innate in our characters by understanding what we need. This stone is important for people who have a self-destructive tendency. It helps them reach emotional balance, and dispels anger and non-positive emotions. Citrine encourages us to discover our inner strength and acknowledge it, and see the beauty that is inherent in new beginnings.

The mineral's effect on the chakras: Citrine is very suitable for treating the solar plexus chakra, and balances its action very well by increasing creativity, initiative, and inner strength. When it is placed on the base chakra, it helps us stimulate the joy that is within us, eliminate and free ourselves of fears, and see the world in a brighter light. It is also suitable for placing on the sex chakra.

Spiritual effect: Citrine is used for cleansing the aura. It contributes to the balance between the masculine and feminine energies and between yin and yang. It can be used for coordinating the chakras with the etheric layers, and for coordinating the physical body with the spiritual bodies. It opens the bridge between the higher mental layers and the intuitive levels of the mind.

Money, profession, occupation: Citrine has a long history of being used for increasing abundance. Some people even call it "the trading stone" or "the money stone" because of its property of augmenting material prosperity and money. Some people are in the habit of placing a citrine crystal in their wallet in order to increase their wealth, or putting it into their cash register in order to accumulate larger sums of money, and even to safeguard the cumulative profits. This is a wonderful stone to give as a gift to a friend who is opening a business, or is in the throes of a financial crisis (during a financial crisis, other circumstances in addition to the obvious material ones must be examined, and an attempt must be made to get to the root of the problem, with the assistance of the crystals). It is very good to put it in the work area of teams and in places in which cooperative work is essential. Moreover, citrine is a wonderful stone for students, researchers, and people who require perpetual learning and intellectual development in their profession. It is also considered to be a suitable stone for government employees, and helps them increase their productivity, as well as improve their work relationship with their colleagues and with the public. Because of citrine's marvelous ability to improve spontaneous verbal expression, it is an excellent stone for radio and TV announcers and entertainers. It is also appropriate for salespeople.

Coral

Coral is not a stone, but rather an organic substance that originates in the sea. Since it comes from a living creature, only coral that has been washed up onto the shore has healing properties. Coral that has been taken from a coral reef is liable to possess harmful properties, and to contain sorrow and suffering, so it is important to verify the origin of the coral before purchasing it. Under no circumstances must coral be broken off the reef. Coral occurs in a range of colors, each of which has its own unique action. Corals occur in blacks, whites, pinks, reds and blues. Horn Coral also belongs to this family. In addition to the properties of the various corals, they are also blessed with the properties of shells, because of their common origin.

Coral is considered to be the holy stone of the Tibetans and the Native Americans. It symbolizes the life force energy and liquidity and solidity together. It was used as a protection against spells and the evil eye (especially red coral). Some people claim that when the wearer suffers from a lack of energy or blood, the coral becomes pale. In general, wearing coral is recommended for states of depression, defective nutrition, exhaustion, and indifference.

Physical healing properties: Coral helps strengthen the bones, stimulate the regeneration of the body in order to nourish the blood cells, and is used in fortifying treatments, and for stabilizing and treating spinal column disorders.

Red coral is used to treat disorders of the kidney cells, of the bladder, and of the parathyroid glands, as well as for regulating the monthly period. In addition, it helps catalyze the body's metabolic processes, treats heartburn, flatulence, and hiccups.

White coral helps with the regeneration of all the cellular structures in the brain, and for treating olfactory disorders.

Blue coral is used to treat liver disorders, and to fortify the liver, especially after recovering from liver diseases, and for treating problems of the pituitary and pineal glands. Moreover, it is used effectively for treating throat problems and for cleaning out phlegm.

Horn coral is used to treat hearing disorders, bone structure problems, mainly weakness and flaccidity, carpal tunnel syndrome, and muscular disorders.

Pink coral helps treat heart problems, problems with the sexual and reproductive organs (female in particular), and chest disorders.

Black coral is used to treat skin and pore problems, and problems with the body's internal organs. It is used in detoxification processes, whereby toxins from the body's various systems are expelled.

The mineral's effect on the emotional and mental layers: Coral helps instill a feeling of tranquillity and harmony. It stimulates the imagination and the intuition, the ability to visualize, and promotes the talent of diplomacy.

Black coral inspires creativity and original thinking. It helps us cope with the dark sides of our personalities and of other people's personalities, and to liberate repressed emotions.

Blue coral improves communication skills.

Pink coral stimulates unconditional love and affection, and helps strengthen the intuitive sides of the understanding of love.

Red coral inspires a feeling of harmony and understanding vis-à-vis the forces of nature. It promotes practicality, helps dispel depressions and dependencies, and assuages fears.

White coral cleanses the brain of negative thoughts and distractions. In addition, it helps develop more effective communication with the subconscious.

The mineral's effect on the chakras: Red coral is placed on the base chakra during a laying on of stones. **Black coral** stimulates and activates the throat energy. Moreover, it can be used for cleansing and purifying the sex chakra. It stimulates the third eye chakra, and strengthens the intuitive abilities that derive from it. **Pink coral** stimulates and activates the heart chakra. **White coral** stimulates and purifies the crown chakra, and links the chakras with the energy of the astral layer.

Spiritual effect: Coral acts as an aid to visualization and guided imagining, as a stimulant of mystical abilities, and for channeling with strong spiritual figures from the past. **Black coral** protects its user from negative energies by absorbing them. It is very effective when placed in a hostile environment, in order to provide protection against non-positive energies. **Horn coral** was used to understand and accumulate knowledge concerning ancient civilizations, for linking up to the personal totem and to the person's vital strength. **Red coral** balances the material and the spiritual, and helps the person link up to sources of divine knowledge and wisdom. **White coral** is used for developing prophetic and predictive abilities for the good of mankind in general. Moreover, it fills in holes and gaps in the aura, and stimulates the flow of energy.

Money, profession, occupation: Red coral is considered to be a very suitable stone for anyone who engages in hard physical labor, because it promotes and augments physical strength. In addition, red coral is also suitable for singers since it is thought to strengthen the voice.

Cuprite

Cuprite crystallizes in the form of cubic, octahedral, and dodecahedral crystals. It is coppery and shiny, and occurs in very dark shades of red, deep red, and sometimes red that is almost black. Cuprite may also occur in shades of purple, green, and silver. Among the red crystals, there are crystals whose color is slightly reminiscent of that of the ruby. The stone itself tends to be opaque, but after polishing, it becomes transparent with a dark red color that resembles the deep red of blood.

Physical healing properties: The color of cuprite is likely to remind us of blood, and it is, in fact, an excellent stone for purifying the blood. Some people recommend that heavy smokers carry it in their pockets on a permanent basis in order to promote the regeneration of the pulmonary cells. It is a superb stone for treating a broad range of physical problems that derive from or are linked to the base chakra, disorders in the reproductive system, AIDS (it also bolsters the immune system), and also problems that are connected to the accumulation of fluids in the body, and to kidney and bladder disorders. Since it has grounding and linking abilities to the base chakra, it is an excellent stone for treating altitude diseases and vertigo.

The mineral's effect on the emotional and mental layers: Cuprite is good for providing stability and a link to the earth, and is very effective for people who experience fear and loss of control. Moreover, it is worthwhile holding it when the person is in a situation over which he has no control, so that he can go with the flow more easily, without useless worries that make the burden heavier and the situation even more difficult.

It helps transform worthless guilt feelings into forgiveness and self-love. It is good as an antidote to pain (together with chrysocolla), and during menopause, as well as for infertility, and for terminal patients who want to live.

The mineral's effect on the chakras: Cuprite is very suitable for treating the base chakra. Sometimes, when its color is dark red, almost red black, it constitutes a combination of both colors of the chakra. By using the stone to treat the chakra, it is possible to strengthen the body's posture and the required positive grounding by reinforcing the energy of the physical body. Its mode of action on the base chakra helps balance the survival needs of the person, and helps him realize them in the proper way.

Spiritual effect: The main function of the stone in this field is providing grounding and a link to the earth by increasing the energy of the physical body. This action, of course, influences the manner of the development and the balance of the rest of the bodies.

Diamond

The diamond, the most precious gemstone, is formed at a temperature of 2,000 degrees Celsius. It is the highest and most exalted manifestation of white light, universal light, and is considered to be the "king of the minerals." It represents brightness, purity, and enlightenment. Its process of creation, from coal, via many natural processes and tremendous heat and pressure, symbolizes the light at the end of the tunnel, the embodiment of the greatest beauty from the blackest depths, the essence of transformation, and the prodigious vicissitudes that cleanse the soul and purify it. The diamond is the hardest mineral in nature. It cannot be cut, except by means of another diamond (as is the case in the diamond industry). The diamond crystallizes in an octahedral (eight-faceted), dodecahedral (twelve-faceted), and trapezohedral forms. It occurs in a variety of colors, including transparent, black, white, pink, yellow, red, blue, green, orange, and brown.

The diamond has an extensive history. It was evidently one of the stones in the High Priest's breastplate (though many people contest this opinion), identified with the tribe of Zebulun, and mentioned several times in the Bible. During the days of the Black Plague in Europe, during the Middle Ages, the aristocrats wore diamonds in order to protect themselves against infection. This proved to be a false hope, since the diamonds did not save them or protect them from contagion. At other times, it was the custom to grind diamonds and sprinkle the dust over the food of enemies as a poison. Again, there is no way of knowing if this worked...

Today, the diamond symbolizes love, innocence, and fidelity in love. It is one of the most common stones in engagement rings, wedding rings, and gifts of love. Many people do not know this, but those very diamonds that are set in rings and other items of jewelry to be given as gifts of love, are liable to carry non-positive energies. The people who excavate them are sometimes subjected to difficult and depressing conditions, and a lot of greed-filled energy is liable to reach the diamond via the numerous hands through which it passes until it reaches the jewelry store. When you buy a diamond, or an item of jewelry with a diamond set in it, make sure to purify it. It is advisable to place the diamond in a glass bowl for about three hours (better still, a crystal bowl that can be placed in the sunlight afterwards). Before placing the diamond in the bowl, fill the bowl with about a liter of water, pour in a level teaspoonful of sea salt and a level teaspoonful of baking soda. Place the bowl in the sunlight. After about three hours, dry the diamond well (or the piece of jewelry in which the diamond is set). It will be purified and clean, and will have a greater glow and shine.

Many legends have been spun around the mystic power of the diamond to protect the wearer from dangers, devils, ghosts, and nightmares. This is because of its shininess, which is attributed to the powers of "good" of the universe. Despite these legends, charoite, for example, provides far more effective protection against unwanted entities and nightmares, and other protective stones tend to be more powerful in the field of protection against dangers than the diamond. Nevertheless, this is one of the stones with the strongest powers of absorption. It absorbs everything - thoughts, emotions, and even body heat. For this reason, it must be cleansed and purified of negative energies frequently. Together with these absorptive properties, it also sucks up white, pure, healing light from the universe, which is an exalted property that is unique to it in its intensity.

Physical healing properties: The diamond is used for balancing the metabolism in the body, as an antidote to poison, and for improving and purifying the vision. In an elixir, the diamond is used for treating illnesses and problems that are connected to the head, tumors, and epilepsy. In addition, it is used to treat sexual problems and sexual dysfunction in men. Because of its tremendous healing powers, the diamond constitutes an effective help in treating any kind of disease.

The mineral's effect on the emotional and mental layers: The diamond stimulates self-love and love of others. It strengthens, and spreads a feeling of harmony and serenity. It encourages fidelity, purity, and openness. In relationships, the diamond inspires a feeling of trust and security. It stimulates the intellect, the imagination, creativity, and the innovative and inventive ability.

The mineral's effect on the chakras: The diamond balances and opens all the chakras, via the crown chakra. It is one of the most suitable stones for opening and activating the crown chakra by linking it to the powers of the universe and to the divine power.

Spiritual effect: The diamond reinforces and expands the strength of other stones, and strengthens and stabilizes their energies. It protects the wearer from negative energies. Some people claim that it does that by thrusting those energies out, thus protecting the electromagnetic field. In addition, the diamond promotes the link between the energies of the heart, the will, and the superego. Wearing diamonds as earrings helps create a balance between the right hemisphere and the left hemisphere. The balance is not only on the mental levels, but also on the spiritual levels.

Profession, occupation: Various channelers and healers tend to wear a diamond in order to strengthen their healing and channeling powers, to safeguard their purity, and to link up to the divine healing power.

Dioptase

Dioptase crystallizes in masses, grains, and clusters. This greenish stone (its color is a kind of "venomous" green) is thought to be a relatively rare stone, and an extremely powerful healing stone.

Physical healing powers: Dioptase, when worn, held, or in elixir form, is very good for alleviating general pains of all kinds. The elixir prepared from the stone has a significant action for alleviating headaches, migraines, post-operative pains, and other pains. It not only soothes pains, but also works on the cellular level that is conscious of the pain. It is good for treating heart problems, high blood pressure, tension, pulmonary problems and disorders, cellular and structural problems in the body, and problems that were created by or result from unsuitable nutrition. In addition, it is excellent for treating vertigo and problems of equilibrium. Some people use it for treating AIDS patients. Moreover, it helps smooth wrinkles in cosmetic treatments.

The mineral's effect on the emotional and mental layers: The stone heals the deepest wounds in the heart, as well as the bruised ego. It is wonderful for people who suffered from heartaches as a result of break-ups and disappointed love, and for "mending" broken hearts. It is an excellent stone for all the situations and feelings of lack, both physical and emotional. It helps the person realize his full potential and abilities, as well as use his material resources correctly in order to accomplish his objectives and realize himself. It helps the person understand and live for today and for the moment, without getting stuck in the past or worrying about the future. It reveals the person's hidden abilities and powers, of which he was unaware, and that could help him on his path toward his objectives.

The mineral's effect on the chakras: Dioptase is wonderful for treating the heart chakra. It opens, fills, and balances it, and gets all the love energy from it flowing through the body. As a rule, when treating the chakras, it cleanses and stimulates them, and brings them to the highest level of action and awareness.

When a person has a problem of whose root he is ignorant, and does not know what to do in order to improve the situation, placing the stone on the third eye chakra is likely to help him understand the root of the problem, and stimulate his desire to improve the situation actively.

Spiritual effect: Dioptase stimulates the memory of past lives, and helps the person understand the connections between those lives and his situation in his present life. By holding it, meditating with it, or placing it on the third eye, he can request to understand lessons. This is a stone that is used in meditations promoting peace on earth, and its cure; by means of dioptase, it is possible to link up to the earth's vibrations and be aware of them. It can be used in treatments in which we seek to liberate the cells from unpleasant memories (every single cell in the body contains the memory of the physical or mental traumas that we have suffered) by general work toward liberating those memories or traumas, and the stone is a very profound aid in every treatment.

Profession, occupation: The stone is suitable for people who engage in the spiritual healing professions, healers and trainee healers, either for treating themselves, or for treating their patients.

Dolomite

Dolomite can be found in the form of grains, masses, and prisms. Its range of colors includes gray, white, greenish-white, green, red, scarlet, pink, black, and brown.

Physical healing properties: Dolomite is a good stone for improving and promoting all the processes of building the body - the muscles, the bones, the teeth, the blood corpuscles, the nails, and the skin. It helps improve the supply of oxygen to the cells and the lungs, and helps treat problems in the adrenal glands, the reproductive system, and the urinary tract. It is possible to use it to ease problems involving or causing shudders.

The mineral's effect on the emotional and mental layers: Dolomite helps stimulate quick and spontaneous thought processes, helps people express their opinions, and promotes originality. In contrast, just as it stimulates quick thinking and thought impulsiveness in people who need it, it is very helpful in getting hyperactive people and children to develop tolerance, endurance, and the ability to sit still. It sparks the compassion that is in a person, and the ability to look empathetically at others who are suffering or need help. In this way, it helps him see his own suffering in proportion, and understand with forebearance that there is a reason and time for everything in the world.

The mineral's effect on the chakras: In treating the chakras, dolomite is suitable for cases in which a loss of energy through the chakras has been diagnosed. The stone helps curb the energy loss in order to balance the chakras, and remove the blockages in them.

Spiritual effect: Dolomite is not usually used for meditation, but it can help the person experience the properties of compassion and charity that are in him, and stimulate them. In so doing, it relieves his subjective difficulties by helping him understand that in fact, he has no reason to wallow in sadness or bitterness.

Emerald

The emerald is a stone from the beryl family. Its color is light green, and it can be found in prismatic crystals. Its unique green color is a result of the presence of the mineral chromium in the beryl.

The name "emerald" comes from the Persian word for "green." Because of its great beauty and prestige, various legends have been embroidered around it, and it was shrouded in a great deal of mysticism both in ancient times and even today. The emerald was one of the stones in the High Priest's breastplate. The emerald was identified with the tribe of Levi, the priestly tribe. The ancient Greeks dedicated the stone to Venus, and believed that it ensured continuing and secure love. Various eastern cultures believed that the emerald contained the memory, augmented the intellect, and stimulated prophetic and predictive abilities. In the Middle Ages, it was thought that the emerald could safeguard women's chastity, as well as her fidelity to, love for, and esteem of her husband. The Incas worshipped it, and in many cultures, it was considered to be a symbol of extrasensory powers and immortality.

Physical healing properties: The emerald is used to treat problems connected with the heart, of course, because of its compatibility with the heart chakra. In addition, it is used to treat various pulmonary problems as well as problems of the spinal column and muscles. It can be placed on tired or inflamed eyes to soothe them. Some people use the emerald to treat diabetics - they place it in the region of the pancreas, in a place where the sunlight can reach the patient and the stone, and make sure that the rays of the sun pass through the stone. Some people recommend that it be worn by paranoid and schizophrenic patients, or that they drink an elixir prepared from it, in order to relieve the many side effects of those diseases, and to create a feeling of protection for the patient. The elixir can be used in order to cleanse the blood vessels.

The mineral's effect on the emotional and mental layers: The emerald causes its wearer or bearer to feel enveloped in love. It is a marvelous stone to give as a gift to couples or to one's partner, since it reinforces the bonds of love and family, encourages the feeling of fidelity, and inspires the person's sensitivity toward himself and toward those around him. It induces a feeling of calmness, harmony, and protection, and helps dispel worries and troublesome thoughts. It has a very good influence on the memory, strengthens it and stimulates it, and helps the person make greater use of intellectual tools. This is a good stone for helping decision-making, as it directs the person toward the right choice. It is very helpful for people who require a "shot" of motivation, spurs them on to action, and helps them focus on the action and work intensively. It strengthens the ability to express oneself and make speeches, makes the person's thought more fertile, and helps him attain thinking that is open and aspires to the truth. Moreover, it stimulates and encourages creativity.

The mineral's effect on the chakras: The emerald is a wonderful stone for working on the heart chakra. It opens, activates, and stimulates the chakra, and simultaneously soothes the feelings, so that there is no problem of being swept away in a burst of emotions as a result of opening the chakra. Its green color - the color of equilibrium, calmness, and harmony - turns it into a stone that brings harmony to every aspect of life.

Spiritual effect: This is a good stone to use while meditating in order to maintain the special breathing that meditation requires and to breathe at the right pace. As a result, it helps attain very profound meditative sensations. In addition, it is used for raising messages from the subconscious to the conscious. It helps the person understand and feel the laws of the universe, and open his intellectual layers to exalted messages.

Profession, occupation: The exquisite emerald is thought to be the stone that brings its bearer luck and fortune. It suits healers because of its ability to promote free thought, and reinforce spiritual comprehension and predictive abilities. Because it enables the person to look one step ahead, out of concern and compassion, it was considered to be a stone that was suitable for nurses in hospitals. In addition, it is thought to be a suitable stone for politicians and statesmen, since it improves oratorical powers on the one hand, and the aspiration to purity and truth on the other.

Feldspar

Feldspar is a family of stones that contains numerous important stones. Besides the properties that characterize the individual stones, they also have the properties of the whole feldspar family. Among the "famous" ones in the family are labradorite, amazonite, moonstone, elbaite, and adularia.

Physical healing properties: In addition to the unique healing properties of the stones in the feldspar family, their great effectiveness in treating various skin problems and a wide variety of muscular problems that derive from different causes - from structural problems to "caught" muscles as a result of prolonged physical effort - must be mentioned.

The mineral's effect on the emotional and mental layers: The stones from the feldspar family help children who are compelled to live far from their parents, whether because of divorce, when they may be separated from one parent, or for other reasons. They also help big "children" who need to go through the process of separation from a parent, whether that parent is alive or just his/her image remains in their spirit and memories. The stones in this family help the person acquire, encourage, and increase self-love and esteem, and help him follow his path as a result of creativity, on the way to fulfilling his heart's desires and his aims.

Spiritual effect: Meditating with stones from the feldspar family helps the person impose renewed order on his life and thoughts, and pay more attention to the messages that emanate from his superego, his inner self, and even from apparently external factors, and be more understanding of them.

Fluorite

Fluorite occurs in a range of colors, including green, blue, green with purple or blue stripes, yellow, purple, red, and colorless, and sometimes mixed stripes of color within its basic color can be seen. This is a "young" stone, a stone that is still in the process of development. It leads its user toward spiritual devotion, cosmic truth, and profound wisdom.

Physical healing properties: Fluorite can be used at the initial stages of a disease, in order to curb the rate of its progress or help prevent its progress. It strengthens the body in general, and helps it attain optimal health. It is effective in the treatment of inflammatory diseases, colds, flu, tonsillitis, infected sores, and herpes. Moreover, it helps protect the person against contagious diseases and infections. **Blue fluorite** is used for treating ear-nose-throat problems, infections in those organs, eye problems, blocked tear ducts, and for communication and speech problems. **Colorless fluorite** should be used for treating vision problems linked to the clouding over of the eye, for problems with the pupil, and impaired vision. **Green fluorite** also helps treat problems that are connected to the throat, but mainly diseases that affect it via the digestive system, such as heartburn. In addition, it is used for treating a wide variety of diseases of the digestive system; it improves the digestion, and helps treat intestinal problems (mainly in the large intestine). **Purple fluorite** can treat bone and bone marrow problems, and **yellow fluorite** is used to treat liver problems and high or unbalanced cholesterol levels. It helps release toxins from the fat cells, thus performing an extremely important function in the detoxification processes.

The mineral's effect on the emotional and mental layers: Fluorite helps achieve emotional, psychological, and mental equilibrium. It helps impose order on chaotic situations, stabilizing and contributing to objectivity. It enhances the learning process, improves concentration abilities, and increases the person's knowledge. It stimulates the intuitive abilities, reinforces the ability to concentrate, and promotes relationships based on equality. It is advisable to use it or to put it in places where there is a feeling that the natural equality is being undermined because of the actions of people who are unaware. It helps nurture stable relationships between the members of a couple, partners, and groups. **The fluorite in the blue shade** helps develop mental fluency. It soothes and strengthens communication skills. **Green fluorite** creates an atmosphere of cleanliness, order, and freshness. It is used in the treatment for dispelling emotional traumas, and inspires love. **The fluorite in the purple shades** is a strong stone not only for spiritual awakening, but also for expressing and understanding the spirituality in the rational layers. It is very helpful for emotional growth and for understanding life's lessons and situations. **The fluorite in the yellow shades** inspires creativity.

The mineral's effect on the chakras: This is mainly according to the colors of the stone. **The fluorite in the purple shades** can be placed on the third eye. **Green fluorite** is suitable for treating, opening, and balancing the heart chakra. **Yellow fluorite** is used to open and balance the solar plexus chakra. **The green fluorite with purple stripes in it** links the heart chakra to the third eye chakra. **The fluorite with the blue shade** opens and cleanses the throat chakra. When there are **purple stripes** or **purple regions** in it, it helps create a link between the third eye chakra and the throat chakra. Because of this property, it is possible to use it to expedite the verbal transmission of messages during meditation with the stone, and to greatly improve communication and speech skills. **Colorless fluorite** is used to activate the crown chakra. In addition, it is used in treatments to coordinate all the chakras.

Spiritual effect: Fluorite helps us differentiate between illusion and reality. It helps a person link up to the universal energies. It is a spiritual purifier, and it expands channeling abilities (especially **blue fluorite**, which is also used for channeling with other worlds). **Colorless fluorite** can be used for cleansing the aura and fortifying it energetically, and strengthening the abilities to transfer the energy of the various stones and minerals during the laying on of stones. **Green fluorite** helps rid places and situations of negative vibrations. **Purple fluorite** is an important and well-known stone for promoting the processes of spiritual development. **Yellow fluorite** can be used during meditation or group spiritual work in order to stabilize the common energies and reinforce the loving bond among the participants.

Profession, occupation: All the fluorite stones, especially transparent and purple fluorite, are important for people who engage in healing and spiritual medicine, as well as everyone who aspires to spiritual development.

Fossil

The fossil is a petrified creature, tree, plant, or marine animal that lived millions of years ago. There are fossilized insects, bones, shells, fish, small mammals, plants, and so on. There are also fossils into which additional minerals, with their own properties, filtered over the course of the years.

Physical healing properties: The fossil is used for treating skeletal and limb problems, for maintaining the health of the mouth and teeth, for states of physical degeneration, and for improving the action of the thymus gland.

The mineral's effect on the emotional and mental layers: The fossil helps to evoke excellent and solid properties. It helps the person open up to his surroundings and to recharge himself with powers of renewal and regeneration. The fossil helps him get rid of old, inhibiting thought patterns, and free himself of the past and of negative patterns whose source is in thought.

Profession, occupation: The fossil helps safeguard business achievements, as well as develop and acquire new ones. It can be of help to people with a busy schedule, or people who have difficulty sticking to a fixed and orderly schedule, since it facilitates the implementation of agreed-upon plans. In addition, it is considered to be very suitable for people who work in the dental professions, when it is placed in the clinic.

Spiritual effect: The fossil serves to create a bond with ancient worlds, distant eras, and other worlds.

Garnet

Garnet crystallizes in masses, grains, or flat strata. It occurs in many colors: ruby red, brown, orange, cinnamon, green, and so on. Garnets are used in many industries throughout the world - in watches, scientific instruments and machines, and even as abrasives in sandpaper. The origin of the word "garnet" lies in the Latin word, *granatus*, which means "similar to a seed," since it can be found in a granular form in many rocks. Having said that, it can also be found in gigantic masses - so large that in ancient times, jars were hollowed out of huge lumps of garnet. In the ancient world, they had the reputation of being extremely powerful protective stones, and they were considered sacred by many tribes in North America, South America, and Africa. It is thought to have been one of the gems in the High Priest's breastplate, and was identified with the tribe of Judah.

Physical healing properties: Garnet balances and strengthens the genitals and the reproductive organs. It is used for treating sexual problems and disorders, mainly excessive sexuality and an exaggerated sex drive. In addition, it helps rid the body of toxins. It is a very good stone for fortifying the body during the period of recuperation from diseases, and in any situation that requires renewed powers and the strengthening of the body. **Red garnet** helps regulate and balance blood circulation, and treats heart problems. It invigorates blood circulation and purifies the blood. It can also be used in cases of anemia and low blood pressure. Moreover, it can be used for treating rheumatism and arthritis. Garnet balances hormonal problems, and is very good during menopause, when it alleviates the symptoms. It also helps regulate menstrual periods. It is used in treating disorders of the spinal column, bone marrow of the spinal column, and the bones. It helps with the absorption of calcium, iodine, and magnesium, as well as of various vitamins. A unique property of garnet is its use as a "natural antibiotic." At the onset of the disease (flu, contagious diseases, all kinds of viruses), an elixir should be prepared from the stone (by placing the stone in a glass of water in the sun for about three hours), and drunk. This must be repeated several times a day. The results are surprisingly effective. While the disease may not be averted completely, it will most likely be much less virulent, and its duration will be much briefer. When preparing an elixir of this kind, which has to be drunk several times a day (preferably every three hours), the elixir should be prepared from a different garnet every time, using two or three garnets - so as not to exhaust the stone. If its powers are overused, it will simply "disappear."

The mineral's effect on the emotional and mental layers: Garnet evokes inspiration and creativity, while helping the person's real talents come to light. It is a very powerful stone for stimulating motivation. In ancient tribes, it was the custom to place a garnet under the bed of a sick or hallucinating person in order to safeguard him from nightmares. It helps dispel depression, and inspires a positive attitude toward life. It balances emotions, prevents and dispels fears, grudges, and impure thoughts, and brings luck in every aspect of life. Since it is balances emotionally, and brings joy and optimism, its bearer often feels popular and well-liked. It raises the person's self-esteem, increases the ability to express oneself anywhere and at any time, and inspires love and devotion. It is very effective in helping a person get over situations of separation and abandonment. An interesting property of garnet is that after absorbing many non-positive energies from the person during its work to balance his emotions and get rid of negative ones, it is liable to fade or even go missing! Also, after giving the person a lot of energies, if it is not purified properly and not recharged, it tends to "disappear."

The mineral's effect on the chakras: Garnet extracts negative energies from the chakras, and transforms negative energies into positive ones. It can be placed on the sex chakra, the base chakra (especially red garnet), and on the third eye chakra, in order to dispel fears, grudges, and negative patterns in the subconscious.

Spiritual effect: Garnet is linked to the fire energy of the Kundalini. It can be used in meditations to evoke the Kundalini, while it balances and stimulates the movement and development of the Kundalini. At the moment of receiving energy, the stone helps distribute it correctly to all the organs of the body. It coordinates and oversees the flow of energy, and creates a balanced energy field around the physical body. Moreover, garnet is good for cleansing and purifying.

Money, profession, business: Garnet has the reputation of safeguarding against losing money. It gives the person a great deal of confidence during business negotiations, even with large corporations and institutions, or with people whose status is considered to be higher. In addition, it is thought to be a stone that brings luck in business and helps in the accomplishment of objectives. It encourages and promotes success in business, and stimulates cooperation even between business rivals.

Hematite

Hematite, with its silvery sparkle, occurs in the form of cubic crystals, cylindrical masses, grains, and so on. The stone has a shiny metallic sheen. It is known mainly in black-gray and silver, but there are also red and brown-red hematite stones that have a metallic sheen, too.

Physical healing properties: Hematite is used for treating problems of the circulatory system, anemia, blood poisoning, lack of iron, and so on. It is effective in the treatment of vertigo, insomnia, and nightmares. Hematite is used to treat states of shock, loss of consciousness, and fainting spells, in order to help the person recover and come to. Its action is the same after accidents, before and after surgery (not during), and after Caesarian sections - both for mother and child. When hematite is placed on the forehead or prepared as an elixir, it is effective in lowering fever and cooling the body. The stone is also used for treating cramps in the legs, for disorders of the nervous system, and for strengthening the spinal column.

The mineral's effect on the emotional and mental layers: Hematite is an excellent stone for promoting thinking, analytical, and memory skills. It is of great help to people who work in fields that demand technological or mathematical knowledge, reinforces the mental skills and abilities required for carrying out both simple and complicated projects, and helps breach the barriers of thought. Hematite helps us see that we ourselves actually set up the barriers and limitations as a consequence of limiting thought patterns, and we are capable of getting rid of them in order to make the most of our abilities and talents. It is a very soothing stone, and should be held when the person feels upset. It helps attain self-control, and is useful in states of agitation in general. It helps the person feel tranquillity, calmness, and inner happiness, it stimulates passion, and has a pleasant, gentle, and enchanting effect on the relationship between the members of a couple.

The mineral's effect on the chakras: Hematite can be placed on the base chakra in order to balance and stabilize it, when it comes to people who are not properly linked to their physical layers. It performs strong grounding work.

Spiritual effect: Hematite links all the bodies - the physical, the astral, and the mental. It balances the feminine and the masculine energies, and the yin and yang. It helps the person enter a gentle meditative state, and gets him out of it smoothly at the end of the meditation. It is recommended for people who tend to enter a meditative state very strongly, and have difficulty getting out of it. When there is a wonderful meditative state, and the person feels that he does not want to get out of it, it is advisable for him to hold or see in his mind's eye a hematite stone in each hand. Meditation guides who notice that one of the pupils is still in a meditative state after he has been instructed to come out of it, can used this technique - tell him to hold or imagine two hematite stones lying next to his legs or held in his hands. The grounding ability of hematite is superb.

Profession, occupation: Hematite is suitable for people who work in or are involved with fields that demand technological or mathematical knowledge: computer people or systems analysts, students of physics or mathematics, engineers, and technicians.

Herkimer diamond

Herkimer diamond is quartz that crystallizes in thick, double-terminated prismatic crystals. Its origin is in Herkimer, U.S.A. Despite its name, this stone is neither a diamond nor a substitute for one.

Physical healing properties: Herkimer diamond helps release tension, cramps, and hardness in the body's tissues. It is used in detoxification processes and for balancing the metabolic processes in the body.

The mineral's effect on the emotional and mental layers: Herkimer diamond is very soothing, disseminates a feeling of pleasant harmony, and evokes spontaneity. It encourages the person to be who he really is, without the fear of external reactions, and without inner shame. It strengthens the awareness, and helps us acknowledge the fact that our reality is the embodiment of our thoughts, wishes, and desires. From that, it helps the person realize his desires, and even change his life significantly. It helps dispel unconscious fears and affords a feeling of well-being and expansiveness. It helps the person tune himself in to various situations, people, activities, and places.

Spiritual effect: Herkimer diamond stimulates the intuition, broadens the awareness, and develops telepathic abilities and the sixth sense. By means of Herkimer diamond, knowledge and insights can be put aside for use at another time, or transferred to someone else.

Profession, occupation: Herkimer diamond is recommended for people who work in an environment where there is radioactivity. They should wear the stone in order to protect themselves from radiation (not instead of conventional means of protection, however!)

Howlite

Howlite is whitish in color, and crystallizes in masses and planes.

Physical healing properties: Howlite helps in all the areas of treatment in which it is necessary to balance calcium absorption in the body. It regulates the body's calcium level, and helps in treating the teeth, skeleton, and bones.

The mineral's effect on the emotional and mental layers: Howlite is an excellent stone for improving and encouraging communicative and expressive skills. It helps people express their feelings more clearly, both to themselves and to others. It greatly improves alertness and hones the senses. For that reason, it is an excellent stone for students, or people who are engrossed in a career that demands intellectual prowess and patience. In those areas, the stone stimulates ambitiousness and the desire to act according to personal goals in order to do one's best. Moreover, it promotes patience, logic, and intuitive and intellectual alertness. When a person wants to move toward a particular goal and achieve it, in his career or studies, this is a superb stone for him. It dispels the hesitations that are liable to crop up on his path, helps develop integrity at the same time as it develops the person's sense of inner justice. Howlite helps assuage anger, tension, and fault-finding. It helps selfish people open up more to the needs of others, alleviates emotional pain, and promotes inner strength and seriousness.

Spiritual effect: Howlite strengthens the basic spiritual properties in the person's soul, develops innocence together with inner strength, inner integrity, and spiritual endurance.

Profession, occupation: Howlite is suitable for anyone who is seeking definite, effective, and successful advancement at work or in his studies. It is suitable for career people of all types.

Jade

Jade crystallizes mainly in green masses, and is also called "the dream stone." It occurs most commonly in a shade of opaque green, but it can be found in white, cream, black, or pink.

In the Far East, jade was greatly admired, and was considered to possess exalted properties. It was used in the manufacture of various expensive items of jewelry and *objets d'art*. It symbolized peace and tranquillity for the peoples of the Far East, because of its exceptional calming properties. The people believed in its ability to grant longevity. In the history of ancient China, jade was linked to mystical abilities and knowledge of the occult. To this day, it is one of the most popular stones in China for setting in jewelry, for carving, and for manufacturing ornaments. The ancient Mayan tribes also attributed lofty properties to the stone. Merchants throughout the ancient world would hold the stone in their right hand while they were negotiating. This was because of its ability to grant the power of making quick decisions, determination, and the ability to bargain. The Greeks used the stone to treat eye problems and to soothe enflamed, burning eyes. Amulets made of jade are common in the tombs of the Pharaohs and other members of the ancient Egyptian civilization. It could be that they believed that the stone would take the souls of the dead to the other world safely and soundly. A butterfly-shaped jade amulet was considered to have the ability to ensure the endurance of love, and to stimulate and encourage conjugal fidelity. It was given the name "the dream stone" because of its ability to recall dreams when worn or placed on or under the pillow during the night, and it also helps interpret and understand the dream.

Physical healing properties: Jade is used for treating heart problems, as well as thigh, spleen, and kidney disorders. It strengthens the endocrine system, and when it is used in an elixir, it can greatly improve the appearance of the skin and hair, and help make them healthy. As a rule, it is considered to have an extremely soothing effect on the nervous system.

The mineral's effect on the emotional and mental layers: Jade helps release repressed emotions, unfulfilled wishes, and subconscious conflicts, by means of dreams. Moreover, this stone promotes self-confidence, determination, and standing up for oneself. It helps the person become more open to and understanding of the needs and feelings of other people, and to take them into account when aspiring to accomplish his objective. It helps the person distinguish between the wheat and the chaff in his life and in his mental and spiritual development. It is a marvelous stone for inspiration, for self-fulfillment, and for attaining a life filled with satisfaction. It stimulates feelings of love, and helps the person become filled with love and bestow unconditional love. It increases practicality, ambitiousness, and wisdom. Its soothing properties are exceptionally effective. It stimulates awareness in a stable and enduring manner. This is one of the most wonderful stones for arousing a feeling of harmony and beauty in the human soul.

The mineral's effect on the chakras: Jade is one of the most suitable stones for placing on the heart chakra. It balances the chakra and brings it into a state of emotional balance. It opens and stimulates it, and causes feelings of unconditional universal love, beauty, harmony, and serenity to flow into it.

Spiritual effect: Here too, jade can be used by means of dream processes. The stone stimulates beautiful, tranquil, harmonious visions, which store those feelings in the mind and spirit. It can be used for creating the physical expression of dreams and aspirations in the material world, while increasing positive ambitiousness - the aspiration for peace and harmony in the world - and granting inspiration and harmony for the realization of the aspirations. Moreover, it is a stone that helps increase self-awareness and spiritual awareness.

Money, profession, business: As we said before, jade is considered to be a very suitable stone for merchants, either held or worn. It is suitable for everyone who is involved in business negotiations. In addition, it is recommended for teachers and people in education, because it supports the practical application of the material that is learned. Also, it is very soothing, and increases self-confidence and openness to the emotions of other people. In ancient times, jade was thought to be a stone that helped healing and practical diagnosis, which makes it suitable for veterinary surgeons, doctors, nurses in hospitals, and holistic therapists who work in diagnostic fields.

Jasper

Jasper occurs mainly in masses and large clumps, and it has a large range of colors. Among the most common colors are red, dark red, brown, light brown, orange, yellow, green, gray, and blue. Sometimes it is adorned with stripes of different colors. This is one of the stones in the High Priest's breastplate, and is identified with the tribe of Benjamin.

Jasper has been mentioned frequently over the course of history. It was a common and well-liked stone both because of its beauty and because some of its forms were not especially expensive. Having said that, polished "Imperial Jasper" is considered to be an expensive stone, and is set in fancy jewelry. A stone of this kind is set in the pope's ring. In some of the Native American tribes, jasper was thought to be a "rainmaking" stone. They would use it in rainmaking ceremonies, as well as in searches for subterranean water sources. It is possible that this particular use of the stone derived from its ability to increase the user's sensitivity to earth energies. The Indians attributed protective properties against the dangers of the night to it. In Peru, red jasper was worshipped as a stone that provided protection against sorcery.

The following properties are attributed to all forms of jasper, while the individual properties of the different-colored stones are also mentioned.

Physical healing properties: Red jasper is especially suitable for general health maintenance and improvement. The other stones are used to treat conditions linked to the destruction of internal tissues, as well as kidney, bladder, liver, spleen, and stomach problems, especially for treating cases of tissue destruction in those organs. The stones soothe the nerves, and some people use them to treat the loss of the sense of smell. Moreover, they have a welcome action on the minerals in the body, helping in their absorption and balance, especially manganese, iron, sulfur, and zinc.

The mineral's effect on the emotional and mental layers: Jasper is suitable for the experience of "rebirth." It helps its bearer renew his ideas and opinions, and find the correct paths of action. It stabilizes, strengthens, and induces a feeling of confidence. It is an excellent stone for people who suffer from fears, guilt feelings, and a lack of confidence. In addition, it promotes restraint and helps preserve energy, so it is very suitable for safeguarding and fortifying energies when the person is suffering from a lack of energy after a disease or during hospitalization. The stone is good for alertness, and helps in states of loneliness, in order to understand the situation, and discover its good points and even its advantages.

Red jasper symbolizes power, stability, basis, vitality, and naturalness. In addition, wearing or holding it helps the person refrain from emotional over-involvement with people who are not positive.

Brown jasper also reinforces stability and confidence, and helps develop the feeling of a firm basis.

Green jasper provides protection against physical or emotional threats. It arouses a strong feeling of affinity for nature, and is considered to be a wonderful stone for placing in the home. It is very soothing, and tends to bestow emotional balance on those who are particularly attracted to it.

Rose jasper is a wonderful stone for balancing the emotions and for providing a feeling of general support. It helps the person feel safe and protected everywhere. It inspires logic and common sense, and realizes the inventive ability in the person's character.

All the types of jasper strengthen the emotional layer and relieve emotional pressure. Moreover, all of them promote a feeling of stability and confidence.

The mineral's effect on the chakras: Red jasper is an excellent stone for placing on the base chakra. It opens and stimulates it while strengthening the person's basis, stability, and link to the earth. **Yellow jasper** is suitable for placing on the solar plexus chakra. **Purple jasper**, which is also called "Jasper Royal Plum," is suitable for stimulating the third eye chakra and the crown chakra.

Spiritual effect: Jasper in its various colors is good for protection against unwanted negative energies. They help ground the person, and encourage linking up to Mother Earth and sensitivity toward her. They help balance the yin and yang energies, and the balanced link between the physical, emotional, mental, and etheric bodies in a harmonious energetic way. Because they provide protection against negative energies, they stabilize the aura, help cleanse it, and remove non-positive energies. Moreover, they help create the link between the material, physical energies and the spiritual and etheric ones. Jasper teaches the person that he lives in the world not only for himself, and encourages him to make others happy, out of an understanding of the bond between all of us, as human beings. This stone, mainly in its yellow shades, helps link up to the energies of the solar plexus, and in the past was used by the shamans to link up to those energies in order to perform their ceremonies.

Blue jasper was used by the shamans to link the person to higher worlds.

Red jasper is an excellent protective stone. Sometimes it fades while it is protecting, because it absorbs the negative energies against which it is protecting its wearer. For this reason, it must be purified and recharged carefully. By means of meditation, red jasper can help find ways to improve situations of injustice and inequity. It is very effective for reconstructing dreams, for causing a recurring dream, and for remembering the contents of a dream if they are significant to the person's life.

Money, profession, business: Red jasper is suitable for people who work at physically or mentally exhausting jobs, such as accounting, computers, law enforcement, law, waiting on tables, and so on, who suffer from great pressure and big work loads, since the stone increases their physical endurance. In the case of people in the performing arts, actors, singers, and so on, who perform in front of a live audience, the stone helps increase their sensitivity to the public and to the feedback they receive, in a non-verbal and sensory fashion. It augments alertness and caution, and so it is suitable for technicians and electricians. It is likely to suit military and law enforcement personnel, wardens, social workers, people who work with juvenile delinquents, and so on, since it promotes emotional stability. It is recommended for people who work with the public - operators, waiters, telephone operators, secretaries, reception clerks, and so on - since it provides them with a great deal of patience with which to cope with the public, and helps them work under great pressure. Because of its ability to increase sensitivity to the earth, it is recommended for people who search for natural resources, quarries, or subterranean water, and for people who work in professions connected with nature, animals and plants.

Green jasper is suitable for people who are involved in gardening, agriculture, and taking care of plants, as well as for environmentalists. As a rule, all the jasper stones are connected with preserving the quality of the environment, and grant people who engage in these areas strength and faith.

Picture Jasper

The beautiful picture jasper stone is found mainly in the United States. When one looks at it, one feels as if one is looking at a special painting or picture. This special stone occurs in color combinations of brown, beige, black, turquoise blue, or ivory. When one scrutinizes the "picture" that appears on its surface, one can discover the hidden message behind the wonderful picture - a message that is unique to the person, sometimes from the past. Some people use it in order to preserve and develop business and economic successes and achievements, and to reach the correct combination of activities leading to the desired scenario in accordance with their aspirations.

Physical healing properties: Picture jasper is used mainly in treatments for stimulating the proper functioning of the immune system, and it is used, in conjunction with various techniques and other stones, for treating the kidneys and the skin.

The mineral's effect on the emotional and mental layers: The stone helps raise thoughts, feelings, fears, and hopes from the subconscious to the conscious level, and helps the person deal with these emotional burdens. It is very helpful for people who suffer from unexplained fears and nightmares. This impressive stone encourages creative vision, which can be sensed as soon as the person looks at the wonderful shapes that appear on its surface.

Spiritual effect: Picture jasper can help us understand how different civilizations operate, whether they are advanced or unknown, and shed a bit of light on those unknown civilizations.

Money, profession, business: This is a wonderful stone for entrepreneurs and business people, and for whomever is interested in preserving and developing his economic and business achievements. It helps the person direct and combine the correct actions in order to achieve business goals.

Jet

Jet is a shiny black stone. Because it is a soft stone, it was widely used for manufacturing carved jewelry, amulets, and ornaments. Its origin is organic: It is ancient coal that has been tightly compressed.

Since the days of the Romans, jet was one of the most popular black stones. Mystical protective properties were attributed to it, and it was called "black amber." The Romans were in the habit of carrying it during their campaigns as protection against the dangers of the road. In medieval Italy, and today too, it was the custom to carve scarabs and beetles out of jet as amulets against the forces of evil. In Ireland, fishermen's wives would burn a small piece of jet while they prayed for the safe return of their seafaring husbands. It is considered a personal stone that cannot be transferred to or exchanged with anyone else. Since jet was also used for non-positive purposes, such as in black magic rituals, and other undesirable procedures, there are sensitive people who do not feel comfortable holding or wearing it. When one purchases such a stone, it is very important to pay attention to whether the energy one feels is "correct," and does not cause negative vibrations. Moreover, it is important to purify it thoroughly, and to recharge it with thoughts of peace and love. Jet must not be purchased in spurious places where non-positive energies can be sensed. Sensitive healers prefer not to use it, but rather use black obsidian or black tourmaline for protective purposes. The use of the stone for non-positive purposes is dangerous.

Physical healing properties: Jet is used to alleviate toothache, and in the olden days, before the practice of dentistry was widespread and well known, it was considered to be a powerful cure for tooth problems. It helps relieve stomach-aches, headaches, migraines, and colds. In addition, it helps treat epilepsy and problems in the lymph glands.

The mineral's effect on the emotional and mental layers: Jet helps dispel unpleasant or frightening thoughts. It is soothing, and effective for states of depression.

The mineral's effect on the chakras: Jet is used to strengthen the base chakra.

Spiritual effect: Jet is considered to be a powerful protective stone, used for protection on the road and during journeys.

Money, profession, business: Jet is thought to be the stone that safeguards stability in business and prevents economic success from being jeopardized.

Kunzite

Kunzite crystallizes in prisms and masses. Its range of colors includes colorless, green, pink, yellow, gray, and purple. Sometimes, there are stones with several colors.

Physical healing properties: Kunzite is used for treating the muscles and strengthening them, for treating diseases that are caused by external tension, and for treating endocrinological and pulmonary problems.

The mineral's effect on the emotional and mental layers: Kunzite stimulates thoughts filled with love and affection toward ourselves and others, and helps establish loving communication with the people around us. It is soothing, spreads tranquillity, and helps create a feeling of powerful and special love on all levels. It stimulates love between the members of a couple, unconditional love and self-love. Kunzite is helpful in promoting punctuality and creativity, and disseminates a feeling of confidence. It promotes thought processes and stimulates intuition. It arouses sensitivity, clarity, and hones the senses. It gives the person a feeling of strength and love, sensitivity and confidence. It is one of the best stones for treating "wounded hearts." It releases old patterns of suffering and pain, while opening up the heart to giving and receiving love.

The mineral's effect on the chakras: Kunzite stimulates and activates the heart chakra, and links it to the throat and third eye chakras.

Spiritual effect: Kunzite cleanses, purifies, and fortifies the energy field. It provides effective protection for the energy field against negative energies and undesirable entities. It is a wonderful stone for profound meditation and for developing channeling abilities.

Work, occupation: Kunzite is an excellent stone for healers and trainee healers in order to promote spiritual growth and development, channeling abilities, and strengthening of the intuition.

Kyanite

Kyanite occurs in rope- or pencil-like configurations, and in masses, sometimes curved and sometimes straight. Its colors include blue, blue with black or white, gray, pink, and green.

Physical healing properties: Kyanite is linked in a special way to the throat chakra, especially in its blue color, and for this reason it is very effective for treating problems connected with the throat and thyroid gland. Moreover, it is used for treating problems linked with the brain, the adrenal glands, the reproductive system, and muscle function disorders.

The mineral's effect on the emotional and mental layers: Kyanite soothes and spreads tranquillity marvelously. It assuages anger and frustration, promotes logic, and helps the person stand firm in situations that, under normal circumstances, would undermine his stability. It is a supportive stone that can encourage the person and support him along his path by stimulating him and supplying him with the necessary energy.

The mineral's effect on the chakras: Blue kyanite has a special effect on the throat chakra. **Pink kyanite** and **green kyanite** are suitable for placing on the heart chakra. When the treatment and laying on of stones are performed by a skilled healer, they can open blockages in this chakra. **Light blue kyanite** placed on the third eye chakra is used during meditation and channeling. In addition, kyanite is used for opening all the chakras.

Spiritual effect: Kyanite is an excellent guiding stone for spiritual development, and is not limited to work in a particular field or path. It develops the intuition and spiritual awareness with great power. Its uniqueness lies in the fact that it does not accumulate negative energies. It has the ability to link up all the chakras at once, even without guiding work. When it is tuned in to the user, it can also open all the chakras. It can be used for linking up all the bodies - physical, emotional, mental, etheric, and astral. The stone is linked mainly to the throat and third eye chakras, and is widely used in healing treatments and channeling. It is very helpful in channeling and for the sensing of things beyond physical reality, and it connects superior knowledge to the inner feelings of the heart, mutuality, and love, so that the application of the divine knowledge and insights that were achieved by means of the stone are distributed and used in order to increase love and awareness in the world. This is one of the most outstanding stones for meditation. It facilitates the entry into the process, and helps when the person feels uncomfortable or frightened during the course of meditation. It can be used to link up to an inner guide, remember dreams, and interpret them. Its spiritual abilities are numerous and divine. It balances the feminine and masculine energies, yin and yang, helps spiritual, emotional, mental, and physical growth, and can be used to eliminate barriers in the various bodies. Its action is gentle but extremely effective. Some people use black kyanite in conjunction with blue kyanite in order to create a stable and spontaneous link between the bodies, and when used in this way, it is very powerful. It repairs holes in the aura and cleanses it (especially blue kyanite). It is not customary to combine color projection while performing healing with kyanite, since the stone itself attracts pure, cosmic light. It is possible to meditate with it in order to return to previous incarnations and mend things.

Profession, occupation: This is an excellent stone for healers, trainee healers, and channelers.

Labradorite

Labradorite is a type of feldspar. It crystallizes in the form of masses and grains. It occurs in white, gray and yellow, copper red, peacock blue, and when the sun's rays are reflected in it, golden particles, reddish gold sunset-like stripes or bright blue sparkles are visible in it.

This stone is famous for its mystical power, and was used throughout history as an effective aid to people who were engaged in mysticism, alchemy and white magic (Wicca). Its special and mysterious beauty contributed greatly to the mystical aura that shrouds it to this day.

Physical healing properties: Labradorite is used for healing brain disorders and digestive problems, as well as for regulating the metabolism in the body.

The mineral's effect on the emotional and mental layers: By means of labradorite, impressions and ways of intuitive thinking can be transformed into practical, intellectual thinking that can be applied. It gives the person a feeling of power, stabilizes, and helps with continuity and consistency. Labradorite helps get rid of troublesome thoughts, thus bringing great relief to people who suffer from them. It increases self-confidence, and helps people who lack confidence muster courage. It has a great deal of value on the mental plane - it inspires lucid thinking, accuracy, originality, and purity. With its help, it is possible to achieve harmony between the intuitive and mystical feelings on the one hand, and knowledge and wisdom that are acquired or learned on the other. It stimulates inspiration and creativity. It diminishes worry and tension, and dispels fears. It is a good stone for facilitating changes and easing distressing, new, or disturbing situations that the person finds himself in during the course of his life. With the help of labradorite, the person can find his vocation in the present incarnation. When making far-reaching changes in life, labradorite helps the person make the correct decisions.

The mineral's effect on the chakras: Labradorite is generally placed on the third eye chakra in order to see visions and engage in channeling.

Spiritual effect: Labradorite is a strong stone for channeling, healing, and spiritual development. It has a protective and balancing effect on the aura, keeping it pure and clean, and protecting it against energy loss. By using labradorite, it is possible to create a harmonious link between the high delicate bodies and the practical physical body. It helps the person understand the way of life he has chosen in this incarnation, and can be used for channeling with superior entities. It is widely used in meditation for channeling in order to open a gate to other worlds for the person, and to inspire visions and scenes. Some people use it to look at previous incarnations, for predicting the future using various techniques, and for many mystical purposes. A unique property that labradorite shares with the opal (even though the latter has changeable colors) is its ability to preserve energies. For this reason, when people are afraid or angry, they should not wear it.

Work, occupation: This is one of the stones that is most recommended for holistic healers, healers, and trainee healers. Having said this, it is possible that if a person acquires Labradorite before he is energetically ready to use it, it will go missing or break. It is of great value to healers - it releases tension from their mind, and gives them confidence about the intuitive actions they perform during the treatment. Since it safeguards against energy loss, and keeps the aura clean and pure, many holistic healers and healers wear a chain of labradorite stones around their necks during a treatment.

Lapis lazuli

Lapis lazuli is one of the New Age stones. It occures in the form of huge masses. Its color is deep blue, and it can contain a little of the minerals pyrite, gold, and calcite.

Lapis lazuli is one of the most ancient stones to be used for mystical and spiritual purposes. In ancient Egypt, it was considered to be sacred, and was used by the nobility and the priesthood; even the Pharaohs themselves wore it, generally cut in the shape of an eye. According to the Egyptian papyri, lapis lazuli symbolized the power of the gods. Because of its pervasive presence in ancient mystical rites, it can be used to experience the significance of those ancient mysterious ceremonies, while helping the person understand the scenes and insights that emanate from visions.

Physical healing properties: Lapis lazuli is used for treating various problems of the throat chakra, such as throat infections, bronchitis, angina, and so on. It is also good for problems connected to the upper chest and the thymus gland. Moreover, it tends to absorb poisonous metals from the body, and therefore it is good for detoxification processes, and for people who work with poisonous metals. The stone is also used for treating problems concerning bone marrow and the immune system. This stone, which is also linked to the third eye chakra, is very good for alleviating insomnia, vertigo, and a feeling of dullness in the senses, as well as for aural and hearing problems. In general, it helps activate the energies of renewal and regeneration in the body, and in its crystalline form, helps rebuild the cells of the muscles and skeleton.

The mineral's effect on the emotional and mental layers: Lapis lazuli can be used in order to alleviate heartaches and feelings of anguish. It encourages the person and gives him renewed strength to continue despite sad events and crises. One of its most important properties is its ability to help us liberate ourselves from old, inhibiting thought patterns. Simultaneously, it is helpful in expanding the wearer's or user's intellectual abilities, helps him be objective toward the information that reaches him, and helps him draw the correct conclusions from the data at hand. In addition, it also guides the person to feel intuitively what is right and suitable for him, and what is not. It is a very important stone for work on getting rid of old, inhibiting patterns of thought and emotion, and it helps dispel the resentment and hatred that lurk in the depths of the subconscious. Lapis lazuli is very good for the various aspects of expression and communication, and is very helpful in treating people who are shy or lack confidence. By holding or wearing it, they can feel more comfortable in company and express themselves more freely. This stone, which gives energy to the throat chakra, stimulates creativity, gives courage, and helps organize routine, everyday actions in the correct way. It is good for relieving states of depression, and helps the person feel self-accepting and serene. It is a good stone to use for balancing conjugal relations, since it promotes equality in the relationship, and helps balance the masculine and feminine energies.

The mineral's effect on the chakras: Lapis lazuli is placed on the throat chakra in order to balance, clean, open, and stimulate it. Moreover, it stimulates the third eye chakra and activates it.

Spiritual effect: Lapis lazuli links the physical, mental, and emotional bodies. It constitutes the "key" to ancient universal and esoteric knowledge, together with the ability to understand this knowledge. It is also suitable for the third eye and throat chakras, and fills these chakras with energy. When it is placed on the third eye chakra, it helps the person understand his dreams in a way that contributes to his emotional and spiritual development. Lapis lazuli balances the yin and yang energies, and is used as a physically and emotionally protective stone.

Work, occupation: Lapis lazuli is considered to be the suitable stone for historians and archaeologists. It strengthens analytical abilities. Moreover, it can reinforce the connection with and the drawing of knowledge from ancient cultures. Lapis lazuli helps strengthen the intellect and powers of expression of writers and people who work in the writing professions, as well as the intuitive layers. Lapis lazuli helps journalists strengthen their power of judgment. It is recommended for directors of companies, since it stimulates the brain and the thought processes, as well as the stream of new ideas. For the same reason, it is wonderful for inventors. Lapis lazuli is also recommended for lawyers and psychologists.

Larimar

Larimar occurs in blue, various shades of turquoise blue, green, red, and white. Sometimes there are white or black dots in it, or mixed colors. It crystallizes in grains and masses.

Physical healing properties: Larimar is used for treating the hair, legs, and cartilaginous regions of the body.

The mineral's effect on the emotional and mental layers: Larimar creates a link between thought and emotion. It helps us recognize the limitations we impose on ourselves, and free ourselves of them. It helps the person acknowledge limiting, old, and unhelpful thought patterns, whether he created them himself, or he was influenced by the fact of their presence in his surroundings. It stimulates determination, tranquillity, love, and the quest for truth. It helps the person be more objective, and to aspire to improve the reality of his life. It stimulates inner wisdom, and permits its expression in a practical manner. This stone greatly helps people who are not prepared or not willing to admit to guilt when necessary. It teaches them that admission of guilt is not so terrible, and that it brings with it a feeling of relief and increased self-esteem.

The mineral's effect on the chakras: Larimar can be used for balancing and encouraging the heart chakra, the throat chakra, the crown chakra, and the third eye chakra.

Spiritual effect: Larimar has an exceptional property. It helps people understand the language of animals, and stimulates the ability to communicate with them. It is used for energetic networking. It reinforces the person's healing abilities and is used for channeling with entities and intelligences.

Money, profession, occupation: Larimar is highly recommended for everyone who works with animals: veterinary surgeons, zoologists, animal researchers, zoo-keepers, farmers, and whoever needs to improve his understanding of animals in his work. Morover, larimar is used to "attract" clients to salespeople. In addition, it is a stone that is suitable for channelers.

Lepidolite

Lepidolite crystallizes in masses. Its colors include various shades of pink and purple, transparent, white, gray, and yellow.

Lepidolite was sacred to the Aztecs, as a protective stone. Some call it the "peace stone."

Physical healing properties: Lepidolite contains a relatively large amount of lithium, which is used for treating manic-depression and other mental diseases, so there are people who use it for those diseases. (Treatment of problems of this kind must only be administered by an experienced therapist and healer, and in the presence of a family member or the patient's regular therapist, since the patient's reactions are unpredictable.) Placing lepidolite near us helps increase the negative ions in the environment, thus helping to safeguard and improve health. It is good for treating diseases that are caused by tension and pressure. It helps soothe the nervous system, helps calm the heart down and stabilize the blood flow. Using an elixir prepared from the stone, it is possible to treat stiff muscles and muscle cramps in the legs and shoulders, as well as tendon diseases. Using quartz and lepidolite on a regular basis (by means of an elixir prepared from both of them, or placing both of them on the abdominal region), it is possible to help treat candida and the symptoms of the disease.

The mineral's effect on the emotional and mental layers: Lepidolite balances emotion and logic. It helps us increase our abilities to be tolerant and patient, thereby causing a reduction in tension and nervousness. It helps people who suffer from insomnia, and is effective in dispelling fatigue. It is used for treating people with a tendency to extremes of mood, and it calms irascible and nervous people down to a great extent. It stimulates joy and optimism, and has a good influence on children who feel sad or depressed. Lepidolite can be used to improve self-love and acceptance, while increasing the belief in oneself and other people. It increases openness and the person's sense of integrity, as well as that of those close to him.

The mineral's effect on the chakras: Lepidolite has a welcome effect on the four upper chakras. It opens and activates the heart chakra, the throat chakra, the third eye chakra, and the crown chakra.

Spiritual effect: Lepidolite helps the person acknowledge his set of old and unhelpful patterns, while helping him to change them and build more useful ones in their stead. It is used in rebirthing processes, and for locating energetic blockages in the body. The healer or crystal therapist must place it on different regions of the body, and pay attention to the resonance that the stone emits when it senses a blockage. This treatment can also be self-administered, without the help of a healer. One of lepidolite's unique properties is its efficacy in energetic networking of regions, rooms, and halls. It "soothes" the energies that are in the rooms, and is very good for networking large spaces such as classrooms, conference rooms, and so on. Moreover, it is very effective in networking places in which ground disturbances have been identified, and helps stabilize subterranean structures. Some people use it in the garden or the field in order to safeguard the crops and the plants from disease, and to ensure an abundant harvest.

Money, profession, occupation: Lepidolite is thought to be a wonderful stone for business, especially where there is a need for negotiation, authority, and diplomatic ability. It strengthens these properties in the person, while improving his modes of business communication and making them more efficient. Moreover, it helps strengthen the integrity both of the bearer and of the person or people with whom he has business ties. It is therefore advisable to keep it in one's pocket during business meetings and economic negotiations. In addition, lepidolite has a welcome effect on the earth and on vegetation, and some people use it in garden and field in order to safeguard crops and plants from diseases, and to ensure an abundant harvest. Also, it is a stone that is widely used in holistic treatments, and is the faithful companion of many healers.

Lodestone

Lodestone, which is slightly reminiscent of pyrite, is also known as "the magnet stone." It occurs in masses and grains. Its colors range from light brown to deep black. Lodestone has polar properties (plus and minus).

Physical healing properties: Lodestone stimulates and strengthens the body's natural movement, flow, and vital strength. It is used in various techniques of magnetic medicine, and increases the person's bio-magnetic powers. When used by therapists who are experienced in magnetic energy, the stone is used for treating many serious diseases: drug addiction, diabetes, benign and malignant tumors, but because of its strength, only a therapist who is experienced in this field must administer the treatment. During a disease, the stone helps the natural powers of the body and the self-healing powers regain their strength, and in this way, contributes to the body's regenerative processes.

The mineral's effect on the emotional and mental layers: This stone facilitates coping with and understanding the ambiguity of life. Because of its polarity, it affords balance between the person's feminine and masculine sides, in a physical, emotional, and cerebral manner. It is suitable for people who feel unmotivated and lethargic, since it helps them move forward by bolstering their self-confidence. It helps the person break dependency, and helps him move in a calm, sure way along his spiritual path by exerting an influence on the different planes of life. This is a good stone to hold when unexpected surprises land on the person, since it helps him cope well with the new conditions.

Spiritual effect: Lodestone links and coordinates the astral body and the etheric body, and helps balance and coordinate the invisible meridians in the physical body with the etheric body. It influences all the chakras.

Malachite

Malachite is a fresh, green stone that occurs in a range of shades of green. It crystallizes in clumps and masses. It is characterized by exceptional examples of "eyes," spiral, and circles.

In ancient times, it was believed that malachite stimulated very powerful hallucinations. It was considered to be a protective stone, and as a stone that stimulated and activated the properties of the mind and personal strength. As a protective stone, "eye" malachite was used to get rid of non-positive occurrences and negative external energies. It was said about them that they warned their wearer of approaching danger - at those times, they would crack and break in two. The ancient Egyptians would grind the stone, and use it as eye-shadow, both for cosmetic purposes and for strengthening metaphysical vision. Moreover, they believed that it was capable of treating all the problems of the circulatory system. They would place it as an amulet on little children in order to safeguard them from external dangers, and in order to increase the child's feeling of safety. When stones were laid on, the Egyptians would use malachite for balancing all the body's energies and for creating harmony in the entire body system.

Physical healing properties: Malachite strengthens the immune system, helps treat arthritis, fractures, torn muscles, and asthma. It also helps treat tumors. Some people give it to women in childbirth in order to ease the birth process. In addition, it helps treat vertigo.

The mineral's effect on the emotional and mental layers: Malachite promotes the inner feelings of hope and peace. It symbolizes change and creativity. It greatly eases changes, and is very powerful in everything to do with understanding the reasons for various emotional states that sparked the disease or debilitated the systems. It helps the person get in touch with his emotions and understand them, and bring repressed memories and experiences up to the conscious level. In such cases, it is a good idea to add a soothing and consoling stone such as rose quartz (when the experiences involve love wounds or a lack of love), or celestite (for instance, when childhood traumas are evoked). This is because its action is not always gentle, and some people find it difficult to cope with the things that are raised to the conscious level. It not only helps understand the root of the problem or the reasons for its occurrence, but also helps the person take responsibility for the situation and work toward changing it. While it helps the person become acquainted with the situation and change it, it provides intuitive answers, inspires instinctive logic, and helps the person act in an effective manner. Moreover, it inspires loyalty in all aspects of life.

The mineral's effect on the chakras: Malachite activates all the chakras. It is mainly suitable for placement on the heart and throat chakras, in order to balance, stimulate, and activate them.

Spiritual effect: As we mentioned previously, malachite is considered to be a very powerful protective stone.

Profession, business: It is said that malachite has the ability to weed out non-positive business partners, thus promoting success in business. Moreover, it is thought to be a stone that helps a person take responsibility in business, operate according to logic and intuition, and reinforce the loyalty between business partners. It is recommended as a protective stone for people who are in the aviation field - stewards, pilots, and people who fly a lot for business and so on. As a protective stone against unexpected dangers, it is considered to be the stone that protects miners.

Moldavite

Moldavite is a kind of tektite - meteoric glass that originates in outer space. Scientists are still discussing the question of whether the tektites are authentic meteors, or a combination of meteoric substances and terrestrial rocks. Moldavite is green in color. These stones fell from the sky in the region of the Republic of Kazakhstan about twenty million years ago. It is rare (in 1987, the total weight of all the moldavite stones was one ton only!) and very expensive as a result. It is not yet known which star it came from.

Moldavite was used for manufacturing vessels and jewelry 25,000 years ago, and it is possible that various energetic and mystical uses were made of it. There is a legend that links moldavite to the Holy Grail, saying that it was an emerald that fell from the heavens. Moreover, it is said that the magic stone of the Grail was guarded by kings who waited for "a knight of exceptional excellence" to discover it and use it as a healing amulet. It is said that the discovery of the stone of the Grail accelerates spiritual development - a property that is very appropriate to moldavite. Among the stones that are to be found on Earth, moldavite is a real gift from heaven. It is considered to be one of the strongest stones in the mineral world, as a vessel for spiritual development and broadening of the awareness. Many people report that working with moldavite is accompanied by the broadening of their spiritual awareness, along with an increase in openness to inner guidance. It works mainly on the spiritual layers and planes.

It seems as if moldavite does not need to be cleansed like the rest of the crystals, even though exposure to sunlight can serve to strengthen and focus the stone's energies for the person's personal aims. Because of its delicate nature, it must not be purified in salt or salt water.

The mineral's effect on the chakras: Moldavite's high level of energy can open and cleanse blockages in the chakras. It is used for treating the heart, throat, third eye, and crown chakras, as well as being placed on them. It should be experimented with in order to know exactly what it will do for each person, in accordance with his spiritual development and potential.

Spiritual effect: It would take too long to describe all the actions of this stone on the person's spiritual layers. It creates a link of cooperation between human beings and the inhabitants of the outside worlds, and affords access to exalted energetic galactic dimensions in order to develop visionary abilities and bring the person to a state of enlightenment. It serves as a powerful channeling stone, and it enables the channeler to see, occasionally, the source from which the channeling message emanates. Moldavite worn anywhere on the body affects the aura.

Moldavite is very powerful in its natural form, and highly focused when it is shaped into a pyramid and other symmetrical shapes. Moldavite creates synergistic energy in combination with quartz, amethyst, rose-quartz, sugilite, larimar, charoite, lapis lazuli, danburite, tanzanite, celestite, aquamarine, diamond, opal, and several other crystals.

Profession, occupation: Of course, this is an excellent and extremely powerful stone for those engaged in spiritual development. It is used by channelers, healers, and mystics in a wonderful way, and promotes their spiritual and therapeutic actions.

Moonstone

Moonstone's color is a shade of pearl, white, milky white or gleaming white. In general, it occurs in stones that belong to the feldspar family. This stone can be worn anywhere on the body in order to cause a general, healing sensation of calmness and tranquillity.

From the dawn of history, moonstone was linked to the magical power of the moon. The ancients believed that a full moon strengthened and fortified the stone's power. For that reason, they thought that a certain "covenant" had been sworn between the stone and the moon, and whoever wore it around his neck when he embarked on nocturnal journeys would be protected, especially when he had to cross water by night. Moreover, it was worn as an amulet to enhance the person's own power, and give him hope. In various regions of the ancient world, moonstone was used to bring back a loved one who stormed out in anger. According to legend, when the owner of the moonstone feels rage and anger, moonstone loses its sheen and brilliance. In the Indian civilization, moonstone is considered to be a sacred stone that symbolizes the link between man and woman and the link between two opposites that make up a whole. The Romans believed that the persona of Diana, which is parallel to that of Aphrodite in the Greek tradition, was imprinted in the stone. For that reason, properties of inspiring love between the members of a couple, happiness, prosperity, wealth, victory, and good fortune were attributed to it. Today, too, it is considered to be a stone that brings good luck to its owner.

Physical healing properties: Moonstone strengthens the body and gives it powers of endurance. It has a very calming effect on the nervous system. It can be used for reducing the tension and pressure that occur during PMS and the actual period. It can also be used for treating spinal problems. For that reason, it must be placed, using a plaster, on the injured or painful vertebrae for a few hours a day. In addition, it is used for treating stomach and duodenal ulcers, as well as for other digestive ailments, such as poor digestion, bloating, and flatulence. The stone stimulates the physical regenerative properties, and thus is used for treating problems of weak or brittle hair, skin (in this case, an elixir is prepared and spread on the skin and hair), eyes, and various organs. It is helpful in the absorption of nourishing substances, vitamins and minerals, helps in the body's detoxifying processes, helps treat problems connected with the lungs, and is helpful in pregnancy and fertility. Moreover, the stone enhances male virility. It soothes mosquito bites and insect stings, even in extreme cases of allergies to stings, malaria, fever, and so on. However, it is not a substitute for medical treatment, but can be applied in parallel to it. Moonstone should be worn or placed on the painful, injured area in order to provide it with renewed energies, reinforcement, calmness and vitality, and an elixir can be prepared from it for drinking or spreading.

The mineral's effect on the emotional and mental layers: Moonstone possesses balancing energy. It is helpful for introspection, and it can be used during emotional, mental, and spiritual changes that occur in the person's life. While it helps these changes occur gradually, it keeps the person in a state of emotional balance. In general, it is a very good stone for attaining and safeguarding emotional balance. It helps the person control his emotions when appropriate, and give vent to them properly at the right time. Many people use it during road travel, and for this reason it is called "the wanderer's stone." It helps us keep what is dear to us near to us, and it is said that it attracts happiness to the place where it is put. Moonstone helps us open our hearts to love, attract love, and experience love. Moreover, it guards and protects sensitive people from emotional injuries.

Spiritual effect: Moonstone helps the person "filter" energetically what he receives from the universe, so that he gets what he really needs. Because it is moonstone, it helps the person understand and accept the various natural cycles, and the effect of these cycles on our emotions. It is a marvelous stone for developing intuitive sensations and reception. It helps us pick up intuitive messages, understand this knowledge, and apply it to our lives. Moonstone cleanses all the chakras of non-positive energies, supports and consoles the person during difficult changes, and emphasizes the feminine sides of each person. In addition, moonstone links the physical, mental, and emotional bodies. It helps remove the obstacles from the person's path, at the same time providing him with guidance and direction for the steps he has to take in order to accomplish his objectives. When the stone is used as a pendulum, it is likely to indicate the place in the body in which the problem lies.

As its name suggests, moonstone embodies lunar properties: rebirth, cycles, understanding the nature of cycles and accepting them with equanimity. It encourages introspection, links us to our natural rhythm, and even helps us balance it.

Profession, occupation: Moonstone is recommended for artists. It reinforces their expressive powers by means of strengthening their faith in themselves, and their self-love. It is very suitable for dancers, and enhances their self-expression via dance. Moreover, it is recommended for teachers and other educators, since it supports cooperative endeavors. In addition, moonstone is good for managers, foremen, and owners of companies. It helps them open their hearts, be more sensitive toward their workers, and use their emotions wisely, without jeopardizing their "cold" efficiency. It is a good stone for psychologists and various healers, since it increases sensitivity toward others. Moreover, it is recommended for people who work at jobs they do not like, in which they feel that they are not expressing their true abilities. Moonstone strengthens self-esteem and the aspiration to find a better place.

Nephrite

Nephrite is a combination of two minerals, jade and actinolite, and it is in fact a type of jade. It crystallizes in masses and in "triangular" shapes that have been smoothed by natural forces. Its colors include olive green, green, gray, brown green, light green, cream, beige, gray blue, black, and pink.

Physical healing properties: Nephrite encourages the action of the white blood corpuscles, thus reinforcing the immune system. It stimulates the flow of adrenaline, and helps regulate metabolism in the body. It is a stone that is widely used in treating the kidneys.

The mineral's effect on the emotional and mental layers: Nephrite helps the person cope with situations of pressure, and alleviates his physical reactions to situations of stress. It helps the person feel in harmony with his surroundings and exhibit sensitivity toward others and their needs.

The mineral's effect on the chakras: Green nephrite is suitable for placing on the heart chakra.

Spiritual effect: Nephrite is superb for all the activities that aim to bring unity and wholeness to opposing energies. It helps create balance and coordination between the masculine and feminine energies, the yin and yang energies, and create energetic balance between the person and other people. In addition, among the tribes of New Zealand, nephrite was used as an amulet against diseases.

Obsidian

Obsidian comes in many different forms, some of which will be described below. Obsidian is transparent volcanic glass, which means that it is found mainly in regions in which ancient volcanic eruptions occurred. They crystallize in a similar manner to diamonds. It can be found in a tremendous range of colors and shapes. Similar to jet, it is also said to be a personal stone, which cannot be transferred to anyone else (but it can be bought especially as a gift for someone else). Ancient amulets and amulets carved from obsidian have been found all over the world. Small statuettes and figurines carved from obsidian have been found in various regions in Central and South America, where they apparently served as lucky amulets. Below are a few properties that are common to the stones of the obsidian family, along with several unique properties of the various-colored stones. (Black obsidian and electric shine obsidian will be dealt with in the next section.)

Physical healing properties: Red obsidian is used for treating gall and blood problems. **Green obsidian** helps treat heart problems, particularly problems that stem from an emotional source, as well as bladder ailments. **Purple shine obsidian** is used for treating Alzheimer's disease. **Snowflake obsidian** is used for making the skin smooth, helps balance the body's systems, and treats arterial problems and skin (especially in the form of an elixir), as well as skeletal problems. **Blue obsidian** is used for treating speech problems, eye problems, and various mental problems.

The mineral's effect on the emotional and mental layers: Obsidian stones present the required repairs and improvements we need to make in our characteristics and personalities. Not only do they inform us of the necessary repairs, but they also support us in the processes of change, and sometimes even chart the simple and easiest way to implement those changes for us. They help us accept our external appearance with love and esteem, and dispel non-positive thoughts toward ourselves and others. They protect the person against emotional exhaustion by others, and support him during times of external pressure. Moreover, they protect sensitive, delicate, and soft people from being exploited. **Red obsidian** promotes stability and politeness. **Gold shine obsidian** helps the person sees the beauty within him, and accept himself completely. It is excellent for people who feel worthless, or who do not appreciate themselves as they should. **Green obsidian** helps the person liberate himself from dependence on others in a gentle, calm way. **Pearl shine obsidian** and **mahogany obsidian**, whose color is red-brown and black, help dispel tension. **Rainbow obsidian** fills the person's life with light, love, and gratitude. **Blue obsidian** reinforces the person's communicative abilities and expressive abilities in writing. Moreover, it helps him understand foreign languages and facilitates expression in those languages. **Snowflake obsidian** helps the person get rid of inhibiting thought and emotional patterns, and adapt to being alone in a pleasant way; it promotes purity of thought and emotion.

The mineral's effect on the chakras: Green obsidian cleanses and opens the heart chakra. **Purple obsidian** opens and activates the crown chakra, and creates a link to the bowels of the earth (it is very effective during meditation). **Pearl shine obsidian** (with a purplish sheen), when placed on the third eye chakra, helps to understand the core of problems and get to their root. **Blue obsidian** stimulates the throat chakra.

Spiritual effect: Obsidian stones have wonderful protective properties both on the physical and on the mental and spiritual planes. They protect the person against negative energies not only from the outside, but from within as well. They can be used for grounding and for creating a link or a grounded connection to the bowels of the earth. They can be placed close to the body when setting out to meditate with stones that activate the crown chakra and cause floating. In healing work, obsidian stones help the person reach the root of the problem and the disease. They protect very well, and help prevent the "sucking" of energy by other people.

Gold shine obsidian and **pearl shine obsidian** are used for observation, and promote people who are engaged in healing and in Shaman medicine and ceremonies. **Purple obsidian** stimulates the intuition, links it to the intellect, and helps express information and knowledge. **Rainbow obsidian** is used to observe mainly matters connected to couples. **Red obsidian** helps balance the yin and yang energies. **Snowflake obsidian** helps see the light at the end of the tunnel, since it is a black stone with white, snowflake-like flecks in it.

Black obsidian, electric shine obsidian

Black obsidian is a marvelous stone that symbolizes the light at the end of the tunnel, the light that is hidden in every thick, primeval darkness. It teaches that even in times of distress, despair and sorrow, we can rise above the limits of our body and ego toward an exaltation of spirit and a link to the spiritual. **Electric shine obsidian** is another, very shiny, form of the stone, which contains a kind of electric blue light.

Physical healing properties: The use of **black obsidian** for treating the body is mainly a healing treatment, using visualization. The healer passes the black obsidian over the sick area of the body, imagines the problem rising above the surface, surrounds it, and transforms its color into shining white. **Electric shine obsidian** is used for treating skeletal and spinal problems. It is helpful in detoxification processes and the elimination of poisons, for soothing cramps in any organ, for improving vision (in the form of an elixir), for reinforcing the immune system, and for strengthening the organs.

The mineral's effect on the emotional and mental layers: This stone develops and stimulates all fields of creativity. It is good for people in whom there is a lot of "black," gloom, and they want to transform it into purity and whiteness. It can teach people who have been through bad and terrifying experiences what the aim of those experiences was, and help them rise up, even by means of black and difficult moments in the present and in the past, to spiritual openness and mental fortitude. Using electric shine obsidian, it is possible to reach the root of the problems and difficulties the person is forced to cope with, and thus try to solve the problems at their root. Electric shine obsidian also helps the person eliminate troublesome, non-positive, and inhibiting thoughts about himself, or of others about him. Both black and electric shine obsidian strengthen the intuition.

The mineral's effect on the chakras: Electric shine obsidian is suitable for placing on the third eye or for meditation with the third eye. It stimulates visions, and activates the chakra, while providing it with energy.

Spiritual effect: A ball of black obsidian is used for observing and seeing events that are likely to occur in the future, as well as for introspection. Among Native American tribes, it was used for ceremonies, since they believed that it honed both the inner vision and the ability to observe and see visions. Electric shine obsidian is also used for observing, for astral travel, for observing events from previous lives, and for communication with entities from other worlds. It helps the person understand dreams and remember them. It has a reinforcing effect on the aura. It not only provides protection against negative energies, but also helps transform them into positive energies.

Onyx

Onyx is actually a type of chalcedony. It generally crystallizes in strata, in shiny black, black with white, red with white, orange with honey-brown, beige with gray and brown, pink with brown and white stripes, and green with brown and white stripes. Since it is very easy to carve onyx, it was used for creating many decorations and ornaments, from jewelry to chess pieces. It was one of the stones in the High Priest's breastplate. In Jewish sources, onyx is identified with the "tribe" of Joseph (the tribes of Ephraim and Menashe).

Physical healing properties: Onyx is used for treating bone-marrow problems; it helps the body absorb vitamins more effectively, balances the hormones, and helps treat problems in the feet and in the body's soft tissues.

The mineral's effect on the emotional and mental layers: The ancient Egyptians believed that wearing onyx around the neck would cool the fevers of love, even to the point of causing a separation between lovers. It can be worn in order to break out of a problematic relationship, when there is difficulty in cooling the emotions down, even though the relationship is neither right nor healthy. However, in any event, it should not be worn on the body for long since it disrupts the flow of natural energy. However, painted onyx does not have that effect. It is very grounding, and helps link the person to the earth energies. Onyx increases self-control, encourages the person to acknowledge his inner strength, and helps free him from fears, pressures, and depressions. It reinforces the power to make the correct decisions, helps him shake off feelings of sorrow, and encourages happiness and good luck. It is a good stone to give to people who "float" or are detached, since it performs powerful grounding work.

Spiritual effect: The stone helps the person understand the balance between yin and yang and the fact that they are one whole. The elixir produced from onyx helps to balance the masculine and feminine energies. When working with the person's inner or higher guide, it hones the person's senses, power of reception, and instincts, and helps him feel and see the guidance that is offered.

Opal

The opal is the stone of water and moon. It is a beautiful and mysterious stone that reflects the entire color spectrum, from milky white to black. There are many shades and types of opal. It crystallizes in masses. In Aboriginal and Native American tribes, the opal was considered to be the visionary stone of the tribe's healers, and they also used it during the "vision quest," in which the apprentice youth or the future shaman sets out to seek his cosmic vocation. This may have been one of the stones in the High Priest's breastplate, and was identified with the tribe of Dan. It must be noted that the stone is very delicate, and can break or crack easily. Moreover, it must not be worn with other stones.

Physical healing properties: The opal is used for alleviating inflammations, purifying the blood, and purifying the kidneys. It is used for regulating the production of insulin in the body and for treating eye problems and disturbances in vision. It facilitates the birth process, and helps in rehabilitation following Parkinson's disease. The elixir produced from **red opal** helps renew the red blood corpuscles. The elixir from **brown opal** helps in the treatment of problems in the genitals, and of sexual problems that stem from the emotional layer. **Pink opal** is used for physical heart problems, but mainly for problems that stem from the emotional layer or as a result of emotional heartache. **Fire opal** in shades of gold is suitable for treating problems in the digestive system, and for strengthening and conveying energy to the digestive organs. **Fire opal** in shades of red is suitable for treating sexual problems. For a lack of coordination or problems resulting from epilepsy, an elixir produced from the **opaque milky white opal** can be used. **Black opal** helps treat problems in the digestive system and eyes, as well as depression. **Blue opal** balances metabolism and is helpful in preventing hair loss. **Green opal** helps in the treatment of flu and colds, as well as in lowering fever and strengthening the immune system. **Red opal** helps treat liver, stomach, and lung problems.

The mineral's effect on the emotional and mental layers: All the types of opal augment the person's properties and the characteristics of his personality. The opal encourages creativity, and stimulates inspiration and imagination. The stone helps the person see things from a different perspective, and for that reason is very effective in coming up with solutions for various problems. It stimulates inner truth, helps release inhibitions, and encourages spontaneity. In love, the opal inspires fidelity and trust, affection and warmth. The opal stimulates the person's aspirations, causing him to dream about beneficial changes in his life, which stem from the high potential that lies within him. These dreams rise from deep inside him to the surface, and become realities. **Pink opal** is used for treating emotional and love problems. **White opal** promotes mental clarity and helps calm the person down in situations of distress and stress. **Fire opal** bestows vitality, energy, strength, and power. **Black opal** stimulates inner knowledge and helps the person examine the information in depth. **Blue opal** reinforces the communicative abilities, and encourages freedom of expression. **Green opal** gives the person a feeling of control over his life, and helps him act wisely and reasonably when he is on a slimming diet. **Red opal** reinforces assertiveness while reducing aggression and hostility. In addition, it is effective for inducing new and positive patterns of thought, and for balancing the right and left hemispheres of the brain. Elixirs prepared from **brown** and **red** opal help in the treatment and relief of depression and emotional pain. An elixir prepared from **transparent white opal** stimulates and augments mental abilities, and stimulates thought. The elixir prepared from **opaque milky white opal** helps treat dyslexia.

The opal's unique property lies in its ability to absorb the person's emotions, intensify them, and reflect them like the reflection of the sun's rays, so that it should not be worn or held when negative or impure emotions prevail.

The mineral's effect on the chakras: All the colors of the rainbow are reflected in the opal, and they balance and open all the chakras. Because of the many colors in which the stone occurs, it is possible to match it to each of the chakras separately, while in several other opals, the colors match the colors of more than one chakra simultaneously. **Blue opal** stimulates the throat chakra, and activates the third eye chakra. **Fire opal**, especially in shades of red, is used for treating the sex chakra and give it energy. **Fire opal** in shades of gold, and **golden opal**, are suitable for treating the solar plexus chakra.

Spiritual effect: The opal opens and develops spiritual alertness and awareness, as well as exalted planes. All the members of the opal family help us feel mind-body unity, while developing the feeling of cosmic unity. When the person so intends, he can wear it or hold it in order to have qualities of seeing but not being seen. He is "absorbed" into the background, and his presence is not felt, when he wants and intends this to be the case. The opal arouses mystical properties in the person, and helps him exploit those powers and properties. **Black opal** is used for "reading" crystal balls, and stimulates visions and scenes. **Blue opal** reinforces the ability to see visions. **Golden opal** helps the person remove and extricate himself from situations of stagnation in his life, and directs him to achieve spiritual wealth.

When the opal does not suit the person at a certain time, it will clearly manifest the crystals' property of "disappearing" when they do not feel at ease in the person's vicinity. It jumps, goes missing, disappears, or hides, and is found only when it is the right time for the person to hold it.

Money, profession, occupation: The opal inspires a relationship of trust and loyalty in business, and contributes to business relationships.

Pearl

The pearl is not a stone, but rather the crystallization of a substance secreted by an oyster after a grain of sand or some other foreign body has penetrated its shell. There are pearls that are produced by oysters in fresh water, as well as ones that are produced in salt water. Pearls occur in a range of colors, the most widespread of which is white, but there are also black, gray, pinkish, yellowish, and light blue ones.

The pearl symbolizes purity, trust, generosity, and innocence. In folk legends, the pearl is linked to femininity and beauty. Some say that the pearl has the power to calm the thoughts so that the person is free to direct all his energy toward loving relationships. Moreover, another common belief is that the pearl that is given to a child, particularly to a little girl, encourages her to grow up pure and beautiful. Apparently, this belief derives from the pearl's property to inspire admiration and self-acceptance in us. Hindu Indians believe that the pearl represents the moon's influence on the earth, and thus it protects the earth against natural disasters connected to the weather. Pearls must not be polished or washed with soap or detergent, since this spoils its beauty.

Physical healing properties: The pearl grants the body purity, is used for treating the soft parts of the body as well as states of swelling and digestive disorders, and helps treat gallbladder ailments. It is also used for improving fertility and for facilitating birth.

The mineral's effect on the emotional and mental layers: Wearing pearls helps the person feel pure and act accordingly, focusing his attention on the thing he needs for development and growth. The pearl reinforces his personal wholeness and purifies his thoughts. It is customary to give a pearl to a person who is unnecessarily loud or vulgar, in order to help him bring out his inner delicacy, purity, and beauty. Moreover, a pearl that is given to such a person, especially if the giver tunes it in an aware and loving manner, is likely to cause the person to become cognizant of his behavior and its effect on his surroundings, and how his surroundings react to it. In women, the pearl stimulates the power of their femininity and increases their self-esteem and their respect for their femininity. As a rule, the pearl helps the person accept himself as he is.

Spiritual effect: The pearl grants wisdom to its user, and opens up channels for receiving spiritual guidance and direction. The pearl enables the person to see how others see him, and it serves as a kind of mirror of his behavior toward other people on the various social levels. The pearl's process of development from a grain of sand that enters the oyster's shell up to its becoming a pearl of perfect beauty represents the story of the "Ugly Duckling." This is a spiritual analogy that shows us that no matter how modest or dull we may think ourselves, we can discover tremendous beauty inside us, similar to the pearl's breathtaking beauty.

Occupation, work: The pearl is thought to be suitable for seamstresses, tailors, and clothing designers, as well as for people who assemble models, build miniatures, and so on - any work that requires attention to the little details, such as sewing, that needs patience. This is because the pearl enhances both the esthetic sense and patience. It should be combined with chrysoberyl, which protects the eyes against strain and pressure.

Petrified wood

Petrified wood is a kind of fossil - wood that was penetrated by a mineral that remained there for eons. The mineral surrounded and penetrated the wood, ultimately replacing it, even though its "woody" properties are still preserved. In general, agate and quartz are found in this role. The minerals that replaced the wood mass are important from the point of view of petrified wood's action.

Physical healing properties: Petrified wood is used for treating the skeleton, the back and its flexibility, and some people also include it in the treatment of aural problems. In general, the elixir prepared from petrified wood is used in cases of sclerotic arteries and high cholesterol, as well as for treating skin and hair (to encourage thickness and shine). In addition, it fortifies the spleen and heart.

The mineral's effect on the emotional and mental layers: Petrified wood that is produced as a result of the replacement by a certain kind of quartz, and is called silicified wood, is mainly used to dispel useless and troubling thoughts and worries that prevent the person from acting in an orderly, clear-cut manner. It helps the person act instead of worry or brood, so as to improve the situation in which he finds himself. Petrified wood is good for giving the person a feeling of stability and connection to the ground, and increases his personal strength in all spheres. Moreover, it has the ability to reinforce the body's powers of endurance. It is good to give it to a person going through crises, difficulties, or diseases, so that he can understand the essence of his situation, the lesson, and the repair that is occurring, and so that he can end it and will not be forced to rehash it over and over again. In addition, it provides support and consolation in these situations. Another interesting property of petrified wood is that if we carry it when there is an unpleasant, unusual, or unnatural odor around us, it alleviates the sensation and dispels the troublesome odor.

Spiritual effect: First and foremost, petrified wood contains the properties of the mineral that is inside it. Don't forget that. One of its most unique properties is that when meditating with it, one can obtain knowledge about previous incarnations and about the work connected to those incarnations, and an understanding of them. It is wonderful for helping us understand what we need, and what we do not need, during our spiritual development and our progress to higher spiritual planes, and it helps us understand that sometimes even things that are not needed have their place and time within the perfect course of development.

Profession, occupation: Petrified wood is very suitable for athletes and sports people, since it stimulates the body's flexibility, its powers of endurance, personal strength, and the feeling of stability. Moreover, because it alleviates a physical workload, it is recommended for people who are engaged in hard physical labor, such as farmers, builders, and porters.

Peridot

Peridot is also known as "olivine," "green chrysolite," and "chrysolite." It can be found in the form of masses and grains. As the name "olivine" indicates, peridot's colors range from shades of green - yellow green, light and dark green, olive green, transparent yellowish green, brown green, lemon yellow, honey yellow - to shades of darker brown and even reddish.

The ancient Egyptians called peridot "topazoz" and believed that peridot glowed in the dark like fiery torches. Some of the Pharaohs liked the stone and wore it, as did the priests and religious functionaries in the ancient Egyptian culture. This was so that they could cleanse themselves of thoughts and feelings of jealousy of the Pharaoh's power. It could be that the intention was symbolic, as a sign of their acceptance of the god-given strength and power of the Pharaoh. The ancient Egyptian healers used peridot to treat diseases that, in their opinion, only the sun could cure, such as lack of control over the muscles and liver diseases. Like the topaz, peridot is also considered to contain the sun's power.

In the Middle Ages, peridot was called "green chrysolite." It was always set in gold in order to ensure its full energetic power. The alchemists believed that the stone should be carved in the form of a bead, a drop, or a sphere, with a hole through it, and worn around the neck, so that it would provide protection against "black" powers and deleterious negative energies. Peridot is a stone that illuminates like the sun, and it "illuminates" the inner darkness while dispelling guilt feelings and fears. It fills the person's consciousness with illuminated and "solar" energies, eliminates sadness, darkness, and depression.

Physical healing properties: Peridot is helpful in detoxification processes and in eliminating poisons; it balances the action of the hormonal system, and is used to treat disturbances of the heart, spine, and lungs. It is very effective in the relief of stomach-aches and ulcer pains that stem from emotional states of agitation and a lack of calmness. Moreover, it is used to help in treatments to strengthen the vision in cases of near-sightedness and astigmatism. It should be given to women giving birth prematurely, in order to ease her contractions, to calm her down, and to help with the opening of the birth canal.

The mineral's effect on the emotional and mental layers: Peridot inspires happiness, optimism, and hope. It stimulates energies of warmth and friendship in the person, and dispels jealousy and quarrels. It helps the person look inside his life and examine the patterns according to which he lives, while recognizing and understanding the patterns that are negative and inhibiting, so as to be aware of their influence on his life, and discard them. It is highly recommended for use, either worn or held, by people who are depressed, or who suffer from mental and emotional pressure. It helps them open their eyes and see the beauty of the world, while arousing inner love for the world and for other people. It does wonderful work on the ego, mainly an ego that is affected by the accumulation of hurt and anger, by dissolving, weakening, and dispelling the anger, resentment, and jealousy.

The mineral's effect on the chakras: Peridot is suitable for treating the heart and solar plexus chakras by helping balance and cleanse these chakras.

Spiritual effect: Peridot creates a protective circle around the bodies and the auras, and it should be worn after an overall treatment for balance, cleansing, and opening the chakras, in order to protect and safeguard the balanced state that has been reached. It is a good stone for accompanying a person during his quest in life for the correct, so that he can understand the incorrect and the unjust in the physical world. Moreover, it can be used in healing treatments for strengthening the body and for stimulating and accelerating its regenerative and rehabilitative processes.

Pyrite

The golden pyrite stone crystallizes in different forms, from grains and masses to balls and pillars, and it can appear in many other forms.

Pyrite is one of the best protective stones. It creates a wonderful protective sheath around the person, and prevents negative energy from all layers from penetrating. When the stone is cleansed, this must be done with water only, without salt.

Physical healing properties: Pyrite is used to prevent harmful changes in the physical body, as well as to repair those damages. The stone is used for treating bone structure, lung problems, bronchitis, and serious infectious diseases. It is useful in states of hyperacidity in the stomach. In the form of an elixir, pyrite is good for treating circulatory problems. Some people use it for cases of fever and inflammations, in order to lower the fever and reduce the extent of the inflammation. Therapists are advised to wear this stone so as to protect themselves from the non-positive energies that are liberated from the bodies of their patients during treatment. Moreover, because of its protective properties, the person is advised to wear it when during volunteer or therapeutic activities in places with negative energy.

The mineral's effect on the emotional and mental layers: The protective sheath that pyrite creates around the person protects him on the emotional level as well, and helps him cope better when he finds himself in difficult situations, or in the company of people with contaminating energies. Pyrite encourages emotional and intellectual well-being, and through it, it is possible to experience anew pleasant memories of friendship and love. From the mental point of view, pyrite stimulates the mental abilities, and contributes to the stimulation of the memory and to the creation of a situation in which it is possible to retrieve the correct information from the memory at the appropriate and necessary moment. It fortifies will power and helps the person concentrate on the truly important levels, not the useless ones. Pyrite encourages people who suffer from depression, frustration and anxieties, calms people who are stressed and tense, and helps them achieve emotional equilibrium. An additional property that pyrite bestows upon the person who wears or uses it is the ability to see through people's masks or false behavior, enabling him to see the true intentions hidden behind the subterfuge.

Spiritual effect: Of course, we will mention once more the protective properties of pyrite that operate simultaneously on the physical, emotional, and etheric layers. For this reason, it constitutes a powerful defense weapon in various energetic activities. Some people discern a certain grounding sensation provided by the stone. In addition, it helps create a link between the intellectual layers and the intuitive ones, for the sake of positive and balanced work with both layers.

Profession, occupation: Pyrite is very suitable for therapists: holistic healers, reflexologists, masseurs, and so on, nurses in hospitals, psychologists and psychotherapists, volunteers who work with juvenile delinquents, workers in shelters for battered women, and so on. It has wonderful protective qualities against the negative energies of pain, sadness, anger, and so on, and also stimulates mental abilities and practicality. Healers do not generally use it on a regular basis for protection during treatments, since it is rather grounding.

Quartz

The quartz family is very extensive, with many stones being related to it. Aventurine, onyx, opal, amethyst, jasper, bloodstone, cat's eye, tiger eye, chrysoprase, carnelian, agate and many other minerals belong to this family. Many other minerals include various combinations of the mineral in different forms. Quartz is considered to be the most common mineral on the face of the earth. It occurs in an enormous range of colors and in different shapes, and it is one of the most energetic stones. Below, we will relate to clear quartz - also known as rock crystal - and later on to its different products and to the colored types of quartz.

Clear quartz is considered to be the "emperor of the crystals." Its color is transparent, but it can be found in various shades and configurations that contain a broad range of additional minerals. It crystallizes in prismatic masses, and in many and varied shapes.

Clear quartz has had many uses in various cultures throughout history. It was used by the inhabitants of Atlantis and Lemuria, the vanished continents, by the ancient Egyptians, the Mayans and Aztecs, the Native Americans, African tribes, Aborigines, Romans, Celts, Scotts, Tibetans, Buddhists, Brahmins, and Hebrews. In those cultures, it served various healing purposes, curing diseases of the body, mind, or spirit. It was used in religious rituals, for diagnosing diseases, for opening and raising consciousness, and for communicating with entities from different worlds. Known as "crystal," it appears numerous times in the Bible.

Physical healing properties: Clear quartz strengthens the body's general energy, and helps protect the person against diseases. Worn around the neck, it serves to stimulate the thyroid and hyperthyroid glands, and for treating throat and respiratory problems. Worn on the chest or the heart (stuck on with a plaster), it helps stimulate the thymus gland and fortify the immune system. In various healing techniques, almost every problem is treated with clear quartz, mainly because it strengthens the body's energy generally as well as the immune system. When one is not sure which stone to use in a treatment, it is possible to use quartz that is tuned to treat the particular problem. The healer requests divine help in solving the problem. The elixir prepared from it can be used in the same way.

The mineral's effect on the emotional and mental layers: Using quartz, it is possible to increase and strengthen the power of thought, purify it, and augment the ability to realize it on the physical level. It balances on all levels: emotional, thought, spiritual. It strengthens the emotional and mental abilities, while balancing them and inducing a feeling of harmony and tranquillity. It is very helpful for people who suffer from emotional instability, or feel that their emotions are influenced by the energies and emotions of people around them. It helps treat insomnia and disturbed or interrupted sleep (especially when it is placed under the pillow), and induces a feeling of serenity and harmony. By means of quartz, a person can recognize negative patterns of thought, emotion, and belief, as well as negative energetic patterns that came into being in consequence. It helps transform those negative patterns into positive ones. It arouses in us the aspiration and the desire for worldwide unity.

The mineral's effect on the chakras: Clear quartz crystal is used for purifying and activating all the chakras. It is suitable for being placed on the head in order to activate the crown chakra. Placing it on the heart chakra helps cleanse the chakra and balance emotional disturbances, and helps stimulate love and self-acceptance. When it is placed on the solar plexus chakra, quartz crystal stimulates energies in the entire body and broadens the emotional fields (this should be taken into account, as well as the nature of the patient's emotional energies, since it might strengthen emotions that are neither necessary nor positive). Placing quartz crystal on the third eye chakra helps empty the mind of thoughts during meditation, and creates a thought-less situation, while creating a sensation of oneness with the universe.

Spiritual effect: By means of quartz, it is possible to channel with the mineral kingdom, with various intelligent entities, stars, animals, and different life forms. During channeling, quartz helps pick up spiritual information from various entities, from ancient healers, from teachers and guides. It helps us recognize our unity with the universe and assimilate it. Quartz crystal, in its different configurations, is widely used in healing treatments. It can help "draw out" physical and emotional pains, and emit strengthening and healing energy. It augments the electro-magnetic field, and protects the aura. It is a wonderful crystal for use during meditation, and serves as an effective and delicate, but powerful, tool for spiritual development and growth.

Profession, occupation: Clear quartz is a wonderful stone for artists of all kinds, since it links up to the pure white light from which all its creative action is drawn. Moreover, it is suitable for consultants in all fields. It is considered an appropriate stone for physicians and healers. An additional quality, unique to crystal, is its ability to increase the sensitivity to tonal frequencies and increase vocal vibrations. Quartz crystal is unique in these actions, and is widely used in music healing and sound healing. For this reason, it is very suitable for musicians, singers, and even radio announcers.

Configurations and types of quartz

There are many different types of quartz. Quartz in its various configurations possesses unique abilities that characterize each crystal configuration. Below are a few common quartz configurations, and various types of quartz that are combined with additional minerals. Smoky quartz and rose quartz appear under separate entries, according to alphabetical order.

Generator quartz

Generator quartz is a configuration of quartz crystal with six crystal faces that are joined together to form an apex. It has many and varied uses in healing, networking, energetic purification and the stimulation of energy. There are natural configurations of generator quartz, as well as crystals that have been polished into this configuration. Both have similar properties. They are used for stimulating other crystals during treatment or laying on of stones, for drawing out negative energy from places and organs (by means of the blunt end of the crystal), and for getting energy to flow into places or organs that lack energy (by aiming the apex at those places).

The different crystals can be placed around the generator when they are not in use in order to charge them and increase their power.

Large generators can be used for projecting thoughts and telepathic exercises. They are widely used in group meditation, when the members of the group sit in a circle around a large generator, and charge it by means of thought.

A small quartz generator is most powerful when used as a pendulum. Today, it is one of the types of pendulum that is most used because of its excellent abilities.

The quartz generator is used to stimulate all the bodies - physical, emotional, mental, and spiritual. It is used to cleanse and purify the chakras and eradicate negative energies in them. Moreover, it fills them with shining white light.

Left quartz crystal

The left quartz crystal is a crystal or generator quartz upon whose left side a kind of small, inclined window shape can be discerned. This crystal is used in all treatments for balancing, stimulating, and activating the right side of the body, and for stimulating the left brain. The right side of the body is activated by the left hemisphere of the brain. Balancing the left hemisphere by means of left quartz crystal strengthens the abilities for which it is responsible, such as rationality, logic, organization, verbal ability, and verbal expression, the analytical abilities, and the intellect. Treating the right side of the body with the left quartz crystal balances, strengthens, and stimulates the energies of the male pole - the active, extrovert one. On the behavioral layer, left quartz crystal is used for treating and balancing aspects that are linked to the person's attitude toward life, to his abilities to give, and to the strengthening of the transmitting abilities. It helps balance the cerebral and intellectual abilities. It is used for treating cerebral disturbances on the left side of the brain.

Left quartz crystal can be used for strengthening the energies of the chakras and for activating them by pointing the crystal at the anterior side of the body.

In combination with right quartz crystal, it is used to balance and synthesize the action of the right hemisphere of the brain and that of the left hemisphere of the brain.

Right quartz crystal

Right quartz crystal is a crystal or generator quartz upon whose right side a kind of small, inclined window shape can be discerned. This crystal is used in all treatments for balancing, stimulating, and activating the left side of the body, and for stimulating the right brain. The left side of the body is activated by the right hemisphere of the brain. Balancing the right hemisphere by means of right quartz crystal strengthens the abilities for which it is responsible, such as intuition, imagination, creativity, liberty, breaching borders and limitations, innovation and inventiveness, abstract understanding, and abilities linked to color and form. Treating the left side of the body with the right quartz crystal balances, strengthens, and stimulates the energies of the female pole - the passive, introvert one. It helps open blockages on this side of the body. Moreover, right quartz crystal is used to treat and balance emotional, intuitive aspects, and to balance and strengthen the abilities to pick up and receive. It is of great help to people whose actions and talents are motivated by the left side of the brain (especially right-handed people), in order to develop the right hemisphere, which is less developed than the left hemisphere in many people.

In combination with left quartz crystal, it is used to achieve harmony and cooperation between both hemispheres of the brain - left and right.

By pointing the crystal at the posterior side of the body, the right quartz crystal can be used to strengthen the energies of the chakras, and to activate them. It can be used for treating cerebral disturbances on the right side of the brain.

Barnacle crystals

This crystal can be identified by tiny crystals joined to the main crystal, like infants. This crystal is used by people who are engaged in treating the community - teachers, social workers, and so on, as well as political or religious leaders who consider the members of their communities to be their "children." The barnacle crystal stimulates profound inner wisdom that induces a feeling of belief in the user. It is used in meditation where stones are laid on, as well as laying on of stones at home, for treating all the problems, conflicts, or questions connected to the family, as well as fertility problems. Some people recommend giving it as a gift to a person who has suffered the loss of a family member, in order to give him a feeling of tranquillity and consolation. Moreover, it is an excellent crystal for placing in locations where group work is performed, whether healing groups or a business project, in which there is a desire to stimulate enhanced working ability, closeness, trust, and mutual help.

Double terminated crystals

The double terminated crystal is a crystal that is pointed at both ends. These crystals stimulate the ability to conduct a whole, harmonious dialogue between people or groups. It is an excellent crystal to carry during negotiations concerning all aspects of peace, and peace on earth, and it must be tuned to this objective beforehand. The double terminated crystal is widely used for transmitting telepathic messages. (A technique for transmitting thoughts by means of a double terminated crystal will be presented in the chapter that deals with developing telepathy by means of crystals.)

These crystals serve to cleanse the body and aura of negative energy, by putting them on places on the body (or places on the body that symbolize the harmful emotional or thought pattern) in order to cleanse the region of negative energy.

A double terminated crystal can be used for transferring energy in a powerful way, or for drawing out non-positive energy and eliminating it.

A double terminated crystal can be used to effectively treat people who suffer from a lack of mental or emotional balance. It can also be used for this without the help of a therapist - a double terminated crystal must be held in each hand for a few minutes, while breathing deeply and calmly.

A double terminated crystal can be used to create balance between the right and left hemispheres of the brain. Placing it on the crown chakra, or on the third eye chakra creates harmony and balance between the actions of the two hemispheres and between the physical and the spiritual layers.

When it is placed on the crown chakra, or on various regions of the brain that are responsible for various actions, it can help the person free himself of useless and inhibiting thought patterns, of addictions, and of negative behavior patterns. Together with the elimination of the negative patterns, the crystal helps create positive, new and effective patterns. Placing the double terminated crystal between the chakras helps create harmony and a balanced action between the various chakras.

Double terminated crystals are excellent for protecting against non-positive energies and dangers, be they physical or mental.

These crystals are also effective for the purpose of astral projection and going more deeply into the various dream situations, as well as for intensifying meditative states.

Some people use double terminated crystals for smoothing facial wrinkles and making them disappear, mainly wrinkles that formed as a result of tension or worry. Placing the crystal releases the tension in the tissues and stimulates their renewal.

"Hieroglyphic" quartz

"Hieroglyphic" quartz is a type of quartz crystal upon which there are grooves that resemble Egyptian hieroglyphics. "Hieroglyphic" quartz crystal contains ancient knowledge and insights from ancient, long-vanished civilizations, from Atlantis, Lemuria, and ancient Egypt.

By means of meditation with the crystal, or placing it on the third eye, it is possible to link up to that knowledge and receive extraordinary information and insights. The information received may be symbols that can be used in Reiki, ancient healing methods, insights connected to human life that derive from those ancient sources, and insights concerning the universe that the appropriate person can use for the benefit of mankind and the earth.

Rainbow crystal

Rainbow crystal is a mass of quartz that contains fragments of light that create all the colors of the rainbow. This special crystal endows its holder with hope and light, and adds color to his life. It reinforces the multifariousness within the person, and inspires purity and awareness. When it is placed on the third eye, and during meditation with it, rainbow crystal links the person to the marvelous celestial layers. It links the person to infinity, and fill him with pure, perfect energy.

When it is placed on the heart chakra, rainbow crystal is used to dispel sadness, depression, and sorrow, just like a rainbow that appears among the clouds.

It fills the heart with happiness, cheer, love, and confidence. It encourages the person to aspire to serve the universe and humanity, and to follow the path to his higher vocation. Rainbow crystal can be used to provide every chakra with light and love, and it is especially powerful in healing. This crystal is a wonderful gift from the universe, and it must be used with love and appreciation.

Twin crystal

Twin crystal is a quartz crystal from whose base two or sometimes more crystals grow. It is a crystal used for discovering and attracting a soul mate, or a twin soul in one's present life.

To this end, it can be used during meditation in order to invoke this soul. It is used for balancing and building up relationships. Moreover, it is used for balancing body and soul and the different or opposing aspects in the person's character.

Blue quartz

Blue quartz is a crystal that includes the minerals rutile, tourmaline, and zoisite. It has the properties of these minerals, as well as the properties of clear quartz, as well as additional unique properties that its blue color gives it.

Physical healing properties: Blue quartz is used for treating endocrine, blood, and gallbladder problems, and for balancing and stabilizing the metabolic processes in the body.

The mineral's effect on the emotional and mental layers: Blue quartz can be used for verbally expressing repressed emotions or emotions that are difficult to express. Blue quartz makes it easier for the person to say what he thinks and express his opinion, and encourages in-depth, clear, and considered thought. It is excellent for creating a relationship and a connection with other people, for improving communicative abilities, and for releasing selfishness and fears that are linked to communicating with other people. It encourages the improvement of the relationship between people, helps the person discard inhibiting social patterns, and stimulates his independence. It helps dispel fears, while bringing their nature and reasons to the conscious surface.

The mineral's effect on the chakras: Blue quartz activates and stimulates the throat chakra.

Spiritual effect: Blue quartz stimulates belief and inspiration.

Green quartz

As its name suggests, this crystal is green in color.

Physical healing properties: Green quartz helps the endocrine glands in their actions to balance the body.

The mineral's effect on the emotional and mental layers: Green quartz arouses love, and stimulates the intuition for the purpose of increasing love. It helps stabilize and maintain conjugal relations as well as the relationship between people in general, in a state of harmony and peace. It promotes creativity, and attracts success and prosperity to its bearer.

The mineral's effect on the chakras: Green quartz can be used for balancing and opening the heart chakra.

Spiritual effect: Green quartz has the ability to transform negative energies into positive ones. It is used in meditation for the purpose of peace on earth, for healing earth, and for requesting peace and unity among its creators.

Yellow quartz
See Citrine.

Harlequin quartz
Harlequin quartz is also called "clown quartz." It is a clear quartz crystal that is dotted with red stripes and spots that originate from the presence of hematite inside the quartz crystal.

Physical healing properties: Harlequin quartz reinforces and improves physical health, stimulates vitality, and provides the physical body with energy. Moreover, it can be used for treating and opening the meridians.

The mineral's effect on the emotional and mental layers: This beautiful crystal inspires and strengthens fidelity, love, and joyfulness.

The mineral's effect on the chakras: Harlequin quartz opens and stimulates the base chakra, and links it to the heart chakra. It can be used to stimulate the heart chakra and to activate the crown chakra.

Spiritual effect: Harlequin quartz contributes to the stabilization and stimulation of the link of the physical body and its systems to the etheric nervous systems.

Rutilated quartz
Rutilated quartz is quartz in which the mineral rutile is present. Another type of rutilated quartz is star quartz, in which there are silver and gold ribbons or threads. These ribbons create an exquisite starry effect. Rutilated quartz combines the properties of quartz with those of rutile.

Physical healing properties: Rutilated quartz is a wonderful stone to use in order to understand the causes of a disease that could be rooted in the emotional, mental, or karmic layers.

The mineral's effect on the emotional and mental layers: Rutilated quartz, especially star quartz, reinforces going in the correct direction and pursuing a goal. In addition, it enhances the sense of direction and orientation. It is an excellent crystal for a person to carry when he is far away from his loved ones. It helps him take care of them in thought and emotions, and feel their proximity. Rutilated quartz helps people who feel lonely to draw love and friendship into the reality of their lives. It is a wonderful stone for finding the reasons for unpleasant situations, or for physical diseases. It directs the person toward the root of the problem in order to repair the situation at its basis.

Spiritual effect: Rutilated quartz, especially star quartz, is used for directing energy from outside the body in a very powerful way. Because of this, it can be used effectively in healing treatments. It has an effect on the etheric and astral bodies.

During the entire course of astral travel, rutilated quartz helps the person understand why he reached the places he reached. It strengthens the understanding of the connection between the specific astral journey and the person's everyday life. Star quartz is used for creating a link with cultures and entities from other worlds and planets.

Profession, occupation: Rutilated quartz is very helpful for cab drivers and truckers, because it reinforces and maintains the sense of direction, and acts as a guide.

Rhodochrosite

Rhodochrosite is rhodonite's "twin sister." Similar to the most common form of rhodonite - pink or deep pink with black residues - rhodochrosite occurs in the form of masses and grains, its most widespread color being pink or deep pink tending to reddish with white stripes and residues. This stone can be found in a variety of shades of pink, from light pink to reddish pink, deep red, yellow, orange, brown, and cream.

There are many legends concerning this unique stone, which is also called "rosa del Inca" - Inca rose - since it was discovered by Inca tribesmen and was worshipped by this ancient tribe.

Rhodochrosite is considered to be the stone of love and equilibrium. It treats the physical and emotional layers in depth, and performs healing on them. On all levels of bodies, the stone contributes to the nurturing of love and equilibrium.

Physical healing properties: In general, rhodochrosite is good for safeguarding the body's health and preventing disease. Since it is a very good stone for the heart chakra, it is widely used for treating various heart disorders, and is suitable for inclusion in treatments for regulating heart rate and pulse. It is good for the treatment of a range of internal inflammations, skin problems, digestive problems, for strengthening the walls of the intestines, and for increasing digestive action. In addition, it helps treat various lung problems, as well as respiratory diseases such as asthma and bronchitis. It cleanses the body of poisons and helps in the treatment of diabetes (mainly in the form of drinking an elixir prepared from it), and of insomnia.

The mineral's effect on the emotional and mental layers: Rhodochrosite is a wonderful stone for creating and attaining emotional balance. It inspires optimism, cheerfulness, and self-acceptance. It is very helpful in cases of insomnia, and induces beautiful and pleasant dreams. Rhodochrosite, like rhodonite, helps balance the emotional layer quickly but gently, and helps stimulate the feminine and masculine aspects of the person's character. It is a marvelous stone for attracting new love into one's life. It is a faithful companion in the person's quest to gain emotional happiness and love. In addition, it simulates and encourages self-love.

The mineral's effect on the chakras: The stone purifies the base chakra, and is also used for treating the sex and heart chakras. It helps balance the chakras and their fields of action. It performs wonderful cleansing, stimulating, and balancing activities on the heart chakra. It is one of the most marvelous "heart healers."

Spiritual effect: Rhodochrosite is an excellent stone for meditation. It envelops the person in celestial energies, energies of love and equilibrium, and it is possible to tune oneself with it during meditation and linking up to our twin souls. It is used for meditations of love toward Mother Earth, who tunes us into caring for the world and willingness to give of ourselves while feeling a sense of responsibility that neither bothers nor grieves us. It can be used for purification, and for balancing various mental processes. Through the stone, it is possible to tune into the superego, while expanding awareness and developing our spiritual side.

Profession, occupation: Rhodochrosite faithfully serves those who are engaged in fields connected to the emotions, treatment, listening, and giving emotional help to others: holistic healers, psychologists, psychotherapists, frail-care workers, and nurses in hospitals. It opens the heart, inspires genuine caring for other people's troubles, and even balances the emotions of the therapist himself, who is sometimes influenced by the difficulties of his work. In addition, it is advisable for beauty consultants and salespeople to carry the stone in their pockets or to wear it while working.

Rhodonite

Rhodonite can be found in a variety of forms: masses, square masses, circular masses, and grains. The most common color in which rhodonite occurs is pink with black spots and stripes, but it also occurs in other colors: reddish, red, reddish brown, yellow, green, and black. Most of the colors feature black spots or stripes mixed in with the dominant color. Sometimes there are veins of silver or gold in the stone.

Physical healing properties: Rhodonite is used for treating enflamed joints and arthritis, emphysema, and bacterial throat infections. Since it is very suitable for the heart chakra, it should be included in treatments of cardiac problems, pains, and disorders (physical and emotional). It is used for treating vertigo and dizziness, in conditions of emotional imbalance, for burns and for pains. In the form of an elixir, rhodonite is used for treating skin problems, in detoxification processes, for digestive disorders, and for infections in the kidneys and bladder.

The mineral's effect on the emotional and mental layers: Rhodonite is a wonderful stone for balancing the heart chakra and for emphasizing the love that is buried deep in the heart of each person. It is an excellent stone to use in various relationships. In a conjugal relationship, it encourages the person to pay attention to the little details, and enables him to view the relationship objectively, and not allow his personality and his self to be swallowed up by it. In addition, it is marvelous for relieving the pangs of dissolving unbalanced or injurious relationships. It is very good for family relationships, particularly for adolescents who are going through a difficult time, and feeling that the whole world misunderstands them. To the same extent, the stone is good for parents, since it improves the communication between them and their children. It is customary to give it as a gift to good friends. It is very effective in helping and balancing situations of emotional and mental imbalance, feelings of confusion and unease, and after traumas that undermined the person's self-confidence. It is a wonderful stone to use when the person feels exhausted or lacks energy because of emotional traumas or after any kind of emotional drama that left the person limp and drained of energy. It helps strengthen and rehabilitate the body's energies that were debilitated as a result of the emotional exhaustion. Rhodonite is excellent for raising self-esteem, self-acceptance, and self-love. It helps the person feel serene, calm, and sure of his path, and helps him make the most of his potential.

The mineral's effect on the chakras: Rhodonite is an excellent stone for treating the heart chakra. It can be used for cleansing, balancing, and stimulating the chakra. It opens the chakra and stimulates unconditional love that is expressed on the physical level.

Spiritual effect: Rhodonite helps balance the energies of yin and yang. During meditations for peace on earth, the stone is wonderful for strengthening self-tuning toward this valuable objective - it helps balance the earth's energies, while simultaneously inspiring a feeling of caring toward one's fellow man and toward the earth, and encourages the generous and loving aspects in each person's personality.

Rose quartz

Rose quartz is an exquisite pink stone that occurs in configurations of masses and grains. It is one of the most common quartz crystals. The ancient Egyptians held its properties in high esteem, and used it for many purposes. It is considered to be a stone of love and compassion in Tibet and the East. The Romans, like the ancient Egyptians, believed that the stone could smooth out wrinkles, prevent them, and promote the beauty of the face and body. Facial masks and cosmetic mixtures containing rose quartz were found in graves from the pharaonic era. In China, it is used to this day as a stone for carving statuettes and for decorating ornaments.

Physical healing properties: Rose quartz is used for cleansing the body's cells, for treating vertigo, the adrenal glands, the kidneys, and heart and lung problems. Its elixir is used for treating the skin and promoting its beauty.

The mineral's effect on the emotional and mental layers: Rose quartz is an excellent stone for arousing self-love. It is the stone of love, and arouses love in all the layers. It opens the heart, dispels non-positive emotions of resentment and hatred, and soothes the emotions. It is very effective after emotional crises, because it helps the person overcome the emotional injury and open up once more to feelings of love. It inspires a feeling of harmony, tranquillity, and gentleness, and is wonderful for improving relationships. In addition, it helps assuage anxieties and tension. It stimulates the imagination and inspiration. It is an excellent stone for treating all emotional problems and injuries. For people who carry love in their hearts, rose quartz reinforces those emotions and makes them permanent. It is a marvelous gift to give a loved one or a friend. At times of separation, divorce, emotional crises, the stone consoles the person, cheers him up, and helps him get through the crisis. It is very helpful for people who find it difficult to show feelings of love, or are afraid to fall in love, because of some past hurt or not having been given love in their childhood.

The mineral's effect on the chakras: Rose quartz has the ability to transmit soft, soothing energy, and spreads serenity over all the chakras. It helps cleanse them of negative energies, and balance them. It is especially suitable for treating the crown and heart chakras. It does wonderful work on the heart chakra: it opens the chakra, cleanses it, balances it, and links it to universal love, which gives it its strength. It links the four upper chakras - the heart, throat, third eye and crown chakras - and causes the energies of love to flow into them.

Spiritual effect: Rose quartz helps create equilibrium between the yin and the yang, and opens the person up to receiving universal love.

Profession, occupation: Rose quartz is recommended for beauty consultants and salespeople. Besides symbolizing beauty and being suitable for people in this profession, it also enhances the self-image and facilitates access to the customer.

Ruby

The ruby, the red stone, is known as the "queen of the stones." Its colors include wine red, pink, and orange red, and it can be either transparent or opaque. It is one of the most expensive gemstones, and it is in great demand in expensive jewelry. It crystallizes in prismatic configurations.

The ancients considered the ruby to be the perfect wedding stone. It symbolized abundant love, a smooth married life, and fidelity. In eastern legends, the ruby was depicted as a spiritual stone that symbolized the beauty of the soul. In ancient Egypt, the ruby was thought to inspire love, to fortify the body, and to attract good luck and beauty. The Indians believed that the ruby burns with an inner fire, and even believed that water could be boiled on it! The Greeks believed that the ruby could melt wax. The legends about the special heat of the ruby stemmed from its symbolizing the sun, and caused the stone to be greatly admired in the ancient world. Moreover, it was believed that when the owner of the ruby was in physical danger, its color would fade as a warning sign. In the Jewish Torah, the ruby was thought to be the symbol of the tribe of Reuben, and is mentioned as one of the twelve stones on the High Priest's breastplate. Today, the ruby is used for producing laser beams and for microsurgery.

Physical healing properties: The ruby strengthens the immune system by increasing the oxygen levels in the blood flow. It liberates thromboses, increases the body's vitality, and strengthens the heart. It purifies and stimulates blood circulation. It is used for treating blood problems and anemia. It is used for treating conditions of fever, heart disorders as a result of defective blood flow, and infectious diseases. In addition, it helps in detoxification processes (by catalyzing the expulsion of toxins from the body).

The mineral's effect on the emotional and mental layers: The ruby encourages honesty and devotion in love. As an elixir, the ruby helps strengthen and enhance the masculine self-image. It increases intuition, grants courage, and emphasizes practicality and practical work for the sake of accomplishing our objectives in life. It brings wealth, abundance, health, and knowledge. It helps concentration, and hones the person's verbal power during an argument or an intellectual debate. Moreover, it protects him from threatening feelings and aggressive attitudes. It inspires vitality and control over mental functions, stimulates creativity, and increases the person's presence.

The mineral's effect on the chakras: The ruby strengthens the heart chakra, and can be placed on the base chakra during healing treatments.

Spiritual effect: The ruby balances mind and spirit. It helps eliminate unwanted dreams, and brings clarity and serenity to dreams.

Money, profession, occupation: The ruby helps achieve and increase economic stability. It is considered to be a stone that symbolizes wealth, abundance, and nobility.

Rutile

Rutile occurs in different forms. The stones can crystallize in bent and twisted shapes, in needle-like shapes, and in prismatic shapes with their apexes resembling a double pyramid. It occurs in many colors: yellow, gold, green, purple, blue, red, red brown, and black. Often this mineral appears, looking like beautiful, golden stalks of hay, inside crystal of other types, such as quartz, amethyst, kunzite, and so on. Rutile adds strength and love to the unique properties of host crystal, and these properties grant the host crystal additional calmness and a feeling of order and reason.

Physical healing properties: Rutile is used for treating problems of the respiratory system, such as bronchitis. It strengthens the blood vessels and helps treat the eyes, giving them a beautiful shine. Some people use it after birth in order to start the mother's milk flow. The stone can be tuned for treating sexual problems and arousing sexual desire.

The mineral's effect on the emotional and mental layers: Rutile helps the person who has a problem to understand and discover the basic roots of his problem, and in this way helps lead him to the correct and profound solution. Because it represents "the hair of Venus" (the thin golden needles of the stone resemble hairs, or golden stalks of hay), it is used for smoothing out marital problems and the relationship between the members of a couple. In addition, it is used for balancing physical and emotional states that have lost their equilibrium.

The mineral's effect on the chakras: Golden or clear rutile in the form of golden needles is used to stimulate the crown chakra. Purple rutile is suitable for balancing the third eye chakra, and for creating a certain order in the way the chakra receives and processes information.

Spiritual effect: Rutile is widely used in healing, in order to balance the aura and eliminate non-positive energies. This stone also has an effect on the physical body, the etheric body, and the astral bodies. Since it tends to dispel unwanted energies, it permits the receiving of clear, interference-free messages from the spiritual worlds. Moreover, it helps remove blockages in the spiritual worlds, even when those blockages have not yet been removed in the physical worlds. This is a good stone to use during astral travel in order to discover the reason why one has reached the particular places one has reached during the journey.

Sapphire

The sapphire is an expensive gemstone that is mainly mined in the Sri Lanka area, where relatively large stones can be found. It is an easy stone to work because of its strength, and this property, together with its great beauty, makes it very popular in jewelry. The sapphire crystallizes in the form of prismatic crystals, in a range of colors that include blue, white, green, black, purple, and yellow. One of its interesting configurations is the star sapphire, a configuration that is considered exalted from the metaphysical point of view. The sapphire has a long history from the religious perspective. It is mentioned in almost every religion, and is considered to attract celestial light to its wearer. The Buddhists believe that the sapphire leads to spiritual enlightenment and spiritual devotion. In Christianity, it was very popular with bishops and cardinals, as a symbol of divine wisdom. The sapphire is often mentioned in the Bible, and is indicated as one of the stones in the High Priest's breastplate. It is identified with the tribe of Issaschar. The star sapphire is considered to be the stone that leads its owner toward the realization of his spiritual goal, for the good of humanity as a whole. The blue sapphire is considered to be the stone which has the highest frequencies of blue light. All the sapphires are thought to be vocational stones, stones that lead the person toward discovering and realizing his vocation.

Physical healing properties: The sapphire is used for treating problems of the circulatory system, for strengthening the arteries, and for staunching bleeding. **Blue sapphire** is used for treating problems of dyslexia. **Yellow sapphire** is used for treating stomach, spleen, gallbladder, and liver problems.

As an elixir, it is used for accelerating the body's detoxification processes. **Indigo sapphire** is used for treating mental disorders, by helping to eliminate negative elements from the subconscious, and building higher and more positive elements.

The mineral's effect on the emotional and mental layers: The sapphire stimulates mental clarity, and the ability to grasp and comprehend. It helps dispel unwanted thoughts, inspires joy, serenity, and openness to the beauty of the world and life. It stimulates intuition and deepens thought. In addition, it helps the person realize his dreams and aspirations. **Blue sapphire** helps strengthen and stimulate communicative abilities. It helps in situations in which a person has to choose among several options, by directing him toward the correct and appropriate choice. **Black sapphire** helps in situations in which the intuition is in doubt, and frees the person from worries. It arouses loyalty and devotion, belief, and the desire to follow God's path. **Green sapphire** strengthens loyalty in all spheres of life. **Purple sapphire** helps assuage unnecessary worries and fears. It grants tranquillity and spiritual understanding. **Indigo sapphire** stimulates the ability to concentrate and be alert, arouses creativity, and attracts inspiration. It is an encouraging stone, and promotes the understanding of the person's personal responsibility for all the events and situations in his life. It strengthens determination, the aspiration to realize dreams and to seek for the truth, rids the intellect of illusions and confusion, and helps the person distinguish between illusion and true knowledge. It reduces the gap between concrete and abstract thought. **Star sapphire**, in addition to all its spiritual abilities, gives its bearer a loving, optimistic and gregarious nature, and helps concentrate the thoughts. **White sapphire** encourages the aspiration to justice and morality, and liberates the person from the greed for mammon. **Yellow sapphire** inspires ambitiousness and its realization, stimulates the intellect and the mental layer, and induces a harmonious feeling in its wearer. It is important to wear it with part of it touching the body.

The mineral's effect on the chakras: Blue sapphire stimulates and activates the throat chakra. It purifies and cleanses it, and is used for healing it. **Green sapphire** stimulates the heart chakra. **Indigo sapphire** can be used for placing on the third eye for strengthening actions of visualization, and for stimulating the imagination, creativity, and inspiration. Moreover it helps remove the negativity from all the chakras. **Purple sapphire** is used for stimulating the third eye and crown chakras. **White sapphire** also stimulates the crown chakra by spurring the person on to seek his vocation and purpose in life.

Spiritual effect: The sapphire accompanies the person along his path toward realizing his vocation. It arouses this vocation in him, leads him, and strengthens him by helping him realize his dreams. **Blue sapphire** is used in healing to treat the entire body. **Black sapphire** is used as a protective stone. **Green sapphire** helps to remember dreams. **Purple sapphire** stimulates understanding and spiritual aspiration. **Star sapphire** can be used in order to better understand people's nature and character, according to a sociable and loving attitude. This very powerful stone also helps the person make contact with entities that are not of this world.

Money, profession, occupation: The sapphire is recommended for people who see their vocations in bringing light, help, and love to the whole of humanity: people who engage in politics out of pure motives, religious functionaries and theologians, judges, lawyers, journalists, people who seek truth and justice and their outward manifestation. In addition, it is considered to be a marvelous stone for writers, helping them to increase the knowledge and wisdom that are required for their work. **Green sapphire** strengthens the abilities of people who deal with physics or combine this field with their occupation. Moreover, it is considered to be a stone that brings abundance and prosperity. **Black sapphire** is a stone that should be carried when a person seeks employment. Also, it helps safeguard the workplace and provides protection. **White sapphire** is one of the most recommended stones for people involved in politics, or in very influential positions, since it releases them from the lust for mammon, inspires morality, and deepens their sense of justice - properties that are essential for people who work in these fields. It is also very appropriate for judges and lawyers, as it strengthens their powers of advocacy and judgment. **Yellow sapphire** is considered to be a stone that brings prosperity, abundance, and happiness, and is thought to be the "merchant's stone."

Selenite

The color of selenite is white or transparent, and sometimes white with black residues. Selenite is actually a form of crystallized gypsum, and it crystallizes in needle shapes and plates.

Selenite is widely used for channeling and for various spiritual activities. It is a stone that links between present and future, and between the material and the spiritual. Selenite with the black residues is suitable for people who feel that there is "black" inside of them - fears, dark sides, and so on - so that the black can be turned into white.

Physical healing properties: Selenite is used for improving the flexibility of the spinal column and the muscles, and is used for treating a large collection of spinal cord problems and postural defects. It helps the regeneration of the body's cells, and the treatment of problems concerning epilepsy. In addition, by means of spiritual work with it, it can help the person better understand his body and the root of his physical problems.

The mineral's effect on the emotional and mental layers: Selenite realizes the person's character, and helps him be more flexible in his decisions. It helps purify thought, and raises the person's awareness of himself and of those around him. It has a wonderful ability to stimulate the aspiration to justice in the person, and also provides him with the energies and the wisdom to judge people and controversial topics justly. It helps the person in his search for the golden path that bridges apparently separate layers. Selenite stimulates the spiritual and mystical layers in the person, while simultaneously helping him to move very easily between the material layers of life. It symbolizes the nature of repair and incarnation that occur on the spiritual layers, on the emotional layers, and on the material layers. Selenite helps the person discard incorrect insights, and non-aware beliefs. It hones his ability to see in depth and to analyze situations, both as they appear on the surface and deep in their hidden interior. It helps the person understand himself better, from all points of view, including his physical body.

The mineral's effect on the chakras: Selenite is used for placing on the third eye chakra, as well as on the crown chakra.

Spiritual effect: As we said previously, selenite is used for many spiritual activities. It can be used for channeling, meditation for receiving information about previous incarnations, and also for receiving information about the future. It links up to insights, just as calcite does, but more strongly. When it is placed on the patient's body, it allows the healer to help the patient reach the incarnation that is affecting his present life. Moreover, via healing, it enables the person to repair the incarnation by detaching himself from emotional and mental inhibitions in that life. During meditation with selenite, visions pertaining to the future can occur, as well as insights about the present, and information that interprets and explains the past.

Money, profession, occupation: Selenite is suitable for judges and people who are involved in the process of justice, arbitration, and bridging.

In addition, it is one of the most wonderful stones for healers and trainee healers. It is widely used by therapist healers, since it helps him attain insights about himself, and broadens his spiritual and physical awareness equally.

Serpentine

Serpentine occurs in a range of green shades, green striped with black, and also brown red, brown yellow, and white. It crystallizes in fibers, plates, and masses. Its shades are sometimes reminiscent of snake eyes, and this, of course, is where its name comes from. Serpentine served as a protective stone for people embarking on journeys, mainly merchants and sailors. Roman merchants would wear it at night in order to protect themselves against invisible dangers. The Native Americans wore it together with coral for physical protection, and for survival in difficult or hostile environments. For this reason, it is considered to be a good stone when setting out on journeys, for safeguarding the person and protection in general.

Physical healing properties: Serpentine is used for improving the absorption of calcium and magnesium in the body, helps treat hypoglycemia and diabetes, and helps rid the body of parasites.

The mineral's effect on the emotional and mental layers: By means of guided healing, serpentine can help treat disorders in the emotional and mental layers, but it must be directed consciously so that the energies are projected onto the region or problem.

The mineral's effect on the chakras: Serpentine stimulates the crown chakra.

Spiritual effect: Serpentine protects the person against external influences. It deepens meditative states, and is one of the strongest stones for work on previous incarnations. For this reason, it can be used in guided healing, placed on the pillow, or simply held. It can repair incarnations, even when it is kept in the person's pocket, and is unaware of its actions.

Profession, occupation: Serpentine is very suitable for people involved in healing or techniques that are connected with healing by means of the repair of previous incarnations. It can be placed on the patient's third eye chakra, passed over the patient, or placed in his hand during the healing. The healer must be experienced in these treatment techniques, and do a great deal of work on himself personally before starting to work on others with serpentine.

Shells

Shells are the abandoned homes of various marine creatures. Shells come in various types, colors, and shapes. Mother-of-pearl, with its varied and shiny colors, is a kind of shell. For thousands of years, shells were used for decoration, for adorning ornaments, and for producing various items of jewelry. Remains of this kind of ornament were found in Egyptian burial caves and in excavations that were conducted in South American Indian sites. For the Indian tribes, shells symbolized wealth and abundance, and were worn around the neck as a sign of the wealth of the wearer. Moreover, shells were used as a substitute for money in trading. Among certain African tribes, shells, especially those that were brought by distant tribes, symbolized beauty, status, and wealth.

Physical healing properties: Some people carry shells when they sail in a boat or on a ship in order to counteract seasickness. In addition, the shell is considered to be a successful amulet for seafarers and people who sail in ships. It is used to treat problems concerning hearing, lack of calcium, the nervous system, and the spinal canal. Some people use it for healing fractures. It helps increase the absorption of vitamins in the body, and protects the muscular system from atrophying.

The mineral's effect on the emotional and mental layers: The shell helps us understand the ups and downs of daily life. It teaches us to go with the flow, and causes other people's negativity to slide right off our backs - to pass, without leaving a trace, just like the sea passed over the shell. The different shells have protective abilities, or symbolize beauty, physical strength, and power. They can be used for raising the self-image, for improving the organizational ability in everyday life, and for increasing personal strength and power. The shell promotes cooperation between people and provides unifying and stimulating energy for groups that work together toward the same objective. It stimulates intuition, sensitivity, and imagination, as well as the ability to adapt to various situations. The shell helps the person make decisions and choices by deepening his integrity and purity while he is making the decisions and thinking about them.

Spiritual effect: Some people use shells for protection, but other people feel differently about this matter. Whoever links up to shells may use them extensively for meditation, and for linking up to the forces of land and sea.

Profession, occupation: Shells are very suitable for sailors, seamen, fishermen, and people who spend a lot of time at sea. Some people attribute properties of stimulating organizational abilities (order from the historical and chronological points of view) to them, a fact that renders shells very suitable for historians and archaeologists. Moreover, shells are recommended for people whose work requires that they improve their organizational abilities and their sense of order - for homemakers as well. Shells are also recommended for construction workers and builders.

Smoky quartz

Smoky quartz, as its name indicates, is a quartz crystal that resembles the color of smoke. It occurs mainly in masses, and its colors range between various shades of smoke gray, including light, dark, and almost black. Smoky quartz transforms negative energies and dissolves them. Keeping a cluster of smoky quartz in a room, home, or office, is very helpful in purifying the place of negative energies.

Physical healing properties: Smoky quartz should be given to people who are undergoing radiation treatment and chemotherapy, because of its action in eliminating negative energies. It can help in regulating the fluids and minerals in the body, and it is very advisable to use it when taking mineral supplements, and the person is not absolutely sure about the exact amount of supplement the body needs. In cases like these mainly, it can ensure the correct intake of the mineral supplements. Smoky quartz is wonderful for alleviating muscle pains, releasing muscle cramps, and bringing relief to regions in the body in which a great deal of tension or pain can be felt. The stone should be placed on the area, using a plaster if necessary. When a smoky quartz generator or a stone with apexes is used, it should be placed with the apex pointing outward. It is especially good for treating the limb chakras (that are located on the hands and feet), and is used for treating disorders in those areas. As we will see in the stone's spiritual and emotional healing properties, it eliminates negative patterns of thought and emotion. In that, it is very helpful in solving the problems, diseases, and states of physical imbalance that stem from these erroneous thought patterns. For this reason, it is likely to be beneficial in treating a wide range of problems and diseases.

The mineral's effect on the emotional and mental layers: This is an excellent stone for people who are "spaced out" and not grounded. As a rule, it is very helpful for focusing, and for that reason, is likely to be of help to people who are in professions that demand a great deal of concentration, or pupils who are being tested in the sciences - but not just for them. It is wonderful for increasing the concentration and for opening up perception and understanding while learning. It is very helpful in getting rid of fears and nightmares, and is effective in getting selfish people to open up and understand the needs of others, and to be less self-centered. Smoky quartz is also very good for people who suffer from depression, or feel mentally exhausted and fatigued by life, by promoting and stimulating *joie de vivre*. It is important to point out that smoky quartz does very good work on the solar plexus chakra. All the problems that stem from an imbalance in this chakra - selfishness, anger, resentment, hatred, jealousy, unbalanced ego, problems of dependency, abuse of power, manipulative and controlling behavior, conceit and fears - can be balanced by means of the constant use of this stone. It is unique in its ability to dispel negative energies and negative emotional patterns that derive from negative and inhibiting thought patterns, such as anger, resentment, and hatred, and its action is gentle and soft. While it works on releasing the negative patterns, it helps acquire more positive, correct, and beneficial patterns of thought and emotion - physical, mental, and spiritual. The stone's action is not particularly fast, but very powerful on the one hand, and very gentle on the other, which makes it an excellent stone for daily use over a relatively long period of time.

The mineral's effect on the chakras: Smoky quartz balances the solar plexus chakra. It has a strengthening, balancing, and stabilizing action on the base chakra. It can be placed on the third eye chakra as well, and used to open the crown chakra.

Spiritual effect: Smoky quartz, especially the darker types, is good for work on the physical and astral layers, during the course of mental development. Although it is not a channeling stone, it is very important for people who are involved in healing, in work methods, and in spiritual development, since it helps them eliminate the negative patterns that are liable to disturb them in their work. It helps the passage between the state of beta waves and the state of alpha waves (the meditative state) and it can be used for entering a meditative state more easily, especially if the person feels that there are disturbances that make it difficult to enter that state. It is very helpful in detaching oneself from daily troubles and worries in order to enter this state more easily. Moreover, during meditation, it serves as a grounding anchor on the one hand, and provides protection on the other. During the laying on of stones, it is an excellent stone for placing on the solar plexus chakra, the base chakra, and even on the third eye chakra. It is very good for stimulating the intuition, and it is used while making contact with other worlds, since it also provides effective protection.

Money, profession, occupation: Smoky quartz can be used while making large and important purchases as well as in the business world. It enables the person to act logically and cleverly so that he makes the best purchase or the most effective business agreement. It is good for encouraging creativity in the business world, and for reinforcing cooperation between workers or various elements. Because of these properties, it is highly recommended for business people, sales and marketing managers, and directors. It is also very suitable for government workers, and helps them improve their public relations.

Smithsonite

Smithsonite occurs in masses and grains and in a variety of colors: gray, white, purple, pink, brown pink, light blue, blue, greenish blue, green, and yellow.

Physical healing properties: Smithsonite is used to strengthen the immune system and enhance its functioning. It helps preserve the walls of the veins and stimulates their regenerative processes. It helps treat alcoholism, digestive disorders, sinus problems, problems with calcium absorption and loss, and skin problems.

The mineral's effect on the emotional and mental layers: Smithsonite soothes and dispels tension and pressure. It stimulates leadership qualities by imbuing the bearer with amiability, grace, and generosity, and helping him operate in situations that require strength and decision. It is used for treating people who went through severe traumas in their childhood. This is a wonderful stone for both adults and children with difficult childhoods, for people who were not given love in their childhood, and for people who lack confidence. It soothes agitated people. Smithsonite is an excellent stone for people who go wandering or undertake journeys in unfamiliar territory, as it fortifies their ability to orient themselves in those places.

The mineral's effect on the chakras: Smithsonite can be used for stimulating all the chakras, but it is especially suitable for healing the crown chakra. When it is placed on the crown chakra, or held above it, smithsonite raises all the chakras to a higher state of awareness. In addition, it has a wonderful effect on the heart chakra.

Spiritual effect: Smithsonite is used in channeling by stimulating the hallucinatory abilities. Besides helping the person pick up messages, it also filters incorrect messages, or informs the person about the correctness of the messages he received. Moreover, some people use it during the laying on of stones as a substitute for a missing stone, by tuning the smithsonite to take the place of the missing stone and play its role.

Sodalite

Sodalite's most common color is blue with white residues (stripes, spots, dots). It also occurs in dark blue, lavender blue, gray, sometimes in yellow, green, light red, white, and clear. It can be found in a range of forms - masses, grains, and even in needle-like formations.

Physical healing properties: Sodalite is good for general treatment of infections; it strengthens the lymphatic system, and is used for treating lymphatic problems ranging from infections to cancer (in which case the treatment must be administered by a healer who is very experienced in crystals). It balances the thyroid gland, in this way maintaining the metabolic balance in the body. In addition, the stone helps cleanse and purify the body. It is used for treating problems concerning calcium lack and absorption, and it is very helpful in sleep disorders.

The mineral's effect on the emotional and mental layers: Sodalite has a welcome effect in releasing old thought patterns by helping us adopt more effective new ones, for the sake of our continued physical, emotional, and spiritual development. It stimulates the intellect, helps resolve mental and emotional states of confusion, and encourages the person to reach effective and logical conclusions. It helps him see things in an effective way, without irrelevant emotional interference, and helps tune him into an objective and a stable and confident way of reaching it, all the while feeling light-hearted and courageous. It stimulates the properties of cooperation, admiration, and trust, both in ourselves and in others. For this reason, it is very good for use in groups, where it bolsters the collective value and the group accomplishment of objectives. One of its unique properties is that it provides a clear link between the conscious and the subconscious, and links emotion to thought. It dispels guilt feelings and fears, and causes well-being. It is a wonderful stone for developing the expressive ability, especially when expressing emotions, and emphasizes true feelings and raises them to the surface in a clear manner.

The mineral's effect on the chakras: Sodalite is one of the most suitable stones for placing on the third eye chakra. It balances and opens it, and provides a link to the intuitive levels.

Spiritual effect: Sodalite is an excellent stone for stimulating the intuition. In a very natural way, and almost effortlessly, it affords access to universal knowledge and to the sacred laws of the universe. By wearing it, holding it, or using it, the person is likely to feel this information seeping into him, and universal ideas uniting with and linking up to his way of thinking and believing, in order to cause spiritual growth, openness, and a higher thought capacity.

Profession, occupation: Sodalite is highly recommended for holistic healers, trainee healers, and healers. It is used by them for treatment as well as for stimulating their intuition and energetic healing properties. As a rule, it is wonderful for therapists of all kinds - psychologists, social workers, and psychotherapists. In addition, it can be very effectively used by writers, since it links the intellectual and the intuitive abilities and eliminates cerebral confusion.

Spinel

Spinel occurs in all the colors of the rainbow - red, orange, yellow, brown, green, blue, dark blue, purple, white, and transparent. It crystallizes mainly in the form of pebbles.

Physical healing properties: All the spinel stones purify the body. They are thought to be stones that stimulate beauty and rejuvenate. **Red spinel** stimulates vitality and physical health. **Orange spinel** helps women or men who suffer from sexual frigidity, and is used for treating fertility problems.

The mineral's effect on the emotional and mental layers: The various spinel stones purify the emotional and mental layers. They can be used when the person fails to perform a task and feels that he lacks the energy to try again. Spinel helps raise the person's positive properties to the surface. **Orange spinel** stimulates the desire to create and express emotions by means of creativity. In addition, it strengthens the intuition. **Green spinel** inspires generosity, compassion, love, and loyalty toward others. **Dark blue spinel** inspires the intuition and increases the emotional abilities. **Blue spinel** helps increase the communicative abilities, and moderate excessive sexual desire. **Yellow spinel** stimulates the intellect. It is widely used in color therapy.

The mineral's effect on the chakras: Since the stone occurs in all the colors of the chakras, it is possible to perform healing and balancing of the chakras by means of a set of spinel stones in suitable colors. In addition, most of the spinel stones stimulate the Kundalini, balance it, and broaden its channel. **Red spinel**

helps balance the base chakra, orange spinal balances the sex chakra. **Yellow spinel** balances and stimulates the solar plexus chakra. **Green spinel** is used to stimulate and balance the heart chakra. **Blue spinel** balances and stimulates the throat chakra. **Dark blue spinel** stimulates and balances the third eye chakra. **Purple spinel** is used for stimulating and opening the crown chakra.

Spiritual effect: All of the spinel stones are used for spiritual purification and for filling up with energy. **Black spinel** is used for grounding, and provides protection. **Clear spinel** is used for linking up to the universal energies. **Dark blue spinal** can be used during astral travel. **Blue spinel** is used in channeling, and for opening and stimulating the sixth sense and increasing intuition. **Brown spinel** is used in healing for purifying and cleansing the aura. **Purple spinel** encourages the person's spiritual development. During astral travel, it helps him remember and preserve the information that he received.

Sugilite

Sugilite occurs in small masses, and can be found in a range of colors, from shades of lilac pink to purple. The most common type is deep purple mixed with black. Sugilite is a stone that links the existential emotional energies to the existential physical energies. It is especially important in situations in which people feel as if they are detached from their physical bodies, or as if they do not want to live in this world, as happens, for example, in cases of autism. It is possible to use a stone with black residues in order to "transfer" a headache from the person to the stone. It is important to purify it immediately after this kind of use by placing it in a glass of water prepared in advance, and dipping the fingertips that touched the stone in the water.

Physical healing properties: Sugilite is used for treating epileptic patients as a part of a broad healing program, for treating autism, dyslexia, and headaches.

The mineral's effect on the emotional and mental layers: Sugilite helps the person understand his place on this earth, as well as the lessons he learns, by helping him cope with life on the physical level, especially when it seems unbearable. It strengthens the person's belief in himself and helps him understand the repairs and lessons that he has to apply in this life. It helps the person feel forgiveness and understanding toward himself, as well as toward others, and helps develop and express the hidden potential in every person. This is a wonderful stone for eliminating negative energies that stem from thought and emotional patterns of anger, hatred, hostility, rudeness, prejudice, and so on.

It performs a double action (which is actually a single one) – it helps him eliminate these negative feelings toward himself, thus altering his attitude toward the world. This helps him discard bad emotional patterns toward others. People who suffer from depression or a feeling of despair with life are advised to meditate with the stone placed on their third eye chakra, in order to stimulate the energies of consolation and compassion that are within them, and open them up to receiving those energies from the universe. Meditation with the stone can stimulate and develop the person's hidden creativity by giving him tranquillity, confidence, and precision in his actions.

The mineral's effect on the chakras: Sugilite links and channels the energy from the crown chakra to the base chakra by opening the chakras on its way and clearing a path for the Kundalini energy. It is good for treating the heart chakra. Placing the stone on the third eye chakra can be very helpful in dispelling feelings of despair and depression.

Spiritual effect: Meditating with sugilite is likely to provide the person with a feeling of freedom, confidence, and elation. In addition, some people have extraordinary visions and scenes during meditation with the stone. Besides unique visions, it is possible to receive information from other worlds while meditating with the stone, and this information arrives in a calm and pleasant way, imbuing the person with a feeling of confidence and serenity. It links the physical, mental, emotional, and spiritual bodies, thus providing the person with a feeling of unity, and stimulating creativity.

Profession, occupation: This is a wonderful stone for trainee healers, as well as for holistic healers. It is excellent for artists and creators.

Tiger eye

Tiger eye occurs in a range of colors, all of which stand out and shine when they reflect light, just like a cat's eye. The stones come in brown yellow, reddish, blue, blue black, black, and they generally occur in a combination of two of the colors, creating a special gleam. The ancient Egyptians would use tiger eye for eyes in the statues of their gods. They feared anyone who wore tiger eye around his neck, because they believed that he could see everything. The ancients believed that tiger eye granted its owner unequalled sharp vision that enabled him to "spy" or to observe their deeds, even if he was far away or concealed from them.

Physical healing properties: Tiger eye is used for strengthening the bones of the spinal column. It is suitable for treating problems of the sexual and reproductive system, as well as throat problems. Naturally, it is used for strengthening the eyes and vision.

The mineral's effect on the emotional and mental layers: Tiger eye links the two hemispheres of the brain, the left and the right, and helps the person attain mental clarity. In addition, it promotes the properties of perception and clarity and hones the ability to work with small details. It helps the person achieve stability and practicality, and for that reason is good for people who are detached or spaced out. It is a stone that brings happiness, gaiety and optimism, and stimulates a good mood, and should be placed in locations where groups gather for work or studies. It stimulates courage and helps the person follow his path by softening and eliminating feelings of pride (since it is an excellent stone for the solar plexus chakra). Tiger eye is widely used for treating fears of sex, and should be given to people who create a kind of dichotomy between the sexual act and emotion, because it links the two layers. Carrying or holding tiger eye can stimulate the person's awareness of his essential needs, and, in parallel, can direct his attention to the needs of others.

The mineral's effect on the chakras: Tiger eye can be used to open and stimulate the sex chakra by balancing it. It is used for treating the base chakra, and is excellent for treating the solar plexus chakra. Of course, the color of the stone is very important, and it should be placed on the appropriate chakra.

Spiritual effect: This is a good stone for group meditation, or as a preparation for mutual meditation.

Money, profession, occupation: Tiger eye is considered to be a stone that brings success and wealth. It can be used when requesting increased prosperity, and it also helps safeguard economic stability and abundance. Tiger eye is thought to be a suitable stone for detectives and people involved in stake-outs. It strengthens the sense of sight, not just the physical aspect, and stimulates in them the courage required for their work. Some people claim that tiger eye reinforces underwater vision. For this reason, it is very effective for people who work under water, for divers, and for marine researchers.

Topaz

Topaz occurs in a range of colors: blue, pink, white, green reddish, yellow, gold, red yellow, brown, gray, and clear. It crystallizes in the form of pebbles and prismatic crystals. As we can see, not only does topaz come in a large range of colors, but also in different structures that include other minerals.

Besides the general description of the various types of topaz, we will focus on several colors with unique qualities - blue topaz, multicolored topaz, and golden/yellow topaz.

Topaz is one of the stones that was set in the High Priest's breastplate, and it is identified with the tribe of Simeon. For the ancient Egyptians, topaz symbolized the sun god, Ra, the giver of life and fertility. For this reason, the stone is considered to possess divine powers. In the ancient Indian language, the meaning of the word "topaz" is "fire." Many exalted healing powers were attributed to it, especially the ability to control anger and cure diseases of emotional origin. The ancient healers recognized its exceptional magnetic powers, and during the Middle Ages would place it under the pillow in order to rehabilitate and increase the body's strength and relieve stress. Because of its ability to strengthen the respiratory system, they believed that it was able to cure colds and pneumonia. Moreover, it was thought to strengthen the mental capacities and soothe the emotions simultaneously, when worn around the neck. One of the most famous legends about topaz says that when the owner of the topaz is in danger, the stone loses its rich color. For this reason, the stone was worn on the fingers in many places, in order to serve as a warning signal against accidents or sudden death.

Physical healing properties: Topaz is considered to be the stone that bestows general health on its owner. It helps treat wounds and ulcers, and promotes tissue regeneration. **Blue topaz** helps treat throat problems, throat infections, and hoarseness. **Yellow or orange topaz** is used for treating liver, bladder, and endocrine problems, the nervous system, exhaustion, and frayed nerves. Multicolored topaz is used to treat chronic skin inflammations and lung problems - lung infections, lung congestion, and so on. In addition, it helps regulate the insulin level in the blood.

The mineral's effect on the emotional and mental layers: Topaz helps eliminate non-positive feelings, and convert them into feelings of happiness and optimism. It promotes enjoyment, gaiety, and love. It strengthens faith and confidence, and helps dispel feelings of doubt and lack of faith. It helps the person act with confidence and certainty in accordance with his decisions, and helps in situations in which it is difficult for the person to believe in his decisions and in situations of uncertainty. It stimulates the ability to see and understand interpersonal and conjugal relationships, and stimulates love. It is good for allaying fears and agitation, especially agitation that stems from a lack of confidence in the universe and its processes. Blue topaz is very effective for people who suffer from conceit and pride. It helps them gradually eliminate these inhibiting properties. It is very soothing, and stimulates inspiration. **Golden topaz** is very soothing, and can be used in states of nervous collapse or nervous exhaustion. **Multicolored topaz** has an extremely powerful ability to treat non-positive thought and emotional patterns in the depths of the subconscious. It helps raise these patterns to the conscious level so that the person can relate to them and treat them. Moreover, it helps repair these patterns, and improves unpleasant and inhibiting behavior patterns.

The mineral's effect on the chakras: The various-colored topaz stones can treat the different chakras. **Blue topaz** helps stimulate the throat chakra. Since topaz stones have the ability to transmit requests so that they can be fulfilled, blue topaz helps transmit, express, and define the requests clearly, consciously, and lucidly. **Golden topaz** can be used for activating the base, sex, solar plexus, and crown chakras. Its action on the solar plexus chakra balances the chakra, and helps resolve conflicts.

Spiritual effect: Topaz is a wonderful stone for visualization processes for the sake of prosperity, objectives, or dreams that one wants to realize, and it is used when ordering energies. It helps elevate the wish to a source that makes wishes come true, and also helps "cleanse" the request if there are undesirable shades in it. Using this stone, it is possible to transmit requests pertaining to a particular person, especially requests that involve his personal success (such as arousing motivation in a passive person, and so on). The requests can also be transmitted by holding a small bottle or glass with an elixir prepared from topaz, while visualizing the thing we want realized. It is widely used in meditation and in energetic projections. It broadens the awareness and the ability to receive and absorb the abundance of the universe. **Blue topaz** can be used for clearly and precisely defining and expressing the desire to channel with a particular layer, entity or situation. In addition, it helps unify mind, body, and spirit with the wholeness of the universe. **Golden topaz** charges energy, and encourages spiritual development and the quest for enlightenment. The charging is expressed not just in renewed powers, but also in an increase in the power of concentration, awareness, clarity, and creativity. **Multicolored topaz** is suitable for using during trances, strengthens meditation, and clarifies the information that arrive during the course of meditation.

Work and business: Topaz is considered to be the stone that brings its owner success. It is good for artists and creators who want to reinforce their personal and unique stamp in their word. **Golden topaz** is used for increasing business success and for attracting clients, investors, or other interested parties to the business. **Blue topaz** is recommended for artists. Before starting to work, it helps them link up to inspiration and stimulate it. Moreover, the various topaz stones are suitable for actors, entertainers, and radio and TV announcers, because they strengthen the projection of energy in order to create communication with the audience. Since they are known to strengthen communication among workers and between workers and the public, they are suitable for all offices in which team work is required, or work with the public, and are very suitable for government workers, as well as for salespeople.

Tourmaline

Tourmaline crystallizes in the form of vertical crystals. The tourmaline family consists of many different colors, with each color having its own unique properties. Tourmaline's colors include black, white, blue, brown, green, pink, bicolored, and tricolored, as well as watermelon tourmaline, which is green or blue on the outside, and red or pink inside. Sometimes, layers upon layers of color can be seen in tourmaline stones. These are extraordinary stones, both in their beauty and in their varied healing powers, on all layers. They have a positive effect on everyone, at all times. While these are delicate, sensitive stones, they are also extremely powerful. They are very suitable for sensitive people who are affected by the surrounding energies.

The Romans, as well as people of other ancient cultures, used tourmaline mainly because of its soothing properties. The stone was used to induce good, relaxed sleep, and for soothing body and mind.

Below there are a number of characteristic properties of each of the members of the tourmaline family:

Physical healing properties: Tourmaline is used for physical protection against accidents, diseases, and injury. Because of its electric properties, it is very useful in treating nervous problems and the nervous system. All the tourmaline stones inspire happiness, gaiety, harmony, and an enchanted feeling. An elixir prepared from white tourmaline can be spread on external ulcers, or drunk to treat internal ones. Moreover, the essence helps to increase the number of white blood cells in the body.

The mineral's effect on the emotional and mental layers: Tourmaline promotes cooperation and balance between the right and left hemispheres in the brain. By means of tourmaline, it is possible to understand and see the aim of our lives, as well as the steps necessary it to realize it. In addition, it helps the person attain success in all spheres, and dispels fears of failure. It helps attract inspiration, increases self-confidence, and dispels anxieties. It balances the feminine and masculine energies. It helps achieve balance of thought, and balances the mental processes. It arouses happiness, determination, laughter, and mental clarity.

The mineral's effect on the chakras: Every one of tourmaline's many colors can treat a different chakra. Their energy suits each one of the chakras, and it purifies, stimulates, and preserves the energy of the chakras.

Spiritual effect: Tourmaline is an extremely powerful protective stone, and it balances the energies of the body and aura. Tourmaline was widely used in ceremonies in order to create a link to the powers that bestow blessings. Shamans from all over the world used it in order to increase their power and receive superior healing powers, at the same time receiving the required protection from it during their spiritual work. Magic wands made of tourmaline can be used to purify the aura, balance the meridians, transfer energy to the chakras, and create balance in all the layers.

Profession, occupation: Tourmaline helps those involved in healing, strengthens their power, and provides them with protection. In addition, it is a wonderful stone for artists, as it increases their inspiration and creativity.

Green tourmaline
Green tourmaline occurs in a range of shades of green, and it fills us with the balancing power of nature.

Physical healing properties: Green tourmaline helps with cell regeneration in the body, and reinforces the immune system. Because of its marvelous action on the heart chakra, it is of great help in treating heart problems and diseases. It is used in treatments for regenerating the heart. It balances the thymus gland, the glands of the endocrine system, and the immune system. Some people use it to help in the weight-loss process, as well as for eye problems.

The mineral's effect on the emotional and mental layers: Green tourmaline can help states of fatigue and mental and physical exhaustion. It soothes and balances emotionally and mentally. The stone arouses creativity, and brings inspiration, success, and wealth. It is used to treat psychological problems connected to masculinity and fatherhood.

The mineral's effect on the chakras: Green tourmaline has a beneficial effect on the heart chakra. It opens and stimulates the chakra.

Spiritual effect: Green tourmaline is a stone that should be placed in healing and treatment rooms. It converts negative energies into positive ones. In addition, it should be placed in locations where there are energies of confusion or tension. During meditation with the stone, it is possible to tune the energy that flows between the heart chakra and the third eye chakra. Moreover, it helps the person see visions. It is used in the healing of plants and green healing, and some people use it increase the power and effectiveness of herbal remedies.

Profession, occupation: Green tourmaline is wonderful and suitable for those who are engaged in therapeutic professions: healers, holistic healers, herbal therapists and homeopaths, physicians, nurses in hospitals, psychologists, and psychotherapists. Healers should wear the stone or place it in the room where the treatment is performed.

Pink tourmaline (Rubellite)

Pink tourmaline is also known as rubellite. It comes in pink, red, red purple, or deep purple.

Physical healing properties: Pink tourmaline gives a feeling of relief, openness, and physical "exaltation." It helps heal the meridians, and promotes physical health.

The mineral's effect on the emotional and mental layers: Pink tourmaline stimulates the sense of direction, and strengthens the communicative abilities and the properties of devotion and love. It helps solve conflicts, balances the emotions, and alleviates the pain of despair and sadness. It strengthens self-love, the feeling of self-esteem, and the belief in oneself.

The mineral's effect on the chakras: Pink tourmaline, or rubellite, is considered to be "the queen of the tourmalines." It has a wonderful effect on the heart chakra, balancing and opening it, and strengthening the power of love and closeness. By means of the power of love that it stimulates, it brings about the balancing of all the chakras.

Spiritual effect: Pink tourmaline symbolizes the love of a mother for her child, and stimulates unconditional love in all the layers. Moreover, it is effective in gently balancing the yin and the yang. A special property of this stone is its ability to transmit messages of love to others, and, like a magnet, it attracts loving messages back to the sender.

Profession, occupation: Like green tourmaline, pink tourmaline is also suitable for all kinds of therapists. Many healers wear strings of pink, green, black and white tourmaline beads. This is a very powerful protective tool against the negative energies that emanate from the patient during treatment, and it also reinforces the healer's treatment abilities to a great extent.

Black tourmaline (aphrizite, schorl)

Black tourmaline is an extremely powerful stone as a result of its unique protective powers. It helps protect the person against his own negative energies, against those of other people, and also against different kinds of radiation. It is highly recommended for people who feel that the energies in their surroundings affect them in an extreme manner. Black tourmaline appears under several "commercial" names.

Physical healing properties: Black tourmaline raises the level of the person's vitality and strengthens the body. The elixir prepared from this stone can treat cases of dyslexia. It stimulates the reflex points connected to the lower back, is used in the treatment of joint inflammations, heart diseases, and problems of disorientation, and helps balance and stimulate the adrenal glands.

The mineral's effect on the emotional and mental layers: Black tourmaline encourages seriousness, self-control, discipline, and power. The elixir prepared from it helps assuage feelings of anger, resentment, and anxiety. Black tourmaline helps the person understand and clarify abstract thoughts and perceptions. It helps achieve emotional stability and hones the senses. It is very powerful when it is necessary to cope with difficult and depressing conditions. It evokes practical creativity, and helps treat fears.

The mineral's effect on the chakras: Black tourmaline helps ground and stabilize the first chakra, and tighten the link between it and the center of the earth.

Spiritual effect: Black tourmaline has especially great protective powers. It protects and safeguards the person against negative energies by protecting the aura. It protects against negative energies not just from without, but also from within. Black tourmaline symbolizes mystery, the ungraspable, the abstract. Moreover, it is considered to provide protection against witchcraft.

Work, occupation: This is a highly protective tool for therapists of all kinds who come into contact with the harmful energies of their patients, or work in places where the percentage of mentally or karmically sick or injured people is high.

Watermelon tourmaline

Watermelon tourmaline is an exquisite stone, extraordinary in its coloring. It is green or blue on the outside, and red or pink on the inside. It has a tremendous energetic effect, and is known to possess the quality of transmitting energies between people who love each other or are important to each other.

Physical healing properties: Watermelon tourmaline has a balancing and healing effect on the heart and the nervous system. It stimulates the body's vitality, at the same time soothing it. It is used to treat heart and lung problems.

The mineral's effect on the emotional and mental layers: Watermelon tourmaline helps the person achieve emotional clarity. It develops his ability to be emotionally objective, and lifts his spirits. Since it arouses joy, it is very effective in treating depression and states of despair. It helps alleviate and dispel inner as well as external conflicts effectively. It is a wonderful stone for lifting guilt feelings, confusion, and feelings of guilt concerning sexuality. It stimulates a feeling of self-satisfaction, confidence, and harmony by enabling us to accept the various aspects of our personality. It helps the person attain flexibility of thought, openness, and the understanding of new and different perceptions. Watermelon tourmaline inspires a smiling and humorous view of the world, and opens us up to the beauties of nature. It increases the ability to behave "tactfully" in every situation, and promotes cooperation. In addition, it soothes the nerves and helps people who suffer from emotional imbalance.

The mineral's effect on the chakras: Watermelon tourmaline can heal and open the solar plexus chakra. It stimulates and opens the heart chakra powerfully as well.

Spiritual effect: Watermelon tourmaline symbolizes the wholeness of opposites, and helps balance the yin and yang.

Blue tourmaline

Blue tourmaline is a gorgeous and impressive stone. The following properties also relate to dark blue tourmaline, which is called indicolite, and blue neon tourmaline, which is neon blue in color.

Physical healing properties: Blue tourmaline is used for treating problems of the thyroid gland and lungs - it cleanses and opens the upper part of the lungs. In addition, it is effective in the treatment of all throat diseases and infections, as well as neck, esophagus, and thyroid gland problems.

The mineral's effect on the emotional and mental layers: Blue tourmaline strengthens communicative skills, and reinforces sympathetic and empathetic communication with others. It promotes a harmonious sensation on all levels, everywhere, and at all times. It is a wonderful stone to hold while engaging in social volunteering activities, helping others, and service, since it strengthens those abilities and helps bring them to the fore. Dark blue tourmaline stimulates the intuition.

The mineral's effect on the chakras: Blue tourmaline stimulates the throat and the third eye chakras.

Spiritual effect: Dark blue tourmaline stimulates the third eye, and helps link the person to the upper layers of extrasensory perception. Using this stone, it is possible to inspire visions. Blue tourmaline develops the extrasensory visual abilities, as well as all the other extrasensory abilities.

Profession, occupation: Blue tourmaline is a wonderful stone for all those whose work involves helping others, who take on social tasks, and who provide services to the public at large, especially in the fields of receiving complaints or providing assistance.

Brown tourmaline (dravide)

Physical healing properties: Brown tourmaline is used for treating intestinal problems, and helps skin blemishes diminish and fade.

The mineral's effect on the emotional and mental layers: Brown tourmaline stimulates tranquillity, and encourages a feeling of humility.

Spiritual effect: Brown tourmaline purifies the aura, and promotes the general equilibrium of the energies of the bura and body. It is used as a protection during meditation.

Colorless tourmaline (achroite)

Colorless tourmaline combines all the properties of tourmaline, so we will mention just a few additional ones below.

Physical healing properties: Colorless tourmaline helps treat headaches and infections. It balances the nervous system and the brain.

The mineral's effect on the emotional and mental layers: Colorless tourmaline has an exceptionally soothing and balancing effect both on the emotional layers and on the mental layers.

The mineral's effect on the chakras: Colorless tourmaline is a wonderful stone for activating the crown chakra.

Spiritual effect: Colorless tourmaline combines and crystallizes the properties of all the types of tourmaline. It is excellent for healing, and balances the energy centers and the meridians of the physical body.

Profession, occupation: Colorless tourmaline is a wonderful stone for healers and trainee healers.

Yellow tourmaline

Physical healing properties: Yellow tourmaline is used for treating liver problems and disorders in the spinal column, kidneys, bladder, and stomach.

The mineral's effect on the emotional and mental layers: Because of the great effect it has on the solar plexus chakra, yellow tourmaline causes an increase in personal powers. It stimulates intellectual curiosity, the quest for knowledge, and creativity.

The mineral's effect on the chakras: This is a wonderful stone for cleansing, balancing, and stimulating the solar plexus chakra.

Spiritual effect: Yellow tourmaline is a stone that helps with spiritual development, and directs the person's attention to the spiritual path that awaits him.

Work and business: Yellow tourmaline encourages enterprise, creativity, and determination in work and in business.

Tourmalinated quartz

The color of tourmalinated quartz is white, with kind of thin black or green strips inside it. It combines the properties of colorless tourmaline and those of quartz. Below is a list of properties that do not appear in the general description of tourmaline above or in the description of the properties of quartz.

Physical healing properties: Tourmalinated quartz is widely used in healing for the treatment of problems on all layers.

The mineral's effect on the emotional and mental layers: Tourmalinated quartz strengthens the sense of direction, achievement-orientation, and success. It encourages positive and wise action, soothes the emotions, and simultaneously spurs the person on to action.

The mineral's effect on the chakras: Tourmalinated quartz links all the chakras, and purifies, balances, and activates them.

Spiritual effect: Tourmalinated quartz links the delicate bodies, balances and helps develop and receive superior forces. Like the other tourmaline stones, it also possesses strong protective powers.

Turquoise

Turquoise symbolizes the blue of the sea and sky, the depths of the ocean, and the depths of the soul. It was considered to be a sacred stone in many ancient civilizations - Egypt, Persia, the Aztec culture, and many others - and special because it was common all over the world. The Tibetan Buddhist monks also worshipped it, and the Native Americans believed that it contained the atmosphere that surrounds the heavens and earth. It is thought to be a stone that protects body and spirit, since its color - turquoise - symbolizes protection. It is believed to bring good fortune, and has been set in jewelry and ornaments for thousands of years. It occurs in the form of masses, prismatic crystals, and veins, as well as inside various minerals.

Physical healing properties: Turquoise has broad-spectrum healing properties, and can be used for strengthening, safeguarding, and protecting the body. It is used for treating all diseases (in conjunction with other stones and healing procedures). It helps repair physical damage, relieve headaches, treat problems of defective food absorption, and treat muscles.

The mineral's effect on the emotional and mental layers: Because it is a combination of green and blue, it helps develop emotional communication. It stimulates initiative, motivation, and creativity by introducing the sweet fragrance of love into all the person's actions. It possessive strong protective properties, stimulates mental abilities, and brings clarity to thought. It stimulates trust, understanding, and good communication between people. It is very helpful in solving problems in the emotional and thought realms, and helps assuage anger and bitterness. Some people claim that its marvelous protective abilities stem from the fact that it can absorb the negativity that is transferred to the person who holds it, in this way preventing the negativity from harming him. For this reason, it is occasionally liable to break as a result of the absorption of the negative energies from which it shields its holder. Some people say that when something threatens its holder, or when he is ill, the color of the stone changes. Turquoise bolsters self-confidence and increases the person's strength, grounds him in a positive manner, and helps him keep in touch with reality. It soothes and helps people who are troubled by thoughts or emotions to feel well-being. It is a wonderful stone to carry on a journey.

The mineral's effect on the chakras: Turquoise reinforces all the chakras, linking them to the meridians and the mental bodies. Because of its color, which is a mixture of green and blue, it is wonderful for the throat and heart chakras alike, and can be used for treating the sex chakra.

Spiritual effect: Turquoise can be used for every spiritual activity. It is an excellent stone for healing, for purifying the energy centers and the physical body. During profound meditation, the stone helps maintain a link with conscious thought (and, as we said before, it symbolizes the perfect link between heaven and earth) and provides protection throughout the meditation. For this reason, it is highly recommended during the course of astral travel, since it keeps us in contact with the earth. It is widely used in healing for eliminating negativity and purifying energies.

Money, profession, occupation: Turquoise is considered to be the stone that inspires success and prosperity. It is recommended for accountants. It helps soothe the mental layer during work and afterwards, and eliminates the effects of mental pressure. In addition, it is recommended for computer programmers and software developers. Because it greatly strengthens the body's powers and protects it against injury, it is recommended for anyone involved in hard physical labor.

Unakite

Unakite crystallizes as multicolored masses of rock in which quartz and feldspar components are present. Its colors are pink and green.

Physical healing properties: Unakite is used for treating the reproductive system. It should be worn during pregnancy in order to support the pregnancy and the health of the fetus. Some people use it for promoting weight gain. In this case, the person using it or the therapist must program the stone and indicate the regions of the body in which the person wants to gain weight.

The mineral's effect on the emotional and mental layers: During a disease or suffering, unakite enables the person to understand the causes of and reasons for his illness. It helps him cope better with physical pain, by releasing the energetic blockages and barriers that formed as a result of past traumatic experiences.

Spiritual effect: This stone should be used during rebirthing, since it helps release energetic blockages that stem from traumatic experiences. It releases the meridians from the emotional blockages that have solidified within them, and balances the emotional body. In therapeutic meditation, it can strengthen the ability to see visions that are connected with the etheric layer.

Money, profession, occupation: Unakite is very suitable for holistic healers. By linking up to the stone, and to the patient, it helps the therapist understand the basic reasons for the disease.

Zircon

Zircon's beauty is reminiscent of that of the diamond, and the stone is used as a substitute for diamonds in jewelry. It occurs in the form of prismatic crystals, cubes, and grains. It occurs in all the colors of the spectrum - blue, yellow, red, yellowish orange, green, brown, gray, and clear.

Physical healing properties: Zircon is used for treating broken bones and muscular problems, mainly problems of lack of flexibility or stiffness, and for helping the growth and stability of the bone. It can be used for treating vertigo and dizziness, and serves as an antidote for poison.

The mineral's effect on the emotional and mental layers: Zircon helps overcome the obstacles in the path of life. During the Middle Ages, yellow zircon was used to increase the enjoyment of physical pleasures such as sex and eating. Orange zircon was used for protection during journeys and for inspiring respect for its wearer. Moreover, orange zircon is used for soothing and treating emotional heartaches and states of emotional imbalance. Brown and red zircons were used to soothe the emotions, to restore the appetite, and to treat insomnia. In addition, they were used to treat depression and melancholy. As a rule, the various zircons are used to create emotional balance, and for this reason are very effective for states of sadness and sorrow, anger, and so on. It helps the person become more passive and tough, when necessary, and helps him keep up his efforts to accomplish his objectives. It promotes innocence, purity, stability, and continuity.

The mineral's effect on the chakras: Zircon is suitable for treating the base, sex, solar plexus and heart chakras by helping them rise up and develop.

Spiritual effect: Zircon is a guiding stone that helps the person learn life's lessons quickly and effectively. For this reason, it helps him advance along the path of destiny without the necessity to learn lessons that were not properly understood over and over again. Zircon has the ability to attract and take in energy, like the diamond, and the ability to transmit energy, like the crystal. In healing treatments, it is mainly used for creating emotional and physical balance in the patient. Zircon has a good protective ability against negative energies, and the person should wear it when he feels threatened. It helps achieve unity in all the layers - physical, mental, emotional, and spiritual.

Profession, occupation: Zircon is considered to be a suitable stone for detectives. It helps greatly when there is a need to arrange the facts in an organized manner. In addition, it is thought to be a stone that helps homemakers cope better with the burden of domestic chores and the responsibility for the household. Zircon reinforces the ability to project vocally, which makes it an effective tool for singers.

The qualities and properties of the various metals

The various metals also have a variety of healing properties, especially in their natural state, without too much processing. There are numerous types of metals, and most of them have medicinal qualities in the various layers. Following is a survey of some of the most commonly used metals.

Copper

Copper appears in many forms - masses, strata, veins, and grains. Its color is reddish yellow.

Physical healing properties: Copper helps balance the circulation and the blood flow. It helps treat bacterial infections and clean wounds. It can be used for treating joint inflammations and rheumatism, and for stimulating metabolism.

The mineral's effect on the emotional and mental layers: Copper stimulates motivation, and energizes people who suffer from passivity and laziness. It stimulates initiative and independence, motivates the person to act, and encourages him to achieve in all spheres. It helps the person understand that he is limited by the limits that he has set for himself, and he has to concentrate on getting rid of them, so that he can continue along his path. For this reason, copper releases the person from conservatism very effectively. Moreover, it stimulates philosophical and objective energy and develops diplomatic skills. It arouses *joie de vivre*, balances sexual energies, and strengthens the mental layers.

The mineral's effect on the chakras: Copper is suitable for treating, activating and opening the base and sex chakras.

Spiritual effect: Copper helps create coordination and a link between the physical, mental, and astral bodies. It promotes intuition by balancing it correctly, and uses healing for transmitting electric pulses. By means of copper, it is possible to transmit magnetic frequencies to the stones in a laying on of stones on the patient's body. It helps balance the body's energies and increase general vitality.

Money, profession, occupation: Copper is very suitable for people who are involved in politics, or need to develop their diplomatic skills at work. It helps them stay on the path they chose, while ignoring personal tangents that have no use on the social level. It stimulates achievement-orientation, and helps promote political aspirations. In addition, it is considered to be a metal that brings luck and helps people who suffered a financial loss to rehabilitate themselves and stand on their own two feet once more.

Gold

Gold is a metal that solidifies in the form of chips, grains, and masses. It occurs in several colors: white gold (light, almost silvery in color), red (orangy) gold, and yellow gold.

Physical healing properties: Gold is used in the treatment of problems of the nervous system and multiple sclerosis, and for improving the respiratory cycle, the digestive system, and body temperature. It is helpful in the treatment of joint inflammations, rheumatism, and paralysis, disorders in blood circulation and problems in the blood vessels, skin problems (some people even used it to treat skin cancer), eye problems, pneumonia, tuberculosis, spinal problems, and insomnia. Moreover, it is used to treat many problems linked to mental abilities, such as dyslexia, problems such as autism, lack of coordination, and epilepsy. It also helps the regeneration of the endocrine system, and the absorption of vitamins and minerals.

The mineral's effect on the emotional and mental layers: Gold stimulates the mental abilities. It helps improve personal qualities by understanding and learning. Gold is especially effective for treating various problems that stem from an unbalanced ego, a feeling of a lack of self-esteem, emptiness, anger, and guilt feelings. It helps the person attain tranquillity and peace of mind, and also balances his emotions, and encourages good and positive feelings. It helps people who bear a great deal of responsibility manage matters in a more balanced way, by relieving the burden of responsibility. It is very helpful in assuaging anger, excitement, and agitation. The use of gold is effective for preserving the exalted thoughts that reach the person at a time when he is unable to apply or use them at the given moment. It helps him preserve the higher thinking, and use it at the appropriate time. Gold is reputed to have the quality of attracting respect, wealth, and health to its owner.

The mineral's effect on the chakras: In the past, gold was used for treating the heart chakra, in order to open, cleanse, and balance it. It is used for opening and activating the third eye and crown chakras. It helps cleanse all the chakras.

Spiritual effect: Gold is used to cleanse the physical, emotional, mental, and spiritual bodies, and for cleansing the aura. It has the ability to stimulate the person's healing powers and link him up to the healing powers of nature. It has the ability to safeguard and increase the vitality of the gemstones that are set in it, and it helps stabilize their energies.

Tin

The color of tin is grayish white, and in its natural state it solidifies in round grains. It can be used in its natural state for various things, in the same way as the various stones are used; or gemstones can be set in it. The color of processed tin is darker and more metallic, and it should not be used for healing. *Tin must not be used, either in its natural or processed form, for preparing elixirs.*

Physical healing properties: Natural tin is used for treating lung problems and diseases, ulcers, and heartburn, and for eliminating parasites from the intestines.

The mineral's effect on the emotional and mental layers: Tin encourages the person to feel braver, and facilitates his battle with fears. It clarifies his thinking ability and promotes logical thinking. It should be carried when starting a new job or project, in order to stimulate perseverance. It encourages flowing and pleasant relationships, and contributes to the mutual consideration of the members of a couple.
In addition, it dispels feelings of sadness and pessimism.

Money, profession, occupation: Some people use natural tin in order to get rid of parasites and harmful insects from the home and the plants in the home and garden.

Iron

The color of iron is dark metallic gray to black. It solidifies in grains and masses. It is possible to use processed iron, but natural iron is more effective. In addition, iron that originates from meteors contains more of the following properties than processed iron.

Physical healing properties: Iron is used to treat disorders in the circulatory system (because it is one of the components of the red blood corpuscles) and internal bleeding. It is used for treating kidney stones and muscular atrophy, for relieving hoarseness, for fortifying the reproductive system, and for strengthening and promoting renewed nail growth.

The mineral's effect on the emotional and mental layers: Iron helps the person understand his life experiences effectively. It helps him liberate himself from obsolete patterns, especially traditional and environmental patterns, that do not suit his present life. As a result, it helps him apply new and courageous ideas. Iron symbolizes the principle of "thou shalt beat thy swords into plowshares." Iron can be used for manufacturing weapons of war (and indeed, this use was very common in the past, as was the production of instruments of torture and oppression), and it can be used for manufacturing plows, spades, and so on - tools that symbolize creation, renewal, an affinity for nature, and an aspiration to peace and tranquillity. This means that it could serve to eliminate the ideas of hatred and war that have been transmitted to the person via erroneous social channels. In addition, it helps the person understand ancient moral values. It is considered to be the metal that stimulates diplomatic skills, protects against injury, and makes the person more able to cope with legal proceedings and lawsuits.

Spiritual effect: Iron is used when communicating or extracting information from other existential intelligences.

Lead

The color of lead is dark gray, and it solidifies in round masses and strata.

Physical healing properties: The ancients used lead for treating blood poisoning. It helps treat gases and discomfort in the digestive system and stomach because it stimulates the flow. For the same reasons, it helps in detoxification processes, especially in the cells of the muscle tissue, Moreover, it is thought to strengthen the physical body. *Lead must not be used for preparing an elixir.*

The mineral's effect on the emotional and mental layers: Lead is considered to be a metal that stimulates movement. In this way, it helps people who suffer from apathy and indifference. It stimulates group unity and cooperation, and causes the members of the group to work together toward accomplishing the common objective.

Spiritual effect: Lead is used for linking up to spiritual guides, mainly in order to receive answers about various paths of action in life. In various cultures, lead is used to eliminate the evil eye, melting it to checking the evil eye using various techniques.

Money, profession, occupation: Lead is helpful in the entrepreneurial realm, when new and original enterprises in the business world are undertaken. In addition, it increases aspiration, initiative, and motivation in everything concerning music and musical creation and marketing. In the same way, it stimulates motivation in sport, either in athletes or in people who engage in the business aspects of sport.

Platinum

The color of platinum is gray to whitish gray. It solidifies in grains and small, thin scale-like strata.

Physical healing properties: Platinum helps safeguard the body's health, balance and maintenance. It helps improve the absorption of foodstuffs, and balance the functioning of the digestive organs. Moreover, it improves the health of the eyes.

The mineral's effect on the emotional and mental layers: Platinum is considered to be a metal that stabilizes and focuses. It helps the person achieve stability in relationships by bolstering his self-esteem and eliminating nit-picking and fault-finding with his partner. It increases mental focus - during extrasensory activities as well. It helps the person work toward his goals, and is very useful for people who start tasks enthusiastically, but lose their focus and energy when it comes to the finishing stages. It develops the intuition, and causes the person to recognize the inner wealth that belongs to everyone.

Spiritual effect: Platinum is considered to be a stone that has the ability to strengthen extrasensory skills and the ability to focus during various extrasensory activities. In various treatment methods, it is used to plant the memory of natural and primeval health into the cells in order to heal physical disorders in depth, especially those that originate in the cells.

Money, profession, occupation: Platinum helps managers, examiners, personnel managers, team leaders, and all those who have to measure the intelligence of the person standing opposite them in their job. It helps them measure the other person's intellectual capacity in depth.

Silver

Silver solidifies in scales, threads, plates, and masses. Its color sometimes tends toward silvery white, and sometimes toward gray or black.

Physical healing properties: Silver helps in the detoxification processes by eliminating toxins on the cellular level. Some people use it as a supplement in the treatment of liver inflammation, and it helps in treatments for improving vision (especially blurred vision), and vitamin absorption. In addition, it is used for facilitating birth and for treating problems of the nervous system.

The mineral's effect on the emotional and mental layers: Silver contributes to improving verbal, expressive, and conversational skills. It promotes the person's popularity, and refines his behavior. It helps tone down vulgar people or people whose manner of speech or behavior is crude or uncouth. It promotes patience along the person's path toward realizing his aspirations, and increases and regulates the intuition and the emotions. It balances the feminine energies.

The mineral's effect on the chakras: During work on purifying and opening the chakras, silver helps the stones that are used for opening and cleansing the energy centers to aim at the appropriate place, and assists in the balancing process of the chakras.

Spiritual effect: During astral travel, silver helps reinforce the connection between the astral body and the physical body in order to ensure a soft and safe return to reality and wakefulness at the end of the journey. It helps protect the person from becoming detached during the journey. It strengthens the properties and powers of the stones that are set in it, and stabilizes them. Because it is a metal that represents the moon, silver is used in activities pertaining to the full or new moon, ritual ceremonies, and meditation.

Money, profession, occupation: Silver is appropriate for diplomats, politicians, or anyone whose oratorical powers require improvement and strengthening.

Selecting, cleansing, and charging crystals

Selecting crystals

Which crystal suits me? Which mineral will contribute to my spiritual development? Which of the crystals will provide the best answers for the physical/emotional problems from which I suffer?

There are many and varied ways for choosing the appropriate crystal. One of them is, of course, to go through the list of crystals in this book. Understanding the qualities and properties of each of the crystals will help us select the crystal or crystals that are most suitable for us at this time. It is also possible to purchase crystals according to the colors of the chakras, so as to create an initial range.

One of the most highly recommended ways is to choose intuitively. When we go to the crystal store, all we have to do is wander around and notice which of the many crystals "beckons" us. Not infrequently, a particular crystal attracts our attention and causes us to scrutinize and touch it. This is no coincidence. It is almost certain that it has a message to transmit to us, or that we, in the depths of our consciousness, know that it suits us and will be very useful to us.

Selecting a personal stone

Each one of us has a personal stone, which is a gift from Mother Earth for our spiritual development. We are likely to discover our personal stone completely by chance, receive it as a gift, or identify it by instinct in the crystal store. In general, the way our personal stone reaches us is unique and makes a certain impression on our soul.

I discovered my personal stone, clear rainbow crystal, without knowing that it was my personal stone at first. I wandered around the crystal store looking for a large clear quartz stone for healing treatments. On the shelf opposite, I saw two clear crystals, almost identical in size. One of them was well polished, and its shape was standard. The other, in contrast, was more "natural," more massive, and seemed to be more special. It seemed to be very suitable for my purposes. But some vague feeling made me feel undecided, and I couldn't choose between the two (even though the less polished one seemed more appropriate to my needs). I requested permission to go out of the store with the crystals and see them in the sunlight. No special differences "jumped" out at me. However, when I held the more polished crystal, I felt, for no understandable reason, that it was the one I had to purchase.

When I got home with the crystal, I purified it well and placed it in the sun.

When I went to charge it, I was surprised to see an incredible rainbow shining out of the crystal. Although I had examined it thoroughly before the purchase, I had not seen this special rainbow. From that moment on, I simply "fell in love" with the crystal. I had heard a lot about rainbow crystals, but I had never seen one until then. Over the years, the link between us has grown stronger, and it has revealed itself to possess tremendous healing power. Although I had initially designated it for treating patients, it turned out that I felt that no other stone was more suitable for any profound spiritual activity or energetic request or order. Today, I know that it is my personal crystal.

That's how it is with our personal crystal. It attracts us, and we have to trust our intuition and gut feeling, and take it. The personal stone guides, teaches, cures, purifies, and uplifts us. As a result of a deep inner feeling, we feel an especially close link with this stone, even if we possess dozens of other stones.

We must respect and safeguard our personal stone. This can be done by preparing a special pouch for it. In this way, we can take it wherever we go, or put it in a place that has special significance for us. We must always ensure that it is purified, cleansed, and shining.

Our personal stone can symbolize our personality, the way we perceive the world, and the way in which we pick up the energies that reach us from the universe. Our personal stone has the ability to link up uniquely to our energetic frequencies, and to draw new positive qualities from the universe into our lives.

There are various minerals that contain a variety of developmental properties that are expressed in tiny changes. These small changes may be tiny and almost invisible to people who do not know the stone well. However, when we are linked to our personal stone, and know it well, we may see tiny changes occurring in it. These changes are likely to appear as small dots on its surface, as changes in color, as cloudiness on its surface, and so on. This property is especially obvious in the various types of quartz, but can occur in other minerals. These tiny changes can indicate the changes that are occurring in us or in our lives. They can be interpreted intuitively, or we can use the information contained in the chapter about reading crystal balls.

The personal stone can accompany us throughout our lives. In contrast, it is liable to "leave" us at a certain point, after it has given or taught us what it has to give. After transmitting the messages that we had to receive, and performing wonders in our lives, it may go on to someone else in order to give him what he has to receive. If the personal stone goes missing, there is no reason to worry. Another personal stone, no less suitable and unique, but with new messages for us, will soon take its place.

As we said before, we are likely to encounter our personal stone in different and unique ways. They are unique according to our own personal feeling. But we can also "order" our personal stone, which heals and illuminates our lives, by means of an energetic order from the universe. This energetic order should be placed when our general feeling is good, calm, and full of confidence in the universe. We must empty our minds of thoughts that are not connected to the matter at hand, define the energetic order clearly, and concentrate. After taking a number of deep breaths, relaxing and calming our bodies, we must close our eyes and ask the universe to let us meet our personal stone.

Cleansing crystals

One of the properties of crystals is that they can absorb the energies of those with whom they come into contact - not just human beings, but also the environment or the area in which they are placed. When we purchase a crystal, we have to take into account that this crystal was handled by many people. It was quarried, processed, traded, and sold. Even in the store, there is no doubt that many hands touched and held it. These energies are undesirable for us, both from the point of using the crystal for healing, and using it for our own purposes. After a treatment with crystals, or holding them in order to balance our emotional state, relaxation, or any other use, the crystal absorbs the energies that are transmitted to it by the patient or the bearer. It absorbs the frequencies of the disease, the imbalance, or the non-positive energies of the person who is using it or who is being treated by it. For this reason, cleansing crystals is absolutely essential, and must not be neglected. Moreover, a crystal that is used for treatment, and absorbs non-positive energies, is itself liable to be "injured." It absorbs those energies, which affect it when they are present in relatively large quantities, and are liable to damage its structure. As a result, the color of the crystal may dull, its transparency may cloud over, and it could crack. Sometimes, when a small crystal is used to treat an infection or a disease, or to balance negative emotions and so on, it is even liable to break, or "disappear."

For this reason, the crystal must be cleansed thoroughly and deeply before using it for the first time, immediately after purchasing or receiving it (if the giver did not purify it first and tune it for us), and purify it after every use.

The first cleansing is deeper and more prolonged than the cleansing that is performed after each use (even after a "light" use such as keeping the crystal in a pocket). Accordingly, the use of crystals belonging to other people is not recommended, because, unless we purify these crystals before use, we are liable to absorb their frequencies, instead of linking up to their high frequencies. To the same extent, we must purify and cleanse the crystal after it has been standing on our desk or in the house for some time, or after it has been placed close to a plant or animal.

It must be taken into account that there are crystals that tend to absorb and pick up the energies that are emitted by the electrical appliances in the home. By doing this, they do us a great service, and diminish the amount of radiation that these appliances emit. Crystals that are placed in the vicinity of a computer, a TV set, a microwave oven, and so on, must be cleansed and purified very frequently, otherwise they are liable to weaken, fade, or even crack.

There are many methods for cleansing and purifying crystals, and we will present a few of them below. Intuition and gut feeling play an important role when it comes to cleansing the crystals, so it is advisable to choose one of the methods for cleansing a particular crystal intuitively. We may feel that a certain method suits a particular crystal, while another method is suitable for another crystal. Occasionally, the crystal itself may "direct" us toward the most suitable cleansing method.

The first stage is to clean the dirt that is visible on the crystal, if necessary. If we notice traces of dirt, earth, or black, sticky marks on the surface of the crystal, they must be cleaned off gently with a soft toothbrush. Using a toothbrush for cleaning is especially effective when cleaning crystal clusters, because it is possible to get to the bits of dirt between the crystals.

Soft stones, sand crystals, or clusters with a soft base should not be soaked in water for any length of time, but rather rinsed under running water, because they are liable to crumble or break.

Each stone must be rinsed separately, one at a time, for two reasons: First of all, in order not to bump one against the other by mistake, which is liable to crack one or both of the stones, and so that we will direct our thoughts totally toward the specific stone, and concentrate on it alone each time, in order to strengthen the cleansing action.

While cleansing the stones, you must avoid extreme changes in temperature (very hot water following very cold water, and vice versa), both while rinsing the stone and when placing it on the windowsill, and ensure that it does not come into contact with either very high or very low temperatures, since this is liable to damage the structural strength of the stone, and if there is a tiny, virtually invisible crack, it could widen.

The stones must not be washed with soap or detergents. If there really is no choice, and the dirt on the stone cannot be removed with water and a soft toothbrush, it should be cleaned with soap made from natural substances only.

Cleansing with salt and water - the first cleansing

One of the most popular methods for cleansing stones is using salt and water. The use of salt for purifying stones has a long history, and apparently derives from salt's property to absorb the energies of everything with which it comes into contact, while performing cleansing actions. The salt that is used for cleansing the stones is sea salt, and not regular processed salt. The stones must be placed in a dish that is large enough to contain them, preferably a glass dish. After placing them in the dish, pour the sea salt over them, and leave them in the salt for about three hours. Similarly, it is possible to use sea water instead of salt, in the same way. After about three hours, take one of the crystals out and hold it in your hand. Use your intuition and your gut feeling to sense whether the crystal has been cleansed of undesirable energies. If for some reason you feel that it is still not clean, put it back in the dish of salt or sea water for another hour or two. Some people keep crystals that have absorbed many energies for 24 hours in a dish of salt or sea water, but generally speaking this is not necessary. It must be remembered that a long submersion in salt or sea water is liable to weaken the stones and cause them to crack.

After removing the crystal from the salt, hold it in your hand under cold running water (not from the refrigerator, but from the faucet! Water that is too cold is liable to weaken the stone's structure), or pour mineral or spring water from a bottle at room temperature over it. Hold the crystal under the water for about three minutes, directing your thoughts to rinsing off all the unwanted energies into the earth, and the crystal will be cleansed. After rinsing the crystal in water, place it on the windowsill, without a glass partition, for 24 hours to enable it to absorb both the sun's energies and the moon's.

There are stones that must not be placed in salt or sea water, because they are liable to weaken and crack. They include:

* fluorite * kyanite * pyrite * calcite * hematite * malachite *

These stones must be purified using one of the following methods:

Placing on a white quartz cluster
For the initial cleansing, the stone can be rinsed under running water for a few minutes, and then placed on a quartz cluster for three hours. After this time, hold the crystal in your hand, and feel whether it has been cleansed and purified. If not, it is advisable to place it on the cluster for another two hours. After the crystal has been cleansed, hold it under running water for three minutes, and direct the unwanted energies to be rinsed off into the earth.

Cleansing with smoke
Cleansing with smoke is an ancient traditional cleansing method that was common among the Indian shamans. The shamans would purify the stone using

smoke from medicinal herbs such as sage, cedar, or sandalwood. The best way is to prepare a stick of incense from the dried leaves of those plants. However, it is possible to used prepared incense made from these plants, but it must be of good quality, with no synthetic ingredients. The process of cleansing with smoke must be performed on a fireproof surface, because burning leaves or smoke are liable to fall onto the surface. Light the incense stick, the plant stick, or the pile of herbs. Wait until the smoke begins to rise. Afterwards, hold the crystal in your hand, and start to move it above the smoke (if the herbs are placed on the surface), or move the incense stick around it, until it is covered in smoke on all sides. Continue moving the crystal through the smoke until you feel that it has been cleansed and purified. Some people move the crystal through the smoke, or move the incense stick around the crystal five times. Others do so seven or eight times. In any event, you will have to rely on your feelings and intuition, because each stone is likely to require a different length of time for cleansing with smoke.

Cleansing a cluster

The quartz cluster must be cleansed one in three months. Place the cluster in the bath, or in a large basin, filled with sea water or sea salt for about three hours (not more, in order to prevent the soft base of the cluster from disintegrating). Afterwards, take the cluster out, rinse it for three minutes under the faucet or mineral water at room temperature, and direct the negative energies to be rinsed off into the earth. After the rinse, place the crystal in the bath or basin with clean water for about three hours, and then let it dry out for a while in the sun.

Cleansing by tuning, breathing, and power of the imagination

It is possible to cleanse stones by means of the power of our thought frequencies, breathing, and energy field. Personally, I do not recommend this method for the initial cleansing of the stone, but rather for cleansing it after it has been held or used for purposes other than "drawing out" pains, or treating serious traumas or severe states of imbalance. Having said that, people with a particularly strong power of thought may feel that they can use this method to cleanse the stone in many different situations.

First of all, rinse the stone well under running water for three minutes, and direct the negative energies to be rinsed off into the earth. (They do not harm the earth, since it has the power to convert the negative energies into positive ones.) Afterwards, grasp the stone with the thumb and index finger of one hand holding one end of the stone, and the thumb and index finger of the other hand holding the other end. In this way, you create an electromagnetic circuit that passes through the crystal. Now, you have to take deep, slow breaths, and use the power of your imagination. The image that you have to evoke is that of cleansing and purification. It is possible to imagine a strong, purifying light passing through your crown from above, via your forearms to your fingers that are holding the crystal, and through the stone, descending via your legs into the bowels of the earth. You can imagine a cold waterfall washing over your hands and the stone, and purifying it. You can imaging that you are standing in a spring, and flowing rainwater is pouring onto you, cleansing and purifying the stone. With this method, most times, you will also perform a cleansing and purifying procedure on yourself. It is important to remember to breathe deeply and slowly throughout the process, and to concentrate on your aim - cleansing and purifying the stone.

Methods for cleansing the stone after treatment, use, or holding it

As we said before, each time we use the stone, it absorbs our energies as part of the healing and "treatment" process it performs for us. Even after keeping the stone in our pocket, it is important to cleanse it. It is important to notice and pay attention to the strength of cleansing required. A stone that is kept for a few hours in the pocket of a person who feels good and happy, and transmits energy to him without any need to cope with serious physical, emotional, or mental imbalance, does not need the same cleansing as a stone that is used in healing treatments. There are no hard and fast rules about this, and you yourself must be aware of the manner and length of cleansing and purifying that the stone must undergo. Jewelry with stones worn on the body must be cleansed at least once a day. Stones that are used for healing and treatments must be cleansed immediately after the treatment, as must stones that are used for meditation for repairing incarnations. These stones must not be touched after the treatment or meditation! They are liable to be saturated with the same energies that we tried to eliminate. A glass two-thirds full of water must be prepared in advance (preferably a disposable one). After the treatment, the stone must be rolled into the glass, and the fingertips that touched it dipped into the water. After soaking in the water for about 20 minutes, purify it by using one of the methods. There are a number of ways to purify the stone after use:

1. Cleansing the stone by breathing and visualization.

2. Placing the crystal in flower petals - For this, we must used petals from organic flowers that have not been sprayed or fertilized with chemicals. Choose a flower that you especially love, and whose fragrance pleases you and arouses positive feelings in you. Place a number of petals below the stone, on it, and around it, until it is completely covered in petals. Leave it like this for 24 hours.

3. Rinsing the stone under running water, while directing the negative energies from the stone to be washed into the earth - The rinsing takes three minutes. Afterwards, place the stone on the windowsill for a while. This method is good for stones that have been in a room for some time and have not absorbed significant quantities of negative or undesirable energy.

4. Placing the crystal in a bowl of brown rice - Brown rice has the property of focusing and balancing energy. Place the stone in a glass dish filled with brown rice, so that it is completely covered. Leave it in the dish for 24 hours. Some people think that the rice can be eaten after that, but I personally do not think that this is a good idea. In contrast, placing the purified and charged stone - especially a stone that is used to balance nutritional lacks of various kinds or to balance the appetite - in a dish of rice, after which it is cooked and eaten, is healthy and fortifying.

5. Rinsing the stone under running water, and placing it on a quartz cluster - Rinse the stone while tuning it, as in the first method, but afterwards place it on a quartz cluster in order to cleanse it. The length of time the stone remains on the cluster depends on the strength of the "work," the duration of the work, and the energies the stone has absorbed. This method is good for cleansing a stone after wearing it or keeping it in our pocket. After treatment or laying on of stones, we must place the stone on a quartz cluster for a longer time - three to six hours.

6. Cleansing after a difficult treatment - This is performed after a treatment in which numerous non-positive energies were released from the patient, traumas were treated, the stone was present in a room where a quarrel occurred, or held during an extreme situation of lack of emotional or mental balance. In order to cleanse the stone after these situations, we perform cleansing method number 5 after the stone has spent three to six hours on a quartz cluster. We rinse it well once more, and place it on the windowsill for 24 hours. We use the same method after using the crystal for "drawing out" pains, or for treatment of infections or serious diseases.

7. Cleansing in the sea - This is a wonderful way to purify crystals. It can be done for no special reason other than we have the time and we feel like doing so. We gather up all the crystals (except for those that are not supposed to come into contact with salt water), and tie them in a bag of natural fabric or in a wooden box or clean cardboard carton. We go to the sea. This method requires special attention, since there are stones that feel a very strong affinity for the sea and would like to be swallowed up in it. For this reason, the stones must be washed one at a time. We take one stone, while all the others are placed neatly on the sand for a pleasant "sunbathe." We dip the stone in the water for a few minutes. It can be placed in shallow water, making sure it does not get swept

away, and let the ripples play with it for a bit. After washing it for several minutes, we put the stone on the warm sand, away from the other stones, and let the sun's energy charge it. In this way, we cleanse one stone after the other. The stones can also be buried in the sea sand for a while. Using this method, we purify the stone in a natural and effective manner, and also charge them with sunlight and with the positive energies of the sea and the shore.

What do we do when a stone breaks?

When a stone breaks, it is possible that it is telling us that it has fulfilled its purpose, or that the function that it performed exhausted it. Moreover, we may have cleansed it in the wrong way (for example, if fluorite comes into contact with salt, the slightest fall is liable to cause it to break! It might even break in our hand during the first use.). In any case, under no circumstances must a stone be glued together with contact glue or the like. The various adhesives are made of substances produced from dead animals, chemical substances, and other undesirable materials. Instead of transmitting pure and healing frequencies, a stone that has been glued is liable to transmit the pain of its breakage to us, or the negativity that stems from the glue's components. This rule is very important. After the stone breaks, we must follow the following rules:

Hold one of the pieces of the stone in your hand. Feel the stone's energy. Is it still transmitting the same energies as it did in the past, or is it "lacking in energy"? Often, the stone's energies pass into one of the broken pieces. This piece will possess very strong energy that includes all the stone's energy, while the other piece will be entirely devoid of energy. Sometimes, none of the fragments is usable. Each one of the fragments must be felt in order to see if any of them is storing the stone's energy inside it. The fragments that lack energy must be buried in the earth. Sometimes, it happens that after some time, one of the buried pieces emerges and appears in your path when you pass the place where you buried it. It is possible that its power was renewed, so you should hold it and try to feel and check if its energies have been restored. If so, fine. If not, it must be buried in the earth again. It is possible that you will feel the need to bury it in another place. Follow your gut feeling.

Charging the stone

Charging the stone increases its natural power. It is very effective, especially after we have used a particular stone a great deal or in a significant way. Moreover, it is advisable to charge the stone if we notice that its color has faded or dulled, if it lacks luster, or is cracked. There are many methods to charge crystals and strengthen their natural power. Here are a few of them:

1. Place the crystal on a cluster of crystals.

2. Place the crystals in the sun on the shore, or bury them in the sea sand for a few hours.

3. Place the crystal outside for 24 hours so that it can be charged with both sunlight and moonlight. Special days, such as new moon, full moon, the longest and shortest days of the year, and even days that have a personal significance for you, can charge the stone with greater power.

4. Charge the crystal with light - Hold the crystal in your charging hand (the hand used in healing for transmitting energy - generally the right hand for right-handed people, and the left hand for left-handed people - but this varies from person to person). Imagine a light in a color that you choose - pink for universal love, gold for divine protection and filling up with the highest energy, green for healing, purple for stimulating intuition and messages from higher sources, celestial blue, or any other color except black. See the pure colored light descending from above, filling you, and enveloping you. The light reaches the crystal via your hand, envelops it, and fills it with pure energy.

Tuning the crystal

Using the power of thought, we can tune the crystal and direct it toward a certain purpose. Of course, this purpose must be pure. We can ask the crystal to strengthen the properties of love, and direct it to transmit love to everyone who uses it or holds it (including you yourself, of course). It can be tuned to healing purposes, channeling, protection, balance, and so on. The property to which we tune the crystal will become one of its unique qualities. In order to tune the crystal, we must know exactly what the purpose of the tuning is, and formulate this purpose clearly and precisely. Before starting the tuning, it is advisable to request assistance, direction and guidance from the superego, from the forces of the universe, or from God. The crystal must be held in the receiving hand, while you take deep breaths and feel relaxed and serene. Focus your consciousness on your declaration, while feeling linked and united with the crystal that you are holding. See the directed thought flowing from you into the crystal, filling it and enveloping it. Continue transmitting the thought to the crystal for a minute or two, or until you feel that it is enough. Afterwards, put the crystal down in the knowledge that it is tuned into the thought that you planted in it.

Storing crystals

When crystals are not in use, they can be stored in a number of ways. A clean wooden box can be suitable for storing them. Drawers, on the other hand, are not recommended. Many healers feel that crystals do not "feel comfortable" in a dark drawer, and their sheen is dulled. The crystals can be placed in a bag made of natural fabric (not synthetic), but under no circumstances in a plastic bag. A plastic box is also not recommended. Many people are in the habit of placing crystals that are not in use in various places around the house, or on the windowsill. In fact, this is the natural place for crystals, because they enjoy spreading their light and pleasant energies throughout the house. Some people dedicate a special table to crystals, and place them on it in an orderly way.

Having said that, two important points in those cases must be taken into account: First, the crystals interact with the energies of the home in that situation, however clean they may be. For that reason, we must the crystals on a quartz cluster or rinse them well under running water before using them. Second, we must remember that the energies of the crystals affect us. There are crystals that are used in channeling because of their abilities to channel with various entities and establish contact between them and us. There are crystals that can make us "float" or become detached. Crystals of this kind should not be placed randomly around the house if we do not wish to channel or do spiritual work during the day, since their frequencies are liable to disturb our daily activities and occasionally cause a lack of concentration. It is especially inadvisable to place many crystals in the bedroom, in particular crystals used for channeling, unless we have a specific aim and intention for doing so.

One of the best ways for storing crystals is in a closet with glass doors. In this way, the crystals can sense the light, display their beauty, but their energies will not be disturbed by the frequencies in the house, and they will not distract us or perform therapeutic actions on us without us requesting it consciously.

Preparing an elixir from the crystal

Elixirs prepared from crystals have been used for thousands of years in many cultures. Shamans, tribal healers, alchemists in the Middle Ages, and healers used and still use the wonderful powers of elixirs and essences that contain the healing energy of the various crystals.

The elixirs prepared from the various crystals work in a similar way to homeopathic medications and to the energetic herbal essences (such as Bach Flower Remedies). The elixirs that are prepared from crystals are very powerful. For this reason, it is not advisable to use them too frequently, or too casually, and should only begin being prepared after a certain period of acquaintance with and understanding of the stones. Elixirs prepared from stones are widely used for balancing emotional situations, and are especially effective for treating various physical diseases, particularly infections and viral diseases. Garnet, for example, is known for its great power in healing flu and various viral and bacterial infections. The elixir prepared from garnet, especially if it is drunk when the first signs of the disease are manifested, is amazingly powerful, and works just like an antibiotic. An elixir can be drunk for general physical strengthening, for increasing the circulation, for promoting cell regeneration, and, of course, for treating emotional problems.

Remember that if we do not tune the stone before preparing the elixir for the treatment of a particular problem, all the stone's properties will be transmitted to the water without special focus on the specific problem.

In order to prepare the elixir, choose a purified stone that possesses the properties we want. Of course, you do not use stones that are not suitable for preparing elixirs. It is advisable to tune the stone before preparing the elixir, in order to reinforce its power and action for the particular purpose - physical, emotional, or mental - that we mention by name. It is also possible to see the person for whom we are preparing the elixir in our mind's eye, and request that it benefit him and help cure him. Place the stone in a glass, bottle, or transparent glass bowl. In general, a small amount of the elixir should be prepared, and more should be prepared for a second drink. (When a small or not particularly powerful stone is concerned, you should let it "rest" and charge it on a crystal cluster or by some other method before preparing an additional elixir.) The glass container should be filled with spring or mineral water, and covered with a glass lid or transparent glass plate. Now place the glass container with the crystal inside it in a place where the rays of both the sun and the moon can reach it. Wait 24 hours, and then the elixir can be drunk. It is very important to ensure that the water and the container do not come into contact with any metal.

The amount of water used to prepare the elixir differs from stone to stone, and also depends on the size and strength of the specific stone. The amount of elixir we have to drink also varies according to the stone itself, and to the person who has to drink it. For this reason, the best way to test the quantities is by using a pendulum. In the chapter dealing with quartz pendulums, we will see how they can be used to receive answers to questions of this kind.

In addition to the method for preparing elixirs that appears here, some people add brandy or alcohol in order to preserve the energy of the elixir. This method is used for preparing elixirs for lengthier use, but it requires a lot of experience in healing and in preparing elixirs.

Preparing an elixir that is affected by sunlight - An elixir that is affected by sunlight is suitable for situations in which we want to charge the stone with masculine energies, for balancing and strengthening the yang energies, or when we prepare an elixir from a stone with an orientation of masculine energies. We prepare the elixir according to the above instructions, but we place it in a glass container with the crystal in the sun for about three hours.

The following stones are mainly suitable for the preparation of an elixir of this kind:
*citrine
*obsidian
*red jasper
*rhodochrosite
*red agate
*zircon
*clear quartz
*Apache tear
*garnet
*topaz
*fire agate
*onyx
*carnelian
*diamond
*hematite
*bloodstone

Preparing an elixir that is affected by moonlight - An elixir that is affected by moonlight is suitable for situations in which we want to charge the stone with feminine, lunar energies, for balancing and strengthening the yin energies, or when we prepare an elixir from a stone with an orientation of feminine energies. We prepare the elixir according to the above instructions, and we place the glass container with the crystal outside at sunset. Of course, nights with a full moon are the best for preparing this kind of elixir. Sometimes, nights with a new moon can also be suitable. After placing the glass container with the crystal outside, we leave it for a few hours, from sunset to midnight, and bring it in at midnight.

The following stones are mainly suitable for the preparation of an elixir of this kind:
*sapphire
*green jasper
*black tourmaline
*pink calcite
*opal
*malachite
*petrified wood

*jet
*lapis lazuli
*blue calcite
*azurite
*sugilite
*pearl
*jade
*fossil
*chrysoprase
*amethyst
*celestite
*clear quartz
*turquoise
*moonstone
*chrysocolla
*emerald
*smoky quartz
*blue quartz
*green tourmaline
*moss agate
*rose quartz

In addition, it is possible to use water in which a stone has been submerged for treating plants and animals as well. In order to prepare irrigation water that is strengthened with the stone's energies, we can select various green stones, or stones that are suitable for treating plants, and, of course, clear crystal. The method of preparation is identical to that for preparing an elixir, except that we use a larger amount of water, as needed.

For treating animals, the crystal can be placed in their drinking water for about three hours. Many people report that after soaking the stone in the animals' drinking water, the animals drank much more than usual.

Moreover, it is possible to purify water by placing a clear quartz crystal in it. In order to purify water, there is no need to place the stone in it for long. Place a medium-sized clear crystal in a vessel containing about a liter of water, and cover the vessel with a transparent glass plate or lid. Put this in the sun or outside for several hours (between three and six hours), and you get clear, fortified water. Having said that, it is not advisable to try this method with especially "problematic" water, such as water in which there is a suspicion of a high level of toxic substances or bacteria. In cases like that, do not take a chance. The method is good for purifying regular water for domestic use, when there are no alternatives such as water filters or mineral water.

Treating animals

Diagnosing and treating animals must be done by a qualified and professional veterinarian. Having said that, we have the ability to improving the quality of our animals' life, whether they are healthy or suffer from various problems. By using stones, it is possible not only to relieve physical symptoms, but also various behavioral problems. Animals respond wonderfully to the energies of stones, and can be treated in a number of ways.

It is important to understand and define to ourselves the problem from which the animal is suffering (the use of crystals is not disruptive to any kind of medical treatment), and if it is being treated by a vet, it is important to ask and understand what the nature of the problem is.

There are three main ways for treating animals:

1. Placing the stone itself

A suitable stone can be placed in the animal's sleeping place (cat or dog). It can be placed in the vicinity of the animal, especially animals that are in cages, such as rabbits and parrots. It is also possible to place the stone in the cage itself. In order to treat various physical problems, such as joint inflammations, muscle weakness, and so on, you can place the stone, or a number of small stones, in a little bag made of fabric, and tie or sew it to the animal's collar. This suggestion is not suitable for cats, since their collar is small, and the stone is liable to be heavy for them. For a calm animal that does not remove things that have been placed on his body, or run wild in the yard, the stone can be placed around his neck. It can be threaded onto a strong leather string and tied around his neck, not too tightly, but not too loosely either, so that he cannot tear it off. For calm, non-volatile animals, the stone can be placed next to them (if you know the animal well, and know that there is no way that he will swallow it). Often, the animal responds marvelously to the stone, placing his chin on it and lying on it, leaving it when he feels that he has received the correct amount of healing vibrations. It is important to program the stone to the animal so as to establish a link between the mineral and the animal, and cause accelerated healing.

After placing the stone, you must observe the animal's behavior. If it expresses resistance of any kind to the stone, moves away from it, exhibits movements of discomfort, or refrains from sitting in the place where the stone is lying, weigh up the following possibilities: It could be that the required transmission of frequencies from the stone to the animal, which is suitable for a certain length of time, has been completed. It could be that the stone is too close to the animal, and the frequencies are bothering him, in which case it should be moved a bit further away. It could be that the stone is not suitable for treating the animal at this time. Observe his reactions, and act accordingly.

2. Administering an elixir prepared from the stone

The dosages for large animals such as horses and big dogs are identical to those given to human beings. For small animals, such as small dogs, cats, and rabbits, half the amount must be used. For very small animals such as mice, hamsters, and so on, and birds, half the amount for an adult human must be placed in its drinking water, exchanging it the next day for regular water, so that one day there is elixir, the next, plain drinking water, and so on. The best way to verify the exact amount is to use a pendulum (see the chapter on the pendulum).

3. Placing the stone in the drinking water

It is possible to place the stone in clean water (that has been filtered) or in mineral water for about three hours. Often, after placing the stone in drinking water, the animal drinks more than usual. If you see that the animal does not touch the water or is put off by it, it could mean that the stone you chose is not suitable. Exchange the animal's water for regular water, and try a different, more suitable stone the next day.

Common physical problems in animals, and the stones that are suitable for treating them

To fortify and preserve the health of the bones - calcite, fluorite

To relieve pain - lodestone

Inflammations and joint problems - azurite

To strengthen the teeth - diamond, fluorite

To treat cancerous tumors (of course, this does not replace veterinary care!) - Herkimer diamond

Adult dogs with kidney problems - nephrite, jade

For eye problems and to strengthen the vision - light opal

To strengthen the immune system - jade

For detoxification processes - moss agate

For infectious problems - obsidian

For respiratory and throat problems - lapis lazuli

For bitches prior to giving birth, during gestation, after miscarriage - pearl

For heart problems - rose quartz

Dogs with eating problems, overeating, and weight gain - apatite

Common behavioral problems in animals, and the stones that are suitable for treating them

Stressful situations that affect the animal - black tourmaline

For animals that suffered from a lack of love and attention - rose quartz, aventurine

For cheering animals up and dispelling depression - star sapphire, carnelian

For changing behavior patterns, especially when another animal is brought into the home - green calcite

For an animal that was physically or emotionally abused - celestite

To treat fears and anxiety - garnet

For animals lacking in energy - carnelian

For jealous animals - peridot

In order to better understand the animal, his behavior, his feelings, and even his "language," you should meditate with larimar. Wearing larimar or carrying it in your pocket is recommended for people who work with animals, and for anyone who wants to understand the animal better and more profoundly.

Treating plants with crystals

Plants, gardens, trees, and fields respond wonderfully to crystals. Often, you can see how a weak or dying plant revives and returns to its former self after a clear quartz crystal or some other suitable crystal has been placed beside it. The quartz crystal's electromagnetic energy has the ability to stimulate the chlorophyll in the plant's structure, thus encouraging new growth.

There are a number of ways in which to treat plants and the soil of the garden using crystals:

Watering the plant with water in which the crystal has been immersed.

Mixing sand (sand has a high concentration of quartz crystal).

Planting quartz crystals around the plants with only their apexes peeping out of the ground.

Placing any mineral or quartz crystal next to or opposite the plant, having tuned it to strengthen and treat the plant.

Networking the garden by means of the crystal.

Minerals that are suitable for treating plants and the garden

There are many crystals that can be used to strengthen garden plants, fruit trees, and field crops. Below are some of the most commonly used ones, but if you intuitively feel that a particular mineral you have on hand will do the job well, give it a chance.

Clear quartz crystal - Placing clear quartz crystal and using it in the ways described below produces excellent results in the treatment of plants. It helps make them healthy, strengthen them, and improve their growth.

An elixir for watering plants can be prepared from clear quartz crystal. This is not exactly an "elixir," because in this case, you can use a much larger quantity of water. The water is very effective for watering weak plants, plants that did not take well, or plants that were very slow in their growth, as opposed to other plants of the same type that were planted at the same time. When the plant is suffering from lack (that is, it is weak, slow in its growth, etc.), the quartz generator is generally suitable. However, you have to use your intuition. Link up to each of the quartz stones and ask to receive a sensory clue in order to know which of them is suitable for treating a certain plant. When you perform this intuitive test, stand next to the plant and link up to it, or see it in your mind's eye when you close your eyes, holding the clear quartz.

The elixir can be prepared in a large glass container, but also placing the stone in an opaque bucket will suffice. It is enough to place the stone in the water for about three hours. Afterwards, water the plant in exactly the way it should be watered – not too little and not too much. If it is a single plant, or plants that do not require much water, prepare a small amount each time. In addition, when preparing the soil for planting seedlings or seeds, you should wet it a few days before planting with water in which quartz has been immersed. However, make sure that the soil is not too moist to disturb the plant's growth. Quartz stones can also increase your "understanding" of the plants and the ability to link up to them and know them better.

Green tourmaline – Green tourmaline is wonderful for increasing the healing power of medicinal herbs. If you have a garden of medicinal herbs, you should place green tourmaline in the center of the garden, or water it with water in which green tourmaline has been immersed. Moreover, you can use green tourmaline to perform healing on a weak or sick plant. You can place the tourmaline opposite the plant, programming it to help heal the plant, or hold it above the plant for a few minutes, exactly as if you were performing healing on human beings (but for less time). You should perform the healing process several times – preferably on alternate days – or use your intuition to devise the appropriate treatment for the plant.

Lepidolite – It is a good idea to use lepidolite when we have doubts about the quality of the soil – not the actual "hole" in which the plant is planted, but rather the basic structure of the soil. An energetic networking must be performed using five lepidolite stones. Place one stone in the center of the garden, and four additional stones, one in each corner. You can also use four stones, without placing one in the center, or form a circle or triangle around the flowerbed or area of the garden that is not growing. In any event, use your intuition and your imagination and place the stones in a way that seems appropriate for your garden. In addition, lepidolite helps protect the plants against diseases and pests, and is good for increasing abundance in the case of fruit orchards, vegetable beds, beds of medicinal plants, and so on. You can place it next to the plant in order to protect it and increase the fruit or vegetable harvest, or water the plant with water in which lepidolite has been immersed.

Moss agate – Moss agate is a wonderful stone for fortifying and protecting plants. It can be placed in the pot in which the plant that is in need of strengthening is growing, opposite it, or you can water the plant with water in which moss agate has been immersed. It encourages good and healthy growth, and helps increase the fruit or vegetable harvest.

Dendritic agate – Dendritic agate operates in a similar way to moss agate. It can be used in the same ways. Moreover, it helps link up to and channel with the plant kingdom. You can hold it, or you can meditate with it when you want to discover things about a certain plant – how to take care of it and nurture it – or its special properties. The meditation must be performed in the vicinity of the plant, or you must visualize it in your mind's eye while holding the stone; then you can ask certain questions about it.

Green jasper – You should carry or wear green jasper when working in the garden, field, or orchard. Like dendritic agate, green jasper helps the person sense the plant's needs better, and opens a door to a more profound understanding of the plant world.

You must tune the crystal you select into strengthening the plants, protecting them against pests, absorbing minerals from the earth well, and so on. After that, you can place the crystal next to a particular plant, or use it to network the garden. In the same way, you should network around the trunks of trees or bushes. When it comes to medicinal plants, the crystal should be programmed to reinforce their properties. It is important to strengthen plants with crystals when moving them from one place to another, after they have been uprooted in order to be replanted in another place, or when they have undergone extreme changes in their growth environment (such as from a shady place to a sun-drenched location and so on).

Networking the garden using a quartz crystal

This method is good for treating every plant, and helps solve a broad range of problems that occur in plants. You must select five medium-size quartz crystals. Then, choose a particular square in your garden and plant four of the crystals in its corners. You must plant the crystals in the earth with just their apexes peeping out. Place the fifth crystal in the center of the square. If you notice that one of the plants is in a particularly debilitated state, and does not respond to the energy of the crystals you placed, extract one of the four crystals from the corners of the square and plant it next to the roots of the plant. It is important to leave the crystal in the center of the square where it is.

Taking care of pot plants

A plant that shows signs of wilting, is not strong enough, is not growing in a healthy manner, or is growing too slowly or distortedly, can be treated in two ways. One is to place a large or medium-size quartz crystal next to its roots. The second is to place a medium or large quartz generator opposite the plant, with its apex pointing at the plant. Often, the results of this treatment are surprising. The action of quartz crystal is very powerful, but if you are linked to or intuitively prefer one of the crystals mentioned previously, use it. Again, intuition is very important in treating plants, and there are many functions that are liable to be unbalanced and cause problems in the growth of the plant. Therefore, if you possess another crystal that you feel is suitable for treating the plant, cleanse it, charge it, and program it to do so. Place it next to the plant in any way you deem correct, or prepare irrigating water with it for the plant, and follow the progress of the procedure.

Wearing the stones – jewelry

The beauty of precious stones has made them expensive, heartwarming ornaments for thousands of years. They were worn in various ways and set into expensive metals. In various cultures (possibly in all), from ancient times up till today, jewelry containing stones was one of the most widespread forms of adornment, from strings of pebbles or shells to diamonds and sapphires set in gold or platinum. In various ancient civilizations, jewelry-makers were not only knowledgeable about how to cut and process stones, but also about the unique properties that were attributed to them, and the legends that had been spun about their tremendous power. They were set in earrings, pendants, necklaces, amulets, brooches, bracelets, rings, and crowns. The stones set in jewelry were used for protection, healing, recuperation, adornment, seduction, and many other properties. In some of the ancient cultures, the priests or tribal healers were the ones who matched the person with the stone he should wear. The stones were set into the crowns of kings and emperors, priests, rajahs, czars, and popes – as well as in the breastplate of the High Priest, so that he could communicate with the highest power. In the royal crowns, the good stones were used to "charge" the king, in the same way as a good stone is placed on the crown chakra in order to protect it and increase its power. The Tibetan sages cherished and admired five sacred stones and metals: quartz, which symbolizes light; turquoise, which symbolizes the eternity of sea and sky; coral, which symbolizes the power of life and the existence of form; gold, which symbolizes the suns life-giving rays; and silver, which symbolizes the light of the moon. The Native Americans would wear turquoise for protection, and believed that it stored the earth's atmosphere inside it; they would wear coral for strengthening the blood and the life force. Before Christianity, the Holy Grail, from which Jesus drank before his death, was set with a marvelous stone, similar in appearance to the emerald (some people think that the stone was moldavite). The High Priest wore a breastplate with emerald, diamond, amethyst, jasper, topaz, sapphire, agate, onyx, garnet, ruby, opal, and aquamarine set in it.

Unfortunately, a large part of the knowledge and wisdom concerning healing and using stones disappeared together with the traditions of those ancient cultures, and has only recently begun to return. During those years, precious stones became objects or ornaments that people were proud of, and would show off, with absolutely no idea of their tremendous power and properties that far exceeded their beauty. Nowadays, when this knowledge is being rediscovered and is returning to us, we can again use stones as marvelous, healing, developing, and balancing jewels.

When we choose to wear a stone as a jewel, set it in a jewel, or create a string of several stones, there are certain rules that we must pay attention to. Certain stones link up to certain metals, while others are liable to harm their power. Certain method of setting are liable to diminish the stone's power. Moreover, we have to think what our aim is in wearing the stone, and, accordingly, wear it on the appropriate area of our body.

There are a few points that we must take into account when we set about creating jewelry from stones:

The color of the stones has a significant influence on the energies of the bodies and the chakras. The correct matching of the colors of the various stones in a jewel or string must be performed – energetically suitable colors, colors from the same family, or complementary colors (see the chapter on color energy).

Glue – Contact glue and other glues made of organic materials, animal components and so on, are in no way suitable for gluing the stone to the jewel, and must not be used.

Gold – Gold is a metal that is suitable for setting all stones. Because it is so expensive, it is worthwhile checking to see if the stones can be set in another metal, especially if the stone is not a polished gemstone and is not one of the most expensive stones. Although gold is suitable for all stones, some of them should rather be set in other metals.

Brass – Brass, like gold, is suitable for setting all stones, and can be used for less expensive stones. It is preferable not to set stones that are highly polished in brass.

Silver – Silver is particularly suitable for setting the various types of agates, amethyst, stones that belong to the moonstone group, diamonds, opals, cat's eye, and lapis lazuli. In addition, it is suitable for setting all the "mineral" stones, but stones that are not minerals, such as petrified wood and amber. The tourmaline stones and zircon are also not suitable for being set in silver.

Copper – Copper is suitable for setting all the stones that contain copper (such as chalcopyrite, turquoise, and so on). It is suitable for chrysocolla, tiger eye, mica stones (sparkling), rhodonite, aventurine, and amethyst. It is not suitable for setting quartz crystals and polished stones (except for amethyst, which belongs to the quartz family, but is suitable for setting in copper, which actually strengthens its power). Pearls, fossils, and corals are not recommended for setting in copper.

Platinum – This expensive metal is suitable for setting all the precious stones – the tourmalines (especially if they are highly polished), zircons, topaz (especially polished), sapphires, diamonds and rubies.

To make a necklace, thread of organic origin, such as silk, cotton, or leather can be used. Strong nylon thread is also very suitable.

It is possible to use various metal threads – copper, silver, and gold – to make a grip for a stone. Precious stones should not be set in this way, but more common stones, such as carnelian, tiger eye and so on, blend well with copper threads or a leather string.

The energies of the stones of organic origin, such as petrified wood, fossils, amber, coral, or shells, link up harmoniously to natural energies, earth energies, and natural substances such as feathers, wood furniture, fresh and dried leaves, fresh and dried flowers, and leather. (Bear in mind that some people are not comfortable wearing leather). For this reason, they can be combined to create beautiful and interesting assemblages. This kind of composition links up to certain people, especially those who work with various shamanic methods or according to Native American traditions.

When the stone is set in silver or gold, the metal generally supports the crystal in order to increase the power of its properties.

Gold is the best conductor of energy, It stimulates and strengthens the stone's energy, similar to the action of the sun on the stones. It possesses exalted qualities of its own, and is preferred by many people because of its beauty, and the fact that it emanates wealth and power.

Silver, on the other hand, represents the moon's energy. It stabilizes the energies of the stones set in it, and guards these energies, but does not strengthen them. For this reason, the main difference between gold and silver is that gold stimulates the stone's energy and fortifies it, while silver stabilizes the stone's energy and preserves its natural properties. We must take these things into account when deciding between setting the stone in silver or gold.

Platinum is the most expensive metal. For this reason, the stone that is set in it must be of great value, great power, high energy, and a strong shine, in order to cope with the power of the metal itself. Diamonds, of course, are very suitable for setting in platinum, but rubies, emeralds, and sapphires also have sufficiently strong energy and shine to be set in platinum. We are referring, of course, to polished, shiny, high-quality stones. (All the above mentioned stones also occur in a raw, unpolished form, and are significantly cheaper than polished stones.)

Copper acts as a conductor when it is worn on the body. In that way, it helps the stone's energies interact with the body's energies. In the main, it is customary to set minerals with a high copper content in it. When malachite, turquoise, azurite or chalcopyrite is set in copper, the jewel can be effective and very powerful. When gold or silver is combined in a copper jewel, the copper increases the energies of the other metals. A jewel that includes those metals increases the power of the stone, and will preserve and strengthen its beauty.

Brass, a golden metal that is not expensive, is sometimes used as a substitute for gold. Brass, similar to copper, strengthens the interaction of the stone's energies with the body's energies. Setting stones in brass and bronze emphasizes the wealth of the stones' colors.

When we set a number of stones together, or make a string of stones, we must pay attention that their properties do not clash, contradict, or disturb one another. For this reason, it is a good idea to read, check, and activate one's intuition before setting several stones together. The best way is to feel the stones we want to set, link up to their energies, and try to sense whether they operate harmoniously together or whether they create different sensations entirely. In addition, "channeling" stones, such as moldavite, labradorite, selenite, and so on, whose main action is to open spiritual channels, should not be worn together. Each one of them has such a strong action that the person who wears two of them, or holds more than one of them at the same time, is liable to "float." In principle, these stones should not be worn as a "decoration," but rather for a certain purpose, since they are liable to interfere with the practical, everyday activities because of their tendency to induce a meditative or linked-up state in the person.

Where must the stone be worn?
After surveying the various ways of setting the stone or creating a clasp for it, the question arises about where to wear it. As we said before, stones can be used as earrings, pendants, necklaces, rings, and so on. There is great significance to the location of the stone on our bodies. As we saw in the chapter on the chakras, when we wear a stone in the vicinity of a certain chakra, it influences the action of that chakra. Of course, certain stones can activate all the chakras, while others are suitable for stimulating, balancing, and opening certain chakras, and strengthening their power.

The right side of the body and the left side of the body
When we wear a bracelet, an ankle bracelet, a brooch or a ring, the side of the body on which we wear the jewel is significant. The left side of the body is the more receptive, sensitive side. The left side tends to pick up the energies that are poured into it more quickly. Wearing the stone on the organs of the left side of the body is effective for controlling and neutralizing external energies (especially stones with protective properties). The right side is the "giving," projecting side. Wearing stones on the organs of the right side of the body strengthens our abilities, the ability to project our personality, to accomplish, and to produce.

The hands

We use our hands for all our everyday actions. We express ourselves with them, perform tasks and actions, create, give love and warmth, and heal with them. They constitute a kind of "visiting card" of the person, but that is not all. The hands, like the feet, are body parts that contain all the organs of the body on their surface, like a map.

Every hand (and every finger) has a different receiving and transmitting ability.

The right hand, for most people, is the transmitting, radiating, giving hand.
The left hand, for most people, is the receiving, sensing, feeling hand.

Rings

Rings of all kinds attract the eye. Their uniqueness lies in the fact the we ourselves can easily look at the stone that we are wearing, focus on it, and feel it visually. There is a great deal of significance to the finger on which we wear a ring.

The thumb represents mainly will power, but also logic and thought. Because of this, it is generally free of rings and independent. Moreover, from the practical point of view, a ring on the thumb is not particularly comfortable.

The index finger represents direction, action, expression, and self-esteem. Wearing a ring on the index finger can affect the ability to express oneself and to communicate, as well as wishes, passions, objectives, and dreams. The index finger on the left hand helps internalize these abilities, and increase inner communication and self-understanding. Wearing a ring set with a gemstone on the index finger of the right hand externalizes these abilities in preparation for their realization and activation. There are several stones that people are in the habit of wearing on the index finger. Garnet, moonstone, mother of pearl, when worn on the index finger, inspire self-love and self-acceptance, as well as love of others; carnelian stimulates achievement-orientation, accomplishment of objectives, and action; lapis lazuli stimulates wisdom, intelligence, and knowledge; turquoise, sodalite, and chrysocolla induce calmness and a feeling of serenity.

The middle finger represents intuition, inspiration, and equilibrium. It is customary to wear a ring on it only when we want to stimulate inspiration and develop the intuition. Amethyst is very suitable for wearing on this finger, in order to stimulate intuition and creativity. In order to increase inner beauty, rubies are customarily worn on this finger. Crystals and sapphires that are worn on the middle finger help us find our direction and vocation in life, and reach exalted goals.

The fourth finger represents creativity. When we want to stimulate creativity, receive and absorb, we wear a ring on the fourth finger of the left hand. When we want to apply and transmit creative frequencies, we wear a ring on the fourth finger of the right hand. It is customary, as we know, to wear a diamond ring on the fourth finger. A diamond on this finger helps strengthen love relationships. Wearing an emerald on the fourth finger helps stimulate creativity as well as receive new and original ideas. In order to express and give love, it is customary to wear moonstone on this finger. Tiger eye and cat's eye help focus the creativity into the required action. In order to link intuition to practicality, turquoise should be worn on this finger. In order to stimulate and strengthen abilities and desires to help others, opal should be worn.

The pinkie represents change, acceptance and understanding of change. Wearing a ring set with stones on the right pinkie helps us use our power to influence the changes that we are undergoing. Wearing a ring on the left pinkie helps us accept them. Wearing a pearl on the pinkie soothes the nervous system and the mind. When we want to get new opportunities, it is advisable to wear aventurine on this finger.

Despite everything that has been said above, it is very important to heed inner feelings. When we want to decide on which finger to wear a ring with a fine stone in it, it is important to feel if it is indeed suitable, if the feeling is good, and, especially, what feeling is transmitted to us.

In left-handed people – but in others, too – there is sometimes interchangeability between the functioning of the left and right sides. There are cases in which people report a receiving right side and a giving left side, and this must be taken into account.

Bracelets

Bracelets are generally worn in the region of the pulse. It is interesting to note that there are people who cannot wear a wristwatch. Often, the reason for this is the quartz in the mechanism of the watch.

When choosing a stone for a bracelet, it is advisable to choose protective or soothing stones. Bracelets or strings of stones for the wrist made of shells, mother of pearl, turquoise, or tourmaline, can help release the cumulative energies of stress.

A bracelet made of small tourmaline beads or fragments in green, white, black, and pink, threaded onto fishing line (nylon thread), provides excellent protection, and is used by people who are engaged in healing and various treatments.

A chain that is worn on the upper part of the arm can help stimulate courage and power.

The neck

In the region of the neck, and below it, in the area of the hollow between the clavicle bones, is the throat chakra. For this reason, any jewel that is worn in the region affects the functions of the throat chakra (see the chapter on the chakras). In addition, the throat is the center where our thought and emotional patterns are stored, because it is the physical link between emotion and reason. Wearing jewels around the neck is likely to positively affect our ability to liberate ourselves from old, non-positive patterns. The neck is the center that represents the ability to change, the ability to accept changes, and flexibility.

Pendants and necklaces

Pendants, necklaces, and strings of beads that are worn around the neck affect the throat chakra and the communicative and expressive abilities, both with oneself and with others. There are wonderful stones to wear around the neck – green calcite, for instance, worn around the neck on a string or as a pendant close to the neck, helps change non-positive thought patterns. Stones that stimulate the throat chakra are suitable for wearing on the throat. Stones that stimulate self-love and inspire self-esteem and a positive self-image, such as rose quartz, are also excellent. A string of pearls helps build a positive personal image.

Medallions

A medallion is a wonderful way of wearing gemstones and minerals. The length of the chain can be adjusted so that the medallion touches the throat chakra, the heart chakra, or the solar plexus chakra. The stones that are suitable for a medallion are many and varied, and we can match the stone to the chakra we want to open and balance, and wear a medallion at the appropriate length. A medallion that hangs onto the chest can contain rose quartz, which is marvelous for calming down, for opening up the heart, and for increasing self-love and love for others. Tiger eye can increase courage and charisma, mainly when it hangs below the area of the diaphragm (the solar plexus chakra). A pyrite medallion grants protection, as does black tourmaline. The combinations and the possibilities are many, and, of course, intuition and inner feelings play an important role in deciding on a suitable stone and the length of the chain.

The ears

The ears symbolize our ability to hear, both in a physical and an extrasensory manner. Wearing stones in the ears as earrings can help us strengthen physical hearing and the extrasensory hearing ability. In addition, wearing stones on the ears has an effect on the upper chakras and on the action of the brain.

Earrings

Earrings made with precious stones have an effect on the entire body. They help create balance between the right and left sides of the brain. Stones of the third eye, such as amethyst and sodalite, are highly recommended. Diamonds, too, are good as earrings, especially before any kind of spiritual activity. On the other hand, opals and lapis lazuli are sometimes unpleasant and are not suitable for wearing in earrings, since they are liable to cause dizziness. Sapphires, pearls, and zircons are also stones that are suitable for wearing in earrings. Sapphires stimulate wisdom and knowledge. Wearing tiger eye as earrings increases the person's charisma and courage, and is wonderful before becoming friends with people. Rose quartz in earrings is considered to be a stone that prevents wrinkles and stimulates facial beauty. Jade is also a wonderful stone for earrings and it instills a feeling of calmness and tranquillity in the wearer. Stones that stimulate various mental abilities can be worn as earrings, as can stones that augment personal power and charisma, and stones that stimulate feelings of love. It is important to try earrings on before purchasing them, or check to see how you feel when the stone is close to the ear before setting it in an earring.

Hairpins and tiaras

A tiara is an item of jewelry that is worn on the head or on the forehead, similar to a crown. When we choose to set a gemstone in a tiara or a hairpin, we must take into account the fact that it is placed on the crown chakra. Therefore, various grounding stones, stones that are suitable for the base chakra and more earthy stones, are not suitable. In contrast, channeling stones are suitable for setting in a hairpin that we use during the course of healing treatments, meditation, and so on, but are liable to cause us to float and to be impractical in everyday life. Smoky quartz, sodalite, amethyst, sapphires, zircons, and emeralds are suitable. Zircons are especially suitable for setting in tiaras. In any case, a stone should not be set in a hairpin, nor a hairpin with a stone set in it purchased before checking thoroughly and with full concentration what sensation the stone causes. An unsuitable stone is liable to cause dizziness or unpleasant sensations. Stones that are suitable for setting in hairpins and tiaras are mainly the stones that contribute to the development of the personality and to spiritual growth, but do not cause significant floating.

Belts

Belts inlaid with stones and minerals can affect our level of vitality. Orange stones such as garnet and carnelian on a belt that is worn relatively low may be suitable. Belts inlaid with turquoise can cause an energetic or a soothing feeling. Carnelian helps raise motivation when it is worn in the region of the waist, agates increase energy, and jaspers and shells help achieve a sense of equilibrium. Quartz stones are generally not suitable. Some people say that wearing coral and bloodstone at the waist helps increase health.

Carrying stones in one's pockets

While this is not, in fact, a way of wearing stones, it is a very effective way to use them. It is advisable to put stones that are suitable for the heart chakra, such as aventurine or rose quartz, in the breast pocket of a shirt. Stones kept in pants pockets, in the thigh area, can affect our actions and deeds. It is advisable to keep a stone in our pocket when seeking employment (orange, reddish, and golden stones, such as tiger eye, red moss agate, carnelian, garnet are all highly recommended), attending a business appointment, going on a date (stones of love, self-love, and confidence, if need be), participating in events in front of an audience or stressful events, meeting with people who stimulate non-positive energies, or are inclined to "suck" our energy (protective stones, of course), and many other possibilities.

Ankle bracelet

After discussing most of the body regions where jewelry can be worn, we are left with the ankles. Wearing an ankle bracelet is fashionable today, but was also popular in ancient times. On the ankle, it is customary to wears stones that strengthen the body and increase physical abilities. Moreover, grounding stones on the ankle can be of assistance to "spaced-out" people, or for people who engage in meditation and mysticism, and need to come down to earth and be more practical and grounded. In addition, some people put stones in their shoes or wear them on their ankle in order to treat various addiction problems. People who come out of a healing lesson or meditation, and feel as if they are walking on air can put a stone such as jasper in their shoe in order to return to physical reality.

Meditation using crystals

One of the most widespread uses of crystals is for purposes of meditation and expanding awareness. Crystals have a marvelous ability to help us during meditation – to calm down, to enter a state of alpha waves, and to sink into deep meditation.

Various crystals are used for this purpose – to facilitate meditation. Other crystals can help us see various visions, receive exalted information, and even channel with superior spiritual beings. There are crystals that enable us to treat body and mind while meditating with them. There are many ways to meditate using crystals. The simplest is just to hold a purified and charged crystal, close your eyes, relax your body, take conscious breaths – and surrender to the feeling. I have chosen a number of interesting forms of meditation, and, according to them, and your imagination, you can prepare various meditations and undergo marvelous spiritual experiences using crystals.

There are a number of rules that should be applied during any form of meditation. While performing the meditations, we must ensure that the surroundings are clean of negative energies. It is possible to purify the room by means of incense or an essential oil burner. The oils of absolute jasmine and frankincense are excellent for creating a calm atmosphere and spiritual opening. Meditation should be performed in a room in which there are no interfering energies from electrical appliances such as microwave ovens, TV sets, or computers. Designating a corner in a room for meditation can prove to be especially effective. This corner will gradually adopt soothing, meditative frequencies that will make it easier for us to enter a meditative state. In addition, telephones should be turned off, and we should ensure that we are not disturbed during the time allocated for meditation. Some of the meditations can be performed either lying down or seated. People who are inclined to fall asleep during meditation are advised to do it sitting up. Whether the meditation is performed sitting up or lying down, the position must be comfortable, and the body must be relaxed and at ease. An extremely important point is making sure to breathe consciously – deep regular breaths throughout the whole meditation.

You should read each meditation below twice or three times before applying it, and prepare all the necessary aids.

Crystal meditation for expanding the consciousness

Clear quartz crystal is a wonderful tool for strengthening any meditation, and it can be used for meditating calmly and tranquilly, sometimes with the expectation of seeing splendid visions. The following meditation often evokes visions and pictures of crystal palaces or caves of crystals. The things that happen in those places can be surprising and wonderful.

Perform the meditation in a quite, relaxed place that is clean of unwanted energies. You can pass a stick of incense through the room in order to remove previous energies, and you can, of course, open the windows and air the room well before performing the meditation. You can put on quiet and pleasant meditative music, but it is possible to meditate without music. For the meditation, you need a purified and charged quartz crystal.

Lie comfortably on your back, close your eyes, and begin to take slow, deep breaths. Contract the muscles of your feet, and relax them. Contract your calf muscles, and relax them. Continue in this way, relaxing all the muscles of your body, from bottom to top. Do not forget to contract and relax your facial muscles. The contraction must be substantial, and the relaxation full. When you feel completely relaxed, place the quartz crystal on your third eye. Continue taking deep breaths during the entire process. Now, let your sensations carry you away, without stopping them or trying to control them. Clean your brain of every thought and emotion, and simply accept the feelings and visions that begin to emerge. After about 15 to 20 minutes of meditation, you must remove the crystal from the third eye and begin to get out of the meditative state. You can set an alarm clock with a quiet, gentle ring, or, if you are particularly sensitive to music, you can see that the tape plays only 15 to 20 minutes of music, so that the cessation of the music serves as a sign for you to stop the meditation. Do not leave the meditative state abruptly. At first, shake your feet a little bit, feel your body lying on the mattress, the contact of the mattress with your body, your organs, and slowly open your eyes.

Meditation to clear the mind

Meditation to clear the mind provides mental calmness and quiet. It is excellent for people who are greatly troubled during the day by work matters, studies, child-minding, and so on. It helps dispel mental stress and pressures. To this end it is wonderful to perform before sleeping or resting, when the person is troubled by numerous thoughts and finds it difficult to calm down. The second aim of the meditation is to teach the person to enter a meditative state so that he can perform more complicated meditations, or ones that include mantras or visualizations, more easily. People who find it difficult to enter a meditative state are advised to practice meditation daily for a certain period of time. In this meditation, no visualization, verbal or thought techniques must be used. As its name indicates, it is used for clearing the mind only.

Perform the meditation in a room that is quiet and energetically clean, with a nice and pleasant atmosphere. You can also do it in the office, as long as you are not disturbed. If there are electrical appliances that emit radiation, such as a computer, cover it with fabric. Ensure that you will not be disturbed for 20-25 minutes. You should light an oil burner containing lavender oil, and play quiet, harmonious, meditative background music.

In order to perform the meditation, you will need a straight-backed chair, and two medium-size pieces of amethyst, purified and charged. You can program them to calm down the thoughts and clear the mind.

Sit on the chair with your feet firmly on the floor. Place the pieces of amethyst within reach, on a table or a stool beside you. Contract your foot muscles, and relax them. Contract your calf muscles tightly, and relax. Contract your thigh muscles and relax. Contract your buttock muscles, and relax. Continue contracting the muscles of the various body parts, in order – your back muscles, shoulder muscles, hand muscles (clench your fists tightly and relax them), your forearm muscles, your upper arm muscles, and your shoulders. Contract your neck muscles and relax. Contract all your facial muscles (screw up your face) – jaw, cheeks, lips, eyes, and forehead. Contract and relax your forehead several times.

Take one of the pieces of amethyst in your right hand, and the other in your left hand. Close your eyes (if you have not already done so) and take deep, slow, and steady breaths. Concentrate totally on your breathing. Feel yourself become more and more calm and serene, the longer you concentrate on breathing. Nothing exists other than that, and nothing distracts you. Feel the pleasant and calming currents, the harmonious frequencies, that are transmitted to you from the amethysts in your hands. Continue like this for about 20 minutes.

At the end of the meditation, wriggle around on the chair a bit, turn your ankles around, and stretch gently. Place the pieces of amethyst to one side. Almost certainly, you will feel calm and full of gentle, harmonious, and balanced energy after the meditation. It would be better if you did not get straight down to work or any other practical matter. If you still have ten minutes before the end of your break, or 10-15 minutes until you have to get back to your regular activities, spend them looking at the scenery outside the window. You can go out for a brief walk, weather permitting, or stare at the green lawn, the trees, the passing combinations of cloud and sky. Despite the simplicity of this meditation, it possesses exceptional qualities and exerts a significant effect on everyday life, and on physical and mental health. After the meditation, you might find that your brain operates more clearly or quickly, and much more lucidly. In the longer range, performing this meditation exercise frequently leads to several positive results. The meditation helps increase the effectiveness of the immune system, reduce stress and its harmful consequences, lower blood pressure, loosen the muscles, and clarify and elucidate thought. It facilitates the person's ability to enter into various meditative states more smoothly and profoundly, and it helps develop spirituality and intuitive perception.

Grounding meditation

This unique meditation helps us feel our link with the soil and with the planet Earth. It stabilizes, centers, and grounds, in the positive sense of grounding. It is very suitable for people who are inclined to "float," daydream, or consciously lose contact with reality. In addition, it is good for people who engage in meditation and astral travel regularly.

For this meditation, you need a smoky quartz crystal. Find a pleasant place with positive energies in which there are nice-looking trees. You can even choose a tree that you know and love, but in any event, the tree that is used for charging the crystal must be healthy, stable, and strong. Bury the cleansed and purified smoky quartz in the ground, among the roots of the tree, for a whole day. Mark the place where the crystal is buried so that you can find it the next day. It must be buried and entirely covered with earth. After the crystal has been in the earth for 24 hours, take it out and shake the dirt off. Do not wash it.

Sit in an easy chair in a clean, calm, and quiet place. You do not need music for this meditation. Begin taking deep, slow breaths, and relaxing your body. Hold the smoky quartz crystal in both hands, and stare at it. If the crystal is especially big, you can place it on a table in front of you, or just hold it. Feel the vibrations, and link up to them. Close your eyes. See the smoky quartz crystal moving away, and getting bigger and more powerful, until it reaches gigantic proportions. Send your mind into the smoky quartz crystal. Inside the crystal, see a big, strong, and sturdy tree. You may see the same tree as the one among whose roots you buried the crystal. You may see another tree. If you see a tree that does not look strong and sturdy, or does not have a good appearance, beautify and strengthen it with the power of your imagination. See the roots of the tree. They are strong, long, and thick, and penetrate the bowels of the earth. In your mind's eye, see yourself going up to the tree. Touch it, stroke it, or embrace it, whatever you feel is right. Afterwards, see yourself sitting and leaning against the strong trunk of the tree. Now, slowly and confidently concentrate your awareness on the base chakra. Distinguish the shining red color of the chakra. See how a current of red light descends from the chakra into the bowels of the earth. When you inhale, see how golden light ascends via the current of grounding light into your base chakra. Exhaling, see the chakra revolve, its light and color strengthening and growing deeper. Feel and be aware of the energy of the earth that is below you. Be aware of the confidence it bestows, and the feeling of nutrition and protection that flow from it to you. Feel your link to the earth and to nature, and let yourself draw courage, stability, and confidence from them. After you have strengthened the color of the base chakra several times by revolving it during exhalation, inhale the golden-red energy of Mother Earth via all the chakras. See how the light spreads through all the chakras, fills the body, and flows from the crown chakra to the aura while filling, reinforcing, and strengthening it. When exhaling, see the light that envelops the aura descend toward the bowels of the earth. Now look at the long, strong branches of the tree. See yourself in your mind's eye straightening up, standing, and lifting your hands heavenward, as if they were branches. See a clear and brilliant sun above you. See a ray of white light coming out of the sun, flowing, entering and filling the crown chakra. The white light descends via the crown chakra and passes through all the chakras, purifying, cleansing, and activating them gently. The white light cleanses all the chakras, and continues to descend via the line of light that links you to the bowels of the earth. When it goes down into the bowels of the earth, see how it cleanses and extracts all the negativity, and takes it down to the bowels of the earth. There it is recycled and transformed into positive, nutritious energies. Continue imagining in your mind's eye how the non-positive energies all leave your body and descend to the bowels of the earth. Continue with this until you feel cleansed, purified, and fortified. Afterwards, take a number of deep, slow breaths, and start to see the gigantic smoky quartz approaching, returning to its normal proportions as it does so. Begin to feel your body. Feel your feet, your hands. Concentrate on the sensations of your body. See yourself inside your body. Feel the chair beneath you. Let the smoky quartz crystal that you saw opposite you disappear. Feel yourself here in the room once more. Twist your feet around, and move your fingers. Gradually open your eyes. Turn your calves and arms around slowly, until you feel stable, and can stand up and perform a few movements to limber up. If you still feel a bit "frozen," do a few jumps and arm movements.

Meditation to get to know the crystal's guardian

Every crystal has its own personality. Just like no two human beings are absolutely identical, and there will always be significant differences between them on the various levels, so it is with crystals. Each crystal has a purpose, knowledge and a way that is unique to it. Think about it – the crystal that you are holding in your hand is thousands, hundreds of thousands, or millions of years old! It has come a long way. It may have been held in its present form in the hands of ancient wizards and sages. It may have been used for healing, expanding awareness, receiving knowledge, or establishing contact with various spiritual entities.

Each crystal has a "guardian." The crystal's guardian is some kind of spiritual entity that accompanies the crystal along its lengthy path. This image can be embodied in front of your eyes in some kind of form that can be seen and understood by human beings – as a young or old person, as a man or a woman, or even as an animal. The form it takes is significant, and indicates the qualities and uniqueness of the crystal.

You may possess a crystal to which you feel that you are particularly linked. You like it, appreciate it, and feel an unusual bond with it. This crystal, like other crystals, did not reach you by coincidence. Although you can read over and over again about the properties attributed to crystals of the type that you are holding, they will never be absolutely accurate, and will not express all the "personal" properties of the crystal. This is because among all the amethysts, the clear quartz crystals and so on, each one has its own personal uniqueness. Getting to know the crystal's guardian will help you understand in depth the significance of the appearance of this crystal in your life. It can explain to you the best way to take care of and use the crystal. Why, of all the stones, was this one chosen to be your constant companion? It is likely to reveal wonderful things to you about the crystal kingdom in general, and about yourself. These impressions may well be marvelous and deeply impressive, and you may well want to write them down immediately after the meditation, or record them, or tell a friend about them. If you perform the meditation in the presence of a close and beloved friend, you can ask him to knock on a Tibetan bowl a few times. This special sound can help you enter this unique meditative state much more easily. You could also put on a tape of knocking on a Tibetan bowl, or wind chimes. Music for its own sake is liable not only not to help, but to distract your train of thought to another channel, pleasant as it might be, but not the aim of this meditation.

Perform the meditation in a room with a good atmosphere, physically and energetically clean. A cleansed, purified, and charged amethyst cluster can be very helpful, as can an essential oil burner with absolute jasmine oil or frankincense. Incense or synthetic oils are not recommended. Withdraw into yourself for about half an hour, during which time you are not to be disturbed under any circumstances. Turn off the phones. In order to get better results, perform the meditation when you are calm, tranquil, and comfortable, and not disturbed by anything.

Take your special crystal – the one whose guardian you want to get to know. After purifying and charging it, hold it in your hands, and convey to it lovingly that you want to get to know its crystal guardian. Address it directly; it is well aware of the message that you are sending it. The meditation can be performed seated or lying down, but because it evokes deeper meditative levels, you should do it sitting up if you have a tendency to fall asleep easily.

Sit or lie comfortably. Hold the crystal in both hands. Relax your body (if you are a bit tense physically, perform the physical relaxation described in the mind-clearing meditation), close your eyes, and take a few slow, deep breaths. With every exhalation, feel all the tensions leaving your body, and your mind being emptied of everyday thoughts. With each exhalation, you are becoming calmer and calmer.

See a red light emanating from your base chakra, dividing along your two legs, and, like the roots of a tree, descending into the bowels of the earth while stabilizing you and safeguarding your connection with the earth. Allow your spirit to leave your body. You might see it as an image resembling you, or as a shining etheric substance. Let it go, watching it becoming smaller, until the crystal you are holding is larger than it. Get inside it, and stay there for some time, looking around you. Feel it while you are inside it. You can look outside, from within the crystal.

While you are still inside the crystal, looking and studying your surroundings, notice the passage that has opened up in one of the crystal's walls, or in its floor. Step into the passage fearlessly. Nothing but nice and pleasant surprises await you. While you are walking along the passage, perhaps going up or down stairs, you will see a plume of light appearing in the passage, seeming to call you. The more you advance toward it, the stronger it gets. A turn appears in the passage, and you make the turn. You enter a large hall made entirely of crystals. These can be crystals of the same type you are holding, the very same crystal (so you feel), or different crystals. The huge hall is totally illuminated with very bright light, with sparkles of light that play mischievously among the various crystals. Opposite you stands the crystal's guardian. It can be some kind of human creature – man / woman – or an animal, or an entity with another form. It can also appear as a unique plume of light. It does not matter in which form it appears – it will be able to answer your questions. It welcomes you lovingly, and you can channel with each other easily, via your thoughts. The crystal's guardian will bless you in its way, and will invite you to stay with it a little.

Now you can ask it what the nature of the relationship between you and your favorite crystal is, why it landed up with you, what it experienced in its long life, what its role in your life is, or any other question you may think of. Engrave the answers supplied by the crystal's guardian well in your awareness. You can also asking various questions about yourself, your vocation, your life, relationships, previous lives, or anything else that you feel is appropriate and correct.

When you feel that the time has come to part, thank the crystal's guardian warmly and bid him farewell. Walk toward the passage. Walk along the passage until you reach the crystal room where you were at the beginning of the meditation. Feel your spirit being drawn into your body once more. Your body is growing, until it returns to its original size. Concentrate on your breathing, and feel yourself returning to your regular state of consciousness. If you experience some difficulty leaving the state of consciousness you were in before, see two pieces of hematite in your hands, and feel how they ground you and wake you up. Feel the back of the chair, the chair beneath you, your feet firm on the floor. If you are lying down, feel the heaviness of your body on the bed, and the touch of the mattress and of your clothes. Take a few deep breaths, twist your ankles around, move your toes, stretch your body slightly, and move your limbs gently. When you feel ready, open your eyes. Sit or lie with open eyes for a few minutes. When you get up, you may want to write down what you saw in a special notebook, record your impressions on tape, or tell a friend. In any event, keep the things revealed to you by the crystal's guardian in your mind and memory.

Meditation, crystals, and chakras

As you read in the Introduction, each of the chakras has a specific function that affects our entire lives. Crystals have an enormous effect on the chakras. They constitute one of the simplest and most effective ways of balancing, opening, and cleansing the chakras. When you set out to work on the chakras, you can avail yourself of the chapter that describes the action of each stone on a particular chakra. You can also use the following techniques that help open, balance, cleanse, and activate the chakras by means of meditation with crystals. In the chapter on colors, you can see how to match a stone, even if you do not know its name or actions, to the chakra for which it is suitable. Below are a number of ways for balancing the chakras, and several suggestions for treating each one. I have presented the meditations according to the order of their development, rather than according to the order of the chakras. For this reason, you should read all the meditations, and only then decide which one to start meditating with in order to balance the chakras.

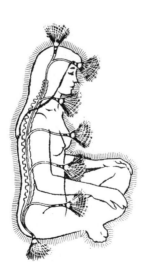

Balancing chakras

Balancing chakras by means of clear quartz crystal

This is a simple and easy technique for balancing the chakras. Choose a medium-size clear quartz crystal. You can use a generator or any other form of quartz crystal to which you feel linked. Cleanse the crystal well and charge it using one of the methods mentioned previously. After charging it, hold the crystal in both hands, and program it for balancing.

You can apply the technique standing up, sitting, or lying down – the main thing being that you are comfortable. Start relaxing your body, while you take deep, slow breaths.

Hold the crystal above the crown chakra. Feel if the area of the chakra feels warm and vibrating. If the area feels lifeless, there is probably a blockage, or an incorrect flow of energy, or some kind of stagnation. In your thoughts, express your desire to balance the chakra, and breathe via the crystal. With each inhalation, see the chakra wheel revolving. Directing the turn of the wheel is intuitive. In general, clockwise is used for opening, and counter-clockwise for closing. Having said that, let the scenes pass in front of your eyes, and see the chakra turning in whichever direction without influencing the direction. If you feel that it is being opened, think, while breathing, that it is opening. See white light descending via the chakra, turning it and descending from it via the other chakras. Do not concentrate on them for the moment, but rather on the crown chakra. When exhaling, aim for the cleansing of the chakra. Every unwanted thing descends from the chakra, via the spinal column, the legs, into the bowels of the earth. Continue in this way for two minutes only. You should not concentrate on the crown chakra for too long.

After you have balanced and opened the crown chakra, repeat the procedure with each of the other chakras. Do not spend too much time balancing the third eye chakra, either. Three to four minutes is the maximum in this technique. You can focus on the lower chakras for a longer time, even ten minutes, as necessary. Continue balancing until you feel a pleasant warmth and vitality in the region of the chakra.

After balancing the chakras, cleanse the crystal, rinse it under running water for about three minutes, and concentrate on washing all the unwanted energies off into the bowels of the earth. Place it on a crystal cluster for about three hours for charging. (If you do not possess a crystal cluster, place it outside, or on a windowsill without a glass partition for 24 hours.)

Using crystals to treat the solar plexus chakra and its functions

Charging the solar plexus chakra
Mediation for developing will power, increasing self-confidence and energy

Using crystals, we can open our awareness, receive exalted insights, and understand and acquire knowledge pertaining to the paths we have to follow. However, taking this path is liable to demand an enormous amount of will power. By means of will power, it is possible to transmit the information from the realm of thought to the realm of action and realization. Will power is linked to the activity of the third chakra – the solar plexus chakra. By means of charging and increasing the strength of this chakra, it is possible to reinforce will power and determination. The meditation for charging the solar plexus chakra increases self-confidence, charges the aura, and fills the entire body and sympathetic nervous system with energy. It increases and strengthens the health and vitality of the body. It is a wonderful meditation for people who feel that they are not in control of their lives, and lack confidence and will power, for people who let others control them and do not know how to say "no." The meditation helps strengthen the ability to focus and concentrate, and the ability to control one's thoughts and desires.

This meditation is not recommended for people with a "serious" ego, for manipulative people, for people who manipulate others in order to attain their wishes, or for people with "exaggerated" self-confidence. These people must use techniques for balancing the chakra, not for charging it. It is possible, of course, that this behavior stems from weakness or a lack in the chakra, but the advantages that are derived from this meditation are liable to be incorrectly understood by them. Check yourself before you start this meditation, and see whether it is really suitable and necessary for you.

You must always be careful not to get out of balance, and not to overcharge one chakra so that the balance between it and the other chakras is upset. In order to prevent this, you can, at a certain point in the meditation, see the light flowing from the solar plexus chakra to the rest of the chakras that are above and below it, and filling them.

In order to apply the meditation, a large citrine crystal or a large clear quartz crystal must be used. It is a good idea, because the crystal will have a basis, and its facets will join into a higher point. Generator quartz or a large citrine with one apex can suit the task well. In order to strengthen its powers, it must be placed in the sun for an entire day, from sunrise until half an hour before sunset. The sun's energy, whose color represents the energy of the yellow solar plexus, exerts a significant action on this chakra. Of course, before placing this crystal in the sun and charging it, it must be cleansed and purified.

Sit comfortably. Start taking deep, slow breaths while focusing on relaxing your body. It you do not feel the optimal relaxation of your body, start contracting and relaxing your muscles, from bottom to top. This action, which is called "The Jacobson Technique," leads to excellent physical relaxation. Now hold the crystal at eye level. Concentrate on it with your eyes open, until you feel focused. Close your eyes the moment you feel a need to do so. After closing your eyes, see the image of the crystal in your mind's eye. Start to imagine the crystal moving away from you, becoming bigger and bigger, until it fills your entire field of vision. See yourself in your mind's eye rising from your chair and approaching the crystal. The nearer you get to the gigantic crystal, almost touching it, the more you feel that it is drawing you to it, until you are drawn right inside it. This action means projecting your awareness inside the crystal. Now you are inside the crystal. Wait for a bit, let yourself feel the special feeling of being inside the crystal. Wait a few moments, until a colored light envelops you. If you do not see this light surrounding you, you can see yourself enveloped by white, golden, or yellow light. It is possible, without you intending it, that you will be enveloped by some color. This color is one of the colors that you need in order to strengthen your will power. You may know what that color is, and you may see it in your mind's eye without meaning to consciously. Feel at ease and calm, and continue to take deep, slow breaths right through the meditation. The light that envelops you vibrates at high frequencies. It is pleasant and soft, and spreads a good feeling. Feel how every millstone, worry, anger, or disturbing thought leaves you and goes outside through the walls of the crystal. You can stand in it, awash with the light that envelops you, or float lightly in it. Let the light fill you, while it cleanses you of non-positive patterns of thought and emotion; see these patterns washed away, outside the walls of the crystal. Do not get involved with them, and do not relate to them – let them be washed outside. Now, lift your head (in your imagination, while you continue sitting calm and relaxed), to the highest points of the crystal. While you look at this point, see yourself washed with enormous rays of white and yellow light. Now, concentrate your awareness on your solar plexus chakra. Imagine it to be like a gigantic sun, yellow and shining. Imagine it revolving. You can turn it in any direction you feel to be the correct one, clockwise or counter-clockwise. Take a deep breath and see the light of the sun that is shining above you drawn into the solar plexus chakra and filling it. It fills up with light, power, warmth, and energy. When you exhale, turn the wheel of the chakra while strongly feeling it fill up with energy. Continue taking deep, slow breaths, all the while imagining the wheel of the chakra revolving and filling up with the sun's energy coming in via the apex of the crystal, until you feel physical warmth in your upper abdomen. Continue with this action for about 10 minutes, while you concentrate totally on receiving energy and the charging of the chakra. Concentrate entirely, and you will see every unwanted and unsuitable thought fly outside, or pass, without attracting your attention. After about 10 minutes, or when you feel a great deal of warmth in your abdomen or your body, see yourself sitting opposite in a chair, and return to your body sitting in the chair. See the crystal opposite you, as you are sitting in the chair; it is getting gradually smaller, until it returns to its original size. Think of your physical body, and slowly begin to feel the sensations in your body, your feet, your fingertips. Feel the chair on which you are sitting. Move your ankles and your wrists in circular movements. Move your arms and legs a bit, until you feel that you are "all here" again. After you get up, drink a glass of water. If you still feel a bit "spaced out," jump up and down lightly, stretch a bit, and eat a snack.

Meditation with crystals of the solar plexus for emotional balance

This is another meditation for the solar plexus chakra. This meditation focuses on the emotional balanced achieved when the chakra is balanced. It helps the person express his emotions more easily, accept them, and balance them. In this meditation, we will relate to the way in which the person expresses his feelings; we will also relate to his temperament, and to his basic character, and according to those parameters, we will match the stones. This is what makes this meditation different than other meditation methods and laying on of stones on the chakras, in which we match the stone to the chakra according to its color. In this meditation, people with a different emotional burden perform the meditation using different stones:

To balance a volatile temperament, a tendency to quarrel and get angry, expressing emotions vociferously, "cool" and soothing stones are held in one hand as follows: aquamarine, blue lace agate, aventurine, moonstone.

For people who have difficulty expressing their emotions, or during situations of a feeling of emotional blockage, the following stones are held in one hand: kunzite, lapis lazuli, garnet, pearl, watermelon tourmaline, rhodonite, or rhodochrosite.

For situations in which there is a need for emotional support, situations of emotional crisis, or for people who tend to suffer from depression, one of the following stones is used: peridot, lepidolite, red jasper, jade, rhodonite, ruby, calcite, or citrine.

Before beginning the treatment, we cleanse, purify, charge, and program the stones to balance our emotions (or the emotions of the patient).

Free up about half an hour for performing the treatment. If you choose an orange stone, or a stone that suits the solar plexus in a special way (you can check this in the chapter on stones and their properties), you must place the stone on the solar plexus chakra. If you choose another stone, you must hold it in both hands.

Choose a quiet place with a calm and pleasant atmosphere, energetically clean. Play pleasant background music that is harmonious and soothing. If you place the stone on the solar plexus chakra, perform the meditation lying down. If it is a stone that is held in both hands, you might prefer to perform the meditation sitting up. However, you can also lie down.

Start taking deep, slow breaths. Place the stone on the chakra, or hold it between your palms, parallel to the base of the diaphragm, in the region of the solar plexus chakra. With each breath, feel how your body becomes more and more relaxed. Concentrate on the crystal that is lying on the chakra, or held between your palms parallel to it. Feel the light vibrations and the resonance it transmits as a sign of its action. Above your head, see a large, golden, warming sun. Golden yellow light flows in a straight line from the sun to you, descends and penetrates your skull. The golden yellow light flows pleasantly through your body, filling it from the top of your head to your toes, and flows via your hands (if you are holding the stone), to the stone. Now, focus on the wheel of the solar plexus chakra. See it as a kind of miniature sun. See the light that is flowing surround the chakra like a wheel, let it turn it in the right direction. With every inhalation, let more light flow into you, and see the wheel turn more vigorously. With every exhalation, see all the unnecessary emotions streaming downward from the chakra, descending to the base of your body via your legs to your feet. From your feet, see a kind of small gate open; the unnecessary emotions flow through it and descend to the bowels of the earth. Continue like this, until you feel a pleasant warmth in the solar plexus chakra, and you will feel intuitively that it's time to stop. Let the golden light play around the chakra for a while. See the wheel revolving more slowly, but steadily and clearly. Notice the sun above your head fading. It does not disappear, of course – it has only completed its role for the moment. Continue taking a few deep breaths without drawing light into you. Lie quietly for a few seconds, feel how you are enveloped in and full of warm light, clean and emotionally balanced. Start to feel the back of the chair and the seat beneath you, more and more conscious of your physical body. Gently remove the stone and place it on once side. Clench and open your hands a few times. Slowly move your ankles in circular movements. Move your arms and legs a bit until you feel that you are "back" again. Slowly open your eyes, and lie for a few more minutes before getting up, enjoying the marvelous feeling.

Afterwards, you will have to place the stone in a glass of water. It may have absorbed non-positive energies from the chakras, and for this reason, when you place it in the glass of water, dip your fingertips, so that the energy residues from the stone will descend into the water. You will have to purify it well and charge it on a crystal cluster for about three hours.

Using crystals to treat the throat chakra and its functions

A meditation of positive thinking to liberate the expressive and creative abilities

Many people feel that there is a lot more inside them than they succeed in expressing, externalizing, developing, and applying. They feel that creativity and inspiration, which have never come to the surface, are bubbling inside them. Sometimes the expressive ability and the ability to communicate with themselves is greater than with those around them. Often, the difficulty in externalizing and expressing these abilities derives from some blockage in the throat chakra. The following meditation combines positive mantras that act on the mental layer with the strength of the crystals.

To perform the meditation, focus on the objectives that you want to accomplish, or on the problems that are bothering you in the field of expression and communication, and choose one of the following stones. Some of them are placed on the throat chakra, and some are held in the hand.

Botswana agate – for expressing emotions, for stimulating creativity. For excessive sensitivity and feeling uncomfortable expressing oneself in front of many people (in class, in front of an audience, and so on) – during meditation, it should be held in the left or right hand.

Blue calcite – stimulates creativity and balances the throat chakra. For improving the expressive ability – for placing on the throat chakra.

Chrysocolla – for stimulating the expressive ability and creativity, and the ability to express oneself artistically – for placing on the throat chakra.

Blue fluorite – for cleansing the throat chakra, when, in addition to "disjointed" communication, the person also feels various physical symptoms in the throat region. Mainly in chronic conditions – for placing on the throat chakra.

Blue kyanite – when communication is angry, either open or repressed – for placing on the throat chakra, or for holding.

Lapis lazuli – for encouraging the different aspects of communication and expression. For shyness and lack of confidence. For freer expression and for stimulating creativity. For promoting courage of expression – for placing on the throat chakra, or for holding.

Blue sapphire – for reinforcing and stimulating the communicative abilities, for soothing and for stimulating inspiration – for placing on the throat chakra.

Blue tourmaline – for reinforcing communicative skills, for stimulating sympathetic and empathetic communication and bolstering self-confidence – for placing on the throat chakra.

Turquoise – for developing emotional communication, stimulating motivation and creativity, and bolstering self-confidence – for placing on the throat chakra.

Apatite – for stimulating creativity and self-confidence, mainly in people who have a low self-image – during meditation, it should be held in the left or right hand.

Aventurine – for stimulating and increasing creativity and optimism - during meditation, it should be held in the left or right hand.

Garnet – for stimulating motivation, inspiration, and creativity, for bolstering self-esteem, for reinforcing the expressive abilities anywhere and anytime - during meditation, it should be held in the left or right hand.

After you have chosen the stone that is suitable for you (while certain properties of the stones are mentioned here, you can also rely on your intuition when choosing!), choose one of the three following positive mantras. It is important to know the mantras by heart during meditation, so memorize them before starting:

I express myself easily.
I make myself heard with love.
I am free to make myself heard.
I am free to express my desires and my emotions.
I make myself heard courageously.
I am sure of myself and of my ability.
I am calm and serene.
I communicate with my surroundings with love.
I love and appreciate myself.
And so on...

You can prepare a similar mantra for yourself, one that suits you exactly. Remember that our subconscious receives and absorbs exactly what is said to it. For this reason, you must phrase the mantras positively, not negatively. In a mantra such as "I am not afraid to make myself heard," the term "afraid" is liable to be absorbed in the subconscious without taking the preceding word – "not" – into account. As a result, you must phrase the mantra positively – "I make myself heard courageously."

After you have chosen a suitable stone and mantra, you can begin the meditation. Find yourself a place that is quiet and energetically clean. If you choose to play music, it should be quiet, and without lyrics, so that nothing disturbs you when you say the mantras. If you tend to get "carried away" during meditation, perform it sitting up, because you will have to remember to say the mantras.

Place the stone you have chosen beside you. Relax your body and begin taking deep, calm breaths. If you have chosen a stone to place on the throat chakra, place it in the point between the two clavicle bones, that is, at the base of the throat. If you have chosen a stone to hold, hold it in both hands, or in the hand you feel to be correct.

Focus on breathing. Now, there are two ways to perform conscious breathing:

If you are a slightly passive type, or are inclined to be heavy (physical heaviness too), tend slightly toward melancholy, and sometimes feel a lack of motivation, perform the conscious breathing as follows: When inhaling, inhale blue light into you. When exhaling, exhale orange light. Breathe consciously, in a way that makes you feel that the breath is circular – the orange light of exhalation pursues the blue light of inhalation. Continue like this when you say the mantras, too.

If you are a cheerful type by nature, nimble, quick, and highly motivated, you can perform the conscious breathing as follows: When inhaling, see blue, turquoise, or white light, enchantingly beautiful, descending from above and entering your body via the crown of your head. It is cool, pleasant, and stimulating. When inhaling, you draw the light of one of the three above-mentioned colors into you, and when exhaling, you wind it around the wheel of the throat chakra. As you persist in the conscious breathing, the wheel of the chakra revolves more smoothly, clearly, and significantly. Continue taking conscious breaths when you say the mantras, too.

Continue breathing consciously in the way you have chosen. After a few minutes, when you feel that you are in a deep and pleasant meditative state, start to recite the mantra. You can say it, sing it, whisper it – whatever you like. Say it over and over again, and be aware of every word that comes out of your mouth.

After about 10 or 15 minutes, or when you feel the time is right, see a pure, white, shining light descending from above, via the crown of your head, entering you and beginning to fill you. It flows via your spinal column, descends to your legs, and from there, descends into the bowels of the earth. At the same time, it fills you completely with white light. You are full of light, until it begins to leave the sides of your body and wrap you in an ellipse of shining light.

Continue taking a few deep breaths, without projecting color. After a few minutes, begin to get out of the meditative state. Turn your ankles and wrists around a bit, and shake your limbs slightly. Put the stone aside, and when you feel ready, you can get up. Give yourself a few minutes to rest before resuming your everyday activities.

Rinse the stone under running water for three minutes, concentrating so that all the unwanted energies are washed off it. Place it on the windowsill so that it can be charged with moonlight or sunlight.

The meditation should be repeated once a day for a week. It will be simpler after the first time. All you have to do is take deep breaths, with your eyes closed, hold a stone or place it on the throat chakra, and link up to it. After you feel calm and relaxed, you must start saying the mantras. There is no need to repeat the balancing of the chakras with color, unless you feel that this is necessary.

You can repeat the mantra as often as you like during the day without using the stone. This action strengthens the effect of the meditation to a great extent, and the results are likely to manifest themselves more quickly.

Meditation to change thought patterns – accepting the change with love

Our thought patterns, some of which we have had since babyhood and childhood, have a significant effect on all of our actions and on the molding of our character. Some of these patterns, which we were taught to believe in since our earliest days, are erroneous, incorrect. These can be general patterns concerning the world, such as "money doesn't grow on trees," "nice little girls don't climb trees," and so on. Some of them are thought patterns that we adopted when we were mentally mature, in accordance with the patterns we learned in childhood, or as a result of various experiences in adulthood. Many of these patterns are not conscious. They can carry messages of an inability to succeed, a lack of belief in the world and in people, fatalism, and of course various fears. Many people are ruled by these patterns without being aware of them. But they do not only affect our abilities and character. It is important to know that when we adhere in our thoughts to a certain belief, this is expressed in our electromagnetic field. As a result, we draw into our lives situations and events that suit that particular thought pattern. Thus, instead of living simple, easy, and harmonious lives, the person invites various unpleasant events and disturbing situations that derive directly from his patterns of belief. This is not to say that fate does not play a role during our lives. But when the person is burdened with negative and inhibiting thought patterns, he is liable to take the very path of fate that leads to the realization of these non-positive beliefs. In order to change these patterns, a lot of mental work is required. The previous meditation, for inspiring the communicative ability, is an effective example of changing thought patterns. Everyone can devise the mantras presented above for himself, according to his needs. They can be used to eliminate inhibiting thoughts concerning money, conjugal relations, work, and self-esteem – in fact, to change any unwanted thought pattern. In the following meditations, too, we will make use of this technique in order to balance the various chakras using the mental layer. In order to promote the process, there must be a genuine desire for change. The throat chakra is responsible for storing various mental patterns, beliefs, thought patterns and even emotional patterns. By opening the chakras up to change, the person can watch the changes benefiting his life. If, in addition to the mantras for accepting change, we also perform meditations for changing the patterns concerning the different levels of life (see the following meditations and the previous one), we will experience far-reaching changes in life, changes that cannot be ignored. Since physical embodiment, in the material world, begins with thought, and operates according to inner beliefs, the "material" world also changes when our thought patterns change.

One of the most exciting points concerning this topic is as follows: The more we display willingness to change our thought patterns, the faster reality itself is likely to change – as a result of practicing and memorizing new patterns. For instance, if we work on changing our thought patterns about money, a certain period of time is likely to pass before we see results. After constant practice, this period of time will become shorter, and we can see, in a surprising way, how quickly the new, positive thought patterns are likely to work. It is important to mention that the new thought patterns with which we load our "computer" – the subconscious – and "save" a certain positive thought in it, must be in positive terms, and not in negative terms. For example: "I operate courageously and decisively," and not "I am not afraid and I do not hesitate." When the subconscious is loaded with new thought patterns, it does not relate to the meaning of the word "not" in the sentence. It picks up the words "afraid," "hesitate," which are subsequently expressed in the mental layer, in the mental aura, and it is those that are manifested in the physical world. For that reason, it is important to pay attention to how we phrase the patterns.

The meditation for accepting change with love prepares us for work with positive thinking. It removes the first barrier that stands in the way of the will to change thought patterns – the fear of change. For years, we have convinced ourselves that "we can't cook," "money burns a hole in our pocket," "nothing works out for me." The result of these statements was far-reaching feedback from life itself. In order to begin the change, we have to welcome it.

A number of stones can be used for work on welcoming change. You can use the following list to choose a suitable stone, but you can choose one of them (even one that does not appear here!) according to feeling and intuition. You can also choose a stone that you think symbolizes change and development, or use your personal stone that accompanies you through life. Some of the stones can be placed on the throat chakra, and some should be held.

Green calcite – a very powerful stone for this purpose. It helps you understand your negative and inhibiting thought patterns, behavior, and emotions consciously. At the same time, it helps cleanse them consciously, purify the unconscious layers of those patterns, and welcome change. It can be placed on the throat chakra or held in the hand.

Lapis lazuli – helps get rid of old and inhibiting thought and emotional patterns. Moreover, it is effective in eliminating the emotions of resentment, hatred, and anger that are found in the subconscious. It can be held in the hand, placed on the throat chakra, or placed on the third eye chakra, if you feel the need.

Lepidolite – helps you recognize inhibiting thought patterns, and encourages change and building more positive and useful patterns. In addition, it stimulates self-love. You can hold it in your hand during the meditation, or place it on the throat chakra. If you feel a special need for this, you can place it on the third eye or the heart chakra.

Kyanite – helps you get rid of unwanted and inhibiting patterns of thought and emotion, especially of resentment, anger, frustration, and hatred festering in the subconscious. Blue kyanite can be placed on the throat chakra, as well as on the third eye chakra. Pink kyanite can be placed on the heart chakra.

Aventurine – links us to creation, and stimulates our confidence in the universe. It helps us liberate ourselves from negative thought and emotional patterns, inspires optimism, encourages a positive attitude toward life, and stimulates self-esteem. You can hold it in your hand, or place it on the heart chakra if you feel a particular need to do so. If the aventurine you are holding is clear, or tends to blue, you can place it on the throat chakra.

Garnet – helps eliminate negative patterns, non-positive beliefs, and inhibiting emotional patterns from the subconscious. Moreover, it helps inspire a positive and loving attitude toward life. You can hold it in your hand or place it on the third eye chakra.

Smoky quartz – dispels the negative emotional patterns that stem from negative thought patterns. Simultaneously with the energetic elimination of the negative patterns, it helps build new thought and emotional patterns that are positive and effective. You can hold it in your hand or place it on any chakra or anywhere on the body that you feel the need to do so.

Sodalite – helps release old thought patterns, and, in parallel, helps you accept, build, and adopt new positive and effective ones. You can place it on the throat chakra. If you feel a need to place it on the third eye chakra, act according to your feeling.

Choose one of the stones, and while you are holding it in your hand and linking up to it (after it has been purified and charged), choose one of the following positive mantras:

I accept myself as I am, and am ready to change.
I accept the change with love.
I am in a state of perfect harmony with the universe.
The universe takes care of me, and provides for all my needs.
I am open to receiving loving messages from the universe.
I love and esteem myself.
I learn every single day.
I flow happily with life.
I am ready to learn new truths happily.
I release the beliefs that I do not need.
I open my consciousness to the wonderful knowledge of the universe.

Memorize the mantra before you start meditating. Set aside about half an hour to perform the meditation, with no interruptions. You can burn aromatic oils such as frankincense, lavender, juniper, basil or jasmine absolute in an essential oil burner. Do not use synthetic oils for meditation. If you are interested in music, play gentle and quiet music, preferably music that contains sounds of nature or knocking on a Tibetan bowl. It is not advisable to play music with lyrics.

Sit or lie down comfortably. Hold the stone, or place it on the region you have chosen. If you feel the need to move the stone and place it somewhere else on your body during the meditation, do so. It is possible that non-positive patterns of some kind are trapped there, and they have to be eliminated. Do not worry yourself with thoughts of "why did I choose that particular region?" while meditation. You can go into it in depth later, and discover the negative patterns that were in that particular region of your body, or the patterns and beliefs that it represented for you.

Close your eyes. Start taking deep, slow breaths. When inhaling, see yourself inhaling pink light. When exhaling, see yourself exhaling green light. Continue breathing in a circular manner.

When you feel calm and linked up, begin to recite your mantra. You can whisper it, sing it, or express it in any way you want, but see that your lips enunciate the words so that you can hear them. While you are reciting the mantra, see your image in your mind's eye. Look at yourself. Do you see a smiling image? What are the emotions you experience when you see your image? Do you see yourself as a child or as an adult? Send love to your image, and make it smile. See twinkling pink and green lights enveloping the image. The shining lights descend to the image like dewdrops of happiness and joy. Let your image dance among the dewdrops of light and color, feel how they envelop its heart and stimulate optimism, confidence, and hope in it.

Very slowly, let your image disappear. Continue taking deep breaths, but faster, without inhaling color. Feel the marvelous sensation of accepting change with love, and the hope that now your life will be sweeter and more beautiful. Catch this feeling in your heart. Put the stone aside.

When you feel ready to wake up, do it slowly and gently. Afterwards, rinse the stone under running water for three minutes, and concentrate on washing off all the unwanted energies. Place it on the windowsill so that it can be charged in the moonlight or sunlight, or both.

Repeat the meditation every day for a week. It is sufficient to hold or place a stone, and say the mantra you chose. You can also, if you feel a genuine need to do so, choose an additional stone, or another stone. You do not have to repeat the whole process, but if you want, you can perform the meditation every time you feel like it.

This meditation is wonderful every time you are faced with change of any kind – beginning your studies in a new place, moving house, the end of a relationship or the beginning of one, and so on. It will clarify to you, and to the universe, that you accept life's changes and surprises with love, and expect the most pleasant surprises.

Using crystals to treat the sex chakra and its functions

Meditation for balancing and opening the sex chakra

The sex chakra expresses both our capacity for pleasure and our creative ability – the physical ability to express what is inside us. When this chakra is not balanced, the person is liable to feel dissatisfied with his life, and he is liable to compensate for this by means of various addictions: to food, work, cigarettes, and so on. A balanced chakra is essential for self-realization. A lack of balance in the chakra, in the various layers, is liable to cause the person to lose his *joie de vivre,* or to feel pessimistic. Moreover, he is liable to discover that life gives him no pleasure – he needs strong and significant stimuli in order to enjoy his life, and is not satisfied by the "little magical things" in life, which should be no less pleasurable. This is liable to cause constant frustration. Many of the sexual functions are attributed to the sex chakra. Because it is located between the solar plexus chakra, which is responsible for the "I" and for the perception of the I, and the base chakra, which is responsible for the physical sexual functions, it is possible to treat problems connected to sexuality that originate in the perception of the I, by means of this chakra. An unbalanced state of the chakra is liable to lead to a feeling of social isolation, solitude, or, alternatively, to dependency and fear of being left alone. Moreover, problems of the sex chakra are liable to prevent the person from applying and realizing his desires. To know more about the functions of the chakra, you can go back and read about it in the Introduction.

In the two following meditations, stones are used to balance the chakra. In the first meditation, orange stones and color projections are used, or orange and blue together. In the second meditation, which should be performed after you have done the first one several times, positive mantras are added, helping you open the chakra and renew its various functions. Since there are liable to be very different states of imbalance regarding the chakra, choose the stone that seems to be the most suitable for this meditation with care. In the next meditation, you can choose the stones more freely, or use your personal stone. All the above-mentioned stones can be placed on the sex chakra. If you choose blue spinel, or any other blue stone, you must place an orange stone (such as orange spinel) with it simultaneously. Besides the stone that you place on the sex chakra, you will have to use clear quartz crystal, large or medium, that can be placed on the table opposite you so that it stands without falling.

Choose one of the following stones:

Orange fire agate – Use this stone if you feel that your sexual lusts are very powerful and unbalanced, and interfere with your everyday life and your spiritual path. You can also use it if you suffer from hormonal problems.

Amber – Use it if you feel a lack of self-satisfaction and do not succeed in expressing your desires on the physical plane. You can also use it if you suffer from kidney or urinary tract problems.

Bloodstone with orange patches – Use it if you have difficulty applying things physically, accomplishing them actively, and making decisions, and if you tend to panic or act selfishly. You can also use it if you want to increase your creativity.

Carnelian – This is thought to be one of the best stones for treating sex problems and the sex chakra. It is suitable for stimulating weak sexual urges, and for people who suffer from sexual frigidity or difficulties in reveling in their sexuality. Carnelian should be used in meditation if you notice that you lack compassion toward others, or feel jealousy, anger, anxiety, agitation, or depression. It is suitable for people who have difficulty in deciding, or who suffer from a lack of motivation and apathy. You can also use it if you want to promote your creativity. On the physical level, choose it if you suffer from physical weakness, from gallstones or kidney stones, from problems in the spleen or pancreas, and from general sexual problems.

Chrysoprase – Choose this stone if you notice that you lack compassion toward others, if you are critical, or suffer from feelings of inferiority or exaggerated pride. On the physical plane, use it if you suffer from prostate problems, problems in the testicles or ovaries, and fertility problems.

Garnet – Use garnet if you feel that you do not esteem yourself as you should, and if you suffer from unconscious fears and anxieties, or from a non-positive attitude toward life. You can also used it in meditation to stimulate creativity.

Fire opal – Use this stone to eliminate inhibitions in your sex life and a lack of spontaneity in sex and in life in general, and if you feel that you have difficulty in accepting warmth and love in your conjugal relationship, or in giving warmth and love. Use it if you feel any lack of balance in the sphere of conjugal fidelity, or if you feel a lack of confidence or a lack of belief in yourself, or in what life holds in store for you. You can also use it in meditation to stimulate creativity, especially if you feel that you are not exploiting your innate potential.

Rhodochrosite – Use this stone if you feel a lack of emotional balance or problems with or confusion about your sexual identity. On the physical plane, use it in meditation if you suffer from problems or weak action of the digestive system.

Orange spinel – Use it to stimulate creativity and sexual vitality.

Blue spinel – Use it if you suffer from strong, unbalanced sexual urges.

Tiger eye – Use it if you feel that your sex chakra is blocked. You can see this if you discover some of the following patterns in your personality: instability, lack of courage, pride, sexual anxieties, or a separation between sex itself and emotion.

Golden topaz – Use this stone if you suffer from uncertainty, a lack of belief in your personal decisions, a lack of confidence, pessimism, difficulty in enjoying sex or life in general, agitation, and fears. You can also use it if you identify patterns of a lack of comprehension in relationships (whether you relate these patterns to yourself or to your spouse).

Aventurine – Hold the stone in your hand if you suffer from sexual problems that are linked to childhood. You can also use it if you identify problems or blockages in creativity, indecisiveness, a lack of emotional balance, or problems in the sexual organs.

Basalt – Hold the stone in your hand during the meditation if you suffer from an inability to control your anger or your emotional outbursts, or if you feel that there is a lot of rage in you that wants to erupt. You can also use it if you suffer from problems in the sexual organs. Basalt should be used in this meditation only if you have "personal" basalt with which you feel a close bond, and preferably at new moon or full moon.

Copper – Hold the unprocessed copper in your hand or place it on the sex chakra if you suffer from a lack of motivation, laziness, a lack of initiative, a lack of *joie de vivre*, and/or sexual conservatism. You can also use it if you feel that your sexual energies are weak, or if you suffer from frequent problems of circulation.

Pink coral – This is suitable for people who suffer from problems in love relationships, and/or problems in the female sexual and reproductive organs.

Kyanite – Use this stone for meditation if you suffer from anger and frustration, agitation, and an inability to calm down. You can also use it if you suffer from muscular problems, from adrenal problems, or from problems in the sexual system. Hold it in your hand during the meditation, unless you feel a need to place it on the chakra or on a particular part of your body.

Brown opal – Use this stone if you suffer from problems in the sexual system, or from sexual problems of an emotional origin. You can also use it for meditation for increasing creativity.

Perform the meditation in a quiet room with pleasant, positive energies. You can play soft, pleasant, and soothing music. It is a good idea to put aromatic oils such as rose absolute, juniper, or jasmine absolute in an essential oil burner. In this meditation, you must perform conscious breathing, inhaling orange light. If you feel that your sex chakra is functioning too much, that is, over-ambition, hypersexuality, and so on, hold any blue stone in one hand, preferably blue spinel, for creating balance. If you feel a lot of heat in the region of the sex chakra during the meditation, transfer the orange light to the rest of your body, or bring the meditation to a close. Since there are many possibilities for maneuver in this meditation, I will mention an additional important point pertaining to men: If you suffer from problems in sexual functioning, such as impotence, a weak sexual urge, problems with erection, and so on, you must see a red light descending and enveloping your sex organ at a moment that I will indicate. If you suffer from premature ejaculation, you must see a blue light enveloping your sex organ, and direct your thoughts to an improvement in your ability to "hold back" for longer. This visualization is very strong and effective. (It may be far less effective when the root of the problem is blatantly physical.) After you practice it during meditation, you can also practice it before or during sex.

Sit comfortably in an easy chair. On the table opposite, place the clear quartz crystal. Relax your entire body and begin taking deep, slow breaths. Place the stone you have chosen on the sex chakra, or hold it in your hand.

Start looking at the quartz crystal opposite you. Concentrate on it with open eyes, and feel as if you are linking up to it. After looking at it for some time, still taking deep breaths, close your eyes. Continue seeing the crystal, clearly and lucidly, in your mind's eye.

Start imagining the crystal moving away from yourself. The further it goes, the bigger it gets, until it fills the entire room with its huge size, and stops growing and moving. Now, imagine yourself, in your mind's eye, getting out of the chair and starting to walk toward the crystal. Feel as if a pleasant force from within the crystal is pulling you toward it. Enter the crystal.

After you enter the crystal, let yourself feel the special and pleasant sensation of being inside the crystal. Examine your surroundings, look at the walls and ceiling of the crystal. After a few moments, see an orange light descending from above and entering the crystal through the ceiling. The orange light envelops you, warm and pleasant. You feel the gaiety and joy that it arouses in you, the power and the independence that are forming in you the more you are wrapped up in the orange light.

Breathe the orange light into you. At this point, you may feel that you want to inhale orange light, and exhale blue light, for balance. Follow your feelings. See an orange circle of light moving and revolving in the area of your groin. Move the orange light to it, fill it with the orange light, and feel how its revolutions become smoother, more harmonious and more powerful. You may feel pleasant and warm sensations in your physical body at the same time. Feel how the orange light balances your sex chakra. It gets rid of everything that it does not need, opens it, and fills it. At this point, you can perform the flow of red or blue light that we mentioned in the introduction to the meditation. It is possible that various scenes connected to the sex chakra and to various memories that are imprinted in it will start emerging. Don't be afraid of them. This is the time to get rid of patterns or memories that you no longer need. Don't let feelings of guilt, sorrow, or anger enter your protected space inside the crystal. See every unwanted memory or emotion rise up and go out through the walls of the crystal, and remind yourself that you love and accept yourself as you are, for you are full of love and compassion. Continue seeing the orange light surrounding and filling your sex chakra, until you feel that it has been filled and balanced.

After about 10 minutes, or when you feel that the pleasant warmth in your body or in the region of the sex chakra has become clear, strong heat, see the current of light disappearing, after filling and balancing you. See yourself starting to leave the crystal. Stand outside the crystal, and look at your body that is sitting in the chair. The moment you see yourself, the crystal will begin to decrease in size, and your image will increase, until both of you return to your normal proportions. Continue returning to your body that is sitting in the chair. Start feeling your body's sensations, the stone you are holding in your hand, or that is lying in the region of your sex chakra, the chair that you are sitting on, and the parts of your body. Begin to open your eyes very slowly. Remove the stone. Continue sitting quietly with your eyes open for a few minutes. If you still feel a bit "spaced out," move your limbs gently, and rub your knees and your calves with your palms. After you get up, drink a glass of water, rinse the stone well, and place it on the windowsill or on a cluster of crystals for charging.

Supplementary meditation – changing patterns and beliefs concerning sexuality

This meditation is a direct continuation of the previous one. In the previous meditation, you opened, balanced, and cleansed your sex chakra. Now you will treat the mental layers connected to the chakra by changing inhibiting thought patterns. Many people have guilt feelings concerning their sexuality, feelings of "It's wrong," fear that derives from religion, and so on. We internalized some of these patterns in our childhood, some from other sources. Various experiences in our adulthood are liable to interfere with our optimal sexual functioning. If you feel that your sexual functioning, or the general functioning of the chakra, is blocked for any reasons that are not physical, but rather emotional, add positive mantras to the meditation.

You must memorize the positive mantra you choose. Perform the meditation exactly as you did the previous one, except that when you begin to activate and direct the orange light to the sex chakra, you must think, in a focused and conscious way, of the positive mantra. You can even say it aloud, during the meditation.

Below are several suggestions for mantras that can be included in the meditation. You can devise your own personal mantra that suits you more than all the others.

I enjoy my sexuality.

I accept myself with love.

I react to love and can contain it.

I enjoy my unique expressions of life.

My body is my own, and I enjoy its functions.

I am free, confident, and liberated.

I let the past go with love.

I enjoy experiencing life and reveling in its expressions.

I revel in my sexuality.

I allow my sexuality to express itself easily and enjoyably.

I revel in my femininity.

I am happy to be a woman.

I love my feminine functions.

I revel in my masculinity.

I am happy to be a man.

I love my masculine functions.

I am now discovering how wonderful I am.

I accept my sexuality with love.

I revel in being a woman.

I revel in being a man.

You should learn your chosen mantra by heart and say it several times a day. You can do that while holding the stone that you use for meditation for the sex chakra, but also at any time and in any place.

Using crystals to treat the base chakra and its functions

Balance, cleansing, and opening the chakra

The base chakra is the chakra that is responsible for all our needs and survival functions. An imbalance in the chakra is liable to be expressed in many and varied ways: Conditions of excess as opposed to lack are liable to bring about situations of over-materialism as opposed to a lack of reality, too much preoccupation with matters of the body as opposed to too much preoccupation with matters of the mind, with the earthly layer being forgotten, and so on. When the base chakra is in a state of lack, the person is liable to lose his connection with the earth. All the earthly functions are liable to seem difficult or unimportant to him. The person is liable to be physically detached, lacking the ability to stand up for himself or make decisions confidently and practically. In contrast, when the chakra is in a state of excess, the person is liable to be lascivious, with a lust for mammon, and concerned about his money and his body in a constant and egocentric manner.

In order to function in an optimal way in this world, the link between spirituality on the one hand and earthiness and physicality on the other must be strong and balanced. This is the role of the base chakra. When the base chakra is not balanced, it makes no difference how developed the upper chakras are. A state of imbalance and lack in the base chakra will manifest itself in all the person's actions.

The following meditation helps balance the base chakra simply and easily. Since it is a relatively simple meditation that is mainly supported by the properties of the stones, it is important to choose the stone wisely. In addition, this meditation should be performed daily for a week. After a week, the person should take a break of a few days, in which he should engage in introspection, and examine the changes that took place. If the situation of lack is significant, the meditation must be repeated daily for another week, and the stone can be exchanged for another suitable one.

Choose one of the following stones, which are the most suitable for the physical or emotional symptoms that you are experiencing.

Bloodstone with crimson spots – Use bloodstone if the lack of balance in the chakra is expressed in physical symptoms of problems in the circulatory system of all kinds, and/or hemorrhoids. Choose it if you suffer from one of more of the following emotional symptoms: selfishness, fears, anxieties, panic, instability and floating, a lack of concentration.

Citrine – Use citrine if you experience existential fears – fears concerning money, food, and so on, conditions of a self-destructive urge, depression, anger, extreme material lust, unhealthy or non-positive relationships with others, and fears concerning death and birth.

Copper – Place a lump of unprocessed copper if you feel that your sexual energies are not balanced, and if you experience a lack of motivation, recurring economic problems, and a fear of economic problems. In addition, use it if you tend to lack objectivity, to be conservative, and to lack the ability to understand philosophical messages.

Red coral – Use this in meditation in order to balance states of passivity and a lack of practicality, dependency, fears, and a lack of affinity for nature.

Cuprite – Choose cuprite if you suffer from a lack of stability, a lack of balance in the survival needs, a lack of grounding, a feeling of detachment, a loss of control, or a fear of a loss of control. You can also use it if you suffer from one or more of the following physical symptoms: fear of heights, vertigo, dizziness, or problems in the reproductive system.

Garnet – Use garnet if you experience fears of abandonment, a feeling of passivity, fears and depressions, angers, and social problems.

Jet – Use jet for strengthening the chakra, and also if you suffer from fears, frightening thoughts, depression, and inner agitation.

Rhodochrosite – Use rhodochrosite for purifying the chakra, and if you experience states of pessimism, detachment, and a lack of connection to the earth, selfishness, and an uncaring attitude toward the world and other people.

Ruby – This stone is recommended for men for reinforcing the sense of masculinity. It is also for women, of course. Use it for balancing the chakra if you experience problems of dishonesty and infidelity in conjugal relationships, a lack of courage, insufficient drive to achieve important goals, fear of conflicts that manifests itself in aggressiveness, and problems of economic stability.

Smoky quartz – If you had difficulty choosing a suitable stone from all the stones for this meditation, smoky quartz is recommended. In addition, you can use it for meditation if you experience feelings of floating, detachment, fears and nightmares, selfishness, egocentricity, mental and physical exhaustion, depression, pessimism, states of anger, an unbalanced ego, dependency, dominance, the use of power toward others, many negative feelings, adherence to old thought and behavior patterns, conservatism, difficulty in cooperating, or a major tendency toward acute or chronic diseases.

Red spinel – Choose this stone if you get ill a lot, feel physically weak, or lack vitality.

Black spinel – Choose this stone if you feel detached or floating, with a low threshold of endurance, and in need of grounding and practical ability.

Dark tiger eye – Use this stone if you experience states of pessimism, difficulty in cooperating with others, a lack of courage, an inability to link sex and love, floating, a lack of stability and practicality, difficulties in coping with little details, problems of comprehension, ignoring essential physical needs, and constant economic instability.

Yellow zircon – Use this stone if you suffer from a lack of enjoyment of food or of other physical pleasures, difficulties in persevering, instability, and repeating the same mistakes in life over and over again.

Red zircon – Use this stone if you feel a lack of control over your feelings, pessimism and melancholy, difficulties in persevering, a lack of innocence, instability, and often experience a lack of appetite.

Alexandrite – If you feel that your base chakra is relatively balanced, and you do not suffer from the emotional or physical symptoms mentioned above, use alexandrite in order to link the third eye chakra, the heart chakra, and the base chakra. Tune the stone to that during meditation.

Harlequin quartz – You can use meditation with this stone for opening the base chakra and linking it to the heart chakra. When using the stone for this purpose, you will have to tune it for this purpose during meditation. Moreover, you can use this stone if you suffer from problems of infidelity and a lack of *joie de vivre*.

Purify the stone you have chosen for the meditation for the base chakra well. Charge it on a quartz crystal cluster, or outside in the sun.

Perform the meditation in a room with a calm and pleasant atmosphere. You can play any kind of music during the meditation – a tape of drumming sounds is especially recommended. The meditation must be performed sitting up, with the legs firmly on the floor and a straight back.

Sit comfortably. Place the stone within reach. Take deep, slow breaths. Begin to relax your body – contract and relax your feet, your calves – and continue contracting and relaxing the muscles of each body part, from bottom to top. Focus mainly on the pelvic muscles, the shoulder muscles, the neck and the face. The contraction must be strong so that the relaxation that follows is full.

After you have relaxed your body, take the stone and place it on the base chakra. You must place the stone on the region linking the rectum and the genitals. The easiest way is in fact to sit on it. Link up to the sensation that the stone transmits to you. See a red light emanating from the stone and penetrating the base of your spinal column. In your mind's eye, see the base chakra as a red wheel. Look at it turning. It is possible that its revolutions are too fast for your feeling – or too slow and tired. Now, when inhaling, draw red light from the stone into the base chakra. When exhaling, send the red light to the chakra, and balance its turns with it. It may energize the turns in a clockwise direction. It may slow them down, or turn counter-clockwise. Let things flow by themselves. Repeat the inhalation and exhalation eight times. On the ninth time, inhale and fill your lungs, and let the red light "spring" upward from the base chakra to the spinal column. See the red light ascending the spinal column, twisting around it like a snake, and stimulating it. You may feel a light prickling in your body or limbs. Continue letting the red light flow up the spinal column, until you feel saturated. Continue breathing consciously, without performing visualization, allowing the sensations and the scenes to disappear by themselves. Keep on sitting in silence for a few minutes, and let the stone perform its action on the base chakra.

When you get up, drink a glass of water. You may feel very energetic and full of life. Moreover, various emotions, feelings, or memories may be aroused in you, some of them unpleasant. This is a natural situation that can occur after the stimulation or balancing of the chakra. You should write down the feelings that emerge in a notebook, and keep track of them. As we said previously, you should repeat the meditation daily, for a week.

Using crystals to treat the heart chakra and its functions

Meditation for cleansing the heart

This meditation helps us free ourselves and cleanse our heart of non-positive emotions: sadness, bitterness, jealousy, sorrow, feelings of inferiority, insults of the heart and so on – every belief, thought, or emotion that does not contribute to our feeling of harmony and self-love, whether it is conscious or unconscious. It is a good idea to repeat the meditation every time non-positive emotions appear in our consciousness, or when we feel that we do not love and accept ourselves totally.

For this meditation, use a medium-size clear quartz crystal, a green quartz crystal, pink-green watermelon tourmaline, or a relatively large piece of aventurine (but it must be in a light shade and fairly transparent). You can also use a relatively large piece of transparent green fluorite, or green calcite that is fairly transparent. Choose one of these stones.

To perform the meditation for the first time, clear quartz crystal and fairly transparent green quartz crystal are the most suitable. To begin with, program the crystal for the purpose of the meditation: reflecting the fact that you are a perfect, whole, and beloved creature, and stimulating self-love and self-esteem in all layers. In addition, it must reveal to you the unpurified and non-harmonious points in your heart that have a negative effect on your self-love. You must raise these points in front of your eyes as dark spots, black or gray, as small bits of dirt, as thick viscous material, or any other symbol of the inhibiting and troublesome feelings and emotions in your heart.

These unclean spots interfere with the enormous and powerful source of love that lies in your heart, and affect your emotions regularly, even if you are not aware of this or try to repress them. During the course of the meditation, allow these images to flow freely, and see them in accordance with your bank of personal associations.

Perform the meditation in an energetically cleansed room, with a pleasant atmosphere. You can perform it on a mattress on the floor, or on a bed, the main thing being that you feel at ease. Set aside half an hour for it, during which time you will not be disturbed. Unplug the phone or any other appliance that is liable to disturb you. You can place natural lavender or juniper oil in an essential oil burner. Play quiet, pleasant and meditative music to help you relax.

Place the crystal at your side, within reach. Lie comfortably, and start taking deep, slow breaths. With each breath, feel how your body parts relax, letting you feel increasingly calm and relaxed. Empty your mind of all thoughts. If irrelevant thoughts pop into your mind, see them pass as if over a screen, without relating to them or going into them in depth. Simply let them go by.

Take the crystal and place it on your heart. Take several deep breaths, letting them out slowly. While breathing, listen to your heart beating. Start to focus more and more on the heartbeats. Feel the heartbeats as the center of your being, and be totally focused on them. As your focus on the heartbeats increases, start to expand your consciousness, and feel the crystal that is lying on your heart. Feel it vibrating at the same frequency as your beating heart, in perfect harmony with its beats.

As you become more and more focused on the crystal, begin to imagine it growing. The bigger it gets, the smaller your body becomes. Ultimately, the crystal will be bigger than your body. Enter it. You are entering your heart, which is represented by the crystal.

While you are inside the crystal, feel the perfect harmony that reigns there. You can hear the beating of your heart there, harmonious, balanced, and pleasant. Feel yourself inside a room, or cave (if you chose aventurine or calcite), which illuminates the crystal with the light of its color. Look at a window in one of the walls of the room or cave (the walls of the crystal). It can be any type of window, but one that can be opened. See yourself small, inside the crystal, going over to the window and opening it.

Through the open window, look out on the cosmos. You must know that none of our thoughts, emotions, or beliefs remains in our body, soul, or consciousness only. They are transmitted and projected to the cosmos, to infinity. We use these emotions and beliefs for learning, for accumulating lessons in life. But now that we are aspiring to live in perfect harmony with the universe, we no longer need every pattern of thought, emotion, or belief that is not in total harmony and balance with the universe.

Look once more inside your heart crystal, in which you are located. Do you see anything wrong, foggy, muddy, black or gray spots, any kind of dirt, wheels of dust?

Look at the base of the crystal. There you will find some kind of tool that is exactly right for cleaning the spots or dirt on the walls or base of the crystal. It could be a vacuum cleaner, a bucket of fresh water with a scrubbing brush, a broom, or any other cleaning implement. You might find a garden hose with a mop next to it for cleaning the walls of the crystal, like you clean windows.

See a green light descending from the top of the crystal to you, the small standing figure. It flows through you, activates and stimulates you to clean and scrub, and fills you with devotion and love. Get to work! Clean every spot and grain of dirt carefully. The more you clean, the more you will feel at ease, and full of well-being and happiness. Clean and polish as much as you can. The moment you finish cleaning, you will see a small spring of flowing water in one of the corners of the crystal. Rinse the cleaning implements in it, and place them in a suitable corner. If there is still some dirt, you can put it in a plastic bag and close it well. Place the dirt or the plastic bag in the spring. The moment you place it there, the spring will suddenly expand for a second, erupt, and swallow the bag, like an airline toilet, making it disappear entirely. Afterwards, the spring will return to its natural size and disappear. Say to yourself, "I am excreting all the unwanted thoughts and emotions through my excretory organs." If there is no dirt left, or if it disappeared by itself together with the cleaning implements, all the better. After you have finished, go to the open window with a smile, conscious of the fact that the universe is watching and appreciating your deeds, and contributing in its own way to the inscription of your deeds and their endorsement in all the layers. Send the universe a loving smile that is full of gratitude, and close the window. Feel clean, purified, and completely full of self-love.

Begin to take increasingly deeper breaths, and focus on your heartbeats. Start to imagine the crystal becoming smaller. The smaller it becomes, the larger your body becomes, until both you and the crystal return to your normal sizes.

Lie calm and at ease for a few more minutes. Close and open your hands, move your ankles in circular movements. Contract your muscles slightly and relax them, quickly but not hard. Remove the crystal from your heart. Open your eyes, and lie for a few minutes, letting the pleasant feeling make you float. When you get up, remember to purify the crystal well, and charge it on a crystal cluster, or in the sunlight and/or moonlight. Drink a glass of water, and remember, when you go to the bathroom, to instruct your heart that you are excreting all the unwanted feelings that you cleaned from inside you. You can repeat this meditation any time you feel the need to do so.

Meditation of the inner child

In the meditation of the inner child, we return to our childhood. This period was supposed to be beautiful and happy, free of worries, and full of joy. However, having said that, the major part of the injuries and negative beliefs and patterns pertaining to ourselves originated in this period. More than once, insensitive adults around us said or did things that hurt us. These could be various clichés, utterances, criticism that undermined our self-confidence, and so on.

Let yourself return to the days of your childhood. Return to a pleasant, sweet place that you remember from that period. That place could be your home, your room, a hiding place that you used as a child, your playground, or any place or other corner of which you have totally positive memories. Reconstruct the feeling of being a child. See yourself playing or resting in your favorite place. Feel and reconstruct your characteristics and feelings. Feel yourself as a little child and feel the presence of your parents beside you. Don't be afraid. The safe place is with you, always accessible and open to you, if anything happens to frighten the little child inside you. Now go back to a certain period of your childhood that you remember as difficult or unpleasant, a period in which you felt that you were not properly understood, or not accepted for what you were, or not allowed to be what you really were. Of course, there could be various periods like that in your life as a child. It is possible that some of them are located deeper in the depths of your consciousness, and are much less pleasant than this one. The more you repeat the meditation, the more you will reconstruct, repair, and bring various periods to the surface, and they are likely to pop up in front of your eyes intuitively.

Now you are in this period that is not easy, as a child. In your mind's eye, raise up from your memory the things that were said to you, the reactions your deeds or behavior evoked, and hurt you. Listen carefully to the words that are spoken. After the meditation, write them down. You can even place a tape recorder next to you in order to go over this material afterwards.

During the week, you can go over this material and see how it affected you during your entire life, how it created your beliefs about yourself and the reality in which you live. You must take into account that the meditation raises these layers to the surface, and even if you do not continue with the conscious work during the week, they are still liable to emerge. Decide whether you are prepared to deal with them.

Let yourself feel the feeling you felt as a child, in the face of those words or reactions expressed by your parents. Don't stop yourself if you want to be angry, protest, or cry.

Now, look at the child that you see – you in your childhood. See the feelings that are expressed on his face – sadness, sorrow, anger, or even indifference. See yourself as an adult, going up to the child and embracing him. Feel yourself hugging him tightly, swamping him with love and compassion.

Now reconstruct the same event once more. This time, however, change the situation. Change your parents' reaction so that it will make the child happy and full of self-acceptance. See them smiling, forgiving, and accepting.

Continue taking deep, slow breaths. Inhale pink light, and exhale green light. Feel a great deal of compassion rising toward your parents who, at that time, did not know how to act differently, and made their mistakes as a result of the inhibiting patterns that were inside them. See the child smiling, happy, and joyful, and feeling strong, whole, and self-confident.

Guard the picture of the smiling child – the child that is you. See it getting smaller, tiny, until you can contain it in your heart. Let him into your heart and lock his smile in it.

Keep on lying down or sitting for a few minutes, until you feel that the meditative state is fading. Remove the crystal, purify and cleanse it well. Write down the material that arose during the meditation, and work with it. One of the best ways to work with it is to check and see how it influenced your life, and what influence it still has on the way your accept yourself, and on your present life. After you form certain insights about this material, you can go back and work on the various meditations for the chakras, which help change thought and emotional patterns.

Stimulating and opening the third eye and crown chakras

As we know, the third eye is responsible for our intuitive and extrasensory powers. This meditation helps stimulate those dormant powers that are found in every one of us by revealing the marvelous intuitive powers of the third eye. Many of the crystals that are used in this meditation stimulate the crown chakra simultaneously, even when they are placed on the third eye chakra.

There are many crystals you can use to perform this meditation. You can perform it often, each time discovering a different crystal's unique properties for stimulating the chakra. Below are a number of crystals from which you can choose the one that is most suited to your character and aspirations. Be honest with yourself. Remember that spiritual development is not a casual matter. If you have not had any extrasensory experiences up to now, do not choose channeling stones, or stones that are used for channeling with entities or for receiving superior knowledge and insights. Know where you stand, and remember that you need a solid basis upon which to build the various layers of spiritual development. If you have had experience in channeling, if you are a trainee healer, or if you have had many balanced and positive extrasensory experiences, choose one of the appropriate stones. The list of stones is arranged in ascending order in order to make it easier for you to find a suitable stone. The list is not accurate, of course, because the effect of the stone on the person depends on the person himself, on his ability to receive high frequencies from it, and on the condition of his third eye chakra. In addition, various stones of the same type are likely to operate in a different manner, since each personal stone is unique in itself. You can always use clear quartz, as well as rainbow crystals, double terminated crystals, and harlequin quartz. The same goes for moldavite. Rainbow crystal is not a common phenomenon, and moldavite is a very rare and expensive stone. If you are lucky enough to possess one of these stones, know that the universe has bestowed a marvelous gift on you. Thank it in your favorite way – love yourself and all creatures, and transmit messages of love and peace wherever you go.

Some of the stones that stimulate the third eye chakra (some of them stimulate the crown chakra in parallel) can be very powerful. You need a stable basis and an excellent grounding ability in order to use them without the guidance of a healer or experienced guide. It is not worth trying if you do not feel confident, since sensitive people are liable to feel unwell after using them. Having said that, don't make the mistake of thinking that even if you have had many extrasensory experiences, the "basic" stones for developing the intuition can't surprise you! For this exact reason, when you "go back" to them after a certain period in which you did not meditate with them, they are likely to transmit wonderful messages to you. Some of them, despite their very delicate nature, stimulate channeling abilities and other higher abilites, and should be used at every stage of spiritual development.

Blue lace agate – If you want to experience a pleasant floating feeling, and enter into new states of consciousness, if you are a shy type, or have difficulty calming down during meditation or in general, this stone will be very suitable.

Amethyst – This is the most highly recommended stone for placing on the third eye chakra. Use it if you are not accustomed to entering meditative states. It is suitable for meditation for any problem of the nervous system and the endocrine system, aural problems, and any kind of mental disturbance. If you are a tense type, it will be especially suitable for you. It is also suitable for people who suffer from dependency, or mental or emotional confusion. In addition, use it for strengthening telepathic abilities, and for increasing spiritual growth and awareness.

Sodalite – This is a wonderful stone for placing on the third eye. It is excellent for people who have not experienced many higher meditations (even those who have may discover new knowledge!) for spiritual development, and for more profound spiritual comprehension.

Indigo spinel, blue spinel, and purple spinel – These are used for strengthening the channeling abilities, for developing the intuition, and for spiritual cleansing.

Sugilite – This is used for receiving superior information, for a feeling of confidence in the universe, freedom, and a feeling of spiritual loftiness. It is very suitable for a person who has not yet experienced a meditation for the third eye.

Purple fluorite with green stripes – Use this stone to stimulate universal love on the spiritual level.

Garnet – Use garnet to eliminate fears from the subconscious and to perform spiritual purification.

Purple fluorite with blue shades in it – Use this stone in order to be able to express what your eyes see during meditations of the third eye. It is also very suitable if you have difficulty distinguishing between reality and illusion, for advancing your spiritual development, and for developing your channeling ability, if you engage in that.

Azurite – Use this stone for developing and strengthening your abilities to pick up either intellectual messages or spiritual-intuitive messages. In addition, it can stimulate your ability to see extraordinary visions.

Lapis lazuli – Use this stone if you suffer from physical problems of the third eye chakra – hearing problems, dizziness, and conditions of a dulling of the senses. Use it to strengthen your intellectual powers and your ability to decide intuitively. Moreover, it is good for cleansing the subconscious of negative patterns. If you are engaged in various fields of mysticism, and want access to ancient knowledge, lapis lazuli is very suitable for you. Also if you are shy or lack confidence.

Lepidolite – Use this stone for balancing emotion and reason, and if you are a tense or impatient person who has a tendency toward extremes of mood or depression. It will help you discern negative patterns in your subconscious.

Indigo sapphire – Use this stone if you are involved in art and want to strengthen your inspiration and creativity. Moreover, use it to strengthen your visualization abilities.

Blue sapphire – Use this stone to strengthen your aspiration to truth and belief. It is a marvelous stone during meditation. Let it lead you – it may give you clues about your true vocation or reveal it to you.

Purple sapphire – Use this stone to stimulate the desire to find your vocation, and receive clues.

Diamond-shaped calcite – If you feel that the spiritual and intuitive messages that are transmitted to you are not clear enough, or require interpretation, use this stone. Use it in order to strengthen your ability to receive answers and to link up to your superego.

Dioptase – Use this stone to receive answers, or to develop the general ability to receive intuitive answers to basic problems that are bothering you. In addition, it helps you develop spiritual awareness.

Larimar – Hold larimar in your hand during meditation in order to strengthen your healing abilities, or to develop the ability to understand "the language of animals." It can also be used in channeling.

Kyanite – This is a wonderful channeling stone. Use it if you experience fears of any kind during high meditation, and to stimulate your spiritual abilities and link up to your inner guide.

Kunzite – Use this stone to make your thoughts more loving, and to hone your senses. Use it when you want to experience deep meditation, or if you are afraid of unwanted entities during high meditations.

Star sapphire – Use this stone to strengthen your channeling abilities with entities from other worlds. It opens the crown chakra, but can be placed on the third eye in order to understand the messages that arrive.

Blue and dark blue tourmaline – Use these stones for developing extrasensory abilities.

Labradorite – This is a very powerful channeling stone. Place it on the third eye if you have already experienced many meditations, feel a special bond with the stone, or engage in channeling. It helps you understand this incarnation, for the sake of channeling and for seeing and understanding previous ones.

Moldavite – This is one of the strongest stones for raising spiritual consciousness in all levels, if you are lucky enough to possess this rare stone.

Electric shine obsidian – Use this stone if you have seen a great deal of "darkness" in your life, and difficult and painful situations. It is used for strengthening the chakra and developing the ability to see visions of the future or of previous incarnations. It is used for understanding why you have been through the trying things you have been through.

Clear quartz – Use clear quartz to stimulate your spiritual development to the precise extent, to facilitate entry into the meditative state, and to experience a marvelous feeling of being part of the universe. Furthermore, use it to strengthen your channeling ability, to receive information from physical and non-physical spiritual guides, and to strengthen your healing powers.

Rutilated quartz – Use this stone to receive information from ancient civilizations. Do not use it if it the first time you are performing meditation for the third eye chakra. You can use this stone to strengthen your comprehension of the Reiki symbols.

Rainbow crystal – If you possess this rare crystal, simply use it. Let it take you where it will.

Charoite – Use this stone if you sometimes tend to confuse imagination with reality to the point that your daily activities are disrupted. Use it if you feel that you are given "difficult lessons" to learn in life, and ask for understanding of the nature of these lessons and the way to cope with them. It develops intuition, and you might see various scenes while using the stone. If you tend to experience any kind of fears during high meditations or channeling, use this stone.

Smithsonite – Use this stone for developing channeling abilities. To this end, you can place it on the crown chakra. In addition, use the stone to remove and expunge emotional injuries from childhood by placing it on the third eye chakra. It stimulates them from inside the subconscious and helps you cope with them.

Selenite – You can use this stone by placing it either on the crown chakra or on the third eye chakra. It develops your channeling abilities, helps you channel on a particular subject, raise your self-awareness, and receive information about previous incarnations.

Apophyllite – If you engage in channeling, or want to strengthen your channeling abilities, your abilities to predict the future, or your extrasensory perception, use this stone. Apophyllite, in addition to strengthening channeling abilities, helps you discover the points in your character that are in need of change, for your physical, spiritual, and emotional wellbeing.

Perform the meditation in an energetically clean room with a calm and pleasant atmosphere. You can place jasmine or frankincense oil in an essential oil burner, but under no circumstances must synthetic aromatic oils or incense be used. Music is a matter of choice, despite the fact that some people prefer to perform third eye and crown chakra meditation without any kind of music. Set aside about half an hour for the meditation. It is impossible to know in advance what will emerge during this unique meditation, since stones are multifaceted and their action on the third eye and crown chakras is special and mysterious. The meditation itself is very easy – all you have to do is place the stone on the third eye or on the crown chakra, enter a meditative state, and open yourself up completely to receiving the visions and the messages. Having said that, you must be very aware of the qualities of the stone you chose, and request consciously, with clear thoughts, that it direct you to receive an answer, a vision, or a solution to a certain subject. In fact, the inner intention is the very heart of this meditation. However, even if you simply place the stone on the third eye or crown chakra, it will perform its action. But if you direct it toward a certain subject, the stone's action will focus on that subject. You should repeat the meditation with the stone for at least three days. In order to strengthen the meditation, after relaxation and breathing, perform the technique of filling up and detaching that appears in the chapter on sets of crystals. After about half an hour, remove the stone, purify it well, and charge it. In a notebook, write down the messages you received or the sensations you experienced. See what you can learn from them.

It is possible, in certain cases, that while you work with certain stones, no unusual visions will appear. There are several reasons for this. Sometimes, the stone operates on certain planes, and at the same time, the person may even fall asleep. It performs its action, and, even if you made a certain request, there may first and foremost be a need to balance the third eye or crown chakra in a certain way. For this reason, do not be disappointed if in these cases you did not feel or see anything. Possibly, after some time, certain insights and understandings will begin to crop up, or you will feel more aware. When the person is not calm and open to receiving the messages, they are liable to arrive in a confused, incomprehensible, or non-sequential way. You must wonder why you are not calm and empty of all thought, and why you are afraid of receiving those messages. In those cases, it is worthwhile trying to meditate with a "lighter" stone if you felt that unconscious fears prevented you from seeing and understanding messages during the meditation.

The visions, sensations, and insights that are received during this ostensibly "simple" meditation are just a part of its action. In the long range, it raises the self and spiritual consciousness enormously. It is worthwhile continuing the meditation, even if you feel as if you are not receiving significant messages. In this case, use one of the first 11 stones on the list, or clear quartz crystal. Even if "immediate results" are not seen, you can rest assured that the stone is performing its function very well. Just be patient.

Sets of crystals

Laying on of stones (sets of crystals) is a treatment and healing method that relates to the person's mind, body, and spiritual layer. This is an ancient treatment method, and was widely used in various ancient cultures.

The sets of crystals balance the energy of the electromagnetic field, link up to it, and work with it. They open the chakras powerfully, and promote the health of mind and body. They develop and reinforce the spiritual abilities to a great extent, and even help the person learn to heal – both himself and others.

The strength of sets of crystals is a result of the different types of minerals that constitute the set, the combination of the various energies, and the way they are placed. In addition, it is possible to combine the laying on of stones with healing, mantras of positive thinking, guided imagining, and other techniques. The correct intention during the set, both of the person who is laying on the stones and of the person who is receiving them, reinforces the stones' combined energetic power. The energies of the crystals that are laid on combine with the person's energy, and transmit messages of light, love, and goodness to him.

When we use sets of crystals for treatment, we do not place our hand physically on the patient's body. We can use our hands to cleanse the patient's energy field, to convey energy from the centers where there is a surfeit of energy to areas where there is a lack, and to project healing. When the healer passes his hands over the etheric body of the patient, he may feel places where there is a surfeit or a lack, places where the energy is stuck or blocked, by sensing hot or cold, a prickling, and various sensations.

The crystals repair defective energies, and create a very powerful electromagnetic field around the patient. They pick up his energetic frequencies, and cleanse whatever has to be cleansed. They draw unwanted energies out of the patient's body, and certain crystals even absorb them. In places where they locate a lack of energy, they radiate additional energy. Moreover, they raise the general energy level of the patient.

Since the laying on of stones is an extremely powerful treatment method, various sensations may be felt during its course. Sometimes there are shivers, hot or cold sensations, jerky limbs, sweating, or an unpleasant feeling. If you are treating another person and prepare a set of crystals for him, you must remain at his side for the duration of the treatment. You must not leave the room. You should prepare a glass of water and a blanket. Keep track of his sensations, and address him if you think that he is not feeling well. If it seems to you that the patient is in any kind of distress, you must stop the treatment by removing the crystals. If you are treating yourself, cover yourself with a light blanket up to your waist, and stop if you feel that the sensations are too intense for you. In general, those sensations, if they appear, pass within a few minutes.

Because of their great power, sets of stones are liable to cause sensitive reactions after treatment. The therapist must explain to the patient the nature of these sensations. The patient is liable to feel disoriented, detached, and weepy. He may feel that difficult, sensitive feelings are emerging. Sometimes, emotions such as a lack of self-esteem, jealousy, anger, and so on, may emerge. You must explain to the patient that these emotions emerge as a result of the sensitive opening that the crystals performed on him. They reactivated old emotional triggers that must be dealt with. Emotional barriers that were located in the mental and emotional body are released, and for that reason, the reactions occur. Explain this to the patient, and calm him down. This is a positive reaction, and there is no reason to be afraid. As a healer, you must encourage him and release these emotions via conversation. Ask him, listen to him, and encourage him. If, as a healer, you notice that a certain chakra is still open, put him back on the treatment bed and perform a closing of the chakra (at the end of this chapter).

In self-treatment, it is highly recommended that a close friend be with you during the laying on of stones. If these emotions emerge, speak to him, and tell him what's on your mind. If you do not have someone close beside you, write down the things in a notebook, or allow yourself to cry and express your emotions. If you feel that you are still in treatment, and one of the chakras is still open, or if you have stopped the treatment in the middle, for some reason, perform the treatment for closing the chakras that appears at the end of this chapter.

Rules preceding the laying on of stones:

The patient must come to the treatment about an hour after eating a light meal – he must not be hungry, but must also not have eaten a heavy meal.

On the day of treatment – before and after – he must not drink alcohol. In certain sets, this point must be emphasized.

The patient must come to the treatment washed, wearing clean underwear and comfortable clothes. Belts must be taken off before the treatment. Women are advised not to wear tight bras.

Both therapist and patient must go to the bathroom before the treatment, and ensure that they wash their hands. Shoes and bags must not be left in the treatment room.

Before the treatment, both therapist and patient must remove all jewelry and watches. Wedding rings can be left on.

The treatment room must be clean, aired, and at a pleasant and comfortable temperature.

If the patient is a person who has difficulty relaxing, music can be played – only quiet music, without lyrics or any meditative instructions. This is because the laying on of stones has its own specific spiritual purpose, and various meditative instructions are liable to "limit" or disturb the unique flow of the treatment.

Aromatic oils can be placed in an essential oil burner. Do not use synthetic oils, and it is not advisable to use incense during the treatment with a set of stones.

All the crystals used in the treatment must be well purified and charged – in the sun or on a crystal cluster. You can charge them with love, tranquillity, with opening of the spiritual awareness, and so on, according to the aims of the set of stones and your knowledge of the patient.

At the end of the laying on of stones, the crystals must be washed well, purified, and charged again.

At the end of the treatment, the therapist must wash his hands well, letting the water flow over his hands (without using soap). It is advisable not to dry his hands before and after the treatment, but to shake them off and let them dry by themselves.

The therapist must not perform the treatment when he is not emotionally clean. In certain sets of stones, in which the therapist is more involved in the treatment, the importance of this point is cardinal. The therapist must be calm, tranquil, and able to discard any thought or emotion easily.

It is not advisable for a therapist to perform this treatment when he is tired or weary.

The therapist must not leave the room while the patient is undergoing treatment, and he must watch the patient's reactions. In certain sets, this is absolutely critical, especially if the therapist does not know how the patient is going to react to the energy of the stones.

After every treatment, the patient must be given a glass of mineral water.

Note: When it is indicated that the apex of the crystal must point upward, it means that the crystal is placed on the floor, and its apex points forward (in the same direction as the head of the patient). When it is indicated that the apex of the crystal must face downward, it means the same direction in which the patient's feet are pointing.

Projecting color in sets of stones

The link between treatment with color frequencies and treatment with crystals is extremely powerful and effective. Color awareness operates on several different levels. Our brains react to every color that our eyes see. Color stimulates feelings in us, evokes associations, and stimulates both the mental layers and the emotional layers.

Often, we feel a need to wear an item of clothing of a certain color, or an item of jewelry of a certain color, to change the color of the walls or the furniture, and so on. This need may come from our subconscious, which feels the need for the effect of a particular color on the soul. Colors affect the aura in an essential manner. The aura contains all the colors, but the lack of a certain color is liable to be expressed. When this color is added to the aura, the person's feeling improves amazingly, and this also influences his physical condition.

In work with crystals, and especially with sets of crystals, we use color projections a lot. Projecting color is extremely simple – all you have to do is see a ray or spot of light in your mind's eye, in the color that you want to project. You can see the ray of colored light directed toward a certain chakra or organ. Below, we will explain the significance of the different colors, their effect on body and mind, and the treatment cases in which they should be used. Having said that, many therapists and healers notice that after a certain amount of experience with color projection, the colors are likely to appear of their own accord when they set about projecting them on the patient. Until such time, you should ask the patient about the physical and emotional problems from which he suffers, and act intuitively to a great extent, in this way choosing suitable colors for projecting on him during the treatment.

In cases where you do not want to project color, you can use stones of that color, programming them to project their color before laying them on the patient. It is advisable that the stone that is being used for color projection be of a rich, deep hue. Moreover, you can program and project into a clear quartz crystal the color with which you want to perform treatment. See a ray of light in that color descending to the crystal, filling it, and "dyeing" it with that color. After the treatment, you will have to purify the crystal well so that it returns to the frequency quality of its transparent (colorless) state.

Projecting the color red

The first thing that we must know is that red is the color of the base chakra. When we come across a red stone, it is almost definite that it will have an effect on this chakra. When we want to stimulate the base chakra and open it, we use the color red. We use a projection of the color red and red stones when we notice conditions of a lack of flow, and conditions of weakness and a low level of vitality.

Emotional and mental effect: The color red stimulates, warms, invigorates, increases vitality, inspires perseverance, increases personal power, strengthens will power, inspires independence, alertness, openness and extroversion, motivation, leadership ability, courage, passion, sexuality, sensuality, and ambitiousness. We project it in situations in which we discern a certain lack or a weakness in these properties in the patient (or in ourselves, in self-treatment).

When it is not a question of stimulating the chakras when we are projecting all the colors, we do not project the color red in the following cases: when the person is agitated and irascible, aggressive, hyperactive, obviously rebellious, overbearing, unusually tense, or has an exacerbated and unbalanced sexual urge.

The color's effect on the body: The color red stimulates physical health and increases the body's vitality and energy. It has an invigorating effect on the heart, on the circulatory system, and the blood flow. Moreover, it has a positive effect on the action of the genitals, the kidneys, and the bladder. It must not be projected on its own if the person suffers from hypertension.

Treating health problems with color: Projecting the color red is used for stimulating the liver, for treating anemic conditions, for increasing red blood cell production, for stimulating the blood and circulatory system, for stimulating the functioning of the nervous system, for accelerating metabolism, for speeding up the expulsion of poisons from the body, for relieving exhaustion, for treating joint inflammations, muscular pains, fractures, bacterial diseases, and impotence. Most of the red stones treat one or more of the above conditions.

Since this color warms and stimulates enormously, it is generally not projected on its own, but together with blue or with turquoise, the complementary color of red – unless the person is in a state of obvious lack and debilitation.

Projecting the color orange

Orange is the color of the second chakra, the sex chakra. When we want to stimulate the sex chakra and open it, we project the color orange and use orange stones. The color orange is also a stimulating and invigorating color. It is a color that symbolizes warmth, independence, practical intelligence, self-confidence, gaiety, happiness, the joy of expression, and a cosmopolitan attitude. This color combines physical energy – like red does, and intellectual qualities – like yellow does. It especially strengthens the etheric body, and promotes health in general.

Emotional and mental effect: The color orange stimulates joy, helps the person attain self-confidence, make the most of his intellectual abilities, and preserve his energy or his motivation. The color orange is projected in cases of sadness and depression, a lack of interest in life, a lack of self-confidence, and a lack of energy and enthusiasm. We also use it when we notice a problem in applying intellectual abilities in a practical way, and for stimulating analytical thought, inventive ability, motivation, and communicative abilities. Most of the orange stones have a similar effect to the projection of the color itself.

The color must not be projected (except in the general balancing of all the chakras) in aggressive, overly ambitious, competitive, and extremely rebellious people.

The color's effect on the body: The color orange has a restful and anti-spasmodic effect on the entire body, and promotes its health. It has a more gentle ability to invigorate and stimulate than the color red, and also supports the blood flow. It invigorates and balances metabolism, and links up to the spleen and pancreas, the digestive system, and the kidneys.

Treating health problems with color: We project the color orange for treating asthma, bronchitis, and problems in the respiratory system and the lungs, for treating stomach problems, joint pains, calcium problems, and feminine problems (such as fertility, menstruation, sterility). In addition, it is used for treating muscle spasms.

Projecting the color yellow

Yellow is the color of the third chakra, the solar plexus chakra. It symbolizes the intellect and mind, organizational ability, discipline, personality, and ego.

Emotional and mental effect: The color yellow stimulates the intellect and the memory. It improves the person's mood and promotes a feeling of gaiety and lightness. It reinforces the person's organizational abilities, strengthens his personality, his analytical and business abilities, his honesty with himself and with others, and is of great help in stimulating learning abilities. We project the color yellow for stimulating these areas, especially when the person (or ourselves, in self-treatment) is suffering from depression, melancholy, mental exhaustion, a weak memory, and problems with learning and concentration.

The color's effect on the body: The color yellow has a stimulating action on the nervous system and the brain. It stimulates the motor nerves and the energy of the muscles, strengthens the digestive system, stimulates the digestive juices and the lymphatic fluids, and purifies the blood. The color yellow is linked to the liver, the gall bladder, the stomach, the large and small intestines, the lungs, the prostate, the thyroid gland, and the bronchial tubes. Most yellow stones link up to these organs and exert a beneficial effect on them.

Treating health problems with color: We use the color yellow to treat the digestive system, the nervous system, hormonal problems (slowing down or a lack of hormone production), conditions of thyroid imbalance, problems concerning the intestine, spleen, stomach, and bladder, and for stimulating the liver and kidneys.

Projecting the color pink

The color pink is one of the colors of the fourth chakra, the heart chakra. It is not one of the basic colors of the spectrum, but comprises a mixture of white (which is light that consists physically of all the colors of the spectrum) and red, but it has good and beneficial healing abilities, and is widely used in color therapy. Because it consists of red, which is a stimulating color that symbolizes, among other things, passion and love, and white, which contains all the colors and symbolizes the link to the divine and the cosmic, pink is the color of healing and cosmic love. It is not advisable to use it for treating nervous or irascible people. In the colors of the aura, pink attests to sensitivity, sentimentality, femininity, yearning, softness, and sometimes over-sentimentality.

Emotional and mental effect: The color pink is one of the most excellent colors for projecting when we discern a situation of a lack of self-love or self-esteem. It stimulates the desire to give, share, and bestow, it warms, consoles, and arouses universal love. We project the color pink when the person feels unloved, lonely, unappreciated, and not good-looking, or fears that his body's aging will cause him to become ugly (fear of physical aging).

The color's effect on the body: The color pink stimulates cell regeneration, youth, and a beautiful skin and body. Although it does not have specific indications, and it works mainly on the mind, it has a superb healing ability.

Pink is not projected by itself for nervous or irascible people.

Projecting the color green

The color green is the main color of the heart chakra. It is the ultimate healing color, and, in fact, when we do not know which color to project for treating physical problems, we can just use green. It promotes growth and development, freshness, energy, hope, and youth. In addition, it is a very powerful stimulating color. As we said, it can be projected for all physical problems, although some people claim that it must not be used for cancer and cancerous growths (because it stimulates growth and development).

Emotional and mental effect: The color green balances body and mind, is very soothing, strengthens, helps the person overcome physical and emotional obstacles, and creates harmony in all spheres. Green helps us accept things as they are, out of confidence in the universe and the processes of nature. It helps us feel more linked to nature, and inspires unity between body, mind, and spirit. It is one of the best colors for treating emotional imbalance.

The color's effect on the body: The color green has a soothing effect on the sympathetic nervous system. It promotes the health of the blood vessels, and encourages the overall regeneration of the body's cells. It helps balance the hormonal system, alleviates various types of pain, balances blood pressure, and soothes inflammations. It is connected with the muscles, the bones, the bronchial tubes, and the lungs.

Treating health problems with color: The color green is excellent for treating hormonal problems because it stimulates the pituitary gland, which is responsible for the functioning of most parts of the hormonal system. It is suitable for treating heart problems, circulatory problems, for regulating hypertension or low blood pressure. Green strengthens the body generally and helps the person recuperate from disease or injury.

Projecting the color turquoise

Turquoise is made up of green and blue. It is not one of the basic colors of the spectrum, but is widely used in healing. It is suitable for treating both the throat and the heart chakras.

Emotional and mental effect: Turquoise is a very soothing color. It is good for projecting on nervous people and people who find it hard to calm down. It provides a wonderful feeling of protection, and strengthens healing abilities. It helps the link between the heart chakra and the throat chakra, and the ability to express emotions verbally.

Treating health problems with color: We use turquoise to lower fever and states of heat in the body, for treating burns, and for relieving headaches.

Projecting the color blue

The color blue is the color of the throat chakra. It is a very soothing color, and symbolizes deep introspection as well as spreading out broadly. This is the color of truth and belief, renewal and purity. The blue stones possess very effective calming properties, too.

Emotional and mental effect: As we said before, the color blue is one of the most soothing colors. For this reason, we use it in any situation where calming down is called for – situations of hyperactivity, agitation, restlessness, and nervousness. Blue stimulates purity and devotion, belief and wisdom. It helps the person break free when he is burdened by activities during the entire day, and rest in order to charge his batteries. It stimulates spiritual development, the meditative ability, and the intuitive ability. It helps treat all the problems connected to communication – problems of expression, problems of an inability to express ideas or emotions, as well as stuttering and physical problems of expressions. In addition, it stimulates the creative ability on all layers. We use the color blue to stimulate feelings of tranquillity, trust, love, wisdom, inner balance, honesty, reliability, manners, rest, confidence, patience, forgiveness, cooperation, sensitivity, belief, and inner quiet. Furthermore, it is used to help us be centered, see things correctly, and develop spiritual understanding and awareness of the divine. It is also used for treating insomnia.

When we treat a person who is characterized by excessive restraint, a lack of involvement, withdrawal, depression, sadness, passivity, a lack of interest in what's going on, emotional frigidity, and self-pity, or a person who suffers from a feeling of physical coldness and overweight, we use blue together with its complementary color, and not on its own.

The color's effect on the body: The color blue has a beneficial effect on the nervous system. It helps lower blood pressure and slow down the heart rate. It helps strengthen and shrink the tissues, and slow down the growth of tumors. The color blue is linked to the organs of touch, nerve cells, brain, spinal cord, skin, and hair.

Treating health problems with color: We project the color blue for treating breathing problems and throat infections, for lowering fever and states of infection, for treating bruises, wounds, and sensory and emotional disorders. It is very effective for treating problems of the nervous system, and helps treat problems of impaired nervous function, including those of organic origin. It is the most effective color for treating female diseases, menstrual cramps, and menopausal problems.

Similar to red, which is located on the other side of the color scale, blue also has a very powerful effect. For this reason, overdoing the projection of blue in a treatment is liable to cause certain people to feel tired and irritable. Therefore, in most cases that we want to treat primarily with the color blue, it is advisable to project a little of its complementary color as well. The way to do so will be described shortly.

Projecting the color indigo

Indigo is the color of the third eye chakra. It is a combination of blue and purple, which creates a kind of deep purple. Indigo symbolizes the healing abilities, morality, purity of intention, the sixth sense, and intuition. It is the color that is responsible for the flow of the energy of the delicate body via the third eye chakra, which constitutes an exalted spiritual energy center.

Emotional and mental effect: Indigo stimulates seriousness, politeness, synthesis between the actions of the mind and the spirit, a feeling of unity, inspiration, balance, inner serenity, and inner quiet. It stimulates the intuition, extrasensory perception, and the healing abilities. Projecting indigo encourages and promotes spiritual development, and develops the person's awareness. One of the special uses of this color in color therapy is liberating the person from negative or superfluous burdens of color.

The color's effect on the body: Indigo has an effect on the sense of hearing, the sense of sight, and the sense of smell. It is linked to the ears, eyes, and nose.

Treating health problems with color: Projecting indigo is used for treating problems of the nervous system, hearing and sight. It helps treat problems of heat that are connected to the lymph glands, purifies the circulatory system, regulates metabolism and the cells in the body, and treats cases of disorders in the respiratory system.

Projecting the color purple

The color purple affects both the third eye chakra and the crown chakra. It symbolizes intuition, art, creativity, belief, imagination, extrasensory abilities, and lack of physicality.

Emotional and mental effect: Projecting the color purple gives the person inspiration and openness from the spiritual point of view. Purple helps develop all the extrasensory and intuitive abilities, as well as strengthen the meditative abilities. It inspires the ability to receive spiritual messages and information, creativity, morality, idealism, a calm attitude toward life, tranquillity, and the ability to change and develop. We project the color purple for treating problems in the person's mental body, and cases in which there is a need to strengthen the person's spiritual aspect.

The color's effect on the body: The color purple stimulates the spleen, purifies the blood, and increases the production of white blood cells. By doing so, it reinforces the immune system.

Treating health problems with color: The color purple possesses the highest healing powers. It helps treat problems of nerves and mental diseases. It can be projected in order to help in weight loss, for stopping diarrhea, and for purifying the blood.

Projecting the color magenta

The color magenta is also not one of the colors of the spectrum, but it is widely used in color therapy. Magenta is made up of pink and red, and it is considered to be one of the colors of the seventh chakra, the crown chakra.

Emotional and mental effect: Magenta can stimulate the person's healing abilities. It stimulates joy and is effective in treating bad moods, melancholy, and sadness.

The color's effect on the body: Magenta possesses an invigorating effect on the arteries and on the kidneys.

Treating health problems with color: Magenta is a cosmic healing color. It is used for treating problems connected with the brain, infections, and problems with the kidneys and arteries.

Projecting the color white

The color white is the color of the crown chakra. White light is created from the combination of all the colors of the spectrum, and contains all of them. White is the color of the high and pure energy. Projecting it stimulates exalted spiritual awareness, purifies and links up to the divine energy. It is a wonderful color for energetic cleansing, filling up, and protection before performing treatments and the laying on of stones.

Emotional, mental and spiritual effect: The color white stimulates spirituality and spiritual abilities, a feeling of unity with the universe, an understanding of the highest layers of awareness, and the link to the divine. It stimulates the higher intelligence and the aspiration to perfection, and induces cleanliness, purity, and filling up with light and energy. It leads to receiving and giving, to the ability to exchange energy between people, and to cooperation.

The color's effect on the body: In general, white is not projected on certain organs.

Treating health problems with color: The color white contains all the colors of the spectrum, and for this reason, cures every problem. In addition, it is especially excellent for treating the pores of the skin.

The principal use of the color white is for cleansing, filling up, and protection. It is not used for energetic projection, since it picks up and absorbs everything.

Projecting the color gold

Gold is also one of the colors that is suitable for projecting on the crown chakra. It is the ultimate healing color, and it is suitable for projection of every kind, in every treatment, and in every situation. It is the energy of divine love, and for that reason, it is the safest color for use in color projection.

Emotional, mental and spiritual effect: Gold strengthens the electromagnetic field, and the energy of all the bodies. It bestows a feeling of warmth and ease, and a feeling of linking to divine love.

The color's effect on the body: Gold strengthens the aura, as well as the energies of the physical body.

Treating health problems with color: Gold helps treat all physical and mental conditions.

Projecting complementary colors

Projecting complementary colors is one of the best ways to use color projection. This is because we have to ensure that we do not create an imbalance in a particular color (when the color opposite it is projected during the treatment). While the energies of the crystals in a laying on of stones balance the color projection, there is still great importance to preserving the color balance.

This point is very important, especially in the projection of red and blue, which can cause strong reactions after their projection. In addition, it is often possible to see that an imbalance in a basic color is parallel to an imbalance in its complementary color. When we project a color on the person lying in the middle of a set of stones, we project the complementary color for about a third of the time of the basic color. For instance, if we project the basic color yellow on the person for 15 minutes, we project the color purple for five minutes immediately after that. It is advisable to memorize the complementary colors before starting to project them in a laying on of stones.

Complementary colors
Red – turquoise
Green – magenta
Blue – orange
Purple – yellow
Indigo – gold
and vice versa.

Basic laying on of stones for balancing the chakras

The stones that are used in the set must be washed well before use, and programmed for balancing, opening, and cleansing the chakras. Prepare 14 stones – two for each chakra. During the placement, you will find out which of the two stones is more suitable for that particular moment. Go back to the list of stones that appears in the first part of this book, describing the action of each stone on a particular chakra, and choose from them. You can, of course, use your intuition, which is the best guide. You can use this set of stones for yourself very easily, and you can also use it for treating your patients.

See that you are lying on clean sheets. You should even shower before laying on the stones, and put on clean underwear. It is possible to perform the laying on of stones fully dressed in thin and very comfortable clothes, but it is preferable to do it in underwear only. Place the stones on clean fabric or on a towel next to you. Place a glass or bowl a third filled with water within reach. It must be large enough to place all the stones in it after the procedure, with the water covering them but not spilling out (you can check this beforehand, before charging the stones).

Lie on your back and start taking deep, slow breaths. Place one of the two suitable stones on the base chakra. Concentrate on the feeling. After a few moments, exchange it for the second stone. Choose the more suitable one. You might feel the need to place both of them. Act according to your intuition.

Continue checking the stones. When you have found seven suitable stones (or pairs of stones), start placing them, one by one, in order on the chakras, starting from the base chakra, and going upward, until you reach the crown chakra. During the entire process, continue taking deep, slow abdominal breaths. Feel golden light shining from the stones, penetrating your body, warming, caressing or healing it. Close your eyes, or leave them open, according to how you feel, but try to keep your mind free of all thoughts. Feel the pleasant vibrations and the warming and healing sensation. Remain like this for 10 to 20 minutes. You can feel, intuitively, when to end and remove the stones. Now, start removing one stone at a time. Start from the crown chakra, and go in order until you remove the stone from the base chakra. Place each stone that you remove in the bowl of water (arrange it in such a way that water will not spill onto the bed, and you do not need to make a movement that is liable to cause the rest of the stones to fall). When you place the stone in the bowl, dip your fingertips in it, with the intention of getting rid of the unwanted energies that were absorbed from the stone.

If, for some reason, you cannot place a bowl of water near you, place the stones on the towel or fabric beside you (separately from the stones you didn't use!), and afterwards place them in the bowl and dip your fingertips in the water. You can continue resting for a while after taking off all the stones, and let the pleasant resonances continue enveloping you with their warm light.

It is possible that while you are lying down, one of the stones will slide off your body. Do not put it back, since this is a sign that it finished its work for the time being.

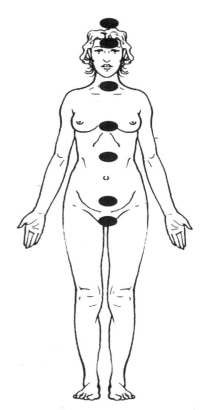

A set of meditative stones for balancing the chakras

In this laying on of stones, we use seven stones, each one for a different chakra. See that the room in which you choose the stones is energetically clean, with a soft and positive atmosphere. You can place an oil burner with several drops of frankincense or jasmine oil, but not synthetic oil. Before you start choosing the suitable stones, spread out all the stones that seem suitable for treating the chakras, and arrange them in groups: a group of red or black stones for the base chakra; a group of orange stones for the sex chakra; a group of yellow or golden stones for the solar plexus chakra; a group of green and pink stones for the heart chakra; a group of blue, light blue, and turquoise (blue-green) stones for the throat chakra; a group of purple, indigo, and lilac stones for the third eye chakra; and a group of transparent, white, or golden stones, that include stones that are especially suitable for the crown chakra (even if their color is different). In addition, you will need a medium-size smoky quartz crystal.

Arrange the groups separately. Sit opposite each group, and concentrate your awareness on finding the stone that is exactly suitable for balancing the particular chakra at this stage in your life. Now you can close your eyes and stretch out your hand to pick up one of the stones. You can hold each one in your hand for a few seconds, and feel intuitively if this is the correct stone. Place each one of the chosen stones on the side, until you have seven stones, one for each chakra. If by chance you feel that two stones are suitable for one of the first five chakras (not the crown chakra or the third eye chakra), you can use both of them.

After you have chosen the suitable stones, you can begin to place them. Look at the rules concerning the laying on of stones once more, and act accordingly. See that no one disturbs you for about half an hour. Do not forget to place a bowl of water next to you in which to immerse the stones after the meditation.

Put a comfortable pillow under your head or neck, and lie on your back. Place the smoky quartz crystal under your legs, about seven centimeters from your feet. The apex of the crystal must face outward (from the body and onward). Relax your entire body, close your eyes, and begin to concentrate on calm and steady breathing. When you inhale, inhale the sensation, the thought of "love" or "peace" or both. When you exhale, focus on the thought or sensation of "everything is as it should be." This method helps you enter a meditative state perfectly, and prepares your being for receiving the welcome energies of the crystals. Each time you feel your thoughts wandering someplace, focus on your breathing again. Continue breathing for a few minutes.

Now, see a white or golden light descending from above and penetrating the crown chakra, descending from it and continuing down along the spinal column, filling your whole body with light, and leaving via the feet.

Take the stone that you chose for the base chakra, and place it on the chakra. In your consciousness, raise the words "stability," "confidence," and "trust." Feel those sensations lifting you, enveloping you, and supporting you. See a red light, delicate but full of life, flowing from the stone into the chakra. Feel its warmth.

Take the orange stone that you chose for the sex chakra, and place it on the chakra. In your mind's eye, see "sensitivity," "sexual expression," "flexibility," and "happiness." Feel these sensations, and feel how they envelop and caress you. See an orange light flowing from the stone into the chakra, shrouding, stimulating, and balancing it.

Take the yellow stone that you chose for the solar plexus chakra, and place it on the chakra. Imagine courage, warmth, and vitality flowing through your body and your being. See yellow light enveloping the diaphragm region, flowing from the stone to the chakra, opening it, and balancing it.

Take the green or the pink stone that you chose for the heart chakra, and place it on the chakra. Think of love, compassion, healing. Ask them and feel them enveloping you and seeping inside you. See green or pink light flowing, pleasant and harmonious, from the stone to the chakra. Feel how it envelops your heart in love and harmony.

Take the blue, light blue, or turquoise stone that you chose for the throat chakra, and place it on the chakra. Ask for good and clear communication, integrity and truth. See blue light flowing from the stone to the chakra region, filling the chakra, balancing it, stimulating it, and opening it. Feel a pleasant coolness in the region of the chakra, cleaning your throat like pure water.

Take the purple, lilac, or indigo stone that you chose for the third eye chakra, and place it on the chakra. See purple-indigo light flowing from the stone to the chakra. In your mind's eye, see the two hemispheres of the brain, and the purple light enveloping them. If you see black or gray spots, imagine how the purple light fills them, until both the hemispheres are completely wrapped in purple light, and their color is white or purple. Feel how the third eye chakra is stimulated, and ask for clarity, spiritual understanding, and spiritual growth.

Take the crystal you chose for the crown chakra, and place it on the chakra, at a distance of about five centimeters from the top of your head. If the crystal you have chosen has an apex, point it toward the top of your head. Concentrate on your breathing, and imagine wisdom, understanding, intelligence, and spirituality. See golden light from above penetrating the crown chaka, descending the spinal column, filling the entire body with light, and continuing via the feet to the bowels of the earth.

With closed eyes, lie for about 10 minutes with the crystals placed on your body. Do not fall asleep, since it is not advisable to leave them on your body for more than 20 minutes in this laying on of stones.

Now begin to remove the stones. First, remove the crystal that is placed on the crown chakra. Place it in the bowl of water, or if there is no bowl of water beside you, prepare a piece of fabric or a towel in advance for placing the crystals. Now remove the crystal from the third eye chakra. Continue taking off the crystals, in descending order, until they have all been removed. Lie for a few minutes, with your eyes open. Turn and stretch your feet. Move your fingers, your hands, and your arms. Very slowly, begin to move your body, while you are still lying down, so that you will not feel dizzy when you get up. Do not get up all at once, but sit up and straighten your body gradually. If you still feel as if you are floating after you have sat up, rub your knees, your calves, your feet, and your ankles. After you stand up, perform a few gentle stretches.

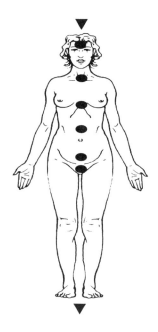

Set of stones – Star of David

This is a well-known and famous set of stones used by many healers. This set generates powerful healing powers around the patient, and the closed circle of healing creates a kind of energetic shield that preserves the healing. This set helps physical and spiritual healing, and greatly increases the patient's awareness. For the set, you need six single terminated quartz crystals and a quartz generator. It does not matter if the crystals are of different sizes. In this set, the therapist has to link the corners of the Star of David using the quartz generator.

Ask the patient to lie down. He must be wearing comfortable clothes that are not too tight and do not bother him in any way. He must take his shoes off outside the room, because the laying on of stones is not performed when shoes are worn. In addition, he must be barefoot, or wearing thick socks. Objects that possess external energy, such as shoes, backpacks, bags, and so on, must not be in the room. The treatment can be performed on an especially large, wide treatment bed, or on a mattress on the floor. Ask the patient to lie down, close his eyes, and begin to take deep, slow breaths. Ask him to feel how his body relaxes and calms down with each breath.

Creating the first triangle
Place the first crystal approximately 15 centimeters above the center of the patient's head. The apex of the crystal must point upward, and not toward the crown of the patient's head.

Place the two other crystals at the side of each of the patient's knees, at a distance of about 15 centimeters. The apexes of the crystals must point upward, toward his head, lying vertically at the sides of his body.

Creating the second triangle
Place the fourth crystal at a distance of 15 centimeters from the patient's feet, with the apex pointing upward, toward his feet. The crystal must be in a straight line with the one above his head.

Place the two remaining crystals at the side of each of the patient's elbows, at a distance of about 15 centimeters. The apexes of the crystals must point upward, toward his head, lying vertically at the sides of his body.

The two triangles must be the same shape.

Filling up and protection
See a pure white light descending from above, and penetrating your crown chakra, via the top of your head. See the light flowing along your spinal column, all the while filling your entire body with pure white light. Think in a clear and focused way: "I am cleansing myself of all emotions and thoughts." Let the light continue filling your body, as it goes down your spine and your legs, and leaves your body to enter the bowels of the earth. It continues filling you until it goes out and envelops you in an ellipse of pure, protective white light.

Now you can continue. Hold the generator quartz in two hands, and invert it so that its apex points downward at the Star of David. Stand for a few seconds above the crystal that is located above the patient's head. Walk in a clockwise direction and in a straight line to the crystal that is lying next to the patient's elbow. Stand for a few seconds above this crystal, while you direct your thoughts to link up the points of the Star of David. In your mind's eye, see the energetic link that is created between the crystals, while you continue to the next crystal, in a clockwise direction. Keep on doing this until you link up all the points of the Star of David. Ensure that you breathe consciously during the entire treatment. See that you do not link up the triangles as separate triangles, but rather as a six-pointed Star of David.

When you have completed the joining of the points of the Star of David, an energetic circle is created around the body of the patient. Now you will have to repeat the procedure five times, so that ultimately, an energetic circle like a Star of David will be created six times – that is, it has six layers.

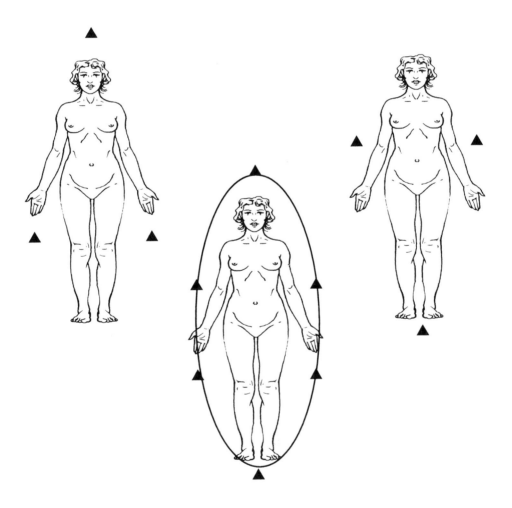

When you have finished circling the Star of David and joining up its points six times, put the generator aside. Look at the patient, and make sure that he is not cold or suffering from any reaction. If you notice that he is cold or shivering slightly, place a blanket on him carefully and gently, without entering the Star of David that surrounds him. Ask him if he feels comfortable, and if everything is all right. At this stage, he may not feel like talking too much, so don't expect more than an acknowledgment.

Let him remain in the Star of David for 10 more minutes, but not more. After that time, begin to collect the crystals, first removing the one above the patient's head and the one below his feet. After you have removed all the crystals, place them in a dish full of water. Then you must wash them and recharge them. After you have removed the crystals, wake the patient gently and softly. If he feels the need, let him lie for five more minutes, and then wake him again.

After the treatment, the patient is likely to feel as if he is floating. Sit him up, and give him a glass of mineral water to drink. Suggest that he go to the bathroom. After he feels more grounded, ask him about his sensations during the treatment.

After the treatment, it is not advisable to smoke for at least an hour, or eat for half an hour. Drinking alcohol on the day of the treatment is forbidden, and the same goes for the 24 hours following the treatment. It is not advisable to wear, hold, or link up to any other crystal.

This treatment should be repeated four to six times, once a week only. Other laying on of crystals must not be performed between Star of David treatments.

Balancing the body's energies

This is one of the strongest sets of stones from the point of view of healing and balancing ability. By using crystals, we create a double Star of David – with 12 points – that symbolizes perfection. With this set of crystals, we balance and purify the body's energies and the energy of the chakras by creating energetic balance and full purification both of the body and of the spirit. In this set, the therapist must be an active participant by projecting colors on the patient by means of visualization or by means of his hands (and color visualization). The therapist must operate in an intuitive and linked-up way, and must ensure that his energies are clean, and that he is in a balanced physical and mental state. This set should not be performed when you are tired, or troubled by thoughts and emotions. This treatment requires a great deal of attention because of its strength. It must only be performed on a patient who has already experienced the laying on of stones. Do not perform it on yourself. During the course of the procedure, various reactions are possible, and for this reason, you must pay heed to the patient. If you think that the patient is experiencing any kind of distress, remove the crystals slowly. Leave only the crystals above his head and below his feet for two to three minutes, and then remove them too. This set is too strong for some people, so you must act judiciously when it comes to deciding whether or not to treat a certain person with it. As we said before, it must only be performed on a person who has experienced the laying on of stones and is accustomed to linking up to the energy of the crystals. People who are in a state of extreme imbalance or who are totally immersed in the material world should be treated with this set. The patient eats a light meal about an hour before the treatment, refrains from drinking alcohol for the entire day of the treatment, and the day after, and arrives washed, calm, and at ease. Before the treatment, remove your watch and all the jewelry from your body, and tell the patient to do likewise. Ask him to go to the bathroom before the treatment.

In order to prepare the set, you will need twelve single terminated clear quartz crystals and a quartz generator.

Perform the filling up, the cleansing, and the protection that are described in the "Star of David" set.

The patient must lie on the floor. Instruct him to take deep breaths, concentrate on his breathing, and feel how his body relaxes more with each breath.

Place the first crystal at a distance of 15 centimeters above the top of the patient's head, pointing upward (that is, not at the top of the patient's head).

Place the second crystal below the patient's feet, at some distance from them, pointing upward, and in a straight line with the crystal above his head.

Place the third crystal at the side of the patient's right shoulder, at a distance of about 15 centimeters from it, pointing upward.

Place the fourth crystal at the side of the patient's left shoulder, at a distance of about 15 centimeters from it, pointing upward.

Place the fifth crystal at the side of the patient's right elbow, at a distance of about 15 centimeters from it, pointing upward.

Place the sixth crystal at the side of the patient's left elbow, at a distance of about 15 centimeters from it, pointing upward.

Place the seventh crystal at the side of the patient's right forearm, at a distance of about 15 centimeters from it, pointing upward.

Place the eighth crystal at the side of the patient's left forearm, at a distance of about 15 centimeters from it, pointing upward.

Place the ninth crystal at the side of the patient's right knee, at a distance of about 15 centimeters from it, pointing upward.

Place the tenth crystal at the side of the patient's left knee, at a distance of about 15 centimeters from it, pointing upward.

Place the eleventh crystal at the side of the patient's right ankle (on the outer side of the leg), at a distance of about 15 centimeters from it, pointing upward.

Place the twelfth crystal at the side of the patient's left ankle, at a distance of about 15 centimeters from it, pointing upward.

All the crystals at the sides of the body must be in a straight line, with their apexes pointing upward.

Now you have created a form that slightly resembles an ellipse around the patient's body. Using your generator, sketch the double Star of David on the surface of the set of crystals:

Hold the generator with its apex pointing at the patient. Stand in front of the crystal above the top of his head. Move in a clockwise direction (from right to left), and start to link the crystals consecutively until you complete the circle and are once more standing in front of the crystal above the top of the patient's head.

Repeat this procedure 11 more times, so that you will have linked the crystals 12 times altogether.

After you have completed the 12 circles, you can begin projecting the colors. Remember not to enter the energetic circle of the set of stones, but rather stand outside it. You can perform the color projection while holding the generator in your hand, pointing at the patient. In this case, you must see the colors passing through the generator to the patient. In my opinion, it is preferable to put the generator aside at this stage, and project colors with your hands. However, act according to your feelings and intuition.

Stand in front of the patient's head, facing him, at a distance you judge to be right. Close your eyes. Aim your hands at the crystal lying above his head and see a golden light projected from them to the crystal. Project the golden light for a minute or two. You do not need to look at a watch, just be aware of the feeling of acceptance or rejection that is transmitted to you from the patient as a result of the color projection, and act accordingly.

Walk around the patient in a clockwise direction, making sure not to enter the set of crystals. Stand opposite the crystal lying below the patient's feet, at a distance you judge to be right. Stretch out your hands and project red light onto the crystal for a few moments.

While you are standing there, see yourself projecting orange light onto the two crystals at the side of the patient's legs. At this point, you must be aware of your visualization abilities. It is possible that you will have to stand opposite each crystal separately, and project orange light onto them. If so, first approach the crystal on the patient's left, and afterwards the one on the right.

Stand opposite the crystal at the side of the patient's right forearm and project yellow light for a few moments. Pay attention to the patient's need for the color projection, and act accordingly.

Stand opposite the crystal at the side of the patient's right elbow, and project green light for a few moments. It is possible that the projection of the green light will take longer, relatively speaking, since this is the projection onto the heart chakra, which affects the general balance of all the chakras.

Stand opposite the crystal at the side of the patient's right shoulder, and project blue light onto it.

When you go to the left side of the patient, do so at some distance from the energetic circle so as not to disrupt the flow of energy above the crown chakra.

Project blue light onto the crystal at the side of the patient's left shoulder.

Project green light onto the crystal at the side of the patient's left elbow.

Project yellow light onto the crystal at the side of the patient's left forearm.

See his energetic circle completed.

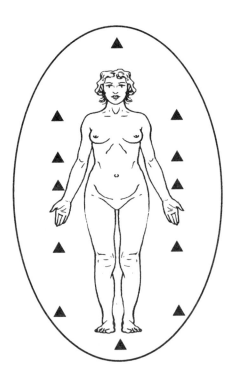

It is possible to project the colors simultaneously onto the two parallel crystals on each side of the patient's body. First you project onto the crystals next to the ankles, then onto the crystals next to the forearms, then onto the crystals next to the elbows, and then onto the crystals next to the shoulders. This method requires that you be able to project simultaneously onto the crystals on either side of the body. In addition, you may feel that one side needs more color projection than the other, and you will have to pay great attention to the patient's acceptance. Know what you are capable of and act accordingly.

After you have completed the color projection, let the patient lie for five to ten minutes. Do not leave the room, but sit at one side and watch his reactions. If you feel any kind of distress on the part of the patient, cut the treatment short by removing the crystals. After about five or ten minutes, begin removing the crystals, starting with the crystal above the patient's head, and then the crystal below his feet. Then remove the crystals on his right side, and finally remove those on his left side.

After removing the crystals, let the patient lie for a while, until he can get up by himself. Since the vibrations of the crystals and the projected colors continue to work after the removal of the crystals as well, the patient may want to continue lying for another 10 to 15 minutes.

When he gets up, give him a glass of water. He may feel a slight floating sensation. It is not advisable to drive for half an hour after the treatment, because of its strength. Sit with the patient and ask him about his sensations during the treatment.

Since the color projection is onto the crystals, you will have to purify them well, because color projection is really like dyeing them in the projected color. Place them in a bowl of water immediately after the treatment, for about half an hour. Afterwards, rinse each one off under running water for about three minutes, with the intention of removing the color. Place them outside for 24 hours so that they can absorb the energies of the sun and the moon.

Upper and lower healing sets

Upper and lower healing sets can be used together for a comprehensive treatment. In addition, each one serves a different purpose:

Upper healing set: The aim of this set is to stimulate the person's more spiritual levels, and lead to his spiritual growth. It is very suitable for people who are grounded by nature, people who live in the "here and now," and are not involved or interested in the layers of spiritual life. This set opens the person up to spiritual experiences, and increases his awareness of what is beyond everyday material life.

Lower healing set: This set is an excellent set for people whose "heads are in the clouds," but their feet are not altogether on the ground. This situation sometimes occurs during spiritual work, when the person is located more in the spiritual layers than in the material layers, but in an unbalanced manner. There has to be a balance not only in physicality, but also in spirituality. When the person does not pay enough attention to matters that are not ostensibly "spiritual," such as work, relationships, and so on, he needs this kind of balancing. One must know how to assimilate the insight, because everything that we do in this world concerns the spiritual layers, or is linked and bound to them. Our relationships, financial affairs, work, and so on, also have a spiritual aspect, for, in the material world, our path toward repairing the soul passes through the material and the spiritual. We use the lower healing set to treat people who are predominantly engrossed in spiritual matters, and neglect physical ones.

The lower healing set and the upper healing set are combined to create balance between the spiritual and the physical. In addition, this combined set helps to effect a deeper opening of the chakras, and an increase of awareness.

Upper healing set

To create this set of stones, you must use seven double terminated quartz crystals and two clear quartz generators. You do not need to use music in this set, unless the patient has a hard time calming down or entering a meditative state. As in the rest of the sets, you must ensure that there are no shoes or bags in the treatment room. The treatment is performed on the floor, where a mattress or a thick blanket can be placed. The patient must lie on his back. Instruct him to breathe consciously, deeply and slowly. Ask him to feel how his body relaxes more with each breath.

Place the seven double terminated crystals around the patient's head, at a distance of about 10 centimeters from his body, to form a kind of semicircle (a three-quarter circle, in fact).

Place the first crystal above the top of the patient's head.

Place the second crystal above the patient's left ear.

Place the third crystal above the patient's right ear.

Place the fourth crystal at the left side of the patient's chin.

Place the fifth crystal at the right side of the patient's chin.

Place the sixth crystal between the left ear and the crystal at the top of the patient's head.

Place the seventh crystal between the right ear and the crystal at the top of the patient's head.

Place one of the generators below the patient's feet, at a distance of about 20 centimeters, with its apex pointing upward. See that it is in a straight line with the crystal above his head. Hold the other generator in both hands.

Now, stand above the patient's head, while making sure not to enter the set of stones. Perform the filling up that is described in the "Star of David" set. After you have done this, invert the generator so that its apex points downward, toward the patient.

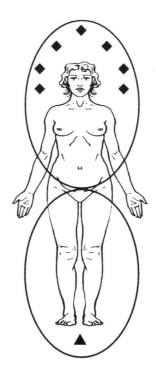

Start linking the crystals, beginning from the one that is above the patient's head, and continuing along the right side of the patient. Link it with an energetic line to the crystal that is located between the crown of his head and his right ear, and continue to the crystal that is at the side of his right ear. Continue in this way until you have linked up all the crystals on the patient's right side. Pull the energetic line that you have created to the patient's base chakra, using the generator in your hand. From the base chakra, continue the energetic line to the left side of the patient, and link it to the generator quartz that is below the patient's feet.

Continue forming the figure 8 by passing the crystal over the generator that is below the patient's feet, to the right side of the patient's body. Pass the crystal again over the base chakra, and draw the energetic line to the left side of the patient. Continue in this way, passing through the crystals on the left side of the patient until you return to the crystal above his head once more. In your mind's eye, see the figure 8.

Drawing the energetic line may sound a bit complicated, but it is very simple. You have to create the shape of the figure 8, which symbolizes infinity, beginning from the crown of the head, via the patient's right side, along his left side, and back to the top of his head.

Repeat the procedure six more times, so that you will have sketched the figure 8 seven times, in accordance with the number of crystals (excluding the generators).

Let the patient lie for 15 minutes, then go over and remove the crystals. It does not matter in what order you remove them. Let the patient lie for a few minutes after the crystals have been removed, Place the crystals in a bowl of water, after which you must wash them in order to purify them, and charge them.

After you rouse the patient, give him a glass of water, and speak to him about his feelings during the treatment.

Lower healing set:

In this set of stones, you must use seven single terminated quartz crystals and two clear quartz generators. There is no need for music here, either, unless the patient finds it difficult to calm down or to enter a meditative state. Instruct the patient to breathe consciously and to relax his body, organ by organ. When the patient has reached a calm and tranquil state, begin placing the crystals.

Place the first crystal about 10 centimeters below his feet, with its apex pointing downward.

Place the second crystal about 10 centimeters from the toes of his right foot, in line with his toes, with its apex pointing outward.

Place the third crystal about 10 centimeters from the toes of his left foot, in line with his toes, with its apex pointing outward.

Place the fourth crystal about 10 centimeters from the middle region of his right calf, with its apex pointing outward.

Place the fifth crystal about 10 centimeters from the middle region of his left calf, with its apex pointing outward.

Place the sixth crystal about 10 centimeters from the region that joins the ankle to the bottom of the calf of the right foot, with its apex pointing outward.

Place the seventh crystal about 10 centimeters from the region that joins the ankle to the bottom of the calf of the left foot, with its apex pointing outward.

Place the quartz generator above the patient's head, with its apex pointing upward. It must be in a straight line with the crystal below his feet.

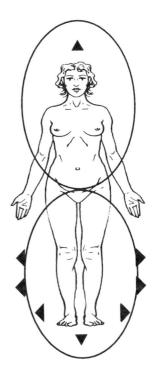

Now hold the second quartz generator in both hands. Perform the filling up that is described in the "Star of David" set. After you have filled up with energy, you must begin to link up the crystals that are placed around the patient. The way to link them up will create the figure 8 (which symbolizes infinity) around the patient's body. Begin with the crystal that is placed next to the right calf. Continue the circle via the crystal that is located in the region between the calf and the ankle. In your mind's eye, see the outline of the linking that you are creating. Remember not to enter the energetic circle that is being formed by the set. Continue to the crystal that is placed below the patient's feet. Continue consecutively until you reach the crystal next to the patient's left calf. By means of the crystal in your hands, draw a line from the left calf to the patient's base chakra, and continue the energetic line to the patient's right side. Continue the energetic line to above the generator that is above the patient's head. In the same movement, continue the energetic line to the right side of the patient, in the direction of the base chakra. Repeat the figure 8 shape six more times, so that by the end of the procedure, you will have created the shape seven times, in accordance with the number of crystals in the set.

Let the patient lie for 15 minutes more, not longer. Begin to remove the crystals in any order you like. Remember to place them in a bowl of water to purify them of the energies that they accumulated during the treatment. Rouse the patient gently, and let him lie for a few more minutes without the crystals, if he needs to. After he wakes up, offer him a glass of water and ask him about his sensations during the laying on of stones, and afterwards.

Combined set – upper and lower:

As we said before, the combined set combines the spiritual and the physical aspects, in order to create perfect balance. For the combined set, you will need seven single terminated quartz crystals and seven double terminated quartz crystals. In addition, you will need a quartz generator.

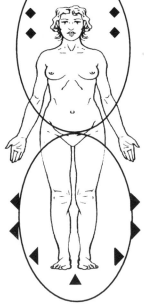

First, place the crystals for the upper set, and then place the crystals for the lower set.

Perform the filling up that is described in the "Star of David" set. Make sure that the patient is taking deep, slow breaths. You can check this according to the swelling and shrinking of his chest and abdomen.

Stand in front of the crystal above the patient's head, and hold your crystal above it with its apex pointing downward. Begin linking the crystals above his head with an energetic line, starting from his right side. Continue to above the patient's base chakra, and draw the energetic line to his left side, to the crystals that are placed around the region of his left leg. From the crystal that is located below his feet, continue drawing the energetic line back in a rightward direction, via all the crystals, and ascend to above the base chakra, in order to create the shape of a figure 8. From the base chakra, continue in a leftward direction, via the crystals that are placed on the left side of the patient's head, until you get back to the crystal that is located above his head.

Repeat the formation of the figure 8 thirteen more times, so that in the end you will have formed the figure 8 fourteen times, in accordance with the number of crystals in the set.

After you have completed the energetic link between the crystals, let the patient lie for about 15 minutes surrounded by the crystals, but no longer. After 15 minutes, begin to remove the crystals in any order. Place them in a bowl of water, and let the patient lie for a few more minutes before gently rousing him. Give him a glass of water when he wakes up, and sit and talk to him about his sensations during the treatment. The conversation after the set is very important, both to therapist and patient. It helps the patient understand and internalize the experiences he has had, with the therapist helping him understand things that he may not have succeeded in interpreting, because he was in the center of the healing procedure. The conversation helps the therapist better understand the action of the crystals, and receive a broader view of their action on different people.

Set of stones for mental stimulation

This set of stones is performed in the shape of a Y. You will need nine medium-size or large single terminated clear quartz crystals for it, and three relatively small additional crystals. Small crystals will also do good work, but it might be less powerful. This set stimulates the person's mental and intellectual development. It increases his awareness, his intuition, and his mental functioning in everyday life, as well as his receptive and learning ability in all the layers. It increases his ability to make correct decisions, and augments his power of concentration and his ability to function well under all circumstances. It helps create a balance between the material and the physical layers on the one hand, and the spiritual layers on the other. In addition, it stimulates creativity and inspiration, as well as his healing abilities. This set can also be performed on oneself, without the assistance of a healer or a partner. The duration of the set is between 20 and 40 minutes.

Purify the crystals well, and charge them to stimulate the mental layers and to increase awareness, insight, and the creative ability. With a bit of effort, you can apply this set to yourself, without the help of a therapist.

Before the treatment, you must perform the filling up that is described in the "Star of David" set. At a certain point, you must instruct the patient to fill up in a similar manner.

Ask the patient to lie on the floor (or on a thin mattress on the floor), with his legs slightly apart, so that you can place the crystals between them. Ask him to take deep, slow breaths, and relax his body.

After performing the filling up and the protection, place the first crystal at a distance of about five centimeters from the patient's right shoulder, with its apex pointing at the patient.

Place the second crystal at a distance of about 10 centimeters above the first crystal and slightly to its right, in order to create the right branch of the letter Y. Place it with its apex pointing at the patient.

Place the third crystal at a distance of about 10 centimeters above the second crystal and slightly to its right, with its apex pointing at the patient. This action will complete the right branch of the letter Y.

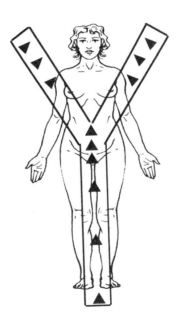

Now, perform exactly the same actions with the next three crystals, in order to create the left branch of the letter Y. Remember to place the first crystal at a distance of about five centimeters from the patient's shoulder, with its apex pointing at the patient.

After placing the six crystals that create the upper part of the letter Y, place the three small crystals as follows:

Place the first crystal below the patient's diaphragm, with its apex pointing toward the patient's head. Right below it, place the second and third crystals, in the same direction. The three crystals must cover the patient's body from the region below the diaphragm to the groin region.

Now place the three last crystals. These crystals will form the leg of the letter Y.

Place the first crystal between the patient's thighs, at a distance of about 15 centimeters from the point of the base chakra (that is, the crystal will be parallel to the lower part of the patient's thigh). Its apex must point at the base chakra. The distance between the next two crystals depends on the length of the patient's legs. Place them at equal intervals, more or less, after the first crystal, so that the end of the third crystal will form a kind of triangle (if you draw an imaginary line) with the patient's feet, and will protrude outward slightly. The apexes of these two crystals must also point at the base chakra.

After you have placed all the crystals, stand at the patient's side without entering the set. Instruct him to breathe deeply, and see a white light descending from above, penetrating his crown chakra, and filling him totally. The white light fills his entire body, descends via the spinal column to the feet, and from there goes down into the bowels of the earth. He is completely full of the white light, which creates an ellipse of light around him, and also encompasses the crystals surrounding him.

After these instructions, let the patient lie quietly for 20 minutes to half an hour. Afterwards, begin to remove the crystal, first removing the right branch of the letter Y, then the left branch, then the lower line, and finally the three small crystals on the patient's body. Place them in a bowl of water, and purify and charge them afterwards.

The patient might feel as if he is floating a bit after the treatment. Give him a glass of mineral water, and ask him to sit for a bit. It is not advisable to drive after this set of stones. After he has come down to earth, ask him about his sensations during the treatment.

Laying on of stones – awakening

The laying on of stones awakens in us the quest for unity with the universe. It imbues us with a feeling of wholeness, of being one with universal love. It increases self-awareness, and helps the person discover the deep and hidden layers of his personality. This set also stimulates the intellectual abilities to a large extent, mainly the logical ability. However, having said that, it helps us understand what is beyond human logic. This set stimulates emotions, the mental layer, and the spiritual quest. It helps the person understand the emotional or physical disorders that he feels, and where they stem from. Moreover, the set helps the person grasp in an essential manner the comprehensive link between mind and body, and the nature of the interaction between the two layers. It creates unity between the intellectual perception and the intuitive perception, and stimulates ancient knowledge and insights.

You will need the following stones for this set:

Twelve medium-size quartz crystals (10-15 centimeters long), two smaller quartz crystals (five centimeters long), and a very small single terminated quartz crystal.

One amethyst that is suitable for placing on the third eye.

A blue stone for stimulating the throat chakra – preferably a small to medium blue crystal. A medium-size blue calcite, blue tourmaline, aventurine, or blue fluorite will do.

Two single terminated rose quartz crystals.

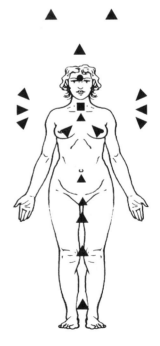

Although the size of the quartz crystals appears here, read the instructions well and "maneuver" with the crystals you have at your disposal. Try to imagine the placement of the crystals on your patient's body when you plan the laying on of stones before performing the first treatment with this set.

Place the two rose quartz crystals on the patient's chest with their apexes pointing diagonally toward the center of the body (in the direction of the shoulders).

Place the first quartz crystal – the tiny one – on the person's chest, above the gap between the two rose quartz crystals, with its apex pointing at the throat chakra, and reaching the hollow between the bones of the clavicle.

Above this crystal, on the throat itself, place the blue stone you chose. If the stone has an apex, it must point toward the patient's face.

Place the amethyst on the patient's third eye chakra (slightly above the point between the two eyebrows).

Place the second quartz crystal above the patient's head, at a distance of about five centimeters from the top of his head, with the apex pointing upward.

Place two quartz crystals – the third and the fourth – above the second one, at a distance of about five centimeters from the second one, and with a gap of about ten centimeters from each other.

Now, place the fifth quartz crystal at a distance of about ten centimeters from the patient's right shoulder, with its apex pointing at the patient's shoulder. Behind it, at a distance of about five centimeters, place the sixth and seventh quartz crystals, with a gap of about 10 centimeters between them, and their apexes pointing at the patient's shoulder. A kind of diagonal flow of crystal is created, indicating the direction of the patient.

Place the eighth, ninth, and tenth quartz crystals in exactly the same way above the patient's left shoulder.

Now use the two smaller quartz crystals. Place the eleventh quartz crystal below the patient's diaphragm. Its apex must point toward the patient's face. Below it, place the twelfth quartz crystal, so that it covers the region of the sex chakra, and its apex points toward the patient's face.

Place the thirteenth quartz crystal at a distance of about 15 centimeters from the patient's base chakra, between his legs, with its apex pointing toward the chakra.

Place the fourteenth and fifteenth crystals at approximately equal intervals until the patient's ankle region, in a straight line with the thirteenth crystal, with their apexes pointing toward the base chakra.

Let the patient remain in the set of stones for 15-30 minutes. Watch his reactions, and ensure that he feels comfortable, If not, shorten the time he spends in the set, and remove the stones earlier.

To conclude the laying on of stones, begin to remove the stones, starting with the quartz crystals, in any order you deem to be correct. Afterwards, remove the amethyst, the blue stone from the throat chakra, and finally the two rose quartz crystals. Place the stones you have removed in a bowl of water. (After the patient has left, or after they have been in the bowl of water for about 30 minutes, rinse them well under running water and charge them in the sun or on a crystal cluster.)

Let the patient lie for a few more minutes before waking him gently. Give him a glass of water, and ask him about his sensations during the treatment with the stones, and after it.

Healing set – crystal clusters

In this healing set, we use the laying on of quartz crystal clusters in addition to that of crystals. Crystal clusters are very power tools for removing emotional blockages and eliminating cumulative stress. They send their healing energy into the healing set, and simultaneously draw non-positive energies out of the patient's bodies. The treatment leads to a releasing of pressures and tension from all the bodies. It releases tensions that are located in the subconscious, and activates, cleanses, and stimulates all the chakras, especially those upon which the clusters are placed.

In order to prepare the set, you will need the following crystals:

Twelve medium-size single terminated quartz crystals.

Three small to medium-size quartz crystal clusters (the cluster that is meant to be placed on the third eye must be relatively very small). The small cluster, for placing on the third eye, can be replaced by a small amethyst cluster.

A generator.

You can use this set for color projection according to your intuition, and according to how well you know the patient. Reread the chapter on the significance and action of colors, so that you know in advance which color to project onto the patient. You may find, to your surprise, that during the actual projection, another color will emerge. The universe helps crystal healing therapists, and sends them the correct knowledge for healing. If you are experienced in healing and color projection, you may be able to rely on your intuition during the treatment, and can project the colors intuitively.

Remind the patient to go to the bathroom before the treatment. He must remove his watch and all his jewelry, and so must you. A wedding ring that does not come off the finger is not a problem, and can be left on.

Instruct the patient to take deep breaths, and direct him to relax his body with each breath.

Begin the treatment with filling up and protection (as is described in the "Star of David" set).

Place the first quartz crystal at a distance of about 10 centimeters above the top of the patient's head, with its apex pointing upward.

Place the second quartz crystal at a distance of about 10 centimeters from the side of the patient's right shoulder, with its apex pointing upward.

Place the third quartz crystal at a distance of about 10 centimeters from the side of the patient's right elbow, with its apex pointing upward.

Place the fourth quartz crystal at a distance of about 10 centimeters from the side of the patient's right wrist, with its apex pointing upward.

Place the fifth quartz crystal at a distance of about 10 centimeters from the side of the patient's right knee, with its apex pointing upward.

Place the sixth quartz crystal at a distance of about 10 centimeters from the side of the patient's right ankle (in a straight line with all the other crystals), with its apex pointing upward.

Now there is one crystal above the patient's head, and five crystals placed at a distance of 10 centimeters from the patient's body, in a straight line, with all their apexes pointing upward.

Place the seventh quartz crystal below the patient's feet, at a distance of about 10 centimeters from them, with its apex pointing upward.

Place the eighth quartz crystal at a distance of about 10 centimeters from the side of the patient's left ankle (parallel to the sixth quartz crystal), with its apex pointing upward.

Place the ninth quartz crystal at a distance of about 10 centimeters from the side of the patient's left knee, with its apex pointing upward.

Place the tenth quartz crystal at a distance of about 10 centimeters from the side of the patient's left wrist, with its apex pointing upward.

Place the eleventh quartz crystal at a distance of about 10 centimeters from the side of the patient's left elbow, with its apex pointing upward.

Place the twelfth quartz crystal at a distance of about 10 centimeters from the side of the patient's left shoulder, with its apex pointing upward.

Crystals eight to twelve are placed in a straight line.

Place the largest crystal colony you have below the patient's pubic bone region (the base chakra).

Place the second largest crystal colony below the patient's diaphragm (the solar plexus chakra).

Place the small crystal (or amethyst) cluster on the patient's third eye chakra.

Stand opposite the crystal that is placed above the patient's crown chakra, and begin to link the crystals with an energetic line, in a clockwise direction. When you stand opposite the crystal above the crown chakra once more, use the generator to link the three clusters that are placed on the patient's body with an energetic line. If you find it difficult to do this while standing opposite the crystal above the patient's head, stand at his side.

Now begin the color projection. As we said before, you can use the generator, or put it aside and use your hands. Stand at the patient's feet, at his side, or opposite the crystal above his crown chakra – wherever is most comfortable for you. Project the color that you planned to project in advance, or the color that comes to you intuitively. If for some reason you do not sense which color to project, project gold or green. Those are the safest colors for projecting. Green is the color of balance, while gold is the safest cosmic energy, the divine light of love. These two colors can be projected whenever you cannot decide which color to project.

After the color projection, let the patient lie in the set for 10 to 15 more minutes.

Afterwards, begin to remove the crystals. First remove the three crystal clusters – the order is not important. Then begin to remove the crystals; here too, the order is immaterial. Act according to your feelings.

Let the patient lie for 10 more minutes.

In this treatment, the patient is liable to feel cold or slight tremors because of the non-positive energies that are leaving his body as a result of the action of the clusters. Conversely, he is liable to feel enormous heat as a result of the energy that is absorbed by the combination of the crystal clusters. These fluctuations in temperature will pass after the treatment, but the patient should be informed that sensations like these might occur.

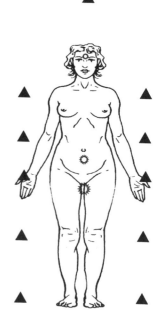

Self-treatment with sets of stones

The sets of stones in the previous chapter, with the exception of the first two sets for balancing the chakras, required the participation of a healer or a partner who could project color or link the crystals' energies by means of the crystal generator in his hands. After you try the self-treatment with the "Star of David" set that appears below, you can try to use the other sets of stones for self-treatment as well. In principle, it is possible to use any one of the sets of stones for self-treatment. This requires knowing the manner of self-treatment with the set, as it is presented in the following set, and also the ability to use your healing powers on yourself. In sets for self-treatment, you will have to breathe consciously and use your powers of visualization in order to "draw" suitable colors to yourself. Again, before you try to use one of the previous sets for self-treatment, try the one below.

The "Star of David" set of stones for self-healing

This set of stones is used for physical and mental self-healing. For the set, you will need the following crystals:

Six clear quartz crystals.

One amethyst that is suitable for placing on the third eye chakra.

A quartz generator.

Use the generator to describe a circle that is big enough to contain your body.

Place the crystals beside you. Lie in the circle, and, while you are lying down, place the first crystal about 15 centimeters above your crown chakra, with its apex pointing upward.

Sit up, your legs straight, and place the next two crystals at the sides of your knees, at a distance of about 15 centimeters from them, with their apexes pointing upward.

You have now completed the first triangle.

Take the next three crystals, and place them as follows, their apexes pointing upward: one between your feet, at a distance of about 10 centimeters from them, in a straight line with the crystal above your head. Place the two that are left at the sides of your elbows, at a distance of about 10 centimeters from them. You have now completed the second triangle. The two triangles must be the same shape.

After you have arranged the set, get up and stand inside it, holding the generator. Turn its apex downward. From inside the set, link the energies of the crystals six times, according to the number of crystals in the set (excluding the generator in your hands and the amethyst that you place on yourself), from the crystal at the top of your head in a clockwise direction.

Put the generator outside the set of stones, as far as you can, so that its energies do not interfere with the treatment.

Lie on your back, place the amethyst on your third eye chakra, and start opening the chakras. Use color to open them (if you do not intend to used a particular color projection while you are lying in the set).

Open them as follows:

Project red light on the base chakra for a few moments.

Project orange light on the sex chakra for a few moments.

Project yellow light on the solar plexus chakra for a few moments.

Project green light on the heart chakra for a few moments.

Project blue light on the throat chakra for a few moments.

Project indigo light on the third eye chakra for a few moments.

Project purple light on the crown chakra for a few moments.

Now concentrate on the base chakra. In your mind's eye, see a ray of light linking all the chakras, from the base chakra to the crown chakra. When it reaches the crown chakra, see it as water flowing, splashing, from a spring, all over your body. See the white light enveloping the whole of you, the crystal that is placed above your head, the crystals that are placed next to your shoulders, elbows, and all the rest, until all of them are linked and illuminated by the light.

Repeat the process until you feel that all the crystals are linked and illuminated.

Now link the crystals on your right side to those on your left side, using the light. Begin to link the crystals on the right and left of your shoulders, go on to the crystals that are on the right and left of your elbows, and so on. Continue in this way until you feel that the entire energetic circle is complete. By means of these actions, you have created a protective electromagnetic field that separates the set in which you are located from the energies of the room, and preserves the energies of the treatment inside it.

Take deep, conscious breaths in order to let the crystals' energy perform their action. Set your biological clock to wake you in 15 minutes' time. After completing the set, get out of it, and place the crystals in a bowl of water. After placing each one in the bowl, dip your fingertips in the water in order to remove the residues of energy that was absorbed in the crystals. After about half an hour, purify them well under running water and place them to charge on the windowsill (without a glass partition) or on a crystal cluster.

Closing the chakras

We perform a closing of the chakras when, for some reason, we need to halt the treatment in the middle, or in a case where the patient experiences strong reactions. It is also done if the patient experiences strong emotional reactions, or feels very "uprooted" and not grounded.

If you have administered self-treatment, and you want to close the chakras, exchange the hands of the therapist (the tool for closing that is described later) with a small smoky quartz crystal, preferably a small smoky quartz generator.

Have the patient lie down on the treatment bed once more. Touch the crown chakra with the index finger of your receiving hand (usually the left hand for right-handed people, and the right hand for left-handed people, but this can differ from person to person).

Now instruct the patient verbally and clearly to see the crown chakra, in the color purple, closing. In your mind's eye, you can see it revolving in a counter-clockwise direction and closing. (If you are performing the closing of the chakra on yourself, say aloud: "The crown chakra is closing now," and see the wheel of the chakra revolving in a counter-clockwise direction for a few seconds, while you turn the smoky quartz above your head in a counter-clockwise direction.)

Afterwards, touch the patient in the region of the third eye chakra with the index finger of your receiving hand. Repeat the instruction for closing the chakra, so that the patient sees the indigo-colored chakra closing. (If you are performing self-treatment, turn the smoky quartz crystal in a counter-clockwise direction for a few seconds.)

Repeat the procedure for the throat chakra as well.

Now perform the following procedure on yourself or on a patient in order to complete the grounding:

Place both your hands, palms downward, fingers slightly apart, on the region of the solar plexus (yours or the patient's). Begin to move your hands downward, in pulling movements, on the surface of the abdomen. Continue performing the pulling movements over the legs, while you direct the etheric energy downward for grounding. With the movements of your hands, slightly spread fingers, pass over the thighs, the calves, and the feet. When you have finished, shake your hands and wash them. If you find it difficult to perform this treatment on yourself, you will have to continue with the closing of the heart, solar plexus, sex, and base chakras in exactly the same way as you closed the three upper chakras. You will have to do it by visualizing each one of the chakras in its characteristic color, and by turning the smoky quartz generator counter-clockwise.

Using crystals to understand the mysteries of the universe and the human soul

Dreams

Dreams have always been a fascinating mystery. Some people claim that "they do not dream." This is not true. We spend a great part of our sleep dreaming, but sometimes we do not remember the dreams. This is the first aspect in which we will prove the efficacy of crystals in the realm of dreams.

The field of dream interpretation is almost as broad and varied as the number of dreams themselves. Various psychological schools of thought tended to attribute different meanings to dreams. In contrast, for thousands of years, dreams were linked to different mystical, superstitious, and predictive contexts. Dreams star in various ancient writings, mainly as symbols and as a way of receiving exalted messages. The best known of them are the stories of dreams in the Bible – the dreams of Joseph, Jacob, and others.

The dreams that occur while we sleep have various sources and functions. Some of the dreams involve motives from everyday life that bother us when we are awake: conflicts, fears, even material that we read in the newspaper or saw on TV. At night, this material is released from the subconscious, sometimes as a means of alleviating the tension that is created by the conflicts or the unconscious fears. Sometimes these dreams take a symbolic form, such as a person seeing himself fall from a tower, while on the conscious level he is involved in business negotiations in which there is a fear of failure and downfall. There are many symbols of this kind. Moreover, our dreams may express hidden or repressed desires, wishes, fears, and memories. Dreams constitute a bridge between the conscious and the subconscious, a link that is generally not clear and conscious during the waking hours. For this reason, we can understand ourselves and look into ourselves with the help of our dreams.

However, there are additional types and levels of dreaming. There are telepathic dreams, a dream that is dreamed by two people who are close, or who are unconsciously energetically close. They dream the identical or similar dream on the same night or within a short time span. Sometimes, this dream carries a message. There are many stories about telepathic dreams in which a person dreams about something that happened to someone close to him, but who is physically far from him. Sometimes the dream occurs at the same time as the event is happening to the person who is being dreamed about. Those dreams are not rare, and can occur in people whose ability to link up to their surroundings, that is, their spiritual openness and receptiveness, is especially high, whether this is conscious or not. Work with channeling stones and opening up the consciousness, strengthening spiritual development, and opening and activating the third chakra, are likely to strengthen the ability to dream dreams of this type.

Another type of dream in which crystals are widely used is the dream that supplies solutions to questions and problems that are troubling the person, reveals additional information about various fields in which he is involved, and provides him with information that comes directly from other entities. At the highest level, these dreams are called "prophetic dreams." Many people involved in religion, humanities, and science used this type of channeling and prophetic dream for their work. An example of this is the story of the famous physicist, Albert Einstein, who related that some of the equations he solved were revealed to him in dreams. The German chemist who discovered the molecular structure of benzene saw the solution in a dream, in the form of a snake biting its own tail, and this vision led him to make his discovery. Many writers and painters were helped by scenes and visions they saw in their dreams, and sometimes based entire works on these dreams.

Although dreams of this type are perceived as a kind of "gift" from the force of the universe, we can stimulate and order them by using crystals, as we will see in the technique that is described below.

An additional and less pleasant aspect of dreaming is "bad dreams," nightmares, and so on. Many people have dreams of this type for a wide variety of reasons, and sometimes the situation is so serious that there are people who are afraid to fall asleep, consciously or unconsciously, as a result of the fear of having "bad" dreams. This aspect of dreaming can also be controlled, moderated, and soothed by using crystals.

Remembering dreams

When relating to the matter of dreams, one of the most common questions is "How can I remember my dreams?" In order to remember dreams, it is advisable to perform the following technique, which is suitable both for ordering dreams and for remembering them. There are certain stones that help us remember dreams. They work very effectively, but they must be cleansed and purified very well before use, charged, and tuned to help the person remember dreams. A partial list of these stones is as follows:

* **Celestite**
* **Jade**
* **Kyanite**
* **Azurite**

* **Clear calcite**
* **Diamond-shaped calcite**
* **Pyrite**
* **Sodalite**
* **Moonstone**
* **Green sapphire**

All of these stones are generally suitable for remembering dreams, but each one has its own specialty concerning the information that it stimulates or the dream work that can be done with it. When we place a stone under our pillow, or on the bed, in order to remember a dream, we will be able to learn and recognize the unique action of each stone. There are stones that help us link up to superior guides and entities by means of dreams; there are stones that help us eliminate negative thought and emotional patterns and traumas by means of dreams; and there are stones that help us understand the dream and solve it, whether after the dream or during the dream. The following stones have unique properties:

Jade – Jade is called the "dream stone." Besides helping to remember the dream itself, jade also helps the person understand and solve it. If we dream a dream at night that we do not understand, it is advisable to hold jade, direct it to understand the dream and its solution, enter into a meditative state, and meditate with it in order to receive the answers. Moreover, with its help, it is possible to release repressed emotions, unrequited desires, and subconscious conflicts through the dream. This dream stone also helps make beautiful and pleasant dreams come true in reality.

Amethyst – Amethyst is excellent for ordering dreams from divine sources and for linking up to spiritual layers via dreams.

Aquamarine – Aquamarine inspires intuitive and spiritual dreams.

Azurite – Azurite inspires visions and scenes during the dream.

Celestite – Celestite helps link up via the dream to spiritual guides and to superior entities of light. It is good for ordering dreams for solving various problems, and for clarifying and understanding dreams.

Kyanite – Kyanite helps the person link up to spiritual guides during the dream, and it also helps solve and clarify dreams.

Diamond-shaped calcite – Diamond-shaped calcite is a wonderful stone for ordering dreams, and for clarifying and understanding dreams.

Smoky quartz – Smoky quartz helps the person dream telepathic dreams.

Fluorite – Fluorite helps the person understand the dream's messages.

Moonstone – While dreaming, moonstone links us to spiritual worlds and induces intuitive dreams and dreams concerning the cycles of the moon, whether from the point of view of the course of our lives or from the universal point of view.

Lapis lazuli – Lapis lazuli helps the person understand his dreams and their connection to his spiritual and emotional development by contributing to the development of those layers. It can be placed on the third eye before going to sleep, and a dream can be ordered to help the person's spiritual and emotional development. It is also a protective stone.

Rhodochrosite – When we place rhodochrosite under the pillow, it inspires pleasant, gentle, and beautiful dreams, and sweet and enveloping scenes.

Red jasper – Red jasper helps reconstruct significant dreams. It can be used to order the dream over and over again. Moreover, it helps the person remember the points of the dream that are very significant in the person's life.

Petrified wood – Petrified wood can be programmed to raise memories from the past during sleep, for channeling with family members who are not in the physical world, and for finding the vocation of the soul. Sometimes, the information appears via dreams, and sometimes it is felt intuitively during waking hours, after sleeping with the stone under the pillow or on the bed.

Double terminated quartz crystal – The double terminated quartz crystal helps make the dream state deeper, and helps the person get into a linked-up state of dreaming so that he can receive exalted messages during the dream.

As we said before, stones can help people who suffer from insomnia as a result of fear of falling asleep – people who suffer from nightmares and bad dreams. The stones that are recommended for these cases are:

Jade – When jade is placed under the pillow, it causes the person to dream pleasant, harmonious, and tranquil dreams, and permits him to wake up with a feeling of serenity, calmness, and harmony.

Hematite – This stone helps eliminate bad dreams.

Garnet – Garnet helps eliminate nightmares and calms fears during sleep.

Charoite – This stone dispels fears and frightening dreams, and is many recommended for people who suffer from bad dreams about entities from other worlds. It is highly effective. It imbues the person with a feeling of spiritual protection while sleeping.

Rhodochrosite – This stone helps cases of insomnia, especially when it is caused by unconscious anxieties and fear of bad dreams. It inspires beautiful, pleasant, and calm dreams.

Citrine – This stone eliminates bad dreams and nightmares.

Jet – Jet absorbs negativity in the bedroom (negativity can stem from arguments, rows, tension, and anger in the home), and helps the person enjoy calm and peaceful rest and sleep.

Moonstone – This stone helps the person calm down and feel tranquil before going to sleep, so as to facilitate good, relaxed sleep.

Ruby – Ruby helps eliminate unwanted, frightening, or disturbing dreams. It causes the dreams to be serene and calm.

Using stones to remember and order dreams:

Basic technique

When we choose a stone for sleeping at night, and want to have an "extraordinary" dream, it is important to define the "purpose" of the dream we want to have, and choose the stone accordingly. If, for instance, we want to have a dream that tells us about our twin soul, we choose rhodochrosite. If we want to link up to our superior guides and teachers, we can choose celestite or kyanite. Someone who suffers from frequent troublesome or unwanted dreams should place a stone for eliminating this kind of dream on his bed in addition to the stone he has chosen (if the latter does not fulfill this function).

The second stage is to purify, charge, and program the stone. The stone is programmed in accordance with its purpose. After the purpose of the dream has been defined, this message must be transferred to the stone in order to increase its abilities and focus its energy on this action.

After the stone has been charged and programmed, it is possible to place it under the pillow, or on the bed (preferably under the pillow, unless the person feels some kind of discomfort when the stone is placed there). It is advisable to go to sleep before midnight, since when we get up early in the morning, our ability to remember dreams is likely to be better. If we want to receive exalted messages via the dream, it is a good idea to place an essential oil burner containing jasmine or frankincense oil in the room, in order to promote spiritual openness. Clean sheets should be placed on the bed, and the person should shower and wear clean sleepwear. This depends on the person's feeling, however. He should set an alarm clock with a gentle but rousing ring for somewhere between six and seven in the morning. Much of the research that has been conducted on dreams shows that waking up at that time is very helpful in remembering dreams. It is advisable to place a notebook and pen next to the bed so that upon waking and recalling the dream, it is possible to write it down very accurately. After the preparations, the person must get into bed and lie comfortably. He should relax his body before falling asleep. Massaging the scalp with shampooing movements also helps a person remember dreams in the morning. He must begin with conscious breathing, and concentrate for a while on the question to which he is seeking an answer, the problem, the request for information, or the knowledge he wishes to attain. When using a stone that leads to exalted messages, he can simply request to see special and lofty visions while he is sleeping. After defining to himself once more what he wants to see in the dream (or the question that he wants answered), he can place the stone on the third eye, ask the particular question (if there is one), and request an answer. The answer is likely to appear in a dream, verbally, or visually. It is possible that he will not have any extraordinary dreams during the night (or for some reason, they are not remembered), but during the day the person will attain a new understanding of or clear knowledge concerning the question he asked. Afterwards, the stone must be placed under the pillow for the duration of sleep.

It is not rare that while the stone is lying on the third eye, some kind of insights concerning the question will arise. A situation in which the answer first arrives in a rather "confused" way is not rare. It is possible that new questions will occur to the person upon waking, or he will remember certain dreams that he does not understand. This is a natural process that sometimes occurs in order to narrow the question that was asked, to direct the person to a new thought channel, or to ask a new question that he did not think of the tiny clue leading to the solution to the problem that he wanted solved in the dream. Sometimes, various clues appear, night after night, and join the completed picture. For this reason, the process should be performed for several nights, until the person feels that he has received the answer to his question. When a person wants to receive exalted messages, the range of possibilities is enormous, and depends on the person and his ability to take in this information. Pictures and insights from previous incarnations, for instance, demand a great deal of patience. As we mentioned before, it is possible to get up in the morning without remembering any extraordinary dream, but with new knowledge and understanding.

Remembering a dream by means of a phantom crystal

We can program the phantom crystal to help us remember dreams. If you happen to have one of these unique crystals, and you feel a bond with it, this may be the most suitable method for you. It is simple. You must remember to purify the crystal well before getting down to work. Before going to sleep, when you feel that you are about to fall asleep, hold the phantom crystal a few centimeters from your third eye chakra. You can hold it in both hands, or in the hand you feel comfortable with. Concentrate on your desire to remember the dreams. Focus on this desire, and transmit it to the crystal. See the thought, "I remember my dreams," flowing, penetrating the crystal, and being absorbed in it. You can see your will power in a shine white light, or any color you like.

Choose the form that is most suitable and comfortable for you intuitively. The moment you feel that the thought has been transmitted to the crystal and absorbed in it, place it under your pillow, and sink into a sweet, calm sleep.

The moment you wake up in the morning, pull the crystal out from under the pillow. Place it on the third eye chakra, and begin to scrutinize the thoughts, scenes, emotions, and images that appear before you.

You can use this method to receive guided dreams, solutions, or knowledge about a particular topic. Before going to sleep, perform the actions described above, but now, transmit your desire to receive an answer, guidance, or a solution about a particular topic to the crystal. Request a guiding dream, knowledge, or vision that will help you solve the problem or provide you with knowledge about this topic. It is important that you think of the topic consciously before you begin to program the crystal, so that you can program it in a clear and lucid way. Place it under your pillow, and when you wake up, put it on your third eye, and receive the message that it transfers to you. You may discover, upon waking, that you remember the dream or its messages, even before placing the crystal on the third eye.

Crystals and Feng Shui

Feng Shui is an ancient Chinese art – about four thousand years old. The meaning of the words "Feng Shui" is "the way of the wind and the water." They hint at the natural flow of the energy in the universe. This ancient art is gaining momentum nowadays, and is become popular mainly because of the beneficial feelings caused by the application of the method. This is the art of life in perfect harmony with the forces of the universe. The technique makes uses of the ancient knowledge of the five elements – wood, metal, earth, fire, and water – in order to create environmental harmony. This technique can be applied in the home, the office, the yard, and the garden, and even on the body itself.

The people who apply and study this method know that all objects and bodies have unique energy fields. These energy fields can benefit the person's personal energy field, or create a conflict with it, and even jeopardize the harmony of the energy field. (We dealt with this subject in depth in the Introduction.)

The "sheh" areas

The "sheh" areas refer to areas in which the energy is not harmonious. In general, these are areas in the house that have little light, or are hardly used. This situation is characteristics of storerooms, stairwells, and so on. These areas are a source of "sheh" – unhealthy energy. To the same extent, bedrooms in which the occupants' sleep is interrupted or unpleasant, or in which they find it difficult to sleep, and places in which arguments and quarrels tend to take place, are also areas that contain "sheh." Feng Shui uses various techniques to change, move, or eliminate negative energy, and/or draw positive energy – chi. In order to change the unhealthy and unharmonious situation, crystals must be placed in these places. Crystals can be used to move, change, or eliminate the unhealthy energy from these areas. There are a number of crystals that are effective mainly for this purpose:

Clear crystal – Clear crystal is an especially balancing crystal. For this reason, it is suitable for placing anywhere in the house. It is mainly recommended for placing in the stairwell.

Rose quartz – The rose quartz crystal is very effective for turning negative energy into calming and tranquil energy. Because of these properties, it is especially suitable for placing in bedrooms in which there is a feeling of unharmonious energy.

Smoky quartz – Smoky quartz crystal has the property of absorbing and drawing in negative energies. In this, it is very effective for cleansing rooms or areas in which there is a feeling of non-positive energy.

Amethyst – Amethyst is very effective for absorbing radiation from electronic appliances. Placing a piece of amethyst on the TV, the computer, the stereo, or any other electronic appliance in the room immediately improves the energy in the room. Amethyst is also effective for placing in workplaces or offices, for protection against unwanted energies.

Citrine – Citrine is especially good for placing in rooms in which quarrels or rows have taken place, or rooms in which some kind of traumatic event occurred.

The stones that are used for Feng Shui in the house must be cleansed meticulously about once a fortnight or once a month, according to your feeling. Some people insist on cleansing and charging the stone even more frequently. Stones that are placed on electronic appliances should not be touched by hand, but rolled from their place into a glass that is one-third filled with water. If you touch the stone with your fingers, you must dip your fingertips in the glass into which you rolled the stone. This must be done whenever the stone seems to have absorbed a serious amount of non-positive energies, so as not to come in contact with those energies.

The various configurations of crystals (most of them are man-made, and not in their natural form of crystallization) help us create more positive and harmonious conditions, in accordance with the art of Feng Shui:

Crystal ball – Crystal balls of various sizes that can be hung on strings throughout the house, in areas where the energy is not positive, convert "she" energy into chi energy. Crystal balls that are hung in a window or placed on the windowsill send positive energy and healthful and healing chi energy all over the room. Crystal balls can be put or hung in passageways, too. When a crystal ball is placed in the entrance hall or passage, pay attention to whether the area is light or dark by nature (this refers to natural light). When light encounters the crystal, it is especially effective in converting "she" to chi. When a crystal ball or a crystal chandelier is hung up, ensure that it hangs above the height of the door. It must be high enough that people will not bump their heads on it.

Obelisks – There are obelisks that are made of a large variety of minerals. They have a significant ability to increase the energies in the surroundings where they are placed. In Feng Shui, they are used to attract energy to a particular area. Obelisks made of quartz crystal are thought to be extremely powerful and effective, since their shape, together with their light color, attracts positive energies.

Clusters – Clusters purify the energy in the room by absorbing the non-positive energy. At the same time, they transmit purifying, pleasant, and calming energy. The light sparkles on all crystals on the surface of the cluster, and significantly strengthens the cluster's action.

The color of the stones

The colors of the crystals that are used in Feng Shui are significant. The use of the complementary color of the color of the room creates a feeling of harmony and serenity. Clear crystal is always a good option, since it reflects all the colors of the spectrum. Red stones stimulate vitality and attract positive energy. Black stones, in contrast, also attract energy – both positive and negative energy. Orange stones stimulate healing energies. Purple stones and stones in shades of indigo attract high spiritual energy, and increase spiritual harmony. Stones in a golden shade stimulate mental abilities and learning abilities. Green stones stimulate creativity and growth. White stones and blue stones reject energy, so they can serve to reject unwanted energy and as protection.

When you place the crystals throughout the house, it is very important to maintain purity of thought, and perform this action consciously and with intent. It is important to use intuition when deciding which crystal or which size crystal to place in a particular location in the house. Moreover, the size of the place vis-à-vis the crystal must be considered. A very small crystal is not suitable for placing in a large room. It is liable not to be effective enough in converting or absorbing energies – and vice versa.

According to the theories of Feng Shui, energy enters the left side of the body, and leaves through the right side. For this reason, carrying a stone in the left shirt or pants pocket, especially a clear crystal, serves as an effective Feng Shui tool for balancing the chi (life energy). The crystal should be programmed for this purpose, for increasing the efficacy of its action.

The use of crystals in telepathy

Telepathy is a form of non-verbal communication by means of which thoughts, emotions, and feelings can be transmitted between human beings, as well as to or from creatures that do not belong to the human species. It is the ability to pick up and receive thoughts and emotions from others, and to transmit thoughts and emotions to others. We can compare energetic reality to a sea of material for thought, on different levels. Everyone can link up to the tremendous store of knowledge and thought in the universe, to various channels that are known and unknown. In fact, we are linked all the time, but sometimes our consciousness does not understand the messages clearly. Often, telepathic messages have a great effect on our lives. We all have telepathic abilities. We frequently use these powers without being aware of it. It is not rare for a person to think of a good friend or relative, and ... the phone rings, and that very person is at the other end of the line. Sometimes we can sense when a person who is close to us is in a sensitive or uncomfortable situation.

Even though everyone has telepathic abilities, some people by nature experience them especially powerfully, and some people develop them. Indeed, this is an ability that lends itself to developing and broadening. There are certain stones, especially channeling stones and stones that activate the third eye chakra, that can develop our telepathic ability without any conscious effort on our part when we use them. Of course, it is possible to program them or to place suitable stones on the sixth chakra and meditate with them. In addition, there are various techniques and methods that constitute conscious activity for developing these abilities. The very desire to develop one's telepathic ability is the first step toward developing it.

When we make use of telepathic abilities, we must remember that what we transmit is an inseparable part of our electromagnetic field. For this reason, we must make sure to transmit loving, illuminated, and positive messages. Telepathic manipulations tend to be more dangerous for transmitting than for receiving, since the transmitter links himself to non-positive energetic channels that are liable to be expressed in his life. Since the use of crystals stimulates and encourages mental and spiritual growth, and actualizes various intuitive abilities and even extrasensory abilities, it causes a strengthening of the telepathic abilities. However, it is also possible to use crystals in a conscious way for applying and performing various exercises for developing telepathy. (Practicing telepathic reception or transmission by means of crystals develops the pineal gland, which is linked to the third eye center.) There is a wide variety of techniques and practice methods. Following are a number of effective methods:

Developing telepathic abilities by means of quartz generators

In order to practice this technique, you need two medium-size, single terminated clear quartz crystals (generators). You can also use relatively small crystals if you use them a lot and feel that they are particularly powerful. You need a partner to practice the technique. Cleanse the crystals well, purify them, and charge them. Program one of the crystals for receiving telepathic messages, and the other for transmitting telepathic messages.

Before beginning the exercise, hold hands for a minute or two so as to create a feeling of closeness and intimacy. Decide who is going to be the transmitter, and who is going to be the receiver. There are people with more powerful receptive abilities, and people with more powerful transmitting abilities. Having said that, it is worth trying both sides in order to strengthen each one's either receptive or transmitting ability. If you can identify which of you transmits more powerfully or receives better (this can be discerned according to certain character traits and various behavioral signs), for the purpose of the first practice, let the transmitter transmit and the receiver receive. Afterwards, you can switch roles. If you do not know, you can decide intuitively or arbitrarily.

Sit opposite each other. Close your eyes and take deep, slow breaths. Concentrate on the third eye chakra. See the region of the third eye flashing and filling with purple light. The transmitter places the crystal close to his third eye (in the center of the forehead) with the apex (the sharp end of the generator) facing outward toward his partner (so that a right angle is created between the crystal and the transmitter's forehead). The receiver holds his crystal in the same manner, with the apex of the crystal pointing at and touching his third eye region. The transmitter holds the apex of his crystal close to the blunt end of the receiver's crystal, so that a continuum is created. Wait for a few seconds, all the while taking deep, slow breaths. Link up to the vibrations of the crystals for a few moments. When you feel calm and serene, and your thoughts are free of disturbing elements, the transmitter must begin the telepathic transmission.

Start by transmitting simple symbols, such as a circle, a square, a triangle, a Star of David, and so on. Every symbol must be transmitted for about 30 seconds. You may need more time to transmit the message, and you may need less. The transmitter must see the symbol leaving his third eye, passing through the crystal he is holding, through the crystal next to it, and penetrating his partner's third eye, which functions as the receiver of the message. He must see the symbol that he is transmitting clearly. After a few seconds, the "receiver" will see the symbol.

Afterwards, you can continue using the same symbols you used at the beginning, but this time "paint" them in your mind's eye in a color, so that both a symbol and a color are transmitted. You can continue with numbers or letters, and get to more complex pictures, such as a moving car, a pine tree, and so on. The sky is the limit with this exercise, and you can even transmit emotions, complex messages, sentences, complex pictures, and abstract ideas. (In parallel, you can increase the distance between the transmitter and the receiver and detach the crystals from each other.)

After practicing this method for some time, you may discover that the telepathic connection between you has been strengthened. You can see this in various "little" and everyday signs. Since this exercise develops the telepathic ability in a powerful way and stimulates the third eye chakra, after some time you can move to higher stages of experimentation.

The next state is telepathic communication from a distance, using the same crystals you used in the basic practice technique. When these crystals are used for practicing telepathic techniques for a long time, they become naturally programmed for telepathic reception or transmission. In order to strengthen this effect, you can make sure to always use the same crystal, one for transmitting and the other for receiving, even when you switch roles.

Decide who will be the transmitter and who will be the receiver. It is possible that at this stage, you can already pay attention to each of your transmitting or receiving abilities. Again, for the first practice, let the person with greater transmitting abilities be the transmitter, and vice versa. Afterwards, you should switch roles.

At the beginning, this exercise should be done in two separate rooms in the same house. Later, you can transmit messages from a distance, and as your abilities increase, from anywhere to anywhere.

For the first practice, each one is in a separate room, facing the other person (even if a wall or door separates you). Perform the opening of the third eye that is described at the beginning of the exercise, take deep breaths, and get into a state of calmness and emptiness of all thought. The transmitter places the crystal on his third eye, its apex pointing at the receiver. The receiver points the apex of the crystal at his own third eye, while the "receiving" end of the crystal points in the direction of the transmitter. Start with transmitting simple shapes, using the same technique that is described in the first part of the exercise. Afterwards, progress to shapes with colors, and so on.

After you achieve success in this exercise, and practice it for some time, it is possible to apply the method without pointing the crystal in the partner's direction. The crystals are already charged and very strongly programmed to be telepathic crystals, receiving or transmitting, even if you purified them after a certain period of use. After purification, all you have to do is program them quickly in order to "remind" the crystal of its role as receiver or transmitter.

Now, all you have to do is hold the crystal (after calming down and opening the third eye), seeing in your mind's eye the image of the receiver or the transmitter. Coordinate between yourselves before starting the exercise, decide who is the receiver and who is the transmitter, and you can even synchronize your watches so that you begin the exercise at exactly the same time. It is a good idea to have a sheet of paper and a pen at hand so that you can draw the shapes that are transmitted or received, in order to check the success of the exercise afterwards. Coordinate between yourselves a fixed "break" between one exercise and the next, or the moment at which each telepathic transmission begins (so that the transmission does not begin when the receiver is noting down what he saw on the paper). When you practice these techniques, you are likely to reach the stage when there is no longer any need of coordination or crystals in order to transmit or receive messages or announcements, and you can forego the crystals altogether. If you want to "be in touch" with your partner during the course of a certain day, for instance, when he is about to take an exam, attend an important meeting, and so on, simply place the crystal in your pocket or bag. During the day, you can transmit positive, reinforcing, optimistic, and encouraging thoughts to him. These will help the receiver successfully accomplish the tasks facing him.

Developing telepathic abilities by means of clear quartz

Another method of telepathic practice also makes use of two clear quartz crystals. In this case, it makes no difference whether or not they have an apex. Sit opposite each other. In this technique, both of you will be transmitters, and both of you will be receivers. Make sure to perform the exercise in a room with a pleasant, calm atmosphere, without any kind of energetic interference from electrical appliances. You can place a crystal or a lump of amethyst on radiation-producing appliances in the room, or cover them with a tablecloth, so that they cannot cause energetic interference. Take deep breaths, and concentrate on the third eye center.

Each of you must hold your crystal in front of you. Stare at the crystal for a few seconds with concentration, and link up to it. Afterwards, close your eyes. Each one must imagine some kind of shape in your mind's eye. Start with simple shapes. See the shape in front of your eyes for a few minutes. Now, see it pass into the crystal, and be absorbed in it. Imagine how it is locked inside the crystal. Now, exchange crystals. Relax your bodies, calm down, and take deep, slow breaths. Hold the crystal that your partner gave you in both hands and link up to it, being completely open to receiving the message that it is transmitting to you. Trust the first impression that occurs to you, the first picture that you will see. If you have opened yourself to receive the message, you can see the picture that your friend imagined in front of your eyes.

Developing telepathic abilities by means of a double terminated quartz crystal

Double terminated quartz crystals are very effective for developing telepathic abilities. This method is slightly similar to the first method we described, but it is likely to suit certain people better. In any case, if you did not achieve satisfactory results in the first method, using quartz generators, try this one.

In order to do this exercise, you will need two double terminated quartz crystals that have been purified and programmed to strengthen the telepathic ability. Decide who will be the transmitter and who will be the receiver. Find a quiet, energetically clean place with a pleasant atmosphere. Sit opposite each other. You can sit as near or as far apart as you want, even in two opposite ends of the room. Sit comfortably, cross-legged, with a straight back, but not uncomfortably so. Take a number of deep breaths. Close your eyes, and concentrate on your breathing. See a white or golden light descending from above, penetrating the crown of your head, and filling your entire body. The white or golden light fills the whole body until it flows outward and creates an ellipse of light around each of your bodies. Each one of you must hold the double terminated crystal with one apex pointing at your third eye, and the second at your partner's third eye. In this method, there is no need for contact or for creating a link between the crystals. The transmitter must concentrate and be focused, and the receiver must be absolutely free of any thought and emotion, and completely open to receiving the message. The transmitter must beginning by transmitting a number. He can see the number sent from his own third eye to the apex of the quartz that is facing it, and from there to the apex of the quartz that his partner is holding. Alternatively, he can simply see the number in his mind's eye, and let it make its own way to the receiver. You can try both methods. If you succeed, do not let the joy of your success cause you to lose your concentration. The moment the receiver receives the number, he must say it, and if it is correct, the transmitter confirms it, and after a few seconds sends the next number, shape, or color. Continue until you can transmit thoughts or messages. If the exercise does not succeed first time round, do not let this cause you to lose your concentration. It is possible that one of you was not yet completely open to receiving, or the transmitter was not sufficiently focused, or various thoughts went through his head, and the message was not clear. Take a few deep breaths with eyes closed, relax, and send another number.

This exercise develops the extrasensory communicative ability in an extraordinary manner. It is not just a nice exercise for checking out the ability. It permits the person to tune into the powerful telepathic properties of the double terminated quartz, and become familiar with the telepathic channels that afford telepathic communication in any situation and at any distance.

Crystal balls

Reading a crystal ball is an ancient art. Crystal balls were used to foretell the future, for prediction, and for developing high spiritual abilities, as well as for various mystical purposes. The use and practice of gazing into crystal balls can greatly develop intuitive and extrasensory abilities. There are different methods and ways of reading a crystal ball. Various experts use it to read the past or the future, and some people do so by observing the reflection of the person's aura in the ball. The resulting images, shapes, and colors are interpreted by experts who use various methods to read crystal balls. The main crystals used for reading are balls made of beryl, quartz crystal, and aquamarine. Many crystal balls are not completely transparent, but a kind of fogginess and cloudiness can be seen in them. Each crystal ball has its own unique personality, and it is likely to suit one particular action or another. Completely transparent balls that have no fogginess or cloudiness are especially suitable for personal meditation for strengthening the spiritual scrutiny ability, and for achieving spiritual clarity. Black opals can also be used as a means for reading and scrutiny, and some people perform these actions with a large piece of labradorite. The reading requires practice, patience, and perseverance. It helps develop extrasensory vision and the intuitive reception ability. There are various ways to charge and program the crystal ball for reading, but the main charging of the crystal is performed by gazing into it.

For the first exercise, you will need a piece of thick, dull black fabric, or a special stand for crystals of a dark matte color, a crystal ball, a chair, and a table. In crystal-ball reading, it is very important to ensure that the room is free of various radiation-emitting electrical appliances. In addition, the reading must not be performed in a room in which rows or arguments took place recently, or in any place where the energy is not positive. After you have found a quiet and energetically clean room, you can light an essential oil burner containing jasmine or frankincense oil, which promote spiritual openness. The lighting in the room should be dim, but not too much so. If you possess a special stand on which to place the crystal ball, use it. If not, fold the fabric in such a way that you can place the ball on it and it will not roll off the table.

Sit with your back to the light source in the room. Before you start gazing into the crystal, perform the following exercise to strengthen the intuitive reception abilities: Sit comfortably, with your feet firmly on the floor, your knees slightly bent, and your arms at the sides of your body. Take a few deep breaths, and transfer the weight of your body downward, so that you feel the link to the earth. Continue taking deep, slow breaths. When inhaling, lift your arms so that they are level with your eyes. Join the tips of your index fingers, middle fingers, fourth fingers, and thumbs to create a kind of diamond shape. Hold them like this in front of your eyes. Let your eyes stare a bit, unfocused. Imagine an eye in the middle of your forehead opening and gazing at the hollow in the center of the diamond shape you have created with your fingers. Continue breathing deeply, and feel the presence of the energy around you. Continue like this for no longer than five minutes.

After performing the exercise for opening the third eye, start gazing into the crystal ball. Now you need a great deal of patience. Patience is essential, because this is an acquired art that demands both natural talent and the ability to sit quietly and gaze at scenes. For the first exercise, do not take too long. Gaze into the ball for no longer than five minutes, with your physical eyes unfocused and staring. After practicing a few times, you can gradually lengthen the time.

After sometime, begin to notice that the crystal is somewhat cloudy. A kind of gauze or cloud passes through it. The cloud clears up, and a colored light appears. This light is the embodiment of the energy of the soul. If for some reason, you leave the meditative state abruptly, stop gazing into the ball. A sharp detachment of this kind is liable to occur if you see some kind of scene, a sign, or a shape, because of the effect of the surprise. After a situation like this, stop gazing into the ball and return to it no sooner than a day later.

In order to finish gazing into the crystal ball, wrap the ball in the black fabric on which you placed it, or in another piece of black material (if you used a special stand). If you used a stand, separate them, and do not wrap the stand with the ball (so as to avoid scratches). Put it in its special place in a glass closet or any other place that is protected and safe, until the next time you gaze.

It is not possible to describe or "promise" what will be seen when gazing into the ball. There are many possibilities. The uniqueness of crystal-ball gazing lies in the fact that it develops the intuition in such a way that there is no need for any written instructions to keep on with it. The correct questions, the ones that have to be asked, will emerge by themselves. In the same way, if you have an affinity for some spiritual topic, scenes that supply answers are likely to occur. Sometimes, the scenes that emerge are likely to seem meaningless. Note them in your memory, or in a special notebook, and come back to them after some time if their significance is not revealed to you intuitively a few days or hours after gazing. The colors that appear in the crystal during the gazing are significant in your life, or in the life of someone you are thinking about consciously (also unconsciously, but it should be done consciously). In the context of this matter, you should not ask questions about other people's lives before you have acquired sufficient experience in crystal-ball reading and gazing. Even then, you must ask the people's permission. However, when you are just at the beginning of your path in crystal-ball gazing, do not attribute earth-shattering significance to these colors. You may need a certain amount of time to learn their true significance. In your notebook, write down the colors that tend to appear when you gaze into the crystal. Try to discover what significance these colors have in your life. Use the chapter that deals with the significance of colors.

Gradually, you will begin to understand the language in which the crystal ball speaks to you, and its unique terminology.

In general, colors that rise up in the crystal ball are considered to be positive, while colors that go down are thought to be non-positive. But again, I would not want to present this as an axiom, since you must trust your inner feelings and intuition in order to discover the unique meaning that your crystal ball gives to the scenes and colors that emerge.

Besides the meaning of the colors that appear in the ball, there are other methods. According to certain ancient methods, it is possible to distinguish a certain "interpretive code" for the colors that occur in the ball.

The color **white** generally indicates positive results. The color **black** may indicate an opportunity for studying, for a lesson, or for learning, in their everyday significance or their spiritual significance.

If the color **purple** appears in the ball, it is considered an especially positive sign, which indicates that spiritual powers are standing at your side, or at the side of the person for whom you are performing the reading. Some people tend to interpret the color **red** as some kind of warning. The color **blue** generally symbolizes matters pertaining to health: an improvement in the state of health, a need to take more care with health, as well as a need to exercise patience in the matter under discussion. The color **pink** is generally interpreted as a sign of love and harmony, or of harmonious results concerning the matter under discussion. The color **yellow**, on the other hand, is liable to indicate rivalry or jealousy. The color **green** is a reminder to remain optimistic and hopeful, or symbolizes optimism and hope pertaining to the matter under discussion. The color **orange** shows a need for energy and decisiveness.

Having said that, go over the significance of the colors in the chapter that discusses color once more, and check these interpretations in depth. After you have noted down the colors that appeared in the crystal ball in your notebook, turn to the interpretations of the colors that appear in this chapter, and see if some kind of insight or knowledge "pops" up intuitively.

Over time, you will get to know the terms used by your crystal ball when answering your questions. Often, the personal crystal ball uses colors according to the associations and the deep inner interpretations that you yourself attribute to them. There are crystal-ball readers who tend to ask the person for whom they are performing the reading what a particular color symbolizes for him, and how he interprets it. In addition, you may see different signs, shapes, and even images. In order to interpret them, you need your own intuition and spiritual powers. Some readers are in the habit of asking the person for whom they are performing the reading what a particular sign or shape symbolizes for him, in order to interpret it.

It must be remembered that one of the reasons why the marvelous knowledge pertaining to crystals disappeared from the world for hundreds of thousands of years is that the people of ancient civilizations made harmful and improper use of them, in contravention of the basic laws of the universe. Under absolutely no circumstances must the knowledge provided by reading the ball be used improperly. It must not be used for any manipulation or investigation of a person, for impure methods of magic or spells, and, of course, not for mediumistic methods of channeling with dead relatives (only experienced mediums are permitted to channel with the dead by means of a crystal ball). Experiments of this kind are liable to be unhealthy for the person performing them, to put it mildly. On the other hand, the crystal ball can be used positively for finding solutions to spiritual, existential, or karmic questions in this world. You can ask it for information pertaining to your previous incarnations, or, in the presence of another person or with his permission, you can ask questions about his previous lives. It is not advisable to do this without the person's consent, since in a case like this, the information is liable to be incorrect. However, in a case where the person is in no state to answer or give permission (for example, a person who is in hospital with a serious disease, and so on), the reading should be performed with spiritual purity and truth.

There is another method for reading a crystal ball. This method can be used for reading the crystal itself, even if it is not shaped like a sphere. It is different than the previous method in that it does not require passive gazing. In this method, the reader "imprints" certain energetic instructions in the crystal that is being used for gazing, for the sake of the reading. What causes the crystal to be imprinted with these instructions is first of all the user's will power and intuition. With this method, you have to charge the crystal by conscious breathing in order to enable the maximum number of messages to be transmitted to the crystal. In this method, balls made of clear crystal, tourmaline, beryl, ruby, moonstone, citrine, amethyst or labradorite can be used, as well as medium to large piece of these stones. In general, a "simple" stone of one of the above crystals will not suit the purpose. For that reason, a stone with a special pattern is required for reading and gazing. How can this stone be found? It may pop out at you at the right time and moment for trying out this unique technique. You can also order it energetically by holding a clear quartz crystal or any other stone you use for placing various energetic orders. While you are holding the crystal, you can concentrate on your desire to find a suitable stone for reading. Afterwards, you can place the crystal under your pillow during the night, or carry it with you when you go to the crystal store. If you are in the habit of doing a great deal of mental work, such as work on thought patterns, positive mantras, and so on, you may need a crystal for placing the energetic order, since exercises of this kind significantly strengthen our ability to order things we want energetically.

This gazing technique is used mainly for producing a mental and spiritual transformation, and for making dreams come true in the material world. It is used less for "reading" and asking questions than the previous method (even though there are people who use this method for the same purpose). There is an endless range of possibilities for work of this kind with a crystal ball.

As an example, one method of gazing is presented below. This unique technique enables you to create the reality of your life to suit yourself. You can develop the method, and invent additional techniques. Of course, you can perform a "realization of wishes" in all spheres – in the economic, health, and mental spheres, as well as higher spiritual development, and so on. The following method focuses on encouraging creativity and on completing creative projects. You can use it, with small "cosmetic" changes, for completing and realizing projects in any field.

During the first stage – the essential one in all the techniques – find yourself a quiet, comfortable place with positive and calm energies in which to perform the gazing. See that there is no energetic interference in the room. Sit in a comfortable chair, and place the crystal ball or the stone you are using on the table. It is advisable to place the stone on dark fabric. Ensure that it is approximately at chest height, or any height at which you can look at it effortlessly. Start taking deep, comfortable breaths. Begin gazing at the crystal without focusing your eyes. Stare at it for a few moments, and forget all about what's happening outside or beyond this exercise. When you feel that the right moment has come, see yourself move into the crystal. You can close your eyes if you feel the need to do so. See yourself inside the crystal. From within the crystal, look at the room you are in, and the objects in it. First, look at the walls, the ceiling and the floor, then look at the furniture, and lastly, see yourself sitting on a chair facing the crystal. This stage, up to here, is identical in all the forthcoming techniques.

Now you can start crystal-gazing in order to inspire creativity and the completion of creative projects.

While you are still inside the crystal, choose any creative field. This field can be writing a book, poetry, painting, film-making, architecture, or anything else. You can focus on a particular creation that you are involved in at the moment. Choose the field or the creation that you are working on at present, or want to work on. Do not choose something that does not appeal to you, or that you are not sure of. Be decisive about the field or the creation that you want to see in front of your eyes. Remember that the aim of the exercise is to realize your dreams in the physical world, so make a true and correct choice.

Before you begin the visualization process, go over the details concerning your creation consciously. Do not leave out even the smallest detail – not just details concerning the creation itself, but also its success – every kind of success you desire. Do not be afraid of letting your imagination soar. Express all your dreams and desires concerning this creation. In order to strengthen the effect, you can write these details down. Spend as much time as necessary doing so. Now, take hold of the crystal ball or special stone that you have chosen for this purpose. Lift it and hold it opposite your third eye. In your mind's eye, begin to see, in a detailed and precise manner, every single detail pertaining to the field of your creation. For instance, if you want to succeed in the field of cinematography, see yourself holding the camera, focusing and pointing it; see yourself arranging the lighting or supervising the lighting of the studio; see the objects moving in front of the camera, and the camera moving toward or away from them. If you are involved in writing a book, and you want to publish it, see the cover of the book in every detail in your mind's eye, the printed pages, your name on the cover, and every single detail, down to the smallest. Relate to the number of copies in the print run and the marketing; see the posters and the articles in the newspapers; see it in bookstore windows or on the shelves. See people buying it and reading it, and so on. Imagine every detail that you can think of, and even more. See all these scenes entering the crystal and being imprinted there. Transmit the scenes, ensuring that you are breathing consciously, slowly, and deeply. See your inhalation as pulling the scenes from your awareness, and your exhalation as sending the scenes into the crystal. The scenes you are transmitting are imprinted in the crystal, and become part of its structure. See your dream come true, and feel the wonderful feeling and the satisfaction that come of completing a project and having a dream come true. Repeat the process three times. Afterwards, place the crystal ball or the special stone you chose for this purpose beside you when you work on your creation. After your success, cleanse and purify the crystal.

You can use this technique for ordering wealth, health, love, or anything else. Spend time thinking about how to act before you apply it. In fact, you should write down your personal idea for ordering something that you desire. Use your intuition in order to plan a personal and unique method for ordering and fulfilling wishes using the crystal ball.

Practicing crystal-ball gazing in pairs

Practicing crystal-ball gazing with the help of another person is very important for developing the practical ability to read the crystal ball. Again, remember that after performing the many gazing exercises, you should not begin reading the ball for others before practicing this exercise several times. The aim of the exercise is to test your abilities in the presence of another person, as well as your ability to transmit the scenes, signs, and colors that are revealed to you in a comprehensible and effective way for your future clients. Here you will have the full cooperation of your partner in the exercise, and he will be conscious of the procedures that are being performed and open to the events. You have to explain to him that this is only an experiment whose aim is to develop your ability to transmit the messages that are revealed in the crystal ball. Thus, your level of expectations must be reasonable; do not expect to "predict the future." While this exercise focuses on the development of the abilities to read and transmit **your** messages, it will also strengthen and develop the intuitive abilities of your partner to a great extent.

Place the crystal ball on the table in the way that was described in the previous exercises. Sit facing the ball, with your partner sitting opposite you, on the other side of the table. (The table, incidentally, should be round or oval, if possible.)

Both of you must sit comfortably. See that your feet are placed firmly on the floor. Bend your knees slightly, and place your arms at the sides of your body. Feel your body relaxed, comfortable, and calm. Take several deep breaths, and transfer the weight of your body downward in order to create a feeling of a link with the ground. Now, both of you must perform **one** of the two following exercises for opening the third eye:

The first is **diamond breathing**, which was described in the first exercise. Remember that your eyes, which are staring at the diamond you have shaped with your fingers, must be unfocused. Imagine your third eye opening in the center of your forehead and gazing into the hollow in the middle of the diamond. Perform this beginning exercise for a few minutes.

The second exercise is **getting the color purple to flow into third eye center**. Sit comfortably, taking deep, slow breaths. After you feel that your body is relaxed and calm, begin to see a purple light descending from above, penetrating the top of your head, and reaching the third eye center, while you are inhaling. While exhaling, see the purple light enveloping the third eye center. In the next inhalation, draw more purple light into the chakra. Now, while inhaling, revolve the chakra wheel that is sheathed in purple light. Continue doing this a few more times. End the exercise by seeing an eye opening in the center of your forehead – the third eye.

After you have performed one of the exercises for opening the third eye, sit quietly for a few minutes with your eyes closed. Your partner must not disturb you by talking or asking questions, but must continue to sit quietly during the reading. The emptier his mind is of thought, the better. Alternatively – and especially if it is not easy for him to sit for a long time without thoughts, or after a few exercises – your friend can raise a certain question in his mind and present it to you. It is advisable to roll or pass this question or request around in your head during the entire duration of the reading and not allow irrelevant thoughts to interfere.

Start gazing into the crystal ball. You may need some time to see scenes in it. If you perform this exercise after practicing by yourself a great deal, the signs are likely to appear more quickly and clearly.

You must be completely engrossed in gazing, and tuned into your partner. Gaze at the ball with half-closed, unfocused eyes. Let the plethora of images, shapes, and colors appear in front of your eyes. Now, when you see a particular image, trust your intuition completely. Say what you feel about the sign or color that appears. Do not be afraid to say whatever comes into your mind, since the exercise to open the third eye has stimulated your intuition to such an extent that most of the things you say will be correct. In any event, his is only an exercise, and you need not be afraid of making mistakes. The first time you perform this exercise, ask your partner not to react to the things you say. Simply look at the scenes, and say whatever comes into your mind. Afterwards, you can both discuss the insights that appeared, or your interpretation of the signs, and their connection to your partner's life. After practicing the exercise in this way several times, begin asking questions when the images arise in front of your eyes (if you feel a need for this in order to narrow your answers). Moreover, with faith and practice, your partner can ask an occasional question about the things you say without breaking your concentration on the crystal ball. You may require patience until you see clear and certain results – but it will pay off.

The crystal pendulum

The use of a pendulum for prediction and revealing the occult is an ancient method that was used in various cultures throughout the world for thousands of years. The pendulum is a tool for receiving answers and information from the superego, which is aware of all the vibrations that we do not pick up, generally speaking, with our regular senses.

Various stones and minerals are used as pendulums. A pendulum made of crystal, and especially clear crystal, is one of the most widespread and effective pendulums. It is possible to obtain pendulums made of citrine, amethyst, rose quartz, onyx, obsidian, and smoky quartz. There are also pendulums made of organic matter such as animals' teeth, ivory, or shells. However, the pendulums that are made from minerals from the quartz family (except for onyx and obsidian), have the most perfect frequencies. These pendulums can pick up the energetic changes that occur in the human body, the astral, lunar, and solar energies, and the earth energies.

You can purchase a pendulum in New Age stores, but you can also make a pendulum out of a suitable stone that you like, or out of one of the minerals of the quartz family. The type of mineral you use for preparing the pendulum can influence or reinforce a certain direction of questions, or can be more suitable for certain topics. Look at the properties of the different pendulums, and choose the one that suits you. Remember that when you work with a particular pendulum for a long time, it is likely to provide satisfactory answers regarding any topic.

A pendulum made of clear quartz – This is **the** pendulum. It is suitable and excellent for any purpose whatsoever, even for uses that go beyond receiving answers, such as establishing a telepathic link using a pendulum, dowsing in order to find objects, work, and an infinite number of other uses. It is very common and also inexpensive.

A pendulum made of amethyst – A pendulum made of amethyst is used effectively for reinforcing the intuitive abilities and the abilities to use the pendulum itself, as well as for asking questions about spiritual matters.

A pendulum made of rose quartz – A pendulum made of rose quartz is used for questions and predictions concerning love and relationships.

A pendulum made of citrine – A pendulum made of citrine is especially effective for questions and predictions in matters concerning business, business and social communication, and studies. They are especially good when it is necessary to make decisions and choose among various options.

A pendulum made of smoky quartz – A pendulum made of smoky quartz is very effective when it is used for receiving answers concerning the mental layers, human behavior, and for questions whose purpose is to lead to a person's better understanding of himself.

Despite their unique properties, you will find all of them effective (to a greater or lesser degree) in all fields, unless you programmed one of them for use in a particular field. Besides these stones, you can also choose a pendulum made out of any other mineral for which you feel an affinity. Likewise, you can use any stone that is dear to you or that you feel possesses unique qualities, if its shape is suitable for use as a pendulum.

Making the pendulum

If you have chosen to prepare the pendulum yourself, you will discover that you can do this very easily. You must remember that the pendulum is cone- or spiral-shaped. A lumpy stone without a clear shape, or a square stone, may not be suitable, or may create difficulties when used, especially if you have only just begun practicing using pendulums. Moreover, the stone must be light and relatively small. Find a stone in a spiral, conical, or elongated shape. You can try using a stone that looks like a disk. Your personal pendulum will recognize your energies and will be linked to them. For that reason, it is not advisable to prepare it or thread it on a suitable chain casually. The ceremony involved in its preparation is not exaggerated, since it will strengthen the link between the pendulum and you, and will facilitate the subsequent programming and use of the pendulum.

You must be calm and serene when you start preparing the pendulum. Place all the materials you need on a clean and empty worktable in a room with as pleasant and clean an atmosphere as possible. You can also play pleasant music (if the procedure takes a long time), and light an essential oil burner. Try to relax your body and empty yourself of thoughts and emotions that are not relevant during the preparation time. You can request guidance and direction, and use your favorite techniques for filling up with energy. If you are rushed, angry, sad, or upset, postpone the preparation of the pendulum. Of course you have to be free of non-positive intentions, thoughts, and emotions, because these energies are liable to make a certain impression on the pendulum you are preparing, and are liable to involve unwanted energies that will affect its work and accuracy.

Prepare a strong cotton or silk thread in white, gray, silver or gold. A gold or silver chain is also highly recommended. If the stone you have chosen does not have a hole, you will have to glue a metal (preferably gold or silver) cap on one of its ends. If it has a hole, thread a small gold or silver loop through it, like the ones used in jewelry. If you have a suitable crystal pendant, or a pendant made of some other suitable stone, you can use that as a pendulum without further preparations.

Fasten the chain to the metal loop or cap by means of the clasp at the end of the chain, or, if you chose a cotton or silk thread, tie it with as small a knot as possible to the metal ring or cap.

Now you must tune the pendulum in order to know what its movement for "no" is, and what its movement for "yes" is. You can do this in two ways. First, you can be the one who determines the pendulum's movement – you decide which way it will turn in order to answer "yes," and which way it will turn in order to answer "no." Second, you can let the pendulum express its natural movement for each of its answers.

Tuning the pendulum by thought and visualization

This method requires a great ability to concentrate the power of thought and the ability to transmit it to inanimate objects. If you have already performed the exercises for developing telepathy by means of generators or a double terminated crystal, you will find that this method is very easy for you. Having said that, because of the crystal pendulum's great sensitivity, even a first attempt at concentrating the power of thought is likely to succeed. This method of tuning reinforces the link between you and your crystal pendulum, and you may be surprised to discover the extent to which it reacts to your thoughts.

Sit in a room with a pleasant atmosphere that is devoid of unwanted energies and electrical appliances that emit radiation. Perform the tuning of the pendulum only when you are free of unwanted emotions such as anger or sadness, and feel calm and tranquil. Moreover, if you are tired, postpone the tuning to another time.

Hold the thread of the pendulum in one hand. With time, you will learn intuitively what the correct length of the thread should be, and in which hand you prefer holding it. Hold the thread in a comfortable, light, and natural way.

Relax your body so that you do not feel any muscle tension that could interfere with the tuning action. Take a number of deep, slow breaths. Get rid of any irrelevant thoughts, and concentrate on the tuning procedure only.

See that you do not cross your arms or your legs. Place your elbow on the table in order to stabilize it. Hold the pendulum in your hand, and stabilize it with the other hand, gently, so that it stops swinging.

Concentrate your entire power of thought on the pendulum Now, begin to transmit the first movement message to it – the "yes" movement. In general, the "yes" movement is a right-to-left turn. You can choose another movement (a horizontal movement, or a left-to-right movement), but the right-to-left movement is the most natural one for indicating "yes," and you should not choose anything else.

Concentrate your power of thought and transmit to the pendulum: "The circular movement from right to left means 'yes,'" or "'Yes' is the circular movement from right to left." It will be a matter of only a few seconds before you see the pendulum performing this movement before your very eyes. Let it perform the movement, stronger and clearer and smoother, for a minute or two. For that entire length of time, continue transmitting the movement message to it.

Now, transmit the movement message for indicating "no" to it. You can choose any movement you want, but the accepted movement for indicating "no" is the circular movement from left to right. (If you chose a horizontal movement for "yes," you can choose the opposite horizontal movement for "no.") Concentrate your entire power of thought and transmit to the pendulum: "A circular movement from left to right means 'no,'" or "'No' is the circular movement from left to right." You can close your eyes and see the pendulum performing this movement, if you feel the need. After a few seconds, the pendulum will obey your power of thought, and will perform the movement you transmitted to it.

In order to avoid confusing the pendulum, it is very important for you to be clear and decisive regarding the movements that you want it to perform to indicate a positive or a negative answer. If the pendulum performs the movement you thought of and transmitted to it in your thoughts, it is a sign that there is a bond between the operator and the tool, and it is prepared to serve you – only for positive and pure purposes, of course. If you discover that the pendulum does not respond to your power of thought, you will have to examine one of the following possibilities:

You are tired or run down. Go and rest, and try again when you are more alert and invigorated, or the next day.

There is radiation interference in the room (computer, TV, microwave), and your power of thought is not yet strong enough to counteract the effect of the disturbing frequencies.

You are not emotionally clean, or you have not succeeded in stopping thoughts that disturb your focus on the tuning. Try again another time, when you are calmer.

You crossed your legs or arms.

Your power of thought is not sufficiently strong yet. Start to practice some of the meditations with stones that appear in the book in order to develop the power of thought and visualization, and/or work on practicing the telepathic ability using generators or double terminated crystals.

If you wish, you can go on to the next method and try it, but you should wait until the next day to do so.

Tuning the pendulum according to its rhythm and confirming it

In this method, ask the pendulum to show you its movement messages that express "yes" and "no."

Repeat the procedure that appears at the beginning of the previous method – the appropriate energetic cleansing of thought, a calm, quiet room with no interfering energies, emptying out of irrelevant thoughts and emotions, relaxation of the body, and concentration on the pendulum. After taking a few deep, slow breaths, see that your legs and arms are not crossed, place the elbow of the hand that is holding the pendulum on the table, and gently stop the pendulum's motions with the other hand, until it is motionless.

Now, concentrate all your thought power on the pendulum. Ask it, "Which is the pendulum's movement for 'yes'?" The pendulum will begin to perform a certain movement, circular or horizontal. Let it perform this movement for a minute or two, until it is clear, smooth, and strong. Engrave this movement in your consciousness and send the pendulum a message of acceptance and confirmation. Now, ask it, "Which is the pendulum's movement for 'no'?" Let the pendulum perform its movement until it is clear, strong, and unequivocal. Engrave the movement and its tuning in your consciousness, and send the pendulum a message of acceptance and confirmation.

The movements must be clear, smooth, and unequivocal. In most cases, the "no" movement, whether it is circular or horizontal, will be opposite in its direction to the "yes" movement. If you do not attain this tuning, look at the list of energetic disturbances that appears at the end of the previous exercise, and act accordingly.

If you have tried both methods, and neither one succeeds, even after you have eliminated the disturbing factors, you will have to leave the pendulum and try again after a certain period of time. Most people can operate a pendulum, but there are rare people who are not suited to it. You will have to try again every now and then, at differing intervals, and see whether you can operate it. During those periods, see that you perform the exercises for balancing the chakras, the meditations, and the work with crystals, all of which appear in the book.

After you have tuned and programmed the pendulum, or have tuned yourself into it, there is no need to program it again. For this, you must ensure that it remains in your possession, and prevent anyone else from coming into contact with it, since alien vibrations are liable to disrupt its programming. It is possible that a pendulum that has been put aside unused for a long time still needs a slight "reminder" about the movements it must perform in accordance with the answers it was tuned to give. If you have chosen to use a crystal pendulum, you should occasionally place it on a purifying quartz cluster, and program it slightly afterwards. If somebody else used your crystal pendulum (which, as we said before, is undesirable), you should rinse it under running water and place it on a quartz cluster for two hours or more (according to your feeling).

The pendulum's tremors

Sometimes, even after you have used the pendulum successfully several times, it performs sort of small tremors or directionless movements in answer to your questions. There are a number of possible explanations for this phenomenon:

The form of the question is incorrect – you must only ask questions whose answer is "yes" or "no" in a clear and unequivocal way, or move the pendulum over a chart, as we will see later on. If you asked it a question that was not formulated correctly, it cannot answer it.

The question is immoral, inappropriate, or this is not the right time to answer such a question.

You are tired, troubled, not calm or filled with non-positive energies as a result of an argument, spending a lot of time exposed to radiation (a computer or TV), and so on. Try again when you are in a better state.

There is strong interfering radiation in the room, or, alternatively, a very powerful crystal is present in the place where you are working with the pendulum.

You crossed your legs or arms, which interferes with the flow of energy.

You experienced disturbing thoughts or an inability to focus, for some reason.

Before every question or working with the pendulum, take the following principles into account, and apply the following rules:

Precise questions – The pendulum will answer "yes" or "no" questions. For this reason, the questions must be formulated in such a way that the answers are only "yes" and "no." Moreover, the questions must be as precise as possible, and you must be decisive and clear regarding the question you are asking.

Objectivity – Your emotions and thoughts while asking the questions must be in a natural state. You must neutralize any opinion or emotion concerning the requested answer, since opinions, emotions, or wishes are liable to influence the answer. You must be prepared to receive the true answer only, and want only a true and correct answer, even if it is unpleasant or undesirable from the subjective point of view.

Cleanliness of thought and emotion – Various irrelevant emotions, anger, worries, disturbances, and uncalled-for thoughts interfere with the smooth, clear movement of the pendulum, and prevent you from receiving an unequivocal answer.

Relaxed muscles – Muscle tension is liable to interfere with the movement of the pendulum. Do not use the pendulum when you are tense and stiff, or after intensive physical activity. Try to relax your entire body before working with the pendulum, and try to enter a relaxed and meditative state, so that you can receive the optimal results.

A blockage in the energy passage – Make sure that neither your hands nor your feet are touching each other, or are crossed, and do not sit with one leg on the other, as this is liable to block the passage of the energy current that is essential for the movement of the pendulum. Sit with your legs apart, and your feet firmly on the floor. Hold the pendulum in your right hand (hold it in your left hand if you are left-handed), with your other hand lying relaxed at your side.

Energetic cleanliness in the room in which the work with the pendulum takes place – High-voltage electrical appliances such as color TVs, computers, microwaves, etc., emit very powerful radiation, which tends to undermine the movement of the pendulum, and make the reading difficult, especially if the reader is inexperienced. In noisy, crowded places such as railway stations, buses, and classrooms, the multitude of frequencies and resonances are liable to affect the pendulum's motions and disturb the reading. The same is true for a room in which arguments or rows took place, or in which people with non-positive, angry or bitter energies were present.

After you have tuned the pendulum and learned to stick to the rules that help you to achieve optimal results, you can start the reading. Reading with a pendulum can help you in everyday life for receiving answers concerning a wide variety of topics – for instance, if you are wondering whether to study with a particular teacher, to go out with a certain person, to purchase a certain object, and so on.

The pendulum can help you predict the future. It must be admitted that you will need a certain amount of experience for this, and a lot of practice and work with the pendulum. You can ask it questions such as, "Will I get this particular job?" "Is this person suitable to be my partner?" and so on. For predictions of this kind, you must take care to formulate the questions very clearly and precisely, and you might need some time to do so. This will enable the pendulum to give you an unequivocal answer. If the pendulum keeps on producing tremors or undefined movements, it is possible that for some reason, it is not a good idea for you to get an answer to the question at this time. The pendulum will not answer questions whose motivation is not absolutely pure, either.

You can ask "choice questions." In this type of question, a question is asked about a number of subjects, out of which one or more must be chosen. The easiest method is working with a list or chart. In this method, too, the importance of a well-formulated question is cardinal.

As an example of a reading with a pendulum and a chart, we will take the subject of the balancing of the chakras. Let's say that you want to perform one of the exercises for balancing the chakras that appears in the book, focusing on a particular chakra. You want to know on which chakra to focus first and foremost.

Take a clean sheet of white paper. Write down the names of the chakras in a neat and well-spaced way, one below the other:

(Crown chakra)

(Third eye chakra)

(Throat chakra)

(Heart chakra)

(Solar plexus chakra)

(Sex chakra)

(Base chakra)

Hold the pendulum above the list. You can ask, "Is this the chakra that I must focus on today?" or "Is this the chakra whose balance is the most essential for improving my life and my awareness in the present?" and so on. You may receive a positive answer for more than one chakra. In this case, you will have to focus on the pendulum's movement, and see which "yes" movement is the clearest, smoothest, strongest, and most unequivocal of all the "yes" answers. You can shorten the list, and ask again, "Is this the chakra that is the most important for me to balance today?" until you have reduced the options.

Using a chart – By using a chart, you can put in many more variables and ask broader questions, especially multiple-choice questions. In one column of the table, write the name or the word about which you are asking the question. You can perform this reading about anything. Below are two examples:

Let's say you want to find the stone that is most suitable for opening your third eye chakra at the present time. You have at your disposal several stones that are suitable for this role, but you want to find **the most suitable one**. Make a chart in the following form:

(Amethyst)
The most suitable for balancing and opening my third eye chakra, at this time.

(Sodalite)
The most suitable for balancing and opening my third eye chakra, at this time.

(Lapis lazuli)
The most suitable for balancing and opening my third eye chakra, at this time.

(Azurite)
The most suitable for balancing and opening my third eye chakra, at this time.

(Sugilite)
The most suitable for balancing and opening my third eye chakra, at this time.

(Fluorite)
The most suitable for balancing and opening my third eye chakra, at this time.

Now, hold your crystal pendulum over the name of the stone. Concentrate on it for a few seconds, and pass the pendulum over the lines that describe your expectation of the stone. Let this line go through your thoughts a few times, or say it aloud. The pendulum will make a "yes" or a "no" movement. It may make a "yes" movement above more than one stone. You can prepare a new chart in which only two or three of the chosen stones appear, or choose the stone above which the pendulum made the clearest, smoothest, and strongest "yes" movement.

You can, of course, avail yourself of the crystal pendulum for making various purchases, when you are deliberating about a number of possibilities, for example. You can apply this technique to any other subject by filling in the columns of the chart in a correct and unequivocal way. As an illustration, let's say that you want to buy a new CD player and you cannot decide which make to purchase. Write the name of the company in the left-hand column, and, if possible, also the name of the model or type. In the right-hand column, write something general – "will best answer my needs," or any other function that is important to you, such as "has the best shock-absorbing capabilities," "the most durable," "uses the least electricity," or any other function that is relevant and important to you. Make a chart similar to the one below (use the sentence "will best answer my needs" or "the most durable" or "has the best shock-absorbing capabilities" or any other relevant question).

"Akai" CD player model/type XXX will best answer my needs.

"Sony" CD player model/type XXX will best answer my needs.

"Aiwa" CD player model/type XXX will best answer my needs.

"Panasonic" CD player model/type XXX will best answer my needs.

Move the pendulum in the same way as for choosing a stone for the chakra. As we said before, you can fill the columns of the chart with any question or subject.

Besides the techniques presented above, the pendulum has endless uses. It is used for sending telepathic messages, for diagnosing the state of the aura, for emotional and health diagnoses, for finding lost objects, and so on and so forth. The more you use the pendulum, the more things you will discover that you can use it for. Be creative, and remember that the more you use the pendulum, the stronger and greater your abilities to use it will become. Moreover, your intuitive abilities become stronger, and your third eye center is opened and stimulated.*

*You can use the book, **"Pendulums"** by Jared O'Keefe (Astrolog, 1999, ISBN 965-494-090-6).

Reading precious stones

Reading precious stones is a method of understanding the present, and planning the future accordingly. It is an ancient method that was widespread in various parts of the world, in a number of variations. In order to strengthen your reading ability, you should go over the chapter on colors in this book a few times. It will give you additional hints, besides the ones presented in this chapter, about the stones' answers to your questions. A greater knowledge of the colors will give you a more profound understanding of the messages that are transmitted in the reading of precious stones.

Reading precious stones is performed according to the color of the stones. This is the first parameter according to which the answers to the questions are received. The type of stone is not particularly important, but it is important that you, as a reader, are linked to the stones that you are using in the reading. The second parameter is the type of stone – active or passive. Later, you will learn how to distinguish these characteristics in stones, or to create for yourself a range of passive stones and active stones for purposes of reading.

The stones must all be clean and purified. They should be charged and programmed with the intention of reading. For reading, you need two stones in each color. One of them must be shiny, rich in color, and glowing, and the second must be more opaque, in the same color, but in weaker shades. The reason for this is that, similar to people, each stone contains two forces. One is the positive (plus) force, yang, giving, masculine, physical, and logical. The second is the negative (minus) force, yin, receptive, feminine, spiritual, and intuitive. (Note that the meaning of "positive" and "negative" here is the same as for electricity and magnetism – a positive pole or a negative pole. There is no value judgment concerning good or bad.) These forces complement each other to create unity and wholeness. The purpose is to find two stones of the same shade – one containing a positive, giving, more conspicuous force than the other, while the second is more conspicuous in its negative, receptive force (the minus and plus aspect). Two stones of the same color will represent these two forces.

When reading, we are required to use our intuition, our powers of perception, and our openness of thought. The reading is performed by asking a question, concentrating on the question, and choosing one of the stones. According to the color of the stone, we can receive clues about the direction on which we have to concentrate in order to solve the problem or find an answer.

As we saw in the chapter on colors, the warm color are the colors that represent action. Therefore, stones that possess a receptive, passive nature in these colors too – red, orange, and yellow – will indicate the extent of the need for action or activity. Stones in green shades can indicate matters of the heart, situations of equilibrium, or an aspiration to equilibrium. Blue stones direct us to the mental layer and thought. Purple stones and indigo stones, the colors of the third eye chakra, direct us to the metaphysical and spiritual layers, such as finding a vocation, and so on. Brown stones are linked to the connection with the earth, to modesty, and grounding, as well as to the need for the use of reason. Pink stones represent the need for healing, rest, or settling conflicts, which can be internal or external. Sometimes, pink stones can advise us to move away from those conflicts when we are not personally involved. White stones and black stones are found at the two ends of the color scale.

How do we decide which stone is passive and which is active?

When we choose an active stone or a passive stone of the same color, we can know which of them is used as an active stone and which as a passive stone by observing the two stones. The active stone must be more dominant. This is the key to the choice. It should be richer in its shade, stronger in color, or shiny and sparkling. The second stone must be less shiny, sometimes faded, and weaker in color. A passive tone should be opaque, slightly faded in color, in matte shades (as opposed to a shiny stone), and less gleaming and dominant. In this matter, you must not just rely on your eye, but also on your intuition and gut feeling. Try to feel which of the stones transmits energy, and which absorbs energy. Observe them for some time, hold them up to the light or to the sun, and feel which is more glowing and dominant.

White stones

White stones represent the creative, giving side in a more significant way. They are supposed to indicate a matter concerning changes, the need for energy, or the need to operate actively and positively. They indicate changes that must be made in the present, or that we want to make, such as the need for changing jobs, residence, relationships, and so on.

An active white stone – This is a shiny or sparkling white stone. When we choose an active white stone, it is a sign of the presence of a tremendous store of energy, which we may be ignoring or repressing. The choice of a white stone when the question of whether to make a certain change in life is asked, provides a positive answer. It indicates new beginnings and forces bubbling under the surface and pushing us to realize our wishes and desires. As an active white stone, you can choose a clear or white quartz crystal. You can also use a transparent zircon.

A passive white stone – A dull, opaque or cloudy white stone. The choice of a passive white stone indicates a slower, more gradual, step-by-step change. It is possible that the results of this change will not be fast, but will require some time to be seen. The change we want to make may have "side effects." That is, moving house will not be easy, quitting a job is liable to result in a tense period, a change in the relationship will hurt the other partner, and so on. As a passive white stone you can use quartz of a dull milky hue, white mother of pearl, white moonstone, or even a white pebble that can be found in a field or on the shore.

Choosing two white stones – Drawing two white stones is a clear indication of change. But it is possible that there is a situation of "all or nothing " – change that is liable to halt with the first obstacle that stands in its path. Choosing or drawing two white stones indicates that in order to implement the desired change, the person will have to face the difficulties in his path courageously. Now that he is aware of the possibility of difficulties that are liable to make him retreat, he must arm himself with courage and not allow them to halt his progress along his path. He must not despair. The choice of two white stones may advise him to take small steps – day-by-day progress – in order to achieve his objective and implement the change. Since it is clearly a matter of change, it is possible that the choice will indicate a need to change an inhibiting and superfluous thought pattern, habit or behavior. Changes in nutrition, work, relationships, and so on must be made step by step, focusing on doing something each day.

Black stones

The color black is the ultimate receptive color. It absorbs all the other colors. For reading, we need two black stone – one active, a shiny, sparkling stone, and one passive, a dull and opaque stone.

In its most positive form, the color black symbolizes the ability to open up to the world around us, to other people. Black stones symbolize conclusion, end, or the closing of a circle. They suggest that we do not run and act, but sit and wait. They can symbolize a period of waiting, or of inactivity in life, an end – of work, a relationship, studies, and so on. Moreover, these stones can symbolize a break in a period in life. For example, before the decision to raise children, or get married, these stones will indicate the end of the era of being single, or of the period when most of the person's attention is directed toward himself or his mate. It could indicate that the end could be painful, such as the end of a relationship, or an end that is forced upon the person, such as being fired from work. But it must be remembered that every end is also a new beginning, and it contains a range of new options, sometimes far better ones. When we know how to welcome the approaching end with understanding and awareness, we can embrace new options with open arms.

An active black stone – For an active black stone, you can choose black hematite in a silvery shade, shiny jet, glossy onyx, or shiny obsidian. These stones, which are rich in black and have a sheen, are different from the usual dull black stones.

Choosing an active black stone can indicate a huge loss of energy as a result of clinging to a situation or a relationship that does not provide an equal amount of energy in return for the energy that is invested in it. It may indicate a depressing or negative relationship or situation. It could be indicative of clinging to inhibiting and non-positive patterns or feelings, such as resentment, anger, jealousy, and so on, that cause a great loss of energy.

A passive black stone – Any dull black or gray-black stone can be used as a passive stone. There are dull black agates, or dark gray-black smoky quartz, very dark, dull garnets, and so on. Even black pebbles that are found on the shore can be suitable for this purpose.

A passive black stone indicates a situation in which the person feels as if he is collapsing under the burden of problems and troubles: demands, requests, or attrition on the part of his relatives, in relationships, or at work. It could be a huge burden in life, such as raising children simultaneously with massive demands at work or in his studies. He may have to shoulder the burdens of people close to him, or a great deal of responsibility. Sometimes, the person does not know how to set limits and say "no," resulting in exhaustion and a lack of energy. Choosing a passive black stone warns us not to overburden ourselves, and not to lose energies in this way, especially for others. It advises us to set limits, to be stronger and more determined, and not to let our energies scatter or dissipate.

Choosing two black stones – If you drew or chose two black stones, this might indicate a feeling of self-oppression, a non-legitimization to feel anger or say no, or guilt feelings. It might also indicate that the person is caught in a situation that drains his energies, especially a situation of continuous worry and helping relatives, which leaves him devoid of energies for his personal growth and development. Moreover, it can be indicative of a person who feels that he has to be strong for his relatives, carry the burden, and deprive himself of personal time, freedom, and the legitimization of his feelings.

Red stones

Red is the color of physical energy and action. It symbolizes strength, power, and courage. A red stone that comes up during the reading can show that the person or someone close to him has been done an injustice – something that arouses in him feelings of anger or aggressiveness. It can indicate a "last straw" situation, where there is a need to change an unfair situation in which the person is involved.

An active red stone – As an active red stone, you can choose shiny red or transparent garnet, red carnelian with abundant color, or gleaming red jasper. Dark red rhodochrosite, with its full and shiny hues, can also suit the purpose, as can red agate or shiny fire agate. An active red stone indicates that the person is aware that he has to go out and battle against unjust or oppressive forces or situations. It shows that this is the time to gird one's loins, and fight for the cessation of unfair situations, or fight for an important aim.

A passive red stone – As a passive red stone, you can use red pebbles that are found in various outdoor places, or on the shore. Red calcite with its somewhat faded color can be suitable, as can red or red brown agate that is not shiny or rich in color.

Choosing a passive red stone indicates the internalization of anger, frustration, and rage. The person might blame himself for the unfair situation in which he finds himself, and eats himself up about it. Moreover, the person could be "punishing" himself, or repression his emotions, by overeating, drinking alcohol, and so on. The choice of this stone indicates an immediate need to stop the circle of self-blame, internalizing anger, and displaying outward passivity. He must begin to take action to change the situation. He can draw another stone for the question of how or in what way he must act in order to change the face of things.

Choosing two red stones – If two red stones came up in the reading, it may indicate protracted inner conflicts, without taking any action, or unhealthy irritation and agitation about something that is not significant. It could involve a feeling of confusion or anger that is not directed at the real problem. Sometimes, there is a problem beneath the surface that causes seething, anger, and agitation. The person does not identify their real source, but instead blames them on reasons that are not the root of the problem. In a situation like this, he must look inward and try to discover the real problem that is troubling and plaguing him.

Orange stones

Orange is the color of independence, uniqueness, and cheerfulness. It represents going along our unique path confidently, feeling strong in the face of obstacles or opponents. It is a color of individuality, even within the group, the family unit, or society. It symbolizes the acknowledgment of the needs of the self and their fulfillment, and the ability to enjoy ourselves, our deeds, and our personality.

An active orange stone – You can choose amber with a rich, orange hue, shiny carnelian, orange jasper or orange citrine, so long as their color is conspicuous and rich.

Choosing an orange stone may occur during a period in which the person feels that he has aims that are unique or exceptional compared to the people around him. Sometimes the stone comes up when the person wants to go on a journey or take a trip to what he considers an exotic place. It indicates that now is the right time to fulfill desires that give us pleasure, a feeling of freedom, and liberty. Some people may not understand or look kindly upon these desires and aspirations, but this is the time to realize them, even if other people do not approve. If the person does not take steps to accomplish these objectives consciously, this is the time to start thinking about what really makes him happy – what he wants to do in life, which path he wants to follow. The active orange stone shows that the person must follow his inner feelings and desires. It may be a question of going back to school, a new career, a trip, or anything else that the person longs for deep in his heart. Even if these ideas come as a surprise to his mate or family members, he must not forego his personal happiness and his feeling of satisfaction with his life. Sometimes, the active orange stone indicates that this is the time for us to start accepting ourselves as we are – for instance, our external appearance after numerous diets, our field of interest, even if others consider it "impractical," and so on.

A passive orange stone – A passive orange stone is likely to appear when the person feels that his personal identity is fading. It appears in situations in which the person "toes the line," acts in accordance with other people's expectations, and surrenders his individuality and his personal desires to others – and he feels as if he is being deprived of his freedom. He might be letting his mate or the members of his family plan his life or his future. In situations like these, when they are protracted, the person is liable to forget his basic aspirations, the things he desired with all his heart to realize and apply. The passive orange stone suggests that he reconsider his priorities, free up some time for himself, time for thinking and observing his life as it is at the moment, while asking the question, "Is this really what I want? Do I feel satisfaction with the way in which things are going? Am I the one who is in charge of my life, or am I being led by others?" This is the time to put personal desires at the top of the list of priorities, not out of bitterness, anger, or a wish to hurt others, but out of tolerance, good communication, and belief in oneself. When a person forms his desires, feels that he is worthy of realizing them, and is sure of his path, the obstacles facing him disappear, sometimes faster, sometimes slower – but his confidence in his personal path enables it to be realized. It is even possible to make a list of priorities or of desires and aspirations, focus on it every day, and take one step daily toward accomplishing one's personal goals.

Choosing two orange stones – If both an active orange stone and a passive orange stone come up in the reading, this may be indicative of a person who lives vicariously. This kind of reading occasionally occurs when there is a talented mother, for instance, who repressed her talents for the sake of raising a family, and now tries to push her children to develop their talents; or a person who experienced poverty during childhood, and now provides his children with everything their hearts desire, but continues to ignore his own needs and wishes, and so on. Another example is the single woman who fixes all her relatives up with mates, while she herself is still single. There are many forms in which people live their lives vicariously, and are unaware that they are doing so, and that they have these innate talents and abilities that are waiting to be discovered and exploited. Choosing two orange stones calls for a profound look at one's present way of life. It requires that the person ask himself if he is making the most of his life, and if he is doing the things that give him a feeling of self-satisfaction.

Yellow stones

Yellow is the color of the sun, and it symbolizes communication. The sun represents opening eyes, the ability to see things as they are, and to differentiate between reality and illusion.

An active yellow stone – As an active yellow stone, you can choose yellow topaz, shine yellow citrine, yellow zircon, golden-yellow tiger eye, yellow jasper, shiny yellow amber, or any other yellow stone that sparkles, gleams, or has rich yellow hues.

An active yellow stone indicates a need for external communication between you and others, a clear and obvious need for communication in order to create movement in life, to shake off stagnation, or to "move things" and start taking action. This does not mean stubborn quarrels, but clear, unequivocal communication. The person has to clarify the seriousness of his intentions and his world view, as well as his perception of things, to those concerned clearly and unequivocally. It may indicate a situation in which the person waits for others to come up to him and ask what happened, what is bothering him, and so on, instead of going to explain his situation. It may also indicate situations in which the person waits for things to change by themselves, or for people to change their attitude or their behavior, and will not go to them and make his standpoint clear. It shows that this is the time to take the reins and lead the negotiations, the conversation, or the exchange of words, in his direction. It is time to take a stand and express thoughts or desires verbally, without waiting for others to give him the opportunity to do so. An active yellow stone sometimes comes up in a situation in which the person feels that he deserves a raise, for instance, but he is afraid to ask for it, and waits for it to be given to him. When his mate behaves in a way that causes him anguish, he expects his mate to "read" his feelings instead of going and expressing them.

A passive yellow stone – as a passive yellow stone, you can choose beryl with soft hues, yellow calcite or yellow fluorite, which are not shiny. You can also collect yellow sandstone with a soft or faded hue in the mountains, on the roads, or at the shore, or yellow shells and pebbles.

A passive yellow stone shows that there is some kind of breakdown in communication with oneself. The person may be confused, and does not know what he wants. Sometimes it can indicate that the person is overly influenced by other people's abilities, to the point that he has no confidence in his own. In addition, the stone can indicate a situation in which the person himself does not listen to, or is unaware of, what others say to him, or try to convey to him, which creates cases of misunderstanding between him and those around him. It can indicate a situation in which the person adheres to his opinions out of sheer defensiveness, and does not let others explain themselves and express their opinions to him. In situations of this kind, the person must shake off previous objections, and listen with an open mind to what other people say, attempting to understand them.

Choosing two yellow stones – If an active yellow stone and a passive yellow stone come up in the reading, they can indicate that an important topic for negotiation is imminent. The person must use the forces of intuition and reason. The reading indicates that the person has to spend some time with himself, thinking and planning how to approach the negotiation, which is likely to occur in any one of life's aspects. It could be that being adamant when requesting a raise may not be the most correct way. He may have to sit down and think logically about how to plan the way in which he will communicate with the other person, and express his feelings, standpoint, or desires to him. Two yellow stones in a reading request that the person sit and think objectively about the matters he is about to raise with another person, and also about the way he will say what he has to say. It is possible that a face-to-face conversation will be useful. However, a letter or a phone-call may help the person get what he wants. It is possible that he must present his case quietly, and be prepared to come toward the other person and compromise, or, conversely, that he must present a determined and uncompromising standpoint. The person must take the time and place for this communication or conversation into consideration. Choosing two yellow stones suggests that the person think well and plan his moves meticulously before going to present his standpoints and opinions to the other person.

Green stones

Green stones are the stones of the heart. When a green stone comes up in the reading, it involves matters of the heart, of emotion. The choice of green stones can indicate great emotional involvement in a certain situation, or an intention that stems from an emotional source, emotions that must be taken into consideration and worked with, not against. Certain situations require that the person act in accordance with his reason and mind, while others call for the guidance of the heart and emotions. To the same extent, people who are close to us can say certain things, but when we are aware of their emotions, which we can sense, we can see that in fact they mean something quite different. In certain situations, green stones can show us that we have the chance to offer emotional support, empathy, and heartfelt understanding to a person close to us. However, it must be remembered that together with empathy, there is sometimes also a need for a certain practicality. Green stones also indicate equilibrium – and this equilibrium must be preserved. Even if we are guided by emotion, we must not abandon thought, reason, or practical action completely.

An active green stone – As an active green stone, you can use a beautiful green emerald, opaque and shiny green malachite, deep green bloodstone, richly colored aventurine, transparent and shiny peridot, green, sparkling, and crystalline dioptase, rich and shiny green chrysocolla, jade with shiny hues, rich green jasper, green topaz, green zircon, dark green spinel, or any other shiny or sparkling green stone.

When an active green stone comes up in a reading, it indicates deep emotional involvement in a particular topic. Even if outwardly the person seems indifferent or unmoved, every fiber of his being is vibrating with emotion about this topic. In cases such as these, the stone suggests that the person trust in his emotions in spite of "reason" or of what other people say. Even if his feelings toward other people, or what they say, seem to prevent him from expressing your feelings about the emotional way in which he interprets the situation, he must permit himself to express them. He must follow his emotions without being afraid to express them and act accordingly.

A passive green stone – As a passive green stone, you can choose green amazonite, or green amazonite that is spotted with white or has a slightly bluish green hue, opaque green jade, apple green chrysoprase, serpentine in an olive-green hue, green moss agate with its slightly faded hue, green fluorite, or green calcite.

Choosing a passive green stone can indicate that things are not exactly as they seem on the surface. People may be presenting a certain opinion or attitude outwardly, while their true feelings are different. The stone can indicate a situation of hypocrisy. It is possible that the person's empathy and sensitivity prevent him from looking into the hidden motives of other people. The situation is not as it seems, and there are "hidden" things. To the same extent, it is possible that a person who makes us angry, or gives us the impression of being insensitive or uncaring, is in fact not like that at all, but has deep emotions that he does not know how to express. His actions may stem from a lack of confidence, from fears or anxiety, and not from malice. In any case, the passive green stone shows that the external behavior of the person or situation in question is not identical to the emotions of that person or situation.

Choosing two green stones – When an active green stone and a passive green stone come up in a reading, it could be an indication of being carried away by emotion, of a situation in which the person is completely captive to his emotions, burdened with emotion, but does nothing practical. Drawing two green stones suggests that the person look inside his emotions. What are his true emotions? Does part of his general feeling stem from a kind of "enjoyment" of being carried away by emotion? It is possible that part of the emotional burden is not really the crux of the matter, but rather stems from a general emotional torrent. Moreover, this kind of reading can indicate a situation in which the person is emotionally "blackmailed" by others. This situation must be prevented, and limits set, so as to be aware of the emotional blackmail, and prohibit it. The reading can describe a situation in which many people rely on the person, economically or emotionally, simply because they are used to receiving constant assistance from him. This exhausts him emotionally. There are also situations in which the person negates himself and foregoes his wishes and desires because others are constantly signaling to him that they need his help. The person must look at the heart of the matter and be honest with himself. Can they really not manage without the constant support that they demand from him? Does this endless support do him any good, or does it cause him to make far-reaching sacrifices? Does he have feelings of emotional exhaustion and blackmail? Drawing two green stones may be indicative of a person who gives of himself unreservedly, is supportive and compassionate, but when he needs support, he discovers, with great pain, that his friends are "busy," or do not know how to support and give properly. The green stones ask the person first and foremost to pay attention to his own emotions, and to go into them in depth.

Blue stones

Blue stones represent knowledge, wisdom, awareness, thought, and understanding. When blue stones come up in a reading, they suggest that one take the path of thought and logic – the conventional path – instead of acting according to emotion or intuition. They indicate a need for clear and lucid thought. Moreover, the matters at hand may be linked to certain ideals or ideas.

An active blue stone – As an active blue stone, you can choose opaque turquoise, which is rich in color, dark blue azurite, falcon eye, the blue type of tiger eye, lapis lazuli in a rich blue color, shiny blue topaz, sparkling blue agate, blue sapphire, or blue zircon.

When an active blue stone is drawn in a reading, it may indicate the need to decide about a matter that is beyond material matters. In this case, the decision must be made based on clear, lucid, and conscious thinking, and the person must consider all the components that affect the situation, and act according to reason. This is the time to let reason, not the heart, decide. The stone suggests that the person not make quick and hasty decisions, but rather consider the steps and act after a great deal of thought. He must weigh up the advantages for the present against the advantages in the long run, and decide in a logical and clear-headed manner.

A passive blue stone – As a passive blue stone, you can use any stone with a light blue or slightly faded color. Blue lace agate is suitable, as are blue fluorite, aquamarine, celestite, sodalite, or moonstone with a blue hue. In principle, any stone that looks less glowing and shiny when compared with the active stone is suitable for this purpose.

When a passive blue stone is drawn in a reading, the main subject once again revolves around matters of intelligence and thought. Having said that, it can indicate a need for greater mental flexibility and softness, and less toughness. Even when the person strides clearly toward the realization of his aspirations and desires, the stone may indicate that he must move more flexibly and thoughtfully. He must still act according to logic and thought, but this may be the place to soften unbending logic with a little bit of emotion. There may be room for compromise so as to obtain the desired result.

Choosing two blue stones – Choosing two blue stones may indicate that the person is expending a great deal of mental energy on the wrong subject. It may also indicate that he is basing his ideals and principles on erroneous conclusions, or that he is adhering to principles obstinately without good grounds for doing so. While all this is going on, the real issue that should be considered slips away, and all the energies are directed toward the wrong place. In situations like that, the person may have to go over the matters from the starting point, step by step, and see where there might be a mistake. In addition, blue stones may stimulate the question of whether the approach taken by the person was suitable. It could be that a determined, stubborn, and uncompromising approach is precisely the one that will lead to the desired results. In contrast, there could be place to ease up a bit, give in here and there, or compromise slightly so as to obtain the same result, but more conveniently and easily. Blue stones may suggest that the person ignore irrelevant topics along his path toward obtaining results or during an argument about a certain matter of principle, and concentrate only on what is really important, on the heart of the matter, and not on peripheral matters connected with it.

Purple stones

Purple stones involve subjects concerning intuition, unconscious layers, inspiration, and abilities that go beyond emotional and physical abilities. They pertain to metaphysical, divine matters, and approach the superego and the intuitive layer. Often, they touch on matters that are beyond everyday life and the usual and conventional layers of the universe. They can appear when the person has to seek another form of answer to his questions – by turning to the subconscious, to dreams, or to meditation with crystals – any way that can raise the answers from the superego, which knows them.

An active purple stone – As an active purple stone, you can use not only purple stones, but also stones in lavender, magenta that tends toward purple, and, of course, indigo. Sodalite in rich shades of purple or indigo is suitable. Sugilite, with its shiny purple color, is also suitable. Richly hued purple lapis lazuli, shiny purple topaz, or shiny polished amethyst are also suitable.

Choosing an active purple or indigo stone can come up in a reading when the person asks questions about the meaning of life: seeking a vocation or his unique mission in life, wishing to apply more spiritual layers to his life, or needing to express creativity. It reinforces the person in his search for his inner truth, and reminds him not to pay attention to the reactions of those surrounding him to this search, but rather to carry on courageously. It may indicate that the person feels that "something is missing in his life," he feels a lack of satisfaction, sometimes without knowing why, even if he is very successful in every aspect of his life. In situations like these, the active purple stone suggests that he seek the answers on the spiritual side, and look inward. Is this side sufficiently developed? Does the person allow himself to concentrate on or pay attention to his spiritual side, to ask questions about the aim of his life, and his self-fulfillment? Sometimes it can help the person make the final decision about shifting various material activities to one side in order to focus on creative activities, or activities that produce a feeling of self-fulfillment and spiritual satisfaction.

A passive purple stone – As a passive purple stone, you can choose an amethyst that is not too shiny as opposed to the active stone you chose, purple fluorite, lilac-colored kunzite, or any purple or indigo stone that is less dominant, shiny, and richly colored than the active purple stone.

Choosing a passive purple or indigo stone may attest to the need for a thought revolution. It suggests that the person put aside his usual "logical" thought patterns and turn to his intuitive side, to his gut feelings. He should operate according to intuition and inner clues. Often, choosing a passive purple stone indicates that the person is trapped in old thought patterns and prejudices about himself, life, or the world. It shows that now is the time to look inside those patterns, to ask himself which patterns he operates by, and to change the obsolete and inhibiting ones that are not necessarily realistic and correct, but rather the fruit of his upbringing and the paradigms of society. When a person asks a question about doing something like this, the purple stone's role is to strengthen him and encourage him to take this path. It does not matter if this does not sit well with social conventions, or is considered unworthy or irregular. The stone promotes self-confidence, allowing the person to go and realize his inner spiritual needs, which demand that he realize himself in his present life.

Choosing two purple stones – Choosing an active purple stone and a passive purple stone indicates that the time has come to leap beyond the regular thought layers. This is the time to act according to intuition. This is the time to bring spiritual truth and the higher layers of the personality to everyday life, and apply them in "ordinary" life. In answer to the question, it is possible that introspection, mediation, and searching in the depths of the consciousness are the answer. Here, emotional patterns and logical answers will not help, but rather intuitive and spiritual activity. An answer of this type is likely to suit every kind of question whose answer is not to be found in the more conventional layers of the universe.

Pink stones

Although pink is not one of the natural colors of the spectrum, it links the lower frequencies of red to the upper frequencies of purple. Pink symbolizes the complementary combination of opposites, as well as the power of love and healing. Pink stones can come up in reading when there is a difficult situation, or a rupture, among family members or friends, or when the situation at work is not harmonious. The color can also appear when the harmony between body and mind is not complete. Pink symbolizes the need for healing, for repairing, and for bringing renewed harmony to the situation at hand.

An active pink stone – As an active pink stone, you can choose pink coral with rich tones, deep pink rhodonite, or its "sister," rhodochrosite, with the various shades of pink; you can also find sugilite and sodalite in a shade of pink, pink tourmaline, or any other pink stone with rich or shiny colors.

An active pink stone can come up in a reading when there is some kind of conflict. It is an external conflict that involves the person, even if he is not the cause of it. It could be an unpleasant situation that a person close to him – a friend or a family member – is in, a situation with a disagreeable atmosphere, friction at work that may not involve the asker of the question personally, but he feels those energies. Often, the effective way of solving situations of that kind when an active pink stones comes up in a reading is by means of peace and love. The person who created the problem or the conflict may be in a difficult situation and needs a gentle hand and a sympathetic approach. In those cases, the way to create good communication is by using gentleness and sympathy.

A passive pink stone – There are many pink stones that can be used as passive pink stones. Rose quartz is very suitable, as are watermelon tourmaline or unpolished pink tourmaline, mother of pearl in pink tones, pink kunzite, pink fluorite or pink calcite. Sometimes, pebbles in a faded or light pink can be found on the shore or in fields, and these are very suitable for this purpose.

Drawing a passive pink stone during a reading often indicates that the lack of harmony or the conflict is internal. The person may feel exhausted, may make many mistakes without knowing why, or may be confused. The stone suggests that he take things more easily and comfortably, not take on unnecessary obligations during this period, rest, and ensure that he eats healthfully. In situations like those, he should refrain from encounters with people or situations that get him into an unnecessary state of stress, disrupt his equilibrium, or arouse non-positive feelings in him. This is the time for inner nourishment, rest, and self-treatment, in order to restore his powers and extricate himself from the feeling of exhaustion or lack of strength. A passive pink stone indicates that the person must focus on and heed his needs, take care of himself, and place himself at the top of his list of priorities. Even if he takes care of children, or has many obligations, if he continues to wear himself out and not pay sufficient attention to his needs, he is liable to collapse.

Choosing two pink stones – When an active pink stone and a passive pink stone come up in a reading, it could mean that the person is getting involved in another person's struggle. While the temptation to make peace, calm both sides down, and mediate between people who are close to him may be strong, it is not advisable at this point. The attempt to mediate and bridge the gap squeezes a great deal of emotional strength from the person. Two pink stones occasionally come up in situations such as quarrels between children at home, when the mother is inclined to interfere and mediate (and gets yelled at by all parties), or when two work colleagues are quarreling, and the person finds it hard to stand by and do nothing, so he tries to calm them down, and so on. Drawing two pink stones tells the person to concentrate on himself, and not to waste his energies on interfering in other people's problems. He may not be especially energetic at the moment, and he needs these energies in order to take care of himself. The interference may distract him from his own problems. The stones advise him not to interfere, and to let the issues and the people involved find their own path to understanding and reconciliation.

Brown stones

Brown stones symbolize the earth, roots, linking up to nature. In addition, they advise us to trust what our eyes can see, and not various rumors and theories. Nowadays, the media bombard people with information, rumors are disseminated at the speed of lightning, and many people are influenced by this inaccurate or incorrect information. Brown stones appeal to us to look at the sure, at the known, at the domestic, and at what we can perceive with our eyes and our senses. They advise us to use simple logic to judge the situations the person is asking about.

An active brown stone – There is a large range of brown stones that can be used as active stones. Of course, the tiger eye with its abundant colors is very suitable. Brown amber, brown chrysoberyl with its strong hues, brown jasper with its dominant shades, or shiny brown agate are also suitable.

Drawing an active brown stone during a reading shows that a matter that requires the person to take logical and practical steps is at hand. In such cases, he must not sit and wait, philosophize or act according to emotions, but take practical action. It might not be easy, and healthy logic must be used. An active brown stone indicates that the problem will be solved by means of practical, logical work, and action on the material and practical layers.

A passive brown stone – As a passive brown stone, you can choose petrified wood, brown smoky quartz, or brown rutilated quartz. Brown pebbles, or simple brown stones can also be suitable, and can be found almost everywhere. Brown flintstones can be found in every field or dirt road. They are very suitable to the nature of the color brown in reading stones, since it symbolizes earthiness and practicality.

When a passive brown stone comes up in a reading, it may indicate a feeling of overwork, or practical demands made by family members or the immediate surroundings. Sometimes, it indicates some kind of loathing of simple work such as housework, when the person feels that his part in the care and maintenance of the home far outweighs that of others. The brown stone can come up in situations in which the person takes upon himself a large work load, especially work connected to the house, or "menial jobs," while his associates do not help as they should. The stone instructs the person that this is the time to move some of these chores to one side. This could result in a certain amount of chaos in the house, dishes in the sink, or eating out instead of home cooking. Having said that, removing some of the burden is essential. It is possible that when the person refuses to do such a huge amount of chores, the others will feel a need or an obligation to cooperate. Often, homemakers who are collapsing under the burden of housework – looking after the children, tidying their rooms and picking up after them, cleaning, cooking, laundry, and so on – draw a passive brown stone. It instructs them that now is the time to let the others work a bit, and to change the distribution of household chores, or to employ household help. A similar situation is liable to occur in the office, when the person feels that he has to do all the "dirty" work – typing, photocopying, calls, and so on, while his colleagues are involved in the more interesting side of the work. The way he should deal with the matter is practical – simply to take some of the burden off his shoulders, even if other people will now have to carry some of it.

Choosing two brown stones – When an active brown stone and a passive brown stone come up in a reading, the reading indicates an insufficient use of simple logic. A situation is described wherein the person absorbs, listens to, and works according to other people's opinions, without contesting them or arguing – sometimes because he feels the situation is confused enough without him adding his opinions. This is a situation in which the person feels that things are not in his control. Other people decide or determine, and even if he does not agree, he acts in accordance with their decisions. Sometimes, this is because the person himself does not know how to act. In this situation, he must use his logic, ask himself how he would advise another person in the same situation to act – and act according to this advice. Sometimes, this is the place to apply "old-fashioned" values in which the person believes with all his heart. He must free himself from going along with other people's opinions and break away from their influence, if it is not positive, or when he does not trust or see evidence of their correctness.

The ways to choose the stones

Choosing the stones can be performed by directed choice, when the stones are revealed, when the stones are hidden, and by making a reading circle.

When a person performs his own reading, he must place the stones in a large or medium-size bag, put his hand in, and choose one or two, according to his feeling. Before doing so, he must ask the question or define the problem aloud. The question must be as clear as possible. He can take out two stones, one after the other, or two together. When two stones are extracted, the situation frequently arises wherein one of the stones shows us the layer in which the problem is rooted, while the second offers us a way to solve the problem. When two stones of the same color are drawn, they are read like one stone, according to the interpretation for taking out two stones of the same color.

When the reading is performed for another person who does not know the significance of the colors of the stones, you can place all the stones in front of him, and ask him to choose two. This is done after he has asked his question. If he feels uncomfortable about asking in the presence of the reader, he can ask the question silently, but he must transmit it by thought. When we perform a reading for a person who knows the meaning of the colors of the stones, the "blind" method of selecting stones from a bag must be used.

It is possible to choose a daily stone, without necessarily asking a question. A stone is drawn from the bag, preferably in the morning, and it will give the person food for thought or a point to focus on throughout the day.

Reading circle

The circle for reading stones helps us read stones even without a prior question (of course, it is possible to ask in order to focus on a certain subject), and it supplies information concerning the different aspects of life.

In order to prepare the crystal, you need dark fabric, preferably thick, about 40 centimeters square. If you have chosen relatively large stones, you might need a larger piece of fabric. You must describe three concentric circles on the fabric (like a dartboard). Use a felt-tipped pen in a color that will stand out on the dark background (such as gold or silver).

The inner circle

The inner circle represents the basic "I," the basic personality, the person himself, without the various external or acquired markers. It represents the basic beliefs and the most basic character traits.

The middle circle

The middle circle represents the person's inner world. It represents his thoughts, hopes, fears, feelings, and passions.

The outer circle

The outer circle represents the person's daily life and his interaction with others. It represents the range of external activities and coping with the practical layers, and sometimes the emotional ones, of life.

The stones are thrown on the fabric, and they fall in the correct place, which shows which sphere they relate to. There are several ways to cast the stones. It is possible to choose a number of stones – a number that is chosen by the person intuitively – and throw them. He can simply put his hand in the bag, take out a number of stones and throw them. It is possible to throw all the stones that he drew together, or throw them one by one. Throwing three stones is preferable at the beginning.

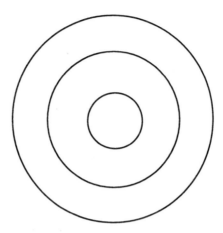

Of course, some stones might fall outside the circle. When a stone falls outside the outer circle, it symbolizes the sphere of repression or concealment. This is an area into which we throw matters that, consciously or unconsciously, we prefer to repress or hide, or are afraid of relating to. Often, these are problems that are too painful to cope with at this time. The person for whom the reading is being performed must be informed of the significance of a stone that falls outside the circle. He can choose to deal with the problem, or not. Often, caution and delicacy are required for reading a stone that fell outside the circle. It is not rare for that same stone to fall outside the circle in reading after reading. This can indicate a repressed problem begging for a solution, awareness, or being related to. Moreover, this can represent a situation in which the solution to a particular problem is liable to cause sorrow or pain to one of the people close to the person. Sometimes, the person's good is liable to cause someone else sorrow. Examples of cases like this include an adult son who wants to leave home, but this will cause sorrow to his aged parents; or a woman who wants to divorce her husband, but this is liable to hurt her children, who are attached to their father, and so on. In cases such as these, the decision is not easy, and requires that the person be very aware of and take responsibility for his actions. In general, the stones that fall outside the circle simply inform us about the problem, and do not demand immediate action, but rather advise us to wait. The best situation is when a stone that fell outside the circle several times falls inside the circle in the present reading. This may indicate that it is possible to take action.

After throwing the stones, we begin to read each one, first of all according to the color and nature of each stone – active or passive. When two stones of the same color have been chosen, and especially when they are in the same circle, it is a sign that the matter under discussion is very important.

A reading that goes on for three days

If the same stone has been extracted from the bag for three days, day after day, it indicates a matter of significance. Often, a situation arises in which the person has difficulty understanding the true significance that the stone wants to convey to him, so it keeps reappearing in reading after reading. One of the best ways to deal with this situation, when we do not succeed in discovering or understanding the meaning of the reading, is to take its opposite stone – the active or passive one – and carry it around for a few days, or place it under the pillow before going to sleep. In this way, a more balanced situation can be achieved, enabling us to see both sides of the problem, which can lead us to understand it.

Using the reading stones

When certain stones came up in a reading in answer to a particular question, the person should carry them with him, and look at them while thinking of the answer he received. He should draw conclusions and engage in soul-searching. It is a good idea to go outside on moonlit nights, spread the stones out, and look at them. They store energies, as well as the answers to the question that was asked, and they can stimulate and encourage the person to take action. They can strengthen him on his path, and remind him what steps he has to take in order to change the undesirable situation.

Crystals and the signs of the Zodiac

Astrology is an ancient science. During its many incarnations, signs and links between various stones and the planets began to crop up, and these influenced the people belonging to these signs. The ancients spent a great deal of time investigating the link between the celestial Zodiac and stones. Sometimes, various stones exerted beneficial effects on the people who were born under a particular sun sign. Various properties found in the stones tend to suit, balance, stimulate, and develop the personal characteristics inherent in people belonging to the different signs. According to one of the accepted theories, man is a microcosm of the universe, that is, the entire universe is embodied in man, on a small scale. This ancient theory became clearer when, with the progress of science, new insights concerning the human body began to be discovered. As we know, the human body is made up of atoms, just like animals, plants, and inanimate objects – as well as the celestial bodies. Gradually, the influence of the stars on people began to be better understood, from the scientific point of view, too. In the beginning, ancient suppositions that the revolving of the celestial bodies affects the forces of nature in different ways were verified – the tides, plant growth, and so on. Afterwards, they began to study the influence of the stars on the more advanced life forms, animals, in greater depth – this subject is still under scientific investigation. The day is approaching when there will also be scientific answers about the influence of the stars on the human body and soul.

Every members of each sign of the Zodiac has certain personal traits that characterize him and distinguish him from the members of the other signs. Some of those traits are useful and progressive, while others can be inhibiting, especially when they are not balanced. The stones that are linked to the members of the different signs help to balance these traits and strengthen the particular and unique positive characteristics of the members of the sign.

There are certain stones that are considered to be basic or foundation stones for the members of the various signs. Those are the stones that are described in various ancient theories as suitable for a particular sign, and are attributed to the stellar power that activates the sign. Moreover, there are many addition stones that suit the members of the sign. There are also stones to which universal force is attributed, making them suitable for the members of all the signs. Some of the stones presented below reinforce the characteristics of the sign, and they possess traits that are similar to those that characterize the sign. In this, they help balance and externalize these traits in states of imbalance, when the person tends to repress the main positive qualities that characterize him. Some of them constitute a complementary factor by stimulating in the person of the sign characteristics that are considered to be "weak" or that are not expressed fully in his character.

Stones that are suitable for all the signs of the Zodiac

The stones that are suitable for all the signs of the Zodiac are plume agate, meteorite, moldavite, clear quartz crystal, multicolored topaz, horn coral, as well as chevron amethyst and azulicite.

Aries

White sapphire – the white sapphire helps Aries people soothe their troubled brains, especially when they get involved in a large number of activities, and try to do the maximum in each one of them.

Fire agate – Fire agate helps the people of this "hot" sign to free themselves of inhibiting lusts and passions on their path to attaining mental and spiritual calmness.

Apache tear – Apache tear helps the people of this sign to be more forgiving toward other people, and not to complain and grumble about them. It helps them accept others whose lifestyle, behavior, and beliefs are different than theirs with greater understanding.

Aquamarine – Because it is the "stone of courage," aquamarine is suitable for Aries people and represents them. Because it promotes forgiveness, mitigates faultfinding, and is very soothing, it helps people of this sign moderate these properties in their characters. It helps them become milder, calms agitation, and stimulates a feeling of responsibility not only for their actions, but also for the things they say.

Aventurine – Aventurine stimulates adventurousness, a property that suits the "pioneers" and the path-breakers of this sign. It is very soothing, and helps them calm down in the midst of all the perturbation and practicality that surrounds them. In addition, it provides emotional balance and soothes agitation, while stimulating love.

Bloodstone – Bloodstone stimulates moderation and cool-headedness, properties that people of this sign sometimes need badly. Aries people, who are talented and charismatic, can use it to harness their talents for the general good, and safeguard themselves from being selfish and manipulative. It also calms them down and helps them get rid of negative thoughts.

Citrine – Citrine hones the communicative abilities of Aries people and helps them communicate with their surroundings with emotional equilibrium. It helps prevent friction and rows (at home and at work) that Aries people are inclined to get into very easily.

Dolomite – Dolomite stimulates the Aries people's spontaneity, and encourages them to express their opinions in an original way. Although it stimulates, it may balance the overly energetic and spontaneous Aries people, and calm them down. Another important property of dolomite is that it helps Aries people extricate themselves from feelings of self-pity or from focusing on their personal sorrow in favor of looking at the suffering of others. When Aries people manage to show empathy for another person who is suffering, they can help him marvelously by providing him with support, a sympathetic ear, and even practical advice. It also helps them be more patient and less snappy.

Emerald – Aries people link up easily to the calmness that the stone provides, and to the feeling of being "wrapped in love," which they sometimes need in situations of a lack of balance. The emerald stimulates intensive activity, similar to the *modus operandi* of the Aries people, when they get down to accomplishing a goal in which they believe.

Hematite – Hematite helps Aries people get rid of obstinacy and the limiting thoughts that they set for themselves. When they remove these thought limitations, there is nowhere they cannot get to. When they feel upset, and are on the verge of venting their emotional outburst on their friends or mates, they should hold hematite in their hands. It calms them down, and helps them extricate themselves from the storm of emotion by bolstering their self-control.

Jade – Jade helps the ambitious members of the sign of Aries not forget the people around them. It helps them act considerately toward others while on the path to accomplishing their objectives.

Kyanite – Kyanite helps Aries people eliminate cumulative frustrations, anger, and agitation. It also provides them with additional energy for achieving positive goals.

Brown tourmaline – Brown tourmaline helps Aries people see the unique path they wish to follow in front of their eyes, and strengthens their particular ambitions.

Taurus

Carnelian – Carnelian, one of the stones that represents this sign, strengthens the properties of initiative, precision, and diligence that characterize it. During the rare moments in which Taurus people sink into pessimism, the stone helps them discover once again their *joie de vivre* and confidence in the universe beneath the doubts that arise occasionally. Carnelian inspires Taurus people with courage, especially in cases in which they want to follow a new path, but are afraid of losing the old, familiar one. It stimulates their innate creativity by encouraging curiosity about and interest in new things.

Black spinel – Black spinel represents some of the Taurus properties – stability, profound perception on the physical plane, and tremendous endurance. It amplifies these properties in the members of the sign, or helps balance them in difficult situations, when the Taurus person feels that those abilities are eluding him.

Copper – Copper's properties characterize Taurus people. It represents determination, independence, initiative, and practicality. Moreover, it balances and stimulates the properties that these people sometimes lack – innovation, willingness to cast off prejudice and conservatism, and leads them to philosophical, objective thought. Copper also teaches Taurus people that the only limitations that stand in their path are the ones that they themselves create by narrow thinking and limited horizons.

Emerald – The emerald represents beauty, tranquillity, harmony, and creativity. The people who belong to Taurus, the sign of Venus, the goddess of beauty and love, can enjoy the pleasant feeling of harmony that the stone transmits. It increases the Taurus people's quality of loyalty and limitless love for their families and friends. It stimulates their innate creativity, and attracts abundance and prosperity.

Kyanite – Kyanite represents Taurus people in its power to help the person stand firm in every situation. When this property, which is natural to these people, is weakened for some reason, kyanite helps them return to their natural balance. In addition, it imbues them with a pleasant feeling of harmony, which is essential for making Taurus people feel good. It balances the feminine and the masculine energies, which occasionally tend to be a bit extreme in the people of the sign of Venus.

Kunzite – Kunzite increases the feeling of unconditional love in these people by expanding their communicative abilities. It promotes sharp senses, a property which is characteristic of Taurus people (especially their sense of touch, which is particularly strong). It strengthens their practical and healthy logic, and also increases their intuitive abilities, which are buried beneath the surface of these people. Because of their fine-tuned senses, their great caring, and their sensitivity toward the needs of others, they often develop broad-based abilities to "feel the other." Taurus people who develop their telepathic talents can turn out to be wonderful receivers of messages. In addition, kunzite stimulates a feeling of confidence and tranquillity, and encourages the creative sides of Taurus people.

Rhodonite – Rhodonite is very suitable for Taurus people. It stimulates the love in them by helping them bestow unconditional love on their loved ones, and helps them realize their innate potential. Moreover, rhodonite can strengthen the spiritual facet in Taurus people that aspires to global love, security, and harmony, as well as their self-confidence. It can make things easier for them in relationships by making them see their contribution to and their behavior in their relationships as if they were objective observers, in conjunction with the contribution and behavior of their mate, and act accordingly.

It provides Taurus people with the feeling of calm, confidence, and serenity that they need constantly. Also, when Taurus people do not break off a relationship with a close but hurtful friend – an unbalanced relationship that their natural devotion does not allow them to end – the stone helps them see how unhealthy the relationship is. These people sometimes carry the baggage of previous love injuries for a long time, and rhodonite helps them open their hearts to a new love, and rid themselves of the painful residues of their previous love crisis.

Chrysocolla – Chrysocolla, which represents love, equilibrium, and creativity, expresses the natural abilities of Taurus people admirably. It helps them spread their net of unconditional love not only over friends and family members, but also over humanity in general. It helps the introverts among them open up more easily and share their feelings. Taurus people have the ability to accept others as they are, no matter how different they may be (as long as they do not hurt them or anyone else). Chrysocolla strengthens this unique property in them. It stimulates harmony in all layers, a very important property for Taurus people. These people love the earth and nature, and link up easily to this stone, which manifests qualities of love of the universe and Mother Earth. It stimulates their creativity and their innate love of art, as well as initiative, the spirit of doing, and also innovative and inventive abilities.

Cuprite – Cuprite helps Taurus people who are afraid of losing control, and for this reason do not permit themselves to let their hair down and enjoy life. It manifests the sign's qualities well, seeing that it symbolizes stability and the link to the earth.

Diamond – The diamond symbolizes the tremendous power that is inherent in Taurus people. The diamond arouses in them feelings of natural harmony, and when this is lacking, it helps them feel tranquil and harmonious once more. It symbolizes belief and confidence, properties that characterize Taurus people. When the diamond is worn or carried, it stimulates these people's imagination, innate creativity, and their inventive and innovative abilities.

Blue sapphire – The blue sapphire, the foundation stone of the sign, stimulates their strong intuition that is sometimes concealed under many layers of "reason" and "practicality." It helps them make decisions more easily, and strengthens their communicative abilities, which are sometimes lacking. It helps them develop their spiritual abilities and aspirations that are sometimes hidden under a layer of conservatism and belief only in that they can "touch" or "see with their own eyes."

Turquoise – Turquoise, which is considered to be "the stone of Venus," stimulates Taurus people's creativity, love, sensuality, and motivation – properties that characterize them when they are in a balanced state. It absorbs every conflict or non-positive emotion experienced by the Taurus person in difficult situations. It spreads peace, harmony, and calmness, which are essential to these people for a feeling of general wellbeing. It is also very beneficial to the introvert and quiet members of the sign by helping them express their emotions.

Selenite – Selenite is very helpful for Taurus people who find it difficult to be more flexible in their way of life and in their perception of life. It helps them tone down their obstinacy, and make decisions in a more flexible and conscious way. Because it is a stone that links the most exalted spiritual layers to the physical layers of our nature, it helps Taurus people broaden their awareness. It helps them in their search for material stability and security while encouraging them to discard mental and emotional inhibitions, and open up to the mystical and spiritual layers.

Gemini

Agate (all types) – Gemini people find agate stones wonderful for strengthening their fidelity, which they sometimes find hard to uphold. Agates help them tune into their innate talents and use them actively. Agate is an important stone for this sign, since it helps these people look inward more clearly. Its ability to balance polar energies helps this "dual" sign tone down the changeable nature that characterizes them. For Gemini artists, agates serve as a stabilizing factor in the creative process. They are also important to them because of their protective properties, seeing that as a result of their non-stop activity, the people of this sign are liable to be prone to various accidents. Agate also contributes a lot to them because of its ability to balance and stabilize emotions and behavior.

Apatite – Apatite, with its exceptional channeling properties, is extraordinarily suitable for Gemini people, the most "communicative" of the signs of the Zodiac. It helps these people use their communicative abilities and their intellect correctly by protecting them from feelings of vanity or condescension. It helps them achieve coordination between the various energies among which these people operate, and the polar energies that characterize them. It also helps them moderate their frenzied activity, which sometimes debilitates them and causes physical diseases.

Aquamarine – Aquamarine helps Gemini people attain better mental equilibrium. It is important for them for relaxation, since they sometimes tend to be frenzied and "hyper." It substantially strengthens these people's outstanding communicative properties, and helps them take responsibility for their behavior, actions, and words.

Celestite – Celestite reinforces the wonderful communicative properties of Gemini people, both on the physical and on the spiritual levels. It also helps balance their polar forces.

Citrine – Citrine represents and stimulates the characteristic sharpness of thought of Gemini people. It is very suitable for the people of this communicative sign. Citrine hones their communicative ability and the great intelligence with which they are blessed by helping them use it correctly and by working in teams. It helps them attain emotional equilibrium, and is important to those among them who have a self-destructive tendency. In addition, it is a stone that helps balance the polar energies.

Chrysocolla – Chrysocolla also helps Gemini people attain emotional equilibrium. It helps them soothe the incessant flow of thoughts, and experience feelings of harmony and unity, which are very important to Gemini people who have a tendency toward this "split."

Emerald – Gemini people can enjoy the strengthening of feelings of loyalty that the stone endows. It hones their superior mental abilities, and, in addition, helps them focus on one thing for a length of time.

Fluorite – Fluorite reinforces the wonderful communicative abilities of Gemini people. It is another stone that helps these people achieve emotional and mental balance, and stimulates their innate spirituality, which does not always come to the fore. It also helps them increase their concentration, and achieve stability in relationships.

Howlite – Howlite is the stone that represents communication and expression. In addition to honing these abilities in Gemini people, it helps them reinforce their patience, which tends to be short-lived sometimes, and their seriousness. This stone can accompany these people faithfully, with their marvelous communicative abilities, by helping them acquire tact that will be useful for them on their path. It helps mitigate and moderate the "two-faced" and "divided" aspects of their character, and can help them both in interpersonal and in professional domains.

Blue sapphire – Blue sapphire is also a stone that represents the ability to grasp quickly and the property of mental clarity. The blue sapphire helps strengthen and stimulate the communicative abilities. It helps in situations in which there is a choice of a number of options, and guides the person to make the correct and suitable choice.

Serpentine – Serpentine strengthens the flow of movement that is one of the characteristics of the members of this mercurial sign.

Pearl – Wearing a pearl helps Gemini people focus their attention better and avoid skipping from subject to subject when they have to focus on a particular activity.

Cancer

Moonstone – Moonstone is very suitable for this sign, whose influencing planet is the moon. Cancer people, whether they are aware of it or not, tend to be influenced by the cycles of the moon – when it is full or partial. Moonstone helps them discover and understand this property and use it properly. Sometimes, they feel depressed and pessimistic, and this is linked to the state of the moon. It helps them attain emotional balance and control their emotions. It makes it easier for them when it is necessary for tnem to make changes, because they are not always quick to adapt to new circumstances. Cancer people love to keep and hold what they love near to them, and moonstone is very effective for this.

Carnelian – Carnelian is an important stone for Cancer people during the pessimistic periods of their lives, when they tend to despair and see the half-empty cup. Carnelian stimulates their *joie de vivre* and helps them overcome sorrow and depression. In addition, it increases their natural caring for other people and the great compassion that is inherent in their characters. It can bring them significant relief when they feel bad or experience despair during their lives.

Pink coral – Pink coral stimulates the natural empathy of Cancer people for other people's troubles, and helps them give love without expecting any concrete reward.

Brown spinel – Brown spinel helps Cancer people cleanse their auras after or during periods of severe pessimism, which causes the aura to be murky and weakens it.

Opal – The opal, which is suitable for all the water signs, stimulates Cancer people's marvelous power of imagination. These people are blessed with a fascinating and exceptional imagination, and by using this power correctly, can change their lives. It helps them use their power of imagination to achieve and accomplish goals, be they spiritual or material. It also stimulates spontaneity in them. In periods of pessimism and depression, they should drink an elixir prepared from brown or red opal in order to alleviate their disturbing mental state. They are not advised to wear an opal when they are in this state, since it is liable to make their non-positive feelings even more extreme (carnelian is the suitable stone for these periods, as is moonstone). Opal has a special effect on

Cancer people – it stimulates the mystical abilities inherent in their characters, as well as the desire to discover and develop these abilities.

Ruby – The ruby is a very important stone for the people of this sensitive and vulnerable sign. It helps them feel protected during a verbal attack, both in a tangible and in a non-tangible way. Since these people tend to develop anxieties and worries, sometimes without a solid, realistic basis, the ruby helps them eliminate the constant feeling of anxiety. In addition, it promotes the attainment of economic stability and security, which are very significant to these people. Cancer people, who are inclined to take their everyday worries and fears to bed at night, will find in the ruby a faithful friend that helps them sleep peacefully and quietly.

Pearl – The pearl, daughter of the sea, is linked to Cancer people. Because it is a stone that symbolizes delicacy of soul and innocence, it strengthens these properties in Cancer people, while helping to balance them. It also helps members of this sign who have a tendency toward acquisitiveness to learn the value and beauty of generosity.

Silver – Silver is the metal that represents this sign, since it symbolizes the moon's power, just as gold symbolizes the sun's power. It helps them become more open and extrovert, and feel more comfortable in company, by bringing their communicative abilities, which are sometimes internalized, to the fore. When the people of this sign feel comfortable in company, their wonderful sense of humor is revealed, and their merriment overflows.

Leo

Amber – Amber, the stone that performs balancing work on the solar plexus chakra, is of great help to Leo people in balancing their egos and eliminating their properties of conceit and domination, which are liable to be obstacles in their paths. In addition, the stone helps them stimulate their capacity for unconditional love. The color of the stone, yellow-golden, is the special color of Leo people.

Golden beryl – Golden beryl reinforces these people's self-confidence, initiative, and courage. It stimulates their desire to succeed. Moreover, it helps them develop better adaptive properties to various situations, and to show flexibility. When a member of this sign faces obstacles, beryl helps him withstand them courageously and not succumb to sorrow. Golden beryl's color suits this sign. It strengthens the positive properties in their character, and helps them balance the solar plexus chakra and the ego. It stimulates and supports their self-confidence and inner strength, and helps their intelligence operate in an integrated way with spiritual messages.

Carnelian – The orange-reddish color of the stone makes it very suitable for Leo people, who tend to be attracted to it because it is a stone that increases sexual energies. It helps them rid themselves of inhibiting fears and the negative emotions of jealousy and anger. In the less pleasant situations of life, these people sometimes tend to sink into apathy and melancholy, when things don't go their way. Carnelian helps restore their characteristic diligence, optimism, and initiative.

Citrine – The golden-yellow color of citrine makes it a favorite Leo stone, because it symbolizes the sun that influences these people. It helps the people who are in managerial positions or who are self-employed tone down the friction between them and their workers. It also helps them make correct decisions. It is wonderful for Leo people because it helps them understand their earthly passions better, balance their survival instinct, refrain from arguments with their family members, and attain emotional equilibrium. It stimulates the spirituality in these people without detaching them from the earthly layers.

Diamond – The diamond is Leo people's favorite stone both because of its beauty and because of its prestige. It helps them balance their feelings of self-love, as well as love for others, and express them in the correct way. It gives them a calm and harmonious feeling, and develops their imaginative talent.

Gold – Gold is the metal that is attributed exclusively to Leo people. They love its color, and the solar power that flows from it. This metal helps them navigate among the many tasks they undertake, and relieve their burden of responsibility. It does wonderful work on the ego, balancing it and the emotional layers. It helps Leo people improve their personal qualities, and cast off anger and guilt feelings. In addition, it engenders respect, a property that Leo people do not tend to take lightly.

Jet – Many Leo people like black jet, which is a stone that protects business and economic success. It helps them shake off melancholy when things don't work out, and increases the courage that is part of their characters.

Jasper – Jasper is very suitable for Leo people, and is the foundation stone of the sign. The sign of Leo is controlled by the sun, whose characteristics are reflected in jasper, especially the gold and yellow types. Jasper helps prevent these people from plunging into selfishness. They sometimes tend to cling to certain ideas, and are not prepared to deviate from them, even when these ideas do not help them in any way. Jasper helps them welcome new ideas and different and useful paths. When a Leo breaks up with his mate, or feels lonely, the stone comforts him wonderfully. One of the biggest services the stone performs for Leo people is its ability to link between physical and material energies and exalted spiritual energies.

Picture jasper – Picture jasper helps Leo people acknowledge their repressed or unconscious emotions by providing them with the strength needed to cope with these emotions. They sometimes tend to conceal them below the surface, because they feel that they cannot cope with them. The stone develops their courage to look inside themselves, and also gives them the tools with which to cope with their inner baggage. Picture jasper also helps them on the business level, especially the people who are in entrepreneurial or managerial professions. It teaches them to use the correct talents, and to perform the actions that are necessary for business and economic success.

Larimar – Larimar helps Leo people acknowledge their mistakes. Many of these people are inclined to consider admitting to a mistake as assuming guilt. Larimar helps them understand that they are not "confessing" to a failure or to an error of judgment, but are assuming the responsibility for their words and actions, which does not diminish their honor – rather, the opposite is true.

Kunzite – Kunzite bolsters Leo people's self-confidence during periods when it is a bit shaky, and helps them feel unconditional love and self-love. It is very suitable for those people who are not particularly tactful in their relationships with those around them, or are inclined to behave in an angry and irritated way. It gives them sensitivity toward other people, and the ability to communicate more gently and lovingly with their surroundings.

Labradorite – Labradorite is wonderful for Leo people, both on the emotional and on the mental and spiritual levels. It strengthens their innate power as well as their self-confidence. It teaches them to see the beautiful side of change and the range of possibilities it offers – despite the fact that Leo people are not known to greet change with open arms. It also removes their worries, tension, and fears.

Onyx – Onyx, another stone that many Leo people love, helps them reinforce their ability to control themselves, especially in periods in which they are prone to outbursts of anger. It helps them see the enormous strength inside them, even in depressing and desperate situations.

Petrified wood – Petrified wood helps Leo people slough off unnecessary worries, and fortifies their personal power.

Peridot – Peridot represents the properties of friendship and optimism of Leo people. In addition, it helps them work on their ego very well, because it is a stone that balances the solar plexus chakra. It helps them eliminate old patterns of anger and negative feelings of which they were not aware, or that they did not think to change.

Rhodochrosite – Rhodochrosite can help one of the most widespread problems of Leo people – insomnia. It strengthens their natural optimism, their love of humor and laughter, and helps them attain emotional equilibrium.

Ruby – The ruby, which links physicality and materialism to spirituality, is a stone that is very suitable for Leo people, especially the men, since it fortifies their masculine properties. This is a stone of wealth and plenty, and strengthens the person's presence.

Green sapphire and yellow sapphire – The green sapphire is also a suitable stone for Leo people, since it stimulates wealth and plenty. The yellow sapphire also strengthens their ability to lay the foundations of the financial and economic layers.

Garnet – The garnet helps Leo people free themselves of angers and negative thought patterns. Its properties suit the popular and gregarious members of this sign, and the stone increases these properties in their personalities. It is recommended for Leo people whose mates have left them, because it helps them get through the rough period in a more optimistic and cheerful manner. It also helps Leo people cope with anger, fear, and resentment.

Pyrite – Pyrite, a golden metallic stone, is also one of the most suitable stones for Leo people. Besides being golden, a color that is beneficial to these people, it helps the naive among them see the hidden intentions behind people's words. It helps them attain emotional balance, and cope with fears and burdens. In addition, it strengthens their motivation to continue along their path toward realizing their aspirations.

Golden spinel – Golden spinel helps Leo people balance their solar plexus chakra and their ego. It strengthens their personal power and intellect by helping them remain objective, and not allowing flattery or insults cloud their view of things as they really are.

Virgo

Moss agate – Moss agate represents some of the properties that characterize Virgo people – refined taste and efficiency. It can help them accept themselves, and strengthen their sensitive and vulnerable egos. It promotes emotional balance and helps those people who suffer from low self-esteem.

Amethyst – Amethyst is a very important stone for Virgo people. It helps them calm their nerves wonderfully, and feel more tranquil and relaxed. In addition, it helps them eliminate their fault-finding characteristics, whether toward themselves or toward others. Virgo people have exalted spiritual abilities, even if they are sometimes hidden beneath the surface. Amethyst helps them stimulate these properties and use them wisely. It tempers their fear of dependence on others, and their anxieties about economic instability.

Amazonite – Amazonite is wonderful for tempering the many worries that plague Virgo people, and its soothing action on the nervous system makes it uniquely suitable for Virgo people who sometimes suffer from sensitive nerves and inner tension. It helps them better understand those around them, and be less demanding and critical of them.

Chrysocolla – Chrysocolla helps many introverted Virgo people to open up socially. It teaches them to accept others as they are, without making too much fuss about the little details. The stone helps balance the Virgo people who vacillate between murderous work on the one hand and apathy and a lack of motivation on the other by stimulating a welcome feeling of motivation. At times when they plunge into feelings of pessimism, chrysocolla gives them the emotional powers to cope with the crises. It is excellent for soothing the thoughts, worries, and anxieties that tend to surround them. It does so by spreading a feeling of harmony and peace. Chrysocolla helps those people who have been hurt in love, and who tend to nurse these sad memories for a long time, by restoring their faith in people in general and people of the opposite sex in particular.

Cuprite – Cuprite can help those Virgo people who have a tendency toward floating and daydreaming by strengthening the link between them and the earth, the element that exerts an influence on them.

Fossil – The various fossils help introverted Virgo people open up more easily to other people. The fossil, like the sign of Virgo, is a symbol of an aspiration to excellence, and strengthens this property. Many Virgo people tend to link up to ancient cultures along their spiritual path, and the fossil guides them efficiently toward spiritual linking-up and receiving information. Moreover, it helps them get rid of superfluous thought patterns, such as the tendency to worry, and helps them adopt other, more beneficial, patterns.

Garnet – Virgo people, who vacillate between extreme frugality and prodigality, can avail themselves of the garnet in order to balance these properties. As for those Virgo people who have a tendency toward idleness (although they loathe this property more than any other), it stimulates motivation. It helps them see life in a rosier light, and be more liked socially. Moreover, it raises their self-esteem, which can help those Virgo people who tend to be so fussy and pedantic with themselves.

Lodestone – Lodestone, too, helps Virgo people when they sink into idleness and a lack of motivation, much to their resentment. It safeguards them against dependency, one of the things they tend to fear, and helps them feel calmer and less troubled. Also, those Virgo people who have difficulty adapting to change will find that the stone is of great help during the unexpected events that happen in life.

Snowflake obsidian – This is a wonderful stone for Virgo people. It helps them see the light at the end of the tunnel when they are sunk in pessimism and a lack of faith in life. It teaches them that there is always a ray of light in the darkness. It helps them eliminate inhibiting patterns of thought and emotion, and adapt to finding themselves alone in a pleasant way. It promotes purity of thought and emotion.

Purple spinel – Purple spinel stimulates the exalted spirituality that is inherent in Virgo people, and encourages them to follow spiritual channels. People of this sign, which is an earth sign, can rise to marvelous heights when they choose to develop their spiritual side. This is how the stone helps them.

Peridot – Peridot stimulates feelings of hope and optimism in Virgo people, and helps them get rid of negative feelings and depression. Moreover, it helps them reexamine their thought and behavior patterns, since these types, who can see the tiniest fleck on someone else's garments, sometimes tend not to notice non-positive patterns in themselves. The stone also helps them discard grudges, anger, and jealousy.

Rhodonite – Rhodonite helps Virgo people attain emotional equilibrium by balancing the masculine and feminine sides of their personalities. It gives them emotional calmness, and helps them eliminate the troublesome things that disrupt their peaceful sleep at night.

Sapphire – The sapphire helps Virgo people see the beauty of life and the half-full cup. It helps them shake off worries and develop better communicative abilities. For those Virgo people who take the spiritual path toward realizing their vocations, it is a faithful companion that helps them develop.

Smithsonite – Smithsonite strengthens Virgo people's properties of patience, grace, and pleasantness. It helps them assuage feelings of pressure and tension, and make their way in and adapt to new places that require a change in their habits more easily. It is a marvelous stone for those Virgo people who take spiritual paths. Virgo is one of the earth signs, but these people, when they realize their vocation in the spiritual realm, tend to reveal themselves as having far-reaching abilities. When they choose this path, they can bring light and blessings to the world. Smithsonite strengthens these facets of their personalities, and reinforces the leadership abilities come to the fore when these people make their way along the spiritual path.

Sugilite – Sugilite is very suitable for Virgo people. By wearing or carrying it, it can help them lighten up with themselves, and balance non-positive emotions. It helps them feel freer and lighter, and balance negative feelings of jealousy, anger, and resentment. It reinforces the compassion that is inherent in their nature, as well as the precision, and helps them become more forgiving and understanding toward others, as well as toward themselves.

Blue topaz – Blue topaz has a calming effect on Virgo people. It helps them recognize non-positive, inhibiting thought patterns, and work toward change.

Virgo people, who are sometimes troubled and suffer from inner agitation (occasionally so extreme that it is liable to cause them to have a nervous breakdown), will find that the blue topaz is a soothing stone that strengthens the nerves. It reinforces their faith in life, and strengthens their decisiveness when they feel hesitant and uncertain.

Watermelon tourmaline – Watermelon tourmaline helps Virgo people in situations in which they plunge into depression and despair. It helps them break away from intellectual stagnation, be softer and more easy-going with themselves, and accept themselves as they are. It stimulates in them the ability to see the beauty of the world, and assuages inner conflicts and guilt feelings. Moreover, it is an excellent stone for calming the nerves.

Libra

Bloodstone – Bloodstone stimulates Libra people's aspiration to high ideals, and the ability to use their range of talents for universal good. It helps them make decision, which is something they occasionally find difficult to do. Bloodstone arouses their innate artistic abilities. Libra people sometimes tend not to be cautious in their eating, and plunge into alternating periods of hyperactivity and idleness. Bloodstone helps balance this.

Citrine – Citrine hones Libra people's intellectual abilities, and is excellent for helping them reach balanced solutions and make decisions. It stimulates their communicative ability, both with individuals and in large gatherings where they sometimes feel uncomfortable. Because it is a stone that "nurtures peace," it is suitable for this peace-loving sign, and helps Libra people when they are trying to make peace and reach a compromise between adversaries, at work or at home. It helps Libra people achieve emotional equilibrium and eliminate irascibility during unbalanced periods.

Green spinel – Green spinel has properties that are similar to those of Libra people – it is a stone of love, loyalty, congeniality, generosity, and compassion. It increases and stimulates these natural properties in Libra people. It also helps them balance the heart chakra, which is very sensitive in this sign.

Chrysoprase – Chrysoprase increases Libra people's superb oratorical powers, and stimulates their quick thinking and their talent for verbal expression. It helps the emotional equilibrium of those Libra people who vacillate between periods of exaggerated self-esteem and days when they feel inferior and worthless.

Red coral – Red coral is liked by Libra people because of the harmony and the natural feeling that flow from it. It helps them free themselves from burdens and feel more optimistic at times when they lose their fundamentally positive perception of the world.

Jade – Jade, with its properties of love of mankind and caring, increases these positive properties in the character of Libra people. Moreover, it helps them differentiate between the wheat and the chaff, and decide where to expend most of their energy by helping them realize themselves.

Lepidolite – Lepidolite is an important stone for this sign, because it affords the establishment of a balance between emotion and reason. Libra people sometimes tend to adhere vehemently to a course of reason, or, alternately, to allow emotion to dominate them. Lepidolite increases their self-acceptance and helps them calm their moods. It also increases their natural properties of openness and honesty.

Moonstone – Moonstone is a balancing stone that helps Libra people moderate emotional ups and downs and mood swings.

Nephrite – Nephrite increases Libra people's aspiration to harmony, and their sensitivity and caring for others.

Rainbow obsidian – Rainbow obsidian helps Libra people during periods of depression or despair by imbuing them with a feeling of gratitude and happiness.

Tin – Tin reinforces Libra people's excellent thinking abilities. It is also of great help to those who find it easy to begin various projects, but tend to lose some of their staying power when it comes to finishing what they started.

Opal – Opal increases Libra people's creativity, and gives them inspiration. It represents the Libra person's ability to see everything from different points view, and increases these unique abilities.

Rose quartz – Rose quartz helps Libra people love and accept themselves more. It transmits calmness, gentleness, and harmony – some of the sign's characteristic properties – and in this way helps them balance and increase these properties when necessary. Moreover, it helps them recover from old love wounds, and attain equilibrium in all layers.

Sapphire – The strong bond between the sapphire, a wonderful stone to which the Buddhists attribute qualities of devotion and spiritual illumination, and Libra people, can be understood in all its glory if we consider the properties of Mahatma Gandhi, who was born under the sign of Libra. The sapphire, which is the sign's most important stone, strengthens Libra people's aspiration to peace, love, justice, and truth. It stimulates in them the desire to bring these attributes to humanity, apply them in their lives, help them find their vocation, and follow the path of their destiny out of belief and devotion. The sapphire increases their intellectual abilities by strengthening their intuitive ability. It helps them dispel situations of confusion and indecisiveness, and stimulates in them the determination to work toward the realization of their dreams.

Tourmaline – Tourmaline is also a foundation stone of this sign. Because it is a very powerful balancing stone that balances the two cerebral hemispheres, it is very useful for Libra people who wear or carry it. Libra people sometimes vacillate, like a pair of scales, and tourmaline, which promotes sensitive and mental equilibrium, brings them great well-being.

In addition, it strengthens their determination to work toward the realization of their dreams. These properties are shared by all the tourmaline stones, but pink tourmaline (rubellite) and blue tourmaline are considered to be especially suitable for Libra people.

Pink tourmaline – Pink tourmaline, or rubellite, stimulates a feeling of direction in Libra people, and helps them cope with and resolve conflicts with themselves. It strengthens their belief in themselves and their self-esteem, which is sometimes lacking. In situations of a surfeit of self-esteem, it helps balance it, and allows them to see things as they are.

Blue tourmaline – Blue tourmaline is also a stone that represents this harmony-seeking sign. It stimulates harmony at all levels, and strengthens Libra people's talents for helping others, caring about others, and the ability to give advice, all of which are so characteristic of them.

Scorpio

Botswana agate – In the past, Botswana agate was used by African tribal healers in fertility rites for strengthening physical and sexual energy. Scorpio people, who are characterized by properties of strong sexuality on the one hand, and an attraction to the various realms of medicine and mysticism on the other, can use it to strengthen their powers, as long as they use it correctly. It helps protect those of the sign who do dangerous jobs, and stimulates feelings of conscience and integrity.

Alexandrite – Alexandrite, which stimulates creativity and sensuality, reinforces these properties in Scorpio people. Because it links the physical, emotional, and intuitive layers, it can direct these people to use their wonderful abilities in a pure and exalted way. These people can rise as high as an eagle from the spiritual point of view. They vacillate between extremes, and can be strong and beneficial beings from the spiritual point of view – or exploit non-positive powers to attain material goals and to satisfy their ego. Alexandrite helps them remember their hearts, which is located between the physical urges and the spiritual aspirations, and when they act out of love, they will make the most of their great power on a positive track.

Black coral – Black coral helps Scorpio people cope with the negative emotions that often well up in them. It helps these people cope with the dark side of their personalities and other people's personalities, and release repressed emotions by helping increase their creativity and original ways of thinking.

Red spinel – Red spinel is suitable for this sign. It reinforces physical strength, and helps balance the base chakra.

Dioptase – Dioptase helps Scorpio people open their hearts and detach themselves from the feelings of "lack" that direct their abilities to negative channels. It strengthens their positive side, which aspires to peace and healing on earth.

Kunzite – Kunzite inspires love and compassion in Scorpio people. It helps them become more sensitive to those around them. Scorpio people can be unreservedly loyal to people who are truly close to them. Kunzite increases this property, and helps them feel a great deal of fidelity toward their mate. It also helps them "open their hearts." This is one of the ways to move these people toward their high and positive qualities, and to keep them from falling into the abyss of resentment and vengefulness.

Labradorite – With the help of labradorite, Scorpio people can bring their mystical abilities to the fore. Because of its ability to stimulate the will, as well as the ability to realize one's vocation, it can be a very powerful balancing factor for these people. Moreover, it helps them eliminate disturbing and obsessive thoughts.

Malachite – Malachite, the stone of change and creativity, symbolizes transformation, one of the characteristics of the sign. It helps Scorpio people link up to their emotions, and helps them activate the heart chakra. It increases their property of fidelity, which is liable to vacillate between one extreme and the other in these people, and helps balance it. It also provides protection for them.

Moonstone – Moonstone helps Scorpio people link up to positive frequencies. It helps them break away from negative energies that accumulate in the various bodies because of non-loving thoughts, and develops their extrasensory absorption and perception abilities.

Opal – The opal also increases the property of unreserved loyalty that is innate in their characters, and helps them extend it over a broader circle of human beings. It helps them see the lofty spiritual possibilities before them, and choose a positive and pure path, by stimulating in them the knowledge of their inner truth. It helps them become more congenial and pleasant. Having said that, when they feel emotions of rage or resentment, and so on, they must not wear or use the stone, as it will make these emotions even more extreme.

Peridot – Peridot acts as a very powerful balancing factor for Scorpio people. It develops the properties of true friendship, optimism, and love in them. When